A *San Francisco Chronicle* Best Book of 2016

More praise for *"Most Blessed of the Patriarchs"*

"A fresh and layered analysis, one centered more on [Jefferson's] interior life than his deeds for posterity. . . . Gordon-Reed and Onuf are not the first to search for other ways into Jefferson's private place, nor will they be the last. But they have provided a smart and useful map for those who are certain to follow."
—Peter Baker,
New York Times Book Review

"Provocative. . . . In *'Most Blessed,'* co-writers Gordon-Reed and Onuf employ their considerable historical and literary skills to collage an unconventional portrait of Jefferson. . . . Few historians are as well suited to examine Jefferson in this manner. . . . The Jefferson who emerges in these pages is a dynamic, complex and oftentimes contradictory human being."
—Walton Muyumba, *Chicago Tribune*

"In their search for understanding rather than for comfortable bromides, Gordon-Reed and Onuf exemplify a virtue that Jefferson admired, even though, in this case, it does not always tend to his advantage."
—Matthew C. Simpson, *New Republic*

"Given that Jefferson believed that no generation can have a rightful claim to govern another, it is fitting that Gordon-Reed and Onuf have given us a new and empowering perspective on the private and public life of one of our greatest Americans. It is a book with which the next generation can judge, and be enlightened by, Jefferson's words and deeds."
—Jeremy D. Bailey, *San Francisco Chronicle*

"With characteristic insight and intellectual rigor, Annette Gordon-Reed and Peter Onuf have produced a powerful and lasting portrait of the mind of Thomas Jefferson. This is an essential and brilliant book by two of the nation's foremost scholars—a book that will, like its protagonist, endure."
—Jon Meacham,
author of *Thomas Jefferson: The Art of Power*

"A peerless team, Annette Gordon-Reed and Peter Onuf pierce the mysteries of Jefferson's character and at last offer a compelling explanation of how the republican statesman and plantation patriarch could coexist in a single soul. Jefferson's flaw was not hypocrisy but conviction, his unswerving belief in paternalism as empowering and beneficent."

—Danielle Allen, author of *Our Declaration: A Reading of the Declaration of Independence in Defense of Equality*

"How did Jefferson's sense of himself and his life missions affect how he handled his many roles, including revolutionary, president, and plantation owner? In this groundbreaking book, Gordon-Reed and Onuf look at Jefferson as a total person and how he set about to fulfill the goals he developed early and held throughout his career. Jefferson is endlessly fascinating, and this book shows why."

—Walter Isaacson, author of *Steve Jobs*

"This inspired collaboration takes us as close as we're likely to get to the way Thomas Jefferson understood himself and his times. Not content with clichés about a man who made his world anew, Gordon-Reed and Onuf show us the world that made the man. . . . Here is Jefferson as he might have painted his own image, a self-portrait comprised of equal parts sun and shadow."

—Jane Kamensky, author of *A Revolution in Color: The World of John Singleton Copley*

"No other recent scholar has done more than Annette Gordon-Reed to illuminate Jefferson's private life; no historian has done more than Peter Onuf to explore the multiple facets of his public life. Together the coauthors' intellectual and personal friendship has produced a remarkable portrait of Jefferson."

—Jack Rakove, author of *Revolutionaries: A New History of the Invention of America*

"Most Blessed

of the

Patriarchs"

"Most Blessed
of the
Patriarchs"

Thomas Jefferson
and the Empire of the
Imagination

Annette Gordon-Reed

Peter S. Onuf

LIVERIGHT PUBLISHING CORPORATION

A DIVISION OF W. W. NORTON & COMPANY

INDEPENDENT PUBLISHERS SINCE 1923

New York • London

Copyright © 2016 by Annette Gordon-Reed and Peter S. Onuf

For information about permission to reproduce selections from this book,
write to Permissions, Liveright Publishing Corporation,
a division of W. W. Norton & Company, Inc.,
500 Fifth Avenue, New York, NY 10110

For information about special discounts for bulk purchases, please contact
W. W. Norton Special Sales at specialsales@wwnorton.com or 800-233-4830

Manufacturing by LSC Communications, Harrisonburg
Book design by Chris Welch
Production manager: Julia Druskin

Library of Congress Cataloging-in-Publication Data

Names: Gordon-Reed, Annette, author. | Onuf, Peter S., author.
Title: "Most blessed of the patriarchs" : Thomas Jefferson and the empire of
the imagination / Annette Gordon-Reed, Peter S. Onuf.
Description: First edition. | New York : Liveright Publishing Corporation, 2016. |
Includes bibliographical references and index.
Identifiers: LCCN 2016000927 | ISBN 9780871404428 (hardcover)
Subjects: LCSH: Jefferson, Thomas, 1743–1826—Philiosophy. |
Jefferson, Thomas, 1743–1826—Political and social views.
Classification: LCC E332.2 .G669 2016 |
DDC 973.4/6092—dc23
LC record available at http://lccn.loc.gov/2016000927

ISBN 978-1-63149-251-8 pbk.

Liveright Publishing Corporation
500 Fifth Avenue, New York, N.Y. 10110
www.wwnorton.com

W. W. Norton & Company Ltd.
15 Carlisle Street, London W1D 3BS

1 2 3 4 5 6 7 8 9 0

FOR LUCIA (CINDER) STANTON

CONTENTS

PART THREE

ENTHUSIAST

PREFACE

In late autumn of 1793, Secretary of State Thomas Jefferson was in Germantown, Pennsylvania, then the nation's temporary capital. A devastating outbreak of yellow fever had driven the government, including President George Washington, out of the capital, Philadelphia, to escape the horrific epidemic, whose origin was a mystery to all. Jefferson had not, in fact, been a part of the exodus. He had decided to leave Philadelphia in the winter of 1792, well before the outbreak. Perhaps he had grown weary of city living or, more likely, wished to find respite from the scene of his metaphorical death match with Secretary of the Treasury Alexander Hamilton, his chief rival in Washington's cabinet. The two men had very different visions about the way the new country should progress, and Washington sided with Hamilton.

Jefferson had taken residence in a house along the Schuylkill River in April. After a brief sojourn at his home, Monticello, he moved to Germantown knowing that he was in his final days in the administration. When he lost the battle with Hamilton, he gave notice of his decision to resign his post. After some difficulties obtaining lodging in the town newly crowded with refugees, he was able to find a home. It was from this place, and against this backdrop of troubled and disorienting times, that Jefferson wrote to his friend Angelica Schuyler Church in the waning days of November.

Jefferson and Church had first met in Paris on the eve of revolution, while he was serving as minister to France. When he wrote to her from Germantown, she was still in London, but she had written to him of her impending return to America and with news of mutual friends they had known there. The marquis de Lafayette had been jailed (which Jefferson knew). Madame de Corny, who ran a salon that Jefferson often frequented, had lost her fortune. Maria Cosway, with whom Jefferson had had some sort of dalliance, had entered a convent. Jefferson reassured Church that efforts were being made on Lafayette's behalf. He lamented Madame de Corny's economic downfall and expressed surprise at the sharply religious turn in Cosway's life. And then Jefferson's love of language took flight:

> And Madame Cosway in a convent! I knew that, to much goodness of heart, she joined enthusiasm and religion: but I thought that very enthusiasm would have prevented her from shutting up her adoration of the god of the Universe within the walls of a cloyster; that she would rather have sought the *mountain-top*. How happy should I be that it were *mine* that you, she and Mde. de Corny would seek.[1]

Church knew Jefferson well enough to recognize what he was doing writing to her in this manner. Even as he flirted with Cosway, he had flirted with her over the years, fully aware that no connection to either woman (both married, Church with two children) could ever be serious or long-term. His suggestion that Cosway, Church, and Corny might repair to Monticello to live with him was on par with other fanciful things he had said to her before.

At this moment, however, matters were more complicated because in addressing Church, Jefferson was talking to the sister-in-law of the man responsible for his current discomfort: Hamilton was married to Church's younger sister, Elizabeth. Open discussion of the implications of this fact in the letters they exchanged was not possible, given Jefferson's sense of propriety and strong dislike of conflict. He could not let on that he even considered that Church knew of the titanic struggle that he and her brother-in-law had waged. Instead, he went back to basics, to a presentation of self that emphasized his attachment to his home, his values, and his faith that, with concerted effort, he could bend the future to his will.

> In the mean time I am going to Virginia. I have at length been able to fix that to the beginning of the new year. I am then to be liberated from the hated occupations of politics, and to sink into the bosom of my family, my farm and my books. I have my house to build, my feilds to form, and to watch for the happiness of those who labor for mine. I have one daughter married to a man of science, sense, virtue, and competence; in whom indeed I have nothing more to wish. They live with me. If the other shall be as fortunate in due process of time, I shall imagine myself as blessed as the most blessed of the patriarchs.[2]

The most blessed of the patriarchs. The strong proponent of republican values, adherent of the Enlightenment, who wrote that "all men are created equal" and was excoriated as a "Jacobin" by enemies, likened himself to a figure from ancient times when republicanism was not even thought of, much less the Enlightenment or revolutionary action to upend the social order on behalf of the downtrodden. Though the word "patriarch" can be used to describe any man who was the "father" of something—Jefferson did this on occasion, himself—his setting of the scene and description of what he would be doing at Monticello suggests that he meant something more particular than just being a father. Indeed, two years later in a letter to Edward Rutledge, Jefferson more explicitly linked himself to the primordial incarnation of such a figure when he said that at Monticello he was "living like an Antediluvian patriarch among [his] children and grand children, and tilling [his] soil."[3] "Antediluvian patriarch[s]" of the highest status— and Jefferson was of high status—ruled over families that included a wife (sometimes multiple ones), concubines, children, and slaves. Depending upon his social position, his authority could extend to a clan or to a surrounding community. A salient feature of his rule was that it was autocratic, a form of leadership at odds with the type that Jefferson championed when he participated in the American Revolution, supported the French Revolution, and worked to build the government in the earliest days of the United States.

In fact, Jefferson had no wife when he wrote to Church in 1793, or when he wrote to Rutledge in 1795, but he did have a concubine, children, slaves, and over five thousand acres of land. And if the members of his surrounding community were not in a truly dependent relationship to him, as those who lived under the aegis of a high-status patriarch of old would have been, they did, in the main, respect him and rely on his capacity to provide things they needed in their lives. Monticello's blacksmith shops, its nail factories, the mills Jefferson built, the jobs he offered for skilled white workers—his property and prestige—helped shape the way of life in the community around Monticello. Indeed, ninety miles away from the mountain, people who lived in the vicinity of his Bedford County retreat, Poplar Forest, took to calling him "Squire." Though lacking the more exotic connotations of the word "patriarch," the title nevertheless acknowledged Jefferson's special status, reaffirming his sense of himself as one who occupied a privileged place—with attendant responsibilities—in his home and community.

That Jefferson called himself a patriarch provides a window into his thinking about his place in the world and his sense of self. But what *kind* of patriarch did Jefferson wish to be, or want others to think he was given the roles he played in his country and in the world at large? At the time he wrote to Church as he prepared to go home, he was closely associated in the public mind with a revolution that was in the process of ripping apart the fabric of society with the announced aim of creating something entirely new. Just eleven months earlier, in service of that revolution, and in the name of its newly constituted citizenry, France had executed the country's patriarch, Louis XVI, an act that left Jefferson unfazed. Even in the face of the chaos in France, the republican revolutionary whose Declaration of Independence deposed America's monarch was cautiously optimistic about the future of republicanism in France and throughout the "civilized" world.

To his extreme enemies Jefferson was a bloodthirsty Jacobin, someone who would disrupt and obliterate traditional lines of authority within society. This characterization went too far, but Jefferson did in fact see himself as part of a vanguard of a progressivism fueled by Enlightenment thinking that would inexorably strip away the old order to make things anew. What has fascinated (and annoyed) many observers of the man, from his time until well into our own, is that he would dare to launch himself into this role from such an improbable base of operations: a slave plantation. Jefferson was a lifetime participant in an ancient system that made him the master of hundreds of people over whom he had near-absolute power. He could buy and sell human beings. If hostility to tyranny was at the heart of his politics and plan for the United States of America, that sentiment had no real currency on his mountain. At the same time, he well understood the basic problem with his way of life and wrote damning and insightful criticisms of the institution that made it possible. An important part of the story we wish to tell is how this progressive patriarch came to rest easy within the confines of a way of life that he believed to be retrogressive.

As the principal author of what has come to be considered America's "creed," the Declaration of Independence, Jefferson is subjected to greater scrutiny than other of his contemporaries—including James Madison, James Monroe, and Patrick Henry—who spoke of liberty as a fundamental right while holding other human beings in bondage, even as they, like Jefferson, claimed to abhor slavery. The distance between Jefferson's words and his deeds on this question, along with other apparently contradictory impulses—the masterful politician also claimed to hate politics—has led some critics to simply brand him a hypocrite and leave matters at that. This is an understandable, even predictable response. But it is ultimately shallow because it is far too easy on his times, on his fellow white Americans, and on all of us today. There is indeed a much richer, more complicated and important story to tell about the world Jefferson inhabited and the way he moved through that world. Even more fascinating is to consider the way he *saw himself* moving through a world he had helped bring into being, for which he felt great responsibility, and for which he had nearly boundless hopes. Jefferson's hopes for the American republic and his firm belief that the United States would create an "empire for liberty" to stand in opposition to the empires of the Old World were products of the empire of his imagination—a place created out of the books he read, the music he played and the songs he sang, the people he loved and admired, his observations of the natural world, his experiences as a revolutionary, his foreign travels, his place at the head of society and government, his religion, and his role as one who enslaved other men and women. From all of this grew a republican patriarch of his own fashioning. It is this process—and its outcome—that we wish to explore.

Jefferson believed that mankind's condition would get better and better as the years unfolded, with the United States taking the lead role in bringing this process to fruition. The path of science—the product of the human capacity to reason—was his template for the future course of human events. As education became more widely diffused, technology and science would advance, retrograde superstitions would fall by the wayside, and republican forms of government resting on the consent of "the people" would eventually cover the earth. The end result of progress would be a state of peace and comity between nations. It is safe to say that modern sensibilities more often than not reject the notion of a future of inevitably rising fortunes for *Homo sapiens*. Indeed, the most pessimistic among us wonder how long—or whether—the species will last at all. Current-day observers are likely, then, to see Jefferson as naïve or, at best, disingenuous—*he cannot really have believed those things he said about progress and inevitable improvement.* Again, the chasm between words and deeds fuels skepticism. But despite mounting evidence in his own lifetime that there would be no straight line to the bright future he envisioned, Jefferson sustained his Enlightenment faith in human progress until his dying days.

Ironically, the historian who helped craft the persistent image of Jefferson slipperiness-shading-into-inscrutability also gave evidence to the contrary. In 1889 Henry Adams very famously set the tone for writing about Jefferson in his magisterial *History of the United States of America* with the following often quoted passage:

> The contradictions in Jefferson's character have always rendered it a fascinating study. Excepting his rival Alexander Hamilton, no American has been the object of estimates so widely differing and so difficult to reconcile. Almost every other American statesman might be described in a parenthesis. A few broad strokes of the brush would paint the portraits of all the early Presidents with this exception, and a few more strokes would answer for any member of many cabinets; but Jefferson could be painted only touch by touch, with a fine pencil, and the perfection of the likeness depended upon the shifting and uncertain flicker of its semi-transparent shadows.[4]

A seductive and poetic image to be sure, but "shifting" also suggests *shiftiness*—a subtle indictment of Jefferson's character from a man whose ancestors John and John Quincy Adams had at best ambivalent relations with America's third president. Henry Adams was a masterful stylist, and there is no wonder that this brief sketch of the supposedly elusive Jefferson has had such staying power in American historiography. Literary and evocative as it may be, however, it is not entirely correct; or one should say it leaves much out of the picture of Jefferson's life—and of the lives and characters of the other early presidents, who were as complicated as most human beings tend to be, a reality that Adams's formulation breezes right past. We invoke other literary figures—actual poets—to comment on the reality of Jefferson's (and humankind's) constitutively multifaced nature. The Portuguese poet Fernando Pessoa, himself a figure of enigmatic repute, put it this way: "Each of us is several, is many, is a profusion of selves. So that the self who disdains his surroundings is not the same as the self who suffers or takes joy in them. In the vast colony of our being there are many species of people who think and feel in different ways."⁵ Pessoa, who wrote poetry in dozens of different voices and personalities, was speaking of the human condition in the early twentieth century, but Jefferson was ahead of his time in many ways and had a personality that would neatly fit within Pessoa's description. And then there is Walt Whitman, whose more famous lines are especially appropriate for Jefferson because they so well capture the restless, ever transforming spirit of American democracy—"Do I contradict myself? Very well, then. . . . I contradict myself; I am large. . . . I contain multitudes."

Pronouncing Jefferson a particularly contradictory figure whose shifts and "uncertain flickers" make him harder to capture than other presidents, or other people, also fails to take into account the numerous and varied roles that he played during his very long life, and what playing those many roles demanded of his personality, in ways good and bad. He served at nearly every level of government that existed in pre- and post-revolutionary America, and retired to found a university. While he was accomplishing these feats, he also maintained a set of personal interests and occupations that were extremely varied as well, enough to sustain a veritable industry of "Jefferson *and*" books and articles—"Jefferson and slavery," "Jefferson and architecture," music, wine, cooking, horticulture, religion, linguistics, paleontology. What can we make of a man who was so many things over such a long period of time?

As it turns out, another of Adams's observations about Jefferson is more on the mark than his intimations of his subject's inherent shadiness. He emphasized Jefferson's capacity for steadfastness of purpose (or outright stubbornness) about cherished principles, even in the face of the disastrous practical consequences that adherence to those principles wrought: "Through difficulties, trials, and temptations of every kind he held fast to this idea, which was the clew to whatever seemed inconsistent, feeble, or deceptive in his administration."⁶ Adams was speaking of Jefferson's attitude about peace, noting that in his desire to avoid war, at what looked to be all costs, Jefferson was willing to appear "inconsistent" to the point of seeming "untruthful." "He was pliant and yielding in manner, but steady as the magnet itself in aim."⁷

With this, Adams deftly distinguishes strategy from tactics, and tells a truth about Jefferson that should be applied to other areas of his life. Whether he was acting as a politician, a father, a master of a slave plantation, or in any other important role, Jefferson almost always had an overall goal (or strategy) in view that can be obscured by the tactics he employed. This was certainly true with respect to roles that were even more central to his life than the pursuit of peace. The revolutionary patriot was willing to do whatever he thought necessary to ensure the bright future he saw for the country he helped found.

Throughout the arc of his long career, Jefferson saw himself and like-minded patriots as being in a never-ending battle to sustain the "Spirit of '76" against the British and "aristocratic" and "monocratic" Americans who sought to make the United States *like* Great Britain and, thus, roll back the gains of the revolution. Rejecting the Old Testament pronouncement "What has been will be again, what has been done will be done again, there is nothing new under the sun," the just inaugurated President Jefferson emphatically declared in March of 1801 when speaking of the nascent American republic, "We can no longer say there is nothing new under the sun." He wrote this in a letter to the eminent scientist Joseph Priestley, the discoverer of oxygen, describing what he thought had been at stake in the bitter struggle that had led to his election.

> The barbarians really flattered themselves they should be able to bring back the times of Vandalism, when ignorance put everything into the hands of power & priestcraft. All advances in science were proscribed as innovations. They pretended to praise and encourage education, but it was to be the education of our ancestors. We were to look backwards, not forwards, for improvement; the President himself declaring, in one of his answers to addresses, that we were never to expect to go beyond them in real science.[8]

The forces of good had triumphed over the forces of evil. Jefferson, in full patriarchic mode, was absolutely sure he was right about this.

And much as he admired George Washington, it seems clear that, deep down, Thomas Jefferson viewed himself as the *real* father of this country. He wrote as if the United States had become its true self only in the 1790s when the Democratic-Republicans, a group that favored the inclusion of the common man in the governance of American society, challenged the prevailing order that the Federalist Party had put in place. These artisans, small farmers, and working people looked to Jefferson for leadership. They went on to become members of what would be called the Democratic-Republican Party, and propel him to the presidency in 1800. With that powerful role came the responsibility to act when necessary. Jefferson's sincere, heartfelt dedication to the fundamental principles that he believed defined the new republican regime justified tactics that skeptical critics—equally convinced of their own patriotism and probity—might rightfully have found questionable.

Jefferson, the republican patriarch: How did he come to think of himself in this role, and how did he conduct himself in it? In what ways did this particular self-construction—this Whitmanesque "large" sense of himself—influence the way he moved through the world as a plantation master, father, grandfather, revolutionary, public official, and, finally, elder statesman? How did he deploy the tremendous resources at his disposal—his talent, ambition, wealth, personal will, and social position—to fulfill the roles he set for himself early on in life? What did Thomas Jefferson think he was doing in the world?

These are the questions we will explore and hope to answer in *"Most Blessed of the Patriarchs."* Our goal is not to critically assess how Jefferson made his way through the world and determine what his life might or should mean for us, for better or for worse—what we think he *ought* to have been doing. We instead seek to understand what *Thomas Jefferson* thought he was doing in the world. Toward this end we do something that we think is absolutely essential: whenever it is at all reasonable to do so, we take Jefferson at his word about his beliefs, goals, and motivations. Readers should be clear: this does not mean that we always endorse Jefferson's formulations of why he did things or what he thought about matters, or that we are not mindful of the very problematic nature of some of his actions and thoughts, and their consequences. With this in mind, we look at the many and varied aspects of his life to try to present a picture of the total man. Jefferson's attitude about slavery, race, and the role of women are as much a part of this story as his actions as a politician, his ideas about government, and his vision of the new nation's future.

It must be said that designating some of Jefferson's positions as "problematic" is not merely a function of failing to recognize that he lived in another time. On some issues of great moment to present-day observers—particularly race and gender—he was at odds with at least a few of his more enlightened contemporaries. It was certainly *possible* for him to have risen above conventional attitudes on such questions. Yet if one is determined to keep score, it should be said that Jefferson was far ahead of his time on other extremely important matters. He was willing to question religious dogma, argue for the separation of church and state, and welcome scientific insights and advances with an open mind. And, as Henry Adams noted, he saw peace as the ultimate goal of statecraft. The quest for dominion and glory through war had wreaked needless destruction and caused "rivers of blood" to flow throughout human history. In Jefferson's view, "Nature's God" clearly had a loftier design for his "Creation," one that was beginning to become intelligible to enlightened people.

WE TURN TO Adams again, writing in another context, to comment further on Jefferson's progress through life. An observation that Adams made about those born at the turn of the twentieth century could fit very well with Jefferson's experiences, though he was a man of the eighteenth century. Pessoa wrote about the fracturing of the modern personality brought on by modern times. Adams wrote of the fractured times themselves. "The child born in 1900 would, then, be born into a new world which would not be a unity but a multiple," a circumstance he lamented in his masterpiece, *The Education of Henry Adams*.[9] This new world grew out of some of the ideals that Jefferson championed, and those that were attributed to him. The worth of the common man, the professed belief in equality as a value in society, skepticism toward old orders, especially organized religion, and faith in science and technology all fired Jefferson's imagination. He had been born in one world, and helped to make a new, more expansive one. His questing and idealistic nature made him determined to use his own life as a model for doing the many and varied things that were now possible in the world that had been born in 1776—and people knew that about him; some loved it, others hated it. The likely apocryphal story that he ate a tomato in front of a courthouse in order to prove that tomatoes were not poisonous, as many Americans believed in the eighteenth century, is just one example of how deeply Jefferson's image as a harbinger of the new took hold in the public consciousness over the course of his career. It has remained there to this day, as Jefferson is cited as having brought to America everything from ice cream to scientific racism.

SO MUCH HAS been written about this republican patriarch, a near-countless number of articles, essays, and books—both nonfiction and fiction. Many stated "truths" about Jefferson are too often merely endlessly repeated opinions—and more or less explicit judgments—about the meaning of his words and deeds. This is not to suggest that many of these opinions have not been useful or correct. It is to say that we are in a particularly critical and, potentially, transformative time in Jefferson scholarship. We now have so much more available information about him that a reassessment of him based on what we now "know" is very much in order. Since the 1990s there has been an explosion of new information about slavery at Monticello, revolutionizing our understanding of his role as master of that plantation and of his home away from home, Poplar Forest. The task of editing *The Papers of Thomas Jefferson* has sped up enormously—the project having been split in two with Barbara Oberg at Princeton University editing the years before his retirement in 1809, and J. Jefferson Looney at the Thomas Jefferson Foundation (Monticello) editing *The Papers of Thomas Jefferson: Retirement Series*. Thanks to their herculean efforts, volumes have been appearing yearly, complete with the most reliable transcriptions of his letters and writings, supplemented by deft editorial notes that provide illuminating details about the people and matters contained in the correspondence. A side project of the *Retirement Series*, *The Family Letters*, presents correspondence of members of Jefferson's family—Jeffersons, Randolphs, Hemingses, Carrs—up until the Civil War years. In it family members provide us with heretofore unknown information about things that happened in Jefferson's life as far back as the 1780s, and clarify the facts surrounding familiar events. More than anything else, these letters show the value of using others' observations of Jefferson to ferret out how they perceived him and, more importantly for our purposes, how he wished to be perceived. Finally, it is impossible to overstate the value of the publication in 1998 of Jefferson's *Memorandum Books*, edited and annotated by James A. Bear and Lucia (Cinder) Stanton. Jefferson's record of his daily life, with notes that explain his references and flesh out context, is perhaps the single greatest contribution to Jefferson scholarship since the publication of his letters began. There is much new material to work with here.

The most familiar narrative of Jefferson's life and the generally accepted understanding of his character were put in place many years ago. Henry Randall's nineteenth-century biography created the arc of the story, though Dumas Malone, writing from the 1940s to the 1980s, certainly improved upon Randall in many ways and refined the presentation.[10] But even without new information, every generation of historians asks different questions about the material that is available to them. They, and their readers, have a set of cultural expectations that form the basis of their engagement with historical persons and events. For example, Randall and Malone came of age in and wrote during a time when the racial views of the dominant culture precluded seeing enslaved blacks, and Jefferson's attitudes about them, as having any great relevance to shaping Jefferson's life or determining how we should view him. Because they were neither inclined nor equipped to ask questions about the role of gender in Jefferson's life and times, they did not delve deeply into his relations with his wife and daughters and their families. Impressed and inspired by Jefferson's central role in the nation's founding, both writers tended toward a hagiographic approach to their subject, although Malone became less so over the course of completing his six-volume work on Jefferson.

There has been a reaction to these earlier portraits of Jefferson, and the pendulum appears to have swung all the way in the opposite direction. "Jefferson the God" has given way to "Jefferson the Devil." We hope to steer clear of both of these presentations, making use of the plethora of new information that broadens our understanding of Jefferson, even as we reassess the material that has been known in light of contemporary understandings of politics, race, and gender. With that said, *Most Blessed of the Patriarchs* is hardly meant to be a conventional biography of Jefferson that runs chronologically from his birth to his death. Instead, the chapters in each of the book's three parts tell his story through our discussion of the most salient aspects of Jefferson's philosophy of life—how it was developed, how it evolved, and how his thoughts and feelings shaped his actions and the course of American history. In Part One ("Patriarch"), "Home," "Plantation," and "Virginia" present the influences that went into shaping Jefferson's life and continued to give meaning to his existence throughout the eighty-three years that he lived. The chapters in Part Two (" 'Traveller' ")—"France," "Looking Homeward," and "Politics"—present Jefferson at work in the world on the business of the newly formed United States as a diplomat and public official, and show how these experiences further molded him into the figure most recognizable to the public during his lifetime and to readers of history, while Part Three ("Enthusiast") contains the final three chapters: "Music," "Visitors," and "Privacy and Prayers." These chapters explore some of the things beyond politics and work that were at the core of Jefferson's identity, helping to shape his relationships with others, and sparking his reflections on the meaning of his life as it was about to come to a close.

We are often asked, "What is left to be known and said about Thomas Jefferson?" The answer, we think, is "Everything." There is little doubt that he was the central figure in the early American republic. No one's contribution to and participation in the formation of the American Union was of longer duration and more sustained influence. This book is designed to be neither a running critique of Jefferson's failures nor a triumphant catalog of his successes. It attempts, instead, to explicate the life of an endlessly fascinating figure of American history who had his hand in so many disparate parts of the nation's beginnings that it is impossible to understand eighteenth- and nineteenth-century America—and the country the United States has become—without grappling with him and his legacy.

Monticello. (Holsinger Studio Collection, ca. 1890–1938, Accession #9862, Special Collections University of Virginia, Charlottesville)

NORTH AND SOUTH

In July 1825 Thomas Jefferson's favorite granddaughter, Ellen, newly married at Monticello to the Bostonian Joseph Coolidge, traveled north to start a new life in her husband's home. She covered territory familiar to her grandfather, for her route through upstate New York, Vermont, and Massachusetts closely tracked the "botanical expedition" that he had taken with James Madison in the summer of 1791, his deepest penetration into the heartland of his archenemies, the Federalists. Jefferson's political foes thought the secretary of state and congressman were in fact politicking against an administration that increasingly appeared to be dominated by the secretary of the treasury, Alexander Hamilton. There is little direct evidence to substantiate that charge. Although the two Virginians did spend some time with politicians (those were the people they knew in the area), they really were intent on escaping New York City, the new nation's miserably hot temporary capital. As enlightened travelers with a bent toward "natural philosophy," Jefferson and Madison could survey the passing landscape and assess its potential for future development. When the two men traveled, Vermont was a new state, having only recently been admitted to the Union a few months before they set out. Its booming population of 85,425 was just beginning to transform forests into fields—where its mountainous terrain allowed.

By the time Ellen, the daughter of Jefferson's eldest child, Martha Jefferson Randolph, and her husband, Thomas Mann Randolph, visited the north country, much had changed. Her first, glowing report on the progress of civilization on the Yankee frontier offered a gratifying image of America's future, a demonstration of the benign effects of the republican revolution that Jefferson, the author of "the great Charter of our Independence," had helped initiate. Ellen reported, "The country is covered with a multitude of beautiful villages." She was amazed that Yankee farmers had wrung such abundance from "the hard bosom of a stubborn and ungrateful land." Despite a cold and forbidding climate, "the fields are cultivated and forced into fertility; the roads kept in the most exact order; the inns numerous, affording good accommodations; and travelling facilitated by the ease with which post carriages and horses are always to be obtained."[1]

The contrast with Ellen's native "country" was striking. Virginians were blessed with the "great gifts of Nature," she wrote, but had squandered the "advantages of soil and climate which we possess over these people."[2] Improvement was the great watchword of an enlightened age, and her grandfather was one of its foremost proponents. There was, however, precious little improvement to be seen in Ellen's native state, more than two centuries after its first settlement. Jefferson's Albemarle County was located on the provincial frontier at the time of his birth, and for decades after that travelers to his mountaintop home still encountered a near wilderness. What had Virginians been doing in those intervening years? Not much, according to one witness who visited Monticello sixteen years before Ellen's plaintive letter to her grandfather decrying Virginia's backwardness relative to New England. The Washington socialite Margaret Bayard Smith, who grew close to Jefferson while he was president, visited him at Monticello several months after he happily retired from public service when his second term ended. Smith's report was bleak. "No vestige of the labour of man appeared," she wrote in her diary in 1809: as she ascended Jefferson's mountain, "nature seemed to hold an undisturbed dominion." She went on, "As we rose I cast my eyes around, but could discern nothing but untamed woodland,—after a mile[']s

winding upwards, we saw a field of corn, but the road was still wild
& uncultivated."[3] Smith was shocked to encounter the progressive
philosopher whom she loved so much in such retrograde physical surroundings. Except for his spectacular house, there was no sign of
civilization.

Ellen had spent a great deal of her early childhood at Monticello, and she had moved there permanently with her parents and
siblings when Jefferson retired. Margaret Bayard Smith almost certainly encountered at Monticello the then thirteen-year-old Ellen,
who knew little of the world outside of rural Virginia. In the years
that followed, Ellen and her sisters Cornelia and Virginia regularly
accompanied Jefferson to his Bedford County retreat Poplar Forest,
spending weeks at a time in relative isolation with him there. Ellen,
considered the most intellectual of Jefferson's grandchildren, had a
special bond with her grandfather. She knew him well enough to
know that he would be particularly interested in her observations
about her new surroundings, for he had devoted his public career to
the improvement of the new nation and particularly of his beloved
Virginia. He would want to know what was happening in other parts
of the Union.

Jefferson was then eighty-two years old. His once robust body
was failing, as were his personal fortunes. The country's first "panic"
(what we call "recessions" or "depressions"), in 1819, the disastrous
co-signing of a loan for a relative who defaulted, and his lack of attention to his spending over the years as he tried to maintain the standard
of living expected of members of his class—all taken together—put
him in dire financial straits. The house he had been building and
remodeling for over five decades was in a constant state of disrepair.
It needed painting and to have the roof fixed. Yet throngs of visitors continued to come up the mountain to pay him homage or, as
his overseer Edmund Bacon wryly suggested in his recollections of
Jefferson and Monticello, to save themselves "a tavern bill."[4] Jefferson had spent decades on the public stage attempting to shape the
contours of both the state he first knew as his "country" and then
the new country that had emerged from the American Revolution.

Conceding defeat in his attempt to turn Virginia into a truly republican society, he turned his attention, in his later years, to creating a state university that would train young men to take up and finish the task he had started. But that was for the future. What had happened in the past to bring them to the present that both Ellen and he found so unsatisfying? Ellen had a simple—and devastating—explanation for the stark differences between New England and Virginia: "our Southern States cannot hope" to match the "prosperity and improvement" of the northern states "whilst the canker of slavery eats into their hearts, and diseases the whole body by this ulcer at the core."[5]

This stark sentiment was not new to Jefferson. Ellen could have read a similar indictment in his only published book, *Notes on the State of Virginia* (1787), in which he decried slavery's "injustice" and its demoralizing effects on the "manners" of white slave owners and their children. How could these self-professed republicans sustain their experiment in self-government when "the whole commerce between master and slave" was, in his words, "a perpetual exercise of the most boisterous passions, the most unremitting despotism on the one part, and degrading submissions on the other"?[6] Slavery turned whites into tyrants and impaired their capacity for self-control. The "masters" could not really master themselves, a critical ability for the kind of responsible citizenship that Jefferson championed and thought would save Virginia.

While living in Paris in 1785, Jefferson fleshed this theme out in a letter to the marquis de Chastellux in which he set forth what he thought were the differences in the characters of northerners and southerners. Although his one-word and short-phrase descriptions posited, in sum, a relative balance of good and bad attributes among the people of the two regions, Jefferson listed some southern traits that had great bearing on his granddaughter's assessment of the different levels of progress in Virginia and New England. Although he did not mention slavery by name, Jefferson referenced the effects of its operation. Southerners, he wrote, were among other things, "Voluptuary," "indolent," and "unsteady" people who were "zealous for their own liberties, but trampl[ed] on those of others."[7] He was speaking of white southerners, but who were those "others" whose rights were being trampled upon? Given that he was prone to displaying his antislavery impulses to Europeans who he knew would be sympathetic, Jefferson was certainly referring to enslaved blacks in Virginia. Indeed, in his *Notes on the State of Virginia*, he uses the phrase "trample on" to describe what whites were doing to blacks in slavery. His take on southern character supports the historian Edmund S. Morgan's famous thesis in *American Slavery, American Freedom: The Ordeal of Colonial Virginia* that the slavery of blacks gave white Virginians the freedom to be as they were. Jefferson implicitly critiques this state of affairs, however, by describing whites as "trampling" on the rights of others. Northerners, free from the malign influence of slavery, were different: they were "sober," "laborious," "persevering" people who were "jealous of their own liberties, and just to those of others."

Jefferson knew that slavery also existed throughout the North, but it was not a slave society as he experienced it. The northern state with which he was the most familiar—Pennsylvania—had just five years earlier enacted a gradual emancipation statute and had for many years before then been the site of antislavery agitation by the state's Quakers. There were never that many black people, or slaves, in New England, certainly not enough to spark competition based upon race or create a need to use slavery as a mechanism to control a large black population. The picture that Jefferson painted of the two regions in the 1780s was close to predictive. Of the two "types" of people he described in his comparison of the North and the South, which group would be more likely to have the inclination—and the drive—to create the tidy villages and farms that Ellen found so appealing in the 1820s? Which people would be more likely to maintain the tradition of the town meeting, that site of participatory democracy that Jefferson so admired? In truth, it is clear from other statements he made over the years that, although it had been the seat of political opposition to his policies and career, Jefferson envied many things about New England. In the empire of this stalwart Virginian's imagination, the perfect republican society looked a great deal like New England, and almost nothing like Virginia.

We do not know whether Ellen Coolidge was familiar with what her grandfather had written about slavery in *Notes on the State of Virginia*, or whether he had ever repeated in her company the sentiments he expressed to Chastellux comparing northerners to southerners. But the Jefferson-Randolph correspondence suggests that slavery was a topic of conversation in the family. Her father was known to express antislavery opinions, as well. From early childhood, Ellen was likely privy to talk around the family fireside where the slavery problem had been discussed, perhaps discreetly because the ever-present "servants," as the family preferred to call the enslaved, would be in earshot. There was cause for concern on that score, for the "servants" did listen.

In 1873 Israel (Gillette) Jefferson, who had been enslaved at Monticello, recalled taking Jefferson and the marquis de Lafayette on daily drives when the great Frenchman visited Jefferson in 1824 while on his famous tour of the United States. During one outing the men's conversation turned to slavery. Gillette recalled that on most days, he could barely decipher what the marquis was saying, but on this day he made a special effort to listen and understand; his "ears . . . eagerly taking in every sound that proceeded from that venerable patriot's mouth."[8] Lafayette said the things one would expect him to say, repeating his oft-expressed conviction that the institution of slavery should be abolished. Jefferson, whose way of life, including his sumptuous hospitality toward Lafayette—indeed, the drive itself—was made possible by slavery, agreed that slavery should end, but ventured no opinion on how or when that might happen. His response is not surprising either.

A younger Jefferson had looked out from his mountaintop home with a mind filled with ideas about creating a truly republican Virginia. As a young legislator with plans for emancipation and as an improving farmer during his brief retirement in the mid-1790s, he had hoped to set an example for his neighbors. Once he returned to politics in the last half of that decade, he was a man obsessed with "saving" the country from the "menace" of Federalism. But when he came home for good in 1809, he turned inward, away from the world. Monticello was no longer a model, and he was not much of a farmer. As his time on earth waned, his vision of the republican millennium receded.

When the sixty-seven-year-old Lafayette arrived on the mountain, the eighty-one-year-old Jefferson was fifteen years into his retirement, a period during which he seldom ventured far from his home and never again left the state of Virginia. When one thinks of Jefferson at home, one thinks of a plantation. This was, however, the longest sustained stretch of time that he had spent in a plantation setting in his entire life, and he was thoroughly enmeshed in the daily rhythms of slavery that he orchestrated at Monticello. The positive benefits that the institution brought to him in the most personal and intimate ways were on constant display. In the winter of life, Jefferson could imagine a world without slavery, but he did not think that world was in sight, certainly not in his "own day." In the rare instance when he allowed pessimism to overtake him, he considered that it might not come "in any age." In the meantime, Monticello—a home, a slave plantation—was a universe at which he was the absolute center. Everything and everyone revolved around him, his wishes, and commands. Here amid his family (legal and extralegal), enslaved people, and the admiring visitors who trekked up the mountain to confirm his much sought-after status in the world, Jefferson was, in a way he had never been before, in the perfect position to keep buried his reservations about the institution that he believed put his region so far behind. As we will see, this period when Jefferson was comfortably ensconced on his slave plantation marked the completion of a personal transformation that began when he was in France.

Although he politely fielded Lafayette's queries and statements about slavery, just as he did later when his granddaughter raised the subject from her new home in Boston, Jefferson found discussing the topic extremely unsettling during the last years of his life. The Missouri crisis, which unfolded between 1819 and 1821, shook him to his core. The thought that slavery might cause the dissolution of the Union he had worked hard to help create—a dissolution that was, perhaps, to be effected by violence—filled him with despair, with "terror," as he put it in a letter to John Holmes in the midst of the crisis. His characterization of this possible outcome as "treason against the hopes of the world" shows the depth of his utter faith that America's republican experiment was to serve as an example for the entire world, just as he viewed his life as a public man and his mountaintop home as examples to others. The overarching idea was right, he believed. Any flaws, even the large flaw of slavery, could be fixed while adhering to republican principles and Enlightenment values. The times, however, were against him. The "sons" of the revolutionaries whose "passions" he deemed "unworthy" knew that slavery was not, as Jefferson and some other members of the revolutionary generation were convinced, a backward institution that was simply going to wither away as people became more "enlightened."[9] Nor was this generation willing to see Jefferson's image of himself as an enlightened slave owner as an acceptable posture to maintain until slavery gradually ended. This was, for a number of Americans, a deep and urgent moral issue.

North and South were developing differently, and in directions that made confrontation likely. It could hardly have come as a shock to Jefferson, then, that Ellen would note the differences in the two regions and cite slavery as the cause of Virginia's relative primitiveness. In this private conversation with his much loved granddaughter, five years after his letter to Holmes, Jefferson was frank in his assessment of the state for which he had had such high hopes. He could only agree that "one fatal stain" deformed "what nature had bestowed on us of her fairest gifts." That "fatal stain" he did not name, and did not have to. Without slavery, Virginia would surely have fulfilled its great potential: "the rustic scenes you have left," he told Ellen, would have long since given way to a "state of society . . . more congenial with your mind."[10] Ellen's mind was very much akin to his, and, whether she knew it or not, she was passing judgment on the fate of her grandfather's early efforts and ambitions for his home state. Through the lens of his severely diminished expectations about his own region and, no doubt, with some embarrassment, Jefferson responded mildly to his granddaughter's energetic and trenchant social criticism by offering up the only thing left to this once very public man: the benefits of the private realm—the consolations of family. He had once had much grander ambitions.

The Jefferson of 1782, who drafted the *Notes on the State of Virginia*, exulted in Virginia's natural endowments and contemplated the role he would play in helping the state realize its potential. His research suggested that the New World environment was perfectly suited to rapid population growth and that its fertile soils would generate unprecedented productivity and prosperity. Bountiful natural resources, however, were not enough. The form of government and the manners of the people were critical, as Ellen's account of how hardworking New Englanders had transformed their unforgiving landscape into a fertile and livable space confirmed. Although New England was not quite a howling wilderness when he and Madison traveled there in 1791, the years between that trip and the time of Ellen's letter showed how a "free and good government" could transform the landscape and "how soon the labor of man would make a paradise of the whole earth, were it not for misgovernment, and a diversion of all his energies from their proper object, the happiness of man, to the selfish interests of kings, nobles, and priests."[11]

Jefferson could identify New England's progress with the promise of American republicanism, the "free and good government" that Virginians, on the surface, shared with their northern counterparts. At the same time he could not deny the increasingly conspicuous discrepancies that Ellen highlighted, or that slavery was at the heart of the differences. Was Virginia perhaps what Scottish Enlightenment theorists called a "stationary" society, incapable of future progress because of the dead weight of corrupt and corrupting institutions—the conventional Western view of the overcivilized and decadent "Orient"? Well into the postrevolutionary period, many Virginians—mostly members of the upper class who had seen their status decline—looked back to a "Golden Age of Virginia," which supposedly existed during the five decades immediately preceding the revolution.

Jefferson, the irrepressible optimist, who very often disagreed with his upper-class cohort about many issues, could never have reached such a dire conclusion about his home state. To accept the myth of a "Golden Age of Virginia" was to betray the meaning of the revolution to which he had devoted so much time and energy, and in which he had invested such fervent hope. Jefferson's image of himself, his life's very meaning, was tied to the central roles he played in the events surrounding the break with Great Britain and the creation of a new country. Monarchy, slavery, retrograde property rules, and an established church dominated prerevolutionary Virginia. There was no romance for Jefferson in any of these institutions. In fact, three of them had been abolished or reformed, in part, through his direct efforts. Only slavery lived on.

Although it is impossible to know what he would have done had he lived a few more years, Jefferson—even at his most dispirited moments—never made the pivot to the nascent proslavery ideology that would have rationalized his life in an instant; he would be deemed understandable *and* consistent had he been a slaveholder who proclaimed that slavery was a moral institution. Instead, he lived a paradox, pushing the resolution of the problem off into a future in which the members of his community (whites, that is) became ready for a "revolution in public opinion" brought on by the "persuasion, perseverance, and patience" of the enlightened advocates of emancipation and expatriation.[12] At this point the only recourse, Jefferson believed, was for white Virginians to remain dedicated to the purest, most undiluted and uncorrupted principles of free government— principles that would eventually make possible and compelling the hoped-for "revolution" in sentiment on the slavery question.

Families

Jefferson could reply to his granddaughter as he did because there was a deep and fundamental source for his faith that the republican character of his fellow white Virginians would eventually emerge, leading to the ultimate success of their experiment in self-government. His conception of national character was grounded in his ideas about the purity and perfectibility of family life and domesticity, in a sense of himself that was cultivated in "the circle of [his] nearest connections." The family was the place where "faithful and lasting affection" could be found, affection that would "adhere . . . under all changes & chances." Virginians may have failed to cultivate their lands—and Jefferson had to acknowledge his own shortcomings as a farmer—but fireside attachments, the warm bosom of his family, amply rewarded a lifetime investment. He had said in an earlier time that family was "the only soil on which it [was] worth while to bestow much culture."[13]

Jefferson knew well how families made societies. The Virginia of his birth had been shaped by planters who controlled the government, as they feverishly acquired land, promulgated property rules that favored the landed, and developed a full-fledged slave society. At the center of all of this, the dynamic driving it all forward, were the strategic marriages that allied families who then went on to set the ethos of Virginia's colonial world. As he helped make a revolution, Jefferson had a hand in changing some of the ways Virginia families worked, with his efforts to abolish primogeniture and entail that give the first public hint of his idealistic vision of correct family relations. Seventeen Seventy-Six and Jefferson's political efforts in the 1790s that culminated in his election as president—what he styled as the "Revolution of 1800"—pushed matters further. The family, knitted together by tender attachments, would constitute the bedrock of republican society. Now it would not just be the planter elite whose families set the tone in this new world. Millions of empowered free white men, with their wives and children playing their roles, would help direct the course of the new republic. The idealized presentation of their fruitful attachments, Jefferson believed, would radiate out to the community, the state, and the nation. The United States would, in turn, become an example to the world of the capacity for relationships based on harmony, bonds of trust, and mutual interest to keep peace in the world.

What of Jefferson's own family? The fire in 1770 that destroyed his boyhood home at Shadwell took with it letters that may have passed between him, his father, and his mother. There is no way to draw an accurate picture of Jefferson as a son. His correspondence with his siblings suggests a normal range of connection between them for that time, but it is not deeply revelatory. Because no letters they wrote to each other are extant, there is no evidence of Jefferson as a husband through the eyes of his wife, Martha, and thus one cannot speak with too great authority about the Jefferson marriage. Others' accounts, however, along with Jefferson's words and deeds, reveal that he made a serious investment in the role of "husband." He was attentive to his wife—so much so that he drew criticism from his colleagues for choosing to be with her instead of his fellow public servants during crucial moments as the revolution unfolded. Certainly his extreme grief upon her death attests to his intense attachment to Martha. His time with her, however, was only ten out of the eighty-three years that he lived.

Important as they were to him, Jefferson's years as a husband pre-dated his time on the world stage as a minister to a foreign country, vice-president, and president. They were also well before he played the roles of father to married daughters, grandfather, and elder statesman working to create a great university for Virginia. Martha never knew the Thomas Jefferson who lived in these roles and was transformed by them. Jefferson's vision of family as it evolved over time, therefore, can best be seen in his role as father and grandfather. The vagaries of life had left him the sole parent to the daughters he had with his wife, the sole surviving grandparent to his grandchildren, and a surrogate father to a son-in-law who had been orphaned by death and effective disinheritance. By his own choice Jefferson was father to enslaved children who had to be maneuvered out of slavery and, if they chose, into whiteness. The texture of his life with them and their mother is all but unknown.

Throughout the years Jefferson, his daughters with Martha, and his grandchildren reaffirmed their family attachments when they gathered at Monticello. When they were apart, they conjured up memories of home. "I now see our fireside formed into a groupe," Jefferson wrote Martha Randolph from Philadelphia in 1797, "no one member of which has a fibre in their composition which can ever produce any jarring or jealousies among us."[14] In both his public and his private lives, Jefferson wrote in order to structure his own life, and to try to bring into existence the world as he wished it to be.[15] By putting things down on paper, it would be so—if all the relevant parties made the right effort. Transmitting this picture of family harmony to his daughter was one part aspiration, one part promise, and one part instruction. Of the astonishing array of Jeffersonian writing and record keeping—Farm and Garden Books, commonplace books, architectural plans, and Memorandum Books—letter writing was the principal means by which he imagined and structured his life. The Jefferson-Randolph letters imparted news, but they were also designed to define who they were as a family. Both Jefferson and his grandchildren were conscious that he would have a place in history and that his family would be brought there with him. Their written presentation of their family life was thus intended not only to shape their mutual understandings about one another. The letters would also provide the evidence historians needed to help them portray the Jefferson-Randolphs.

Despite Jefferson's wishes, there were "jarrings" and jealousies." How could there not be when so much of the family's attention was riveted upon the man who helped shape their sense of themselves, while he was alive and even afterward? During the years in which she corresponded with Jefferson biographer Henry S. Randall, Ellen painted a picture of her family that made it clear she and her relatives measured themselves by reference to their proximity to Jefferson. In one missive, she confided to Randall, quite correctly, that her mother Martha was her grandfather's favorite child, and recounts the efforts Jefferson made to alleviate her aunt Maria Eppes's feelings of insecurity about her father's preference. She noted how hurt her cousin Francis would be to hear that his mother was second place in Jefferson's affections. Why Ellen felt compelled to eschew family loyalty and say this, and then suggest that Randall not use the material, is a mystery unless we conclude that the habit of family ranking was too hard to break.[16]

When Randall mentioned that Wormley Hughes, a member of the enslaved Hemings family, had indicated that everything was not totally rosy in the Jefferson-Randolph clan—indeed, as Randall put it, "that some tragic features mingled" in the family story—Ellen adamantly rejected the notion. She did admit that her father was jealous of Maria's husband, John Wayles Eppes, with whom Jefferson had an easy camaraderie, but characterized that as a minor problem. The real tragedy, she said, was her eldest sister Anne's travails with a husband, Charles Bankhead, who regularly beat her. Recurring to the compulsion to rank, she noted that Anne had been her grandfather's "first favorite and pet—the first born of his firstborn."[17] Sister to sister, cousin to cousin, brother-in-law to brother-in-law—all categories of family members jockeyed to be as close to the patriarch as possible, and suffered at the thought that they were not close enough. Ellen's letters suggest that this not only put stress on Jefferson's family members, it put stress on him, as well, as he did what he could to tamp down on potential conflicts.

There was a problem, however, that seriously complicated Jefferson's republican vision for his region of the country—the "fatal stain." His was a slave society where families came in varied and interesting forms. Indeed, when his own advantageous marriage to Martha Wayles Skelton in 1772 made him a truly wealthy man, he became entangled for the next five decades with the family of Elizabeth Hemings, an enslaved woman who had borne six children by Jefferson's father-in-law, John Wayles. Jefferson deepened the connections when he entered into a long-term liaison with Elizabeth's daughter and Martha's half sister, Sarah (Sally) Hemings. There was no way that Jefferson could publicly fit this family into his proffered vision of the ideal. He had to create a different one tailored to his own circumstances, and that he did. Martha's half siblings could not be written of as who they actually were. Neither could Sally Hemings or the children she bore him. But Jefferson's belief in the need for family harmony—even among those family members with whom he had, in Conor Cruise O'Brien's apt phrase, "veiled and equivocal relations"[18]—was present from the beginnings of his family life at Monticello and continued until his death.

The "veiled" world that Jefferson lived in with the Hemingses was in marked contrast to the world he lived in with his legal white family. The life of this extralegal (private) family was decidedly *not* to be constructed in letters that would betray the substance of their lives with him and compete with his legal (public) family. Nor were the multiple connections of the Hemings-Wayles family to live on in history books. The absence of any mention of a Hemings-Jefferson family tie in Jefferson family letters—it was the norm in southern white families to keep such references out of written records—was for nearly two centuries a strong signal to historians that the long-whispered-about second family at Monticello did not exist.

Consider the role that the Jefferson-Randolph family correspondence related to Poplar Forest has played in shaping their family image for posterity. Ellen and her sister Virginia's letters describing journeys with their grandfather to and from his Bedford retreat paint a general picture of warm family intimacy as Jefferson escaped the throngs of visitors who descended upon Monticello during his retirement—anecdotes about stays at inns and picnics along the way. What the sisters' letters do not reveal is that, depending upon the year, either Beverley and Madison Hemings or Madison and Eston Hemings were along for those journeys, even though their letters often mentioned the boys' uncle John Hemings and cousin Burwell Colbert, who also traveled with them. The sisters' letters to their mother, Martha, describing their trips ask her to assure these men's wives that they had arrived safely. They never, in any letter that is known, sent word back to Sally Hemings to apprise her that her sons—still boys for most of these years—were well.

We know that the Hemings boys were along because in preparation for the trips, and the work that was to be done on the house while he was there, Jefferson would write to his overseer at Poplar Forest to say that he was coming and to mention that he was bringing with him at the same time "Johnny Hemings and his two aids" or "two assistants." When they were between ten and twelve, Jefferson put his three sons in apprenticeships with their uncle John, the enslaved artisan whose work he admired the most and with whom he spent the most time. In doing so, he placed himself in the lives and minds of these boys and, then, young men as they performed tasks that he, a woodworker himself, found valuable and had ordered. They learned to be carpenters and joiners by working on their father's house supervised by their uncle and at times, no doubt, by their father, who took a hands-on approach to overseeing the work he assigned to John Hemings.[19]

While Beverley and his sister Harriet Hemings disappeared into whiteness, Madison and Eston Hemings entered the historical record at the promptings of others. Most famously, Madison's recollections, given in 1873 to Samuel Wetmore, provide the basics of the Hemings family story at Monticello. His brother Eston, who took the last name "Jefferson" for his family when he decided to move to Madison, Wisconsin, to live as a white man, was more reticent, though his taking of his father's last name was telling. Talk of his parentage was open in the southern Ohio area where he, as Eston Hemings, first settled after leaving Virginia. At one point, a group of men who had gone to Washington came upon a statue of Jefferson that looked just like Eston Hemings. After they returned home, they asked him whether Jefferson was his father. He responded "quietly," "Well, my mother whose name I bear belonged to Mr. Jefferson." And after "a pause" he added, "and she was never married." Although he said nothing further to his Ohio inquisitors, he or other immediate family members took the story of his parentage to Wisconsin. His son John Wayles (Hemings) Jefferson, who became a lieutenant colonel in the Union army, pleaded with members of his Wisconsin cohort not to tell his story, lest it be known that he was part African American, and thus would be unable to rise through the ranks as he did. When his younger brother, Beverley (Hemings) Jefferson, died, a friend in Madison mentioned in a letter responding to his obituary that he was the grandson of Thomas Jefferson.[20]

The family decision to live as white Jeffersons made matters tricky, because it was known that Jefferson had no white sons with his wife. Telling the whole truth publicly would reveal their African ancestry and cut them off from the benefits of full citizenship. Madison Hemings's descendants—at least the ones who remained in the black community—kept their family history largely to themselves through the generations. One of those who passed for white made up stories about Italian ancestry.[21]

The only members of the Hemings family with whom Jefferson is known to have corresponded were Robert Hemings and John Hemings, Sally Hemings's older brother and younger half brother, respectively. His correspondence with Robert, the record of which can be found in Jefferson's journal of incoming and outgoing letters, has been lost, and that with John is largely practical and work related. At the start of his presidency, Jefferson's failure to write to his former chef, James Hemings, brother of Sally, Robert, and John Hemings, became a source of conflict between the two men that led to their estrangement, though there was a brief rapprochement before James Hemings's suicide in Baltimore in 1801.

So one sees Jefferson's ideas about family and harmony in the context of his complicated domestic situation with the Hemingses, not in the few words he wrote about the family, but in the decisions he made about their lives. Upon marriage to Martha, he cast aside his long-term personal valet, Jupiter Evans, in favor of his wife's twelve-year-old half brother, Robert, who became Jefferson's constant travel companion and was with him in Philadelphia when he wrote the Declaration of Independence. He later paid to have the young man apprenticed to a barber to learn the trade. In the home, the Hemings sisters served as maids to Martha and companions to the children she had with Jefferson. Martha's deathbed scene, with husband, white sister, white sister-in-law, and enslaved half sisters gathered by her bedside, presents the not uncommon plantation family tableau in all its strangeness to modern observers. The Hemings men were allowed, against the dictates of the law, to hire themselves out and keep their wages. Many times Jefferson did not know where they were as they traveled on their own throughout Virginia.

Because the story of Jefferson's second family did not die with him in 1826 but instead took on a new life as the South came under increasing fire about the institution of slavery and the plight of enslaved women, the Hemingses' mere absence from Jefferson-Randolph family letters was not enough to obscure their connection to Jefferson. Action had to be taken. And from this we can see the most consequential example of literal family fashioning from Ellen Coolidge, who in a letter to her husband, Joseph, in 1856, very famously wrote her half uncles—Beverley, Madison, and Eston Hemings—and her half aunt Harriet out of the Monticello family circle. In a letter placed in a letter book prepared, she said, for descendants who might be interested in what life among the Jefferson-Randolphs was like, she insisted that it was a "moral" impossibility for her grandfather to have had a mistress and children with her.[22] Putting it in those terms, she upheld the picture of her family as devoid of the kinds of "jarring or jealousies" that would certainly have existed when a man had two families living side by side. Ellen offered their great happiness as a family unit as the prime evidence against the notion that her grandfather had a mistress, for his having a mistress would have made them an unhappy family. For many years quite a number of American historians found this an effective argument.

The letter, which Ellen expected to be passed around in Boston circles, also defined what a "good" slaveholding family was like to her northern cohort who would have had little or no experience with this sort of thing. No race mixing was taking place among these people, save for the stray, decadent relative—the so-called black sheep—whose type, after all, could be found in even the best of families, north and south. Her grandfather, the family patriarch, by definition could not be a black sheep.

ELLEN'S CORRESPONDENCE WITH her grandfather in 1825 attested to the powerful attraction of his conception of home, an abstract ideal made real by her nuclear family's devotion to the man they saw as their patriarch. Ellen may have described slavery as a "canker," but she could not at first live comfortably in her new home environment without slaves. Early into her time in the North she complained that good servants were hard to find in New England. What bothered her so? Writing to her sister Virginia in 1826, she gave the answer: "the curse of domestic life in New England is the insolence & insubordination of the servants & the difficulty of getting any that do not give more trouble than they save." At other times she complained that the servants were subpar and "afraid of work."[23] For the first time in her life, Ellen was dealing with maids and nurses who were free people. Being able to take their labor elsewhere, ineligible for the whip or sale away from their families, servants in the Coolidge household had a different view of their relationship to her.

The peculiar institution was a "fatal stain," as Jefferson said, that retarded Virginia's development and corrupted its character. Whatever slavery meant for Virginia's economic development, there is no question that at the level of the personal and domestic, enslaved people helped make Monticello the cherished place it was for Ellen and her grandfather. What Ellen missed in her New England home was the mastery that she had known in her life at Monticello and at Edgehill, the Randolph family home. Ellen and her family could be as "benign" or despotic as they chose toward the black people enslaved on their plantation, over all black people, really. There was tremendous freedom and power in this, even for a woman bound by the limitations of early nineteenth-century gender norms. At various points Ellen sought, without success, to hire black servants for her Boston household, hoping in vain to re-create the atmosphere of racial hierarchy of her formative years. The space that existed between a free white person and a slave (or a black person) over whom she could exercise near-total dominion was, for her, paradise lost.

Journey's End

Although the affective side of plantation life was important, money was also a central concern. Jefferson had been in a parlous financial position for a number of years, but Ellen left Monticello to begin her new life in the north in 1825 just as things were about to unravel completely. By 1826 her grandfather was confronting both the imminent wreckage of his estate and his final days on earth. The two events were hardly unrelated. For as long as the great man remained alive, his creditors could be kept from dealing the final blow. The man who in 1793, three years before Ellen's birth, said he aspired to be "the most blessed of the patriarchs" was racked with guilt, "over whelmed at the prospect of the situation in which [he would] leave [his] family." A mountain of debts threatened the futures of Martha and her children, "rendered as dear to [him] as if [his] own, from having lived with [him] from their cradle, in a comfortless situation."[24] Jefferson's protracted absences, poor management, and unanticipated financial setbacks left the family home at risk; indeed, after his death Monticello and the slaves who had made it as "comfortable" a place as possible were put up for sale. As the historian Herbert Sloan has noted, it was they who suffered the most from the financial catastrophe on the mountain. Many families were shattered, and all but a few were forced from the place they had lived for decades, many having spent more time on the mountain than Jefferson.

Property in land and property in slaves were the engines that drove Virginia society from its earliest days, giving Jefferson and those in his class wealth, independence, and liberty—their sense of identity. It was the dividing line between those who could participate in republican society by voting and those who could not, between those who were respectable and those who were not. While he still lived, the family struggled to relieve Jefferson's "gloom" about the fate of his property, insisting, in his grandson Thomas Jefferson (Jeff) Randolph's words, that "we shall never think of difficulties or loss of property as an evil." Another grandson, Francis Wayles Eppes, the son of his deceased daughter Maria, offered to return the Poplar Forest property in Bedford County that Jefferson planned to leave to him in his will. The cousins suggested that their real inheritance had nothing to do with property. The estate they cherished—the rich harvest of family love that Jefferson cultivated at Monticello—could not be lost to creditors. "How wretched are those possessing large property and unfortunate in the vices and ingratitude of their children," Jeff Randolph exclaimed: "How rich you are in the virtues and devoted attachment of yours." And then, he added, channeling the conventional wisdom, children "make the poverty of rich men"; they "make the wealth of the poor ones." Jeff had been managing his grandfather's affairs for many years, and now he assured him by saying, "Neither My Mother or Yourself can ever want comforts as long as you both live. I have property enough for us all and it shall ever be my pride and happiness to watch over you both with the warmest affection and guard you against the shafts of adversity."[25] Roles were now reversed. The patriarch was dependent on his family, and their love was the comfort of his old age. Their attachment to him modeled the loving relationships that Jefferson imagined would bind the generations in republican families.

In earlier times, Jefferson showered his grandchildren with gifts, reinforcing their devotion and casting a near magical aura over his presence. Yet they did not love him in expectation of future rewards, knowing how little they should expect from his estate upon his death. They would have to be independent and self-sufficient, and they wanted the family patriarch to know that they would be fine after he was gone. Francis wrote to Jefferson saying that he was "young, healthy, and strong," and so would be "able to provide for [him]self, and for those who depend upon [him]." Jeff's "trials and struggles with the world have been so salutary," he assured his grandfather, "as to give [him] a decision of character and confidence in [him]self not to be dismayed at any difficulties which can arise." Jefferson had always thought he would eventually balance his books and provide for the grandchildren. Martha Randolph was long skeptical. In 1808, as her father began planning his retirement, she told him not to worry about the children. Her "happiness" and theirs depended on securing "those comforts" to Jefferson that he had "allways been accustomed to and which habit has rendered necessary to [his] health and ease." "Moderate desires, youth, and health [could not] fail to insure" her children's happiness "as far as they will be capable of enjoying it and wealth it self could do no more."[26]

Jefferson's grandchildren were rich in memories, cherishing keepsakes they had received from him: toys, books, and, most of all, letters. When Ellen traveled north by land, the precious possessions she had accumulated in her twenty-seven years at Monticello, however, were lost at sea. "Your life [is] cut in two," her sympathetic grandfather wrote, and she now had to begin her new life "without any

records of the former."[27] The "cut" marked both the great distance
between Monticello and Boston and the great differences between
New England and Virginia, evoking the growing rift along the "geographical line" between free states and slave states that had nearly
destroyed the Union in the recent Missouri crisis. Among Ellen's
greatest losses, Jefferson learned, was a "beautiful writing desk" that
John Hemings—called "Daddy" by Ellen and her siblings—"had
taken such pains to make for" her. But Jefferson knew that Ellen's
attachment to Monticello would survive any separation or rupture.
John Hemings might be devastated by the loss (Jefferson described
him as having been in despair), but Ellen's wound could be healed by
the offer of another "writing box," the one on which her grandfather
had drafted "the great Charter of our Independence" in Philadelphia
in the summer of 1776.

This extraordinary gift resonated with both national and personal
significance. In the wake of the Missouri crisis of 1819–21, which
exposed sectional conflict over slavery and called into question the
continuance of the Union, relics of the revolution had begun to
"acquire a superstitious value because of their connection with particular persons" who had been involved in creating the Union. In this
"superstitious" way Jefferson was present to his granddaughter in his
desk; his spirit, the Spirit of '76, was also present in Boston, where the
revolution had begun so many years ago when he was still a young
and hopeful man. Ellen's husband, Joseph, had written to her mother
when the newlyweds first arrived in Boston that "public opinion in
this section of our country has changed, of late, much, very much,
in regard to" Jefferson himself: "public and private testimony to his
patriotism and character, are no longer infrequent; to his literary merits they have never been so."[28] The Bostonian recalled Monticello, the
site of his recent wedding, and this comparison worked to Virginia's
advantage. "The crowds of uninteresting men among whom I have
been moving of late," Coolidge told his mother-in-law, "make me
think of *him* with increased veneration." When Jefferson sent his most
treasured writing desk north, it was as a gift to Coolidge, not Ellen—
or, more accurately, to the newlywed couple, confirming the binding

attachment of northerner and southerner, North and South. "All here are well, and growing in their love to you," Jefferson wrote Ellen in his last letter to her, "and none so much as the oldest [Jefferson], who embraces in it your other self [Coolidge], so worthy of all our affections, and so entirely identified in them with yourself."[29]

Here were the durable, "more perfect" bonds of union, within American families and transcending "geographical lines," that Jefferson believed would vindicate his lifework. This was the lasting inheritance that would forever bind Ellen to Monticello and Americans to the sacred legacy of independence and republican self-government to which her grandfather, now facing utter ruin at Monticello, had devoted his life to creating and sustaining.

There was, of course, the other side of the unfolding American story—one that was integral to the "fatal stain" that Ellen and her grandfather invoked, but not one about which they could speak openly or whose effects on their family they could acknowledge. Two years earlier Jefferson had sent a son and a daughter (Ellen's half uncle and aunt, Beverley and Harriet Hemings) out of slavery and into whiteness to become what he described in an earlier letter, written in a different context, as "free white citizen[s] of the United States." This family legacy, the most transformative event Jefferson had engineered for any individuals to that point in his life, and would later repeat for their youngest siblings, Madison and Eston, could not, like his gift to Joseph Coolidge, be celebrated publicly as a mark of family connection. There would be no family letter for this, just terse and utterly misleading references in his Farm Book to the siblings' having run away in 1822. Later, in his last will drawn in 1826, he would describe Madison and Eston Hemings as John Hemings's "apprentices," with no explanation for why two young men, one still a teenager, were joining in freedom other men who had served him for decades. Family in Jefferson's Virginia had many aspects.

Jefferson's long life journey was nearly over by the time he exchanged letters with his granddaughter as she embarked on another phase of her family life. The end was painful for him, both physically and emotionally. A vigorous man throughout his life, Jefferson in 1818 was given mercury to help treat what was likely a bacterial infection. Not surprisingly, he suffered ill effects from the treatment that persisted for years. Through it all he managed to present himself well to the many people who came to visit and marveled at his vitality despite his age. By 1825, however, he developed severe prostate problems that made it difficult for him "to make water." This occasioned the use of devices that had to be introduced through the urethra to allow for the flow of urine. Although this treatment solved his immediate problem, it introduced bacteria that damaged his kidneys. As his health problems mounted, there were also family tragedies to confront: the serious injury to Ellen's brother Thomas Jefferson Randolph, who was stabbed by his brother-in-law during a fight, and the death of Ellen's sister and Jefferson's first grandchild, Anne Cary Randolph Bankhead, just six months before Jefferson's own death.

Yet amid these extremely difficult years there were also some happy moments that Jefferson could savor, like Lafayette's famous visits to Monticello in 1824. The old patriots—fourteen years apart in age—reminisced about earlier times together in the American Revolution and in France, and Jefferson got to show off what he was doing with his new university in Charlottesville, a project that contained all of his hopes that Virginian society would one day catch up to its sister states in the North. But the two men occupied different places in the public consciousness of the day. While the Frenchman was lauded on his tour around the country, and given a princely sum and grants of land by the U.S. Congress in recognition of his contributions to the revolution, Jefferson, strapped for cash, was feeling forgotten and unappreciated. Presidents had no pensions during these times, and he had conducted the social affairs of the presidency—his numerous dinner parties, where he always served the best wine—out of his own pocket, with scant hope of reimbursement. He offered Lafayette his congratulations on receiving the gifts, but the situation cried out for comparison. Still, the Frenchman's visit energized Jefferson, and with his old friend he could look back to a younger self who had held such high hopes for the future and the role he would play in it—hopes that were born and nurtured in the very same place where his life would soon end.

Part One

PATRIARCH

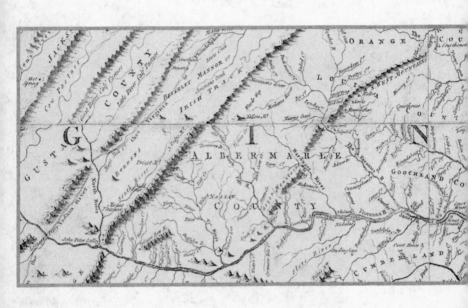

Joshua Fry–Peter Jefferson map. Detail showing Shadwell and surrounding area in Albemarle County. (© The Thomas Jefferson Foundation at Monticello)

CHAPTER 1

HOME

Home was a powerful idea for Thomas Jefferson, a fixed point in a sentimental geography formed from the melded associations of people, places, and events. When he was away from Monticello serving in the national government, he visualized his mountain as a paradise of domestic tranquillity. And as he imagined the future of Virginia and the new United States, his vision of his own family life carried out on cherished space merged with a broader dream of an enlightened republican society grounded in a fruitful attachment to the land. Jefferson was primed to do this. His boyhood home had been carved out of the vast forests that had been a province claimed by the Iroquois Nations. Through the Treaty of Albany in 1722, Virginia purchased from the Iroquois the area that would come to be known as the Piedmont. Thirteen years later Peter Jefferson—Jefferson's father—patented 1,000 acres of land there along the Rivanna River and built a plantation called Shadwell. In that place on April 13, 1743 (or, according to the old-style calendar, April 2), thirty-three years before the American Revolution, his first son, Thomas, was born. Thomas would die eighty-three years later at Monticello, the home he built just across the river and up the mountain from his father's homestead.

This was not, however, the "from time immemorial" connection to place that European aristocrats who were able to trace their families and homes in a particular setting back for centuries could claim. Their deep connections to the land bespoke timeless tradition, settled expectations, and unquestioned authority. The Jeffersons, by contrast, were frontier people, strivers, and a frontier society is, by definition, an unsettled society, built on improvisation, opportunism, hope, and, almost always, a level of insecurity. This was certainly the case in the Jeffersons' territory. There a cohort of European colonials lived uneasily with a dwindling population of Native Americans whose land they had taken by force, deceit, or treaty. They also lived cheek by jowl with a growing number of Africans transported to Virginia as slaves. Indeed, Jefferson's first memory was of being handed up on a pillow to an enslaved person on horseback to make the journey from Shadwell to Tuckahoe, where he spent several years of his boyhood. He also remembered the Native Americans who visited his father at Shadwell, those early recollections of cordiality fueling a form of nostalgia that influenced his later dealings with Native American groups.

Nostalgia masks harsh realities. From the time of his youth, Jefferson's home was a place that mixed gentility with barbarity. Though not large, Shadwell was a well-appointed residence that facilitated gracious living and entertainment. The historian Susan Kern has shown that although Peter and Jane Jefferson lived on the frontier, they entered the more sophisticated world at large via the Atlantic market, shipping out tobacco and bringing in consumer wares. Fine china, clothing, silverware, expensive furniture, and music played on family-owned instruments filled Jefferson's early senses, creating expectations about how life was to be lived.[1] How was this world obtained and maintained? The status and work of Peter Jefferson— slave owner, surveyor, and mapmaker who marked the boundaries of land that had come under the control of the British colonists, the speculator and cofounder of the Loyal Land Company—is instructive. His father's work made the relationship between the races and the land clear to young Thomas from the beginning—whites enslaved one race to work the land as they waited for, and precipitated, the displacement of another race in order to seize control of additional land to be cleared and cultivated by the enslaved.

This is how it was in the land Jefferson so loved, the land that shaped his character. The British colonists, then American citizens, worked their way west throughout the coming decades until Native Americans were expelled from their territories and driven across the Mississippi to reservations and the Union dissolved into a civil war that ended legalized slavery. More than any other member of the founding generation, the very future-oriented Jefferson thought about and grappled openly with the moral and practical implications of the encounters among red, white, and black that had been apparent to him from boyhood. His frank musings on the subject of race in *Notes on the State of Virginia*—the pseudo-science in his comments borrowed largely from books he had read—grew out of his own experiences and his intense engagement with every aspect of the future of the new nation. He understood that the questions of what would become of Indians who stood in the way of European land hunger, and how and whether black former slaves could coexist peacefully with whites as free people in America, were core issues for the American experiment. If others among his cohort of founders were not thinking seriously and writing about these matters, they should have been.

Setting Off

That Jefferson planted himself such a short distance from his boyhood home, on family property, is significant, for his patriotic attachment to his "country" Virginia focused on the land itself. His agrarianism linked his father's property with that of Virginia's founders—the fathers of a prosperous new commonwealth—and, eventually, with God the father. "Those who labour in the earth are the chosen people of God," he famously proclaimed in his *Notes*. Although the locations of Shadwell and Monticello, the beginning and end points of Jefferson's life journey, could not be readily distinguished on the large map of Virginia that Peter Jefferson and Joshua Fry published in 1751, the two home places were, in fact, worlds apart in terms of the aspirations they expressed and fostered.

Despite his relatively humble origins, Peter Jefferson had been an enterprising estate maker with dynastic ambitions within the confines of Britain's North American empire. His son Thomas, the postcolonial, was more ambitious still. He imagined the citizens of independent Virginia as a great family of families that would substitute a harmonious republican commonwealth—a "living generation" speaking with a single voice—for the colonial era's perennial clash of great families seeking advantage over each other while exploiting their humble neighbors. Jefferson did not reject his father. He rejected his father's world. From his mountaintop prospect, he surveyed a vast expanse and saw limitless opportunities for *all* white Virginians. Certainly he was grateful for his father's inheritance and was determined to be a good steward of what had come to him from the old regime. But Virginia was a big country. Elite Virginians had no reason to mimic Old World aristocrats who monopolized the land. In the new republic, the planter's attachment to his own land could be universalized: all white freemen were Virginians, cultivating loyalty to the commonwealth as they improved their land and their families' prospects.

Perhaps Jefferson idealized home and land because he was so often away from his own. As noted above, he first took leave of Shadwell when he was around three years old. Fulfilling a promise made to William Randolph, his wife's kinsman and his friend, that he would move to Tuckahoe and serve as the guardian of Randolph's children and run his plantation should anything happen to him and his wife, Mary, Peter Jefferson uprooted his wife, son, and daughters after Randolph died in 1746. Thomas passed the early part of his boyhood in a place that was home, but not really his home. Another boy, Thomas Mann Randolph, just a year older, was the scion of Tuckahoe, who had several siblings of his own. By the time Thomas was nine, the Jeffersons had returned to Shadwell, but Thomas went off to boarding school and was home only on holidays. For five years beginning in 1752, he lived in the household of the Reverend William Douglas, the head master of the Latin school that his father had chosen for him. After Douglas's school, and his father's death in 1757, there was the Reverend James Maury's, where he also boarded during the week, going home to Shadwell on Saturdays. He soon grew anxious to put himself firmly on the path to adulthood by going to study at "the College."

In his first surviving letter, written when he was sixteen years old, young Thomas sought permission from John Harvie, one of the executors of his father's estate, to attend the College of William and Mary, in Williamsburg, the provincial capital and home of the royal governor. The educational and cultural advantages were obvious, but more importantly, the teenager wrote, "I shall get a more universal Acquaintance, which may hereafter be serviceable to me." Here we see the first evidence of his ambition. Thomas certainly did not lack for acquaintances at Shadwell. To the contrary, he wrote, "as long as I stay at the Mountain the Loss of one fourth of my Time is inevitable, by Company's coming here and detaining me from School."[2] But this was not the sort of "company" that would get him anywhere in life, or fulfill his late father's dynastic quest. In an early show of his understanding of the art of persuasion, Thomas pressed a line of argument that he knew might appeal to those charged with overseeing his financial well-being: going to William and Mary might even save money by limiting "the Expences of the Estate in House-Keeping." Entertaining a constant round of visitors wasted the estate as well as Thomas's precious time. Implausible as his explanation was, it was worth the try. The point was that staying in Albemarle would limit his horizons, fixing him in place and forfeiting the opportunities his father had opened for him. His executors consented.

One can get a glimpse of Jefferson's state of mind during this period from a revealing letter he wrote fifty-one years later to his grandson Jeff Randolph, then sixteen and about to go away to school in Philadelphia. With all the appropriate caveats about late-in-life recollections of early feelings, the passage offers poignant evidence of what the death of Peter Jefferson meant to young Thomas. It was the pivotal moment in his development, he said, when "at 14. years of age, the whole care and direction of my self was thrown on my self entirely, without a relation or friend qualified to advise or guide me."[3] In reality, Thomas was not an orphan and was not "thrown on" himself "entirely": his mother, Jane, and five solicitous male guardians were there to advise and guide him.

What Jefferson was describing was the feeling of being bereft. His father's death had transformed his childhood home, making him into a different person in the process—one who, for the first time in his life, felt he had no one to turn to. This sense of being alone, when he was not truly alone, apparently contributed to his desire to escape to another setting, to put a gain where there had been a loss. So he left his childhood home to live on his own for a time in what he characterized as a dangerous world. Recollecting "the various sorts of bad company with which [he] associated from time to time," Jefferson claimed to be "astonished [that he] did not turn off with some of them"—the "horseracers, cardplayers, Foxhunters"—"and become as worthless to society as they were."[4]

Grandparents are often prone to dispensing advice to their grandchildren and other members of the younger generation through morality tales of falls (or near falls) and redemption. It is their duty. As a young man Jefferson engaged in some of the activities that he expressly warned his grandson against. He went fox hunting with his wife, Jeff's grandmother. And both Thomas and Martha Jefferson played cards—Thomas, backgammon. Still, his advice to Jeff was wise, and correlates nicely with current-day neurological research showing that the part of the brain that controls judgment is not fully formed in most human beings until around the age of twenty-five. Looking back on his younger self, Jefferson warned his young grandson *not*—at his present age—to trust his own "reasoning powers" to guide him through life's hazards, but instead to identify with and model himself on "dignified men" who could serve as substitute fathers.

Jefferson had found such men himself when he went off to college, where he "had the good fortune to become acquainted very early with some characters of very high standing, and to feel the incessant wish that [he] could even become what they were." By asking himself "what would Dr. Small, Mr. Wythe, Peyton Randolph do"[5] in any given situation—instead of relying on his own, still undeveloped reasoning powers—Jefferson could become more and more like them, thus establishing a solid moral foundation for his subsequent development. In this way Jefferson would honor the memory of his own father, preparing himself to assume Peter Jefferson's patriarchal role and take proper care of his mother and siblings. Jane Jefferson's absence in her son's autobiographical letter to his namesake grandson is a measure of Jefferson's strong identification with his father, not of his hostility toward his mother. Peter Jefferson's legacy drew Thomas Jefferson back to Albemarle, to build his own home on his father's land and to make himself into the plantation patriarch he imagined his father to have been.

FOR THE YOUNG JEFFERSON, a provincial Virginian, England in the mid-eighteenth century also signified "home": it was the colony's "mother country," the country where his actual mother was born, and, for a time, a hoped-for destination on his life journey. While a student in Williamsburg, he wrote to his closest college friend, John Page, from "Devilsburgh" to say that he had convinced himself of "the necessity of . . . going to England."[6] Travel was on his mind, but marriage was there too. Around the same period that he spoke of travel abroad, he developed an infatuation, evidently one-sided, with the beautiful Rebecca Burwell that made him think about home in a new way. Perhaps, Jefferson mused when he was twenty, he and friend William Fleming could marry their respective sweethearts, live close by, "practise the law in the same courts, and drive about to all the dances in the country together."[7] He had reached the point where he could imagine settling down and returning to Albemarle, in the midst of enlightened friends. Writing again to Page, the notion of marriage and getting away from Virginia merged: "Why cannot you and I be married too : . . ? Do you think it would cause any such mighty disorders among the planets? Or do you imagine it would be attended with such very bad consequences in this bit of a world, this clod of dirt, which I insist is the vilest of the whole system?"[8]

The young man's frustration and longing are palpable, and not out of the ordinary. Jefferson had no personal knowledge of any other "bit of a world" or "clod of dirt," but he knew, from his extensive reading and the travels of others, that more was out there. At the same time, the desire to find a wife and settle into a life with dear friends nearby was as powerful as his impulse to get away from Virginia. He asked Page in that same letter whether he had any "inclination to travel," because "if you have I shall be glad of your company." The two young friends could sail away on the "Rebecca," for that was "the name" he intended "to give the vessel." The courtship of Rebecca was only slightly less imaginative than the "vessel" he was going to build or have built and named "Rebecca." These ideas were unrealistic, but the feelings that provoked them ran very deep.

Throughout his life, Jefferson's vision of home always included a place with friends nearby, or even in his residence. The historian Rhys Isaac perceptively notes,

> Ardent in his youthful friendships, the young Jefferson made at least four proposals that his favorite companions should upon marriage make joint establishments. They and their wives would live in adjacent households. (Among the small proportion of Jefferson's letters to survive the 1770 fire at Shadwell, this plan is found articulated three times; there was a fourth expression of it through an invitation for Jefferson's brother-in-law to bring his bride to live on the mountaintop at Monticello beside her sister, Jefferson's fiancée, Martha.)[9]

Isaac offers that Jefferson's "fantasy" was out of the ordinary in western Europe. Upper-class married couples did not typically live with other married couples as one household. Presumably, there could be only one patriarch per home.

Where, Isaac asks, would Jefferson have seen this type of arrangement? In the slave "quarters" that he had lived around all of his life. During Jefferson's childhood and youth, barrack-style housing for the enslaved that brought multiple families or unrelated individuals together in one dwelling was a common living arrangement. Even after the switch during the late eighteenth and early nineteenth centuries to more single-family dwellings, it was not uncommon for more than one family to share slave housing. Distant though the laws made them, there is no question that whites and blacks in the South's slave society influenced one another in myriad ways, consciously and unconsciously. Romanticizing aspects of the culture of the oppressed—enslaved people were not choosing to live in multifamily households—is certainly a familiar phenomenon. Isaac's supposition about the most likely source for Jefferson's interest in communal living arrangements that defied the norms of his class is both intriguing and reasonable.

Although nothing came of his youthful entreaties for co-residential living among friends, Jefferson never relinquished the dream. As a middle-aged man in the 1790s, he tried to persuade William Short, his secretary when he was minister to France, to return to the United States and live near Monticello. Short purchased property in the area but never lived there permanently. Jefferson made the same efforts with James Monroe to greater success. When he was in Philadelphia in 1791 serving as secretary of state and renting a very large house, he asked James Madison to leave the boardinghouse where he was staying, and move in with him. Madison declined. In the end it would be his daughter Martha who helped fulfill his dream of having family and/or friends share his roof, when she and her husband and their children moved to Monticello upon Jefferson's retirement from public life. The move signaled disarray in Martha's household and marriage, but the communal living suited both father and daughter.

Young Thomas's clumsy suit to Rebecca Burwell ultimately failed, as did his ill-formed travel plans: Page and other Williamsburg friends married, and the bachelor-lawyer returned to the Piedmont to ply his trade. But the choice Jefferson posed for himself in Williamsburg between marriage and home and a voyage into the wide world took matters out of his own hands. The ultimate result of his indecisiveness was "a perfect resignation to the divine will," and a recognition "that whatever does happen, must happen." He would take his bearings from heart and head, home and world, determined "to bear up with a tolerable degree of patience under this burthen of life, and to proceed with a pious and unshaken resignation till we arrive at our journey's end, where we may deliver up our trust into the hands of him who gave it, and receive such reward as to him shall seem proportioned to our merit."[10]

Settling Down

It would be many years after he suggested to Page that they go traveling before Jefferson crossed the ocean. He found a wife sooner, and when he did it was near the beginning of events that would transform his life and the nation's history, for around this time the American colonists began to express their discontent with some of the actions taken by the British government. As the political discontent simmered, Jefferson married the widow Martha Wayles Skelton on January 1, 1772. It is not clear how the two met, but her father, John Wayles, was a wealthy lawyer-planter in Williamsburg. He had done business with Jefferson, who was just beginning his legal career. The two men also had other friends in common. The world of the Virginia gentry was small, and expectations were high that single people like Thomas and Martha would marry within their social set. However they met, the pair seemed perfectly suited to each other, both of them being accomplished musicians and singers.

Nine months after Thomas and Martha married, the couple had their first child, a daughter named after her mother, who had been named after *her* mother, Martha Eppes Wayles. The infant Martha had serious health problems, and the Jeffersons' response to their baby's difficulties speaks volumes about the couple's relationship to slavery. They had Ursula Granger—their enslaved cook who was nursing her own baby, Archy—nurse Martha. As an adult, Martha would perform the same service for her younger sister, Maria, when she was too ill to nurse her son, Francis. The difference, of course, is that this was Martha's choice; something that she was probably eager and pleased to be able to do for her sibling. It is not known whether Ursula wanted to nurse the Jeffersons' baby or whether she was simply made to do so. We do know that whereas little Martha grew healthy and lived into her sixties, Ursula's Archy did not live past his first year. This mix of social distance from, mastery over, and intense intimacy with enslaved people was a constant in Jefferson's life, from cradle to grave.

Much as he treasured domesticity, Jefferson was not destined to enjoy a stable life at home with his wife and child without significant interruptions. First, there was the matter of a house to live in. Monticello at this time consisted of a building now known as the South Pavilion and the "Honeymoon Cottage." This small two-story structure was a rather rude affair. The couple lived on the top floor, with the kitchen on the first level. This was where their first child was born. For the first few years of their marriage, while the main house at Monticello was being built, the couple spent considerable time at Elk Hill, the home that Martha had lived in with her first husband, Bathhurst Skelton, who was only in his early twenties when he died. Martha seldom remained on the mountain when Jefferson was away on public business. Instead, she went back to Elk Hill, stayed at her late father's home at The Forest, or lived with her sister at Bermuda Hundred.[11] This was an era when young people died and left young widows and widowers. Couples could not expect that they would stay married to each other for decades, and that they would not take a second or, even, a third spouse. Even with those expectations, it must have been difficult for the young Thomas Jefferson to begin married life spending time in the home that his wife had so recently made with her previous husband, by whom she had had a child and who had died far too soon. At this point Monticello was still forming in his mind, and his idea of family life with Martha in a permanent home that was entirely their own was, to a great degree, more a dream of the future.

Although he was eager to be settled at home, the outside world intervened. The American Revolution, in which Jefferson was an eager participant and played a pivotal role, disrupted what he had hoped would be an idyll of family life. In this moment he broke loose from his earlier resignation to leave things to providence and became a man of action, in his own way. There were things to do: patriotism demanded sacrifices in defense of patriot homes and homelands, whether on the battlefield or in Congress. Jefferson had been chosen to serve in the Continental Congress, and was not on the battlefield, a fact that gave his enemies ammunition in later years. But his signature on the Declaration of Independence (his authorship was not well known during this time) put him at risk of his life as a rebel and traitor. His turn as Virginia's war governor made him even more a marked man—the object of at least two attempts at capture.

There was no way for him to see so far into the future, but the tug of war between Jefferson's duties at home and his ambition to play a role in the affairs of the world, begun in these early years of his marriage, would last for decades. There is reason to suspect that his wife did not entirely support his political ambitions. When he became governor of Virginia, in 1779, he had to persuade her to join him in the governor's mansion. She had originally opted to stay at her sister's home very near Williamsburg, where the capital was situated. It took great effort on his part to get her there. During the times he was away representing Virginia in the Continental Congress, his only connection to home was Martha's enslaved half brother, Robert, his teenage manservant. The source of Martha Jefferson's disinclination to travel with her husband, and make their home wherever they happened to be, is not clear. One could offer her precarious health as the reason, but she did travel between Monticello and the environs of Williamsburg where one of her sisters lived in their late father's home. Though not so far as Philadelphia, it was a still a considerable distance from Monticello.

Martha Jefferson's recurrent poor health, linked to her childbearing, was an important feature of Jefferson's home life that became more problematic as his involvement in the revolution grew deeper. Martha needed to have him at home, and he wanted to stay there, especially when she was ill. That he often decided to be at home with her greatly annoyed some of his revolutionary compatriots, who chided him and wrote disparagingly of him behind his back, for choosing home over what they saw as his duties to the revolution they were trying to make. They hinted that Jefferson was acting in something less than a manly fashion, as the home was associated with softness and pleasure betraying a feminine character, while the leadership of a revolution was hard work to be carried out by men. Many present-day observers would likely label this kind of complaint as a form of sexism. At the same time, Jefferson's attitude toward his wife and family would mark him as ahead of his times and more akin to the many husbands and fathers today who strike a balance between work and family that involves accepting substantially less than perfection in both realms.

THERE WAS A practical aspect to Jefferson's longing for home. His extended absences in public service threatened the viability of his plantations. His obsession with returning to Monticello grew out of his chronic anxiety about managing an inefficient and largely unprofitable agricultural enterprise from a distance. As we will see, Jefferson actually had little interest in the day-to-day life of farming. It was, instead, his seemingly endless building campaigns over the years—which subtracted from rather than added to his financial bottom line—that consumed him and allowed him to imagine himself as a plantation patriarch in a prosperous and improving landscape. Construction signaled progress.

Despite his conflicted emotions, Jefferson did his best to operate effectively in what he deemed to be the separate private and public worlds that were critical to his view of himself. And he had to do this for a very long time. No other member of the founding generation served in public life so long and in so many different capacities as he, at almost every level of government. After his turns as a member of the Continental Congress and war governor of Virginia, he accepted an appointment in Paris in the 1780s that took him overseas for five years. When he returned to the United States, he quickly took an appointment as secretary of state in New York and then in Philadelphia that kept him away from home for all but four of the thirty-three months that he occupied the office. Later on, Vice-President

and President Jefferson returned home so often—he was at Monticello roughly half the time he served in these roles—that it drew the
attention of critics who felt his absence damaged the workings of
the government. This was not so, for Jefferson worked compulsively
wherever he was. During his time in office, work was done at home
and in whatever capital he found himself. Once he retired, the public
trekked up the mountain to see him. Home and the world at large
were never far apart.

Jefferson found a powerful—self-abnegating—reason to be away
from home: patriotism, a feeling that had first stirred in him during
the revolution and that grew stronger with the formation of the
United States. It both resolved and sustained the tension between his
public life and private self. It was the mechanism through which he
merged his personal identity with an inclusive, all-embracing corporate identity: that of "the people" whom he represented, who were
the source of his authority and the subject of his dreams. In Jefferson's
view when the people mobilized, as they did in the 1770s, to make
a revolution and establish republican principles for the new government, they (and he) were acting on behalf of all mankind. In this same
way, he viewed his election to the presidency in 1800 as more than
one man's ascent to power; it was a new revolution for the American
people and the universal cause of republicanism, which he believed
was being betrayed in the 1790s. Being a part of this epochal new
development—at or near the head of it—was strong competition for
the home indeed.

Through all his time in public life, Jefferson's patriotic identification with his "country" (Virginia) always pulled him back to versions
of home, depending upon where he happened to be. Representing
Virginia in Congress, and later the United States in the world, fostered this split in consciousness. He felt these dissonant forces pow-
erfully: in Philadelphia, writing the Declaration, he wanted to be
in Williamsburg, helping to write Virginia's constitution; in Philadelphia, Williamsburg, or Richmond, he wanted to be at Monticello, protecting and caring for his family. The family man who loved
nothing more than being on his mountain, a place of fundamental

attachment, also saw himself as a leader. Once he played that role on the national stage, he was utterly confident that his plan for the course the new nation should set was the best one, and he really did not trust others to see things through in the right way—his way. So even as he disparaged life in the public sphere, he actually wanted to be there. He needed to be there.

While he was away from Monticello, Jefferson's idealized vision of home comforted him, serving as a powerful counterweight to the strife and discord he found in political life. The masterful politician, one of the best of his generation, abhorred direct conflict and sought to avoid it in any way he could. This was an almost impossible situation for a politician who was present at the birth of the American party system, and who had helped bring the era into being. Over the years Jefferson gave the people who remained at home in Virginia personas that fit nicely with his longing for peace and tranquillity and, it must be said, control. Because they loved and admired him so, members of his family tried hard to live up to their assigned roles, or at least to maintain the appearance of doing so. Whatever disorder existed in the places where he served in public office, he could hold Monticello in his mind as a site of peace.

It was not just blood relatives who had to toe Jefferson's line. Because he was the master of Monticello in a way that he could never be the master of Williamsburg, Richmond, Paris, New York, Philadelphia, or Washington City, overseers, workers, and particularly the enslaved for the most part had to fit into the program of willed domestic tranquillity. Those who deviated were cast out of the home, lest they continue to sow seeds of discord. Free workers who demanded too much money or drank too much were dispatched. Slaves could not be "fired." Jefferson's ultimate remedy for dealing with enslaved people who went too far outside of the parameters he set for them was to sell them or, in the case of at least two members of the Hemings family, to simply take them off the roll of slaves and let them go.

Much as he sought to shape places and other people, the starting and end point of Jefferson's homemaking project was, of course, Jefferson himself. He began the work as a teenager aching for transformation, but he remained open to change throughout his life, even at great risk. This is shown most clearly in his decision to challenge the authorities in Great Britain with no certainty of eventual success. His legendary optimism aside, Jefferson's prospects and those of his fellow planters were devastated by the revolutionary crisis in Virginia, with the disruption of prewar markets for the province's leading exports, tobacco and wheat, and the destruction of plantations themselves, including his own Elk Hill. The conflict forced him and other slave owners to confront the possibility that they might lose their homes in the wake of slave insurrection as the enslaved sought out the British as possible allies and left plantations to take up with the invading army in a bid for their freedom.

The republic that grew out of this process was itself an experiment with unpredictable results: the only certainty was that defeat would condemn prominent "rebels" such as Jefferson to ignominy and displacement, however mild the terms of a British-dictated peace and reconstruction. This uncertainty about Virginia's economic and political future shadowed Jefferson's thinking about his home even after the nearly miraculous turn of events that secured American victory at Yorktown in 1781 and an unexpectedly generous peace settlement at Paris in 1783. In truth, Virginia's future in the Atlantic trading system and in the American Union would remain uncertain in a world constantly at war, through the Treaty of Ghent in 1814, which ended the War of 1812, and beyond. For almost forty years Jefferson put himself at or near the center of his country's affairs, turning himself into a man who lived a very public life that was anything but settled and orderly. During all of this time, home, a slave plantation on the top of a mountain, would be an idealized place he always insisted he longed for.

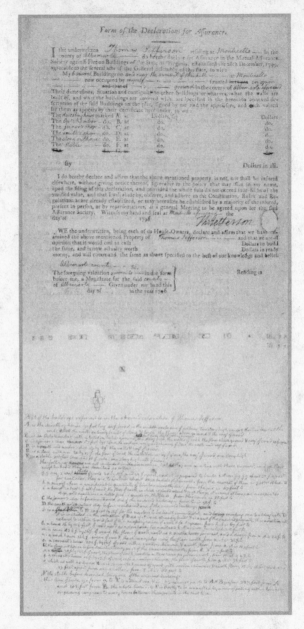

Plat of the buildings at Monticello: Jefferson's "Declarations for Assurance," 1796.

(Original manuscript from the Coolidge Collection of Thomas Jefferson Manuscripts, Massachusetts Historical Society)

CHAPTER 2

PLANTATION

In a letter to his sometime tobacco customer and former landlord Thomas Leiper about troubles he was having with one of Leiper's tobacco orders, fifty-eight-year-old Thomas Jefferson declared that he "never saw a leaf of [his] tobo. (tobacco) packed in [his] life."[1] The confession startles. After all, he had been farming tobacco for a very long time. What of Jefferson the champion of agriculture who pronounced farmers God's "chosen people"? His "chosen people" not only attended to planting; they saw the fruits of their labor through to market. Could the self-described "ardent" farmer, with a well-known tendency to manage, if not micromanage, aspects of his life with an attention to detail that bordered on the compulsive, actually have been so uninterested in the finished product of his farms?

When one considers the matter more fully, Jefferson's statement to Leiper is no surprise at all. Like most Americans until well into the twentieth century—for only then did the United States cease to be a nation of farmers—Jefferson was a farmer by accident of birth. Nothing about Jefferson's actions suggests that he had a natural affinity or love for farming, as he had for music, architecture, and writing—or politics, for that matter. He inherited farms from his father and his father-in-law that were the basic means of his livelihood, and he did what he had to do to make things work, inventing a type of plow and experimenting with contour plowing and crop rotation. These actions can be more properly likened to the kind of tinkering that Jefferson was prone to doing, like making keys, woodworking—looking at a thing and wanting to improve it in some way, preferably something over which he had at least some semblance of control. Control, however, is one of the last things that farmers, who live beholden to the vagaries of nature, can expect to have.

At home in Virginia, Jefferson rode out on horseback around his plantations daily, an activity as a form of exercise (which he did wherever he was—Paris, Philadelphia, Washington) that also allowed him to inspect his domain and to watch the work as it progressed. But he was doing other important work on these daily forays besides being a farmer. Performing this ritual, the six-foot-two-and-a-half-inch rider on horseback, who was the actual master of all he surveyed, reaffirmed his sense of himself and sent a message to all who saw him—enslaved workers, free white workers, and any visitors who happened to be in the vicinity—about his place at the pinnacle of this self-contained world. It also announced his membership in a class of men who were the masters of their own individual worlds and who had controlled Virginia society from the earliest days of the colony. One would not have to love farming as an activity to become attached to the comforts and pleasures of this particular tableau. It should also be kept in mind that these rides were often to a particular destination, one of his mills.

We know little of Jefferson's life at Shadwell and Tuckahoe, the plantations of his boyhood and youth. His father's and mother's account books tell us something of their lives at Shadwell, but do not reveal Jefferson the boy's specific connection to agriculture, nor do the relatively few recollections of his childhood that he conveyed to his grandchildren in his unfinished autobiography. Away at school from the age of nine, he entered college as a teenager and began a more than decade-long focus on being a student, then an apprentice reading law, and then a young lawyer. Upon reaching majority, he gained control over the property—including enslaved people—his father had left him in his will. In 1773 the death of his father-in-law put more land and slaves under his control. That legal event, however, also brought him and his brothers-in-law substantial debt to manage. For many years to come, farms and slaves had to be looked at in terms of their utility as property and how they could be used—aside from the agricultural work that slaves did on the land—to obtain credit or satisfy debt.[2]

Jefferson soon became disenchanted with law as a profession and found his true calling in life as a revolutionary and a politician. The struggle against Great Britain lit a fire within him that would never be totally extinguished. The end of the war brought no permanent settlement for him at Monticello. After his wife died, in 1782, he spent months away in the various seats of the Confederation Congress until he left the country for France in 1784, turning his farm operations over to Nicholas Lewis to manage while he was overseas and while he spent four years at the beginning of the 1790s in New York and Philadelphia serving in the federal government. During this twelve-year period Jefferson was a resident farmer for less than half a year.

Farmer

It was during a brief time, roughly 1794 to 1796—after having fled the contentious Washington administration—that Jefferson spent about two years in the role of "ardent" farmer. The valedictory passage that he sent to Angelica Schuyler Church, noted in the preface, is worth considering again in depth for what it says about how Jefferson viewed Monticello as a plantation and how that shaped the way he conducted his life.

In the mean time I am going to Virginia. I have at length been able to fix that to the beginning of the new year. I am then to be liberated from the hated occupations of politics, and to sink into the bosom of my family, my farm and my books. I have my house to build, my feilds to form, and to watch for the happiness of those who labor for mine. I have one daughter married to a man of science, sense, virtue, and competence; in whom indeed I have nothing more to wish. They live with me. If the

other shall be as fortunate in due process of time, I shall imagine
myself as blessed as the most blessed of the patriarchs.

Madison Hemings, his second son with Sally Hemings, recalled
that Jefferson "hardly ever allowed himself to be made unhappy any
great length of time,"[3] attributing great powers of self-control to his
father, who he also said had a "smooth and even" temperament. Both
Hemings and Martha Randolph used the word "irritated" to describe
how Jefferson acted when things went wrong, both suggesting that
his responses were almost always commensurate to the occasion.[4]
Happiness for Jefferson, apparently, was to a great degree a matter
of choice. Edmund Bacon, overseer at Monticello for nearly seventeen years, gave a concrete example of what Hemings was talking
about. Bacon, then an elderly man, recalled Jefferson's reaction when
brought news of the failure of a dam that he had ordered constructed
to support the operation of his mills. Bacon remembered feeling
completely undone by the event, confessing that he had "never felt
worse."[5] On the other hand, Jefferson, he said, appeared "calm and
quiet as though nothing had happened," when, in fact, the news was
catastrophic. The resulting flood had done great damage to the sea-
son's harvested wheat crop. Instead of dwelling on the loss (at least
not in any way that he allowed Bacon to see), Jefferson immediately
outlined to his distraught employee his plans for solving the problem.
They would put in place a temporary fix and contemplate building
another, better dam when they were able to do so. That was business
related. But Jefferson maintained the same attitude when dealing with
family matters. His revealing letter to Church gives further evidence
of how he accomplished his feat of inward equanimity or, at least, an
outward appearance of equanimity.

The "occupations of politics" were "hated" because Jefferson had
effectively been driven from the field by Church's brother-in-law, the
winner in the contest for Washington's favor. Would Jefferson have
left the cabinet had he been victorious? Church, who was extremely
close to Hamilton, almost certainly knew the basics of what had
transpired between the two men—it was public knowledge that they

were at odds.[6] Jefferson could expect that she would relay his brave-faced self-presentation to his rival. In Jefferson's formulation, the unpleasantness that had gone before was immaterial because he was returning to what he really loved most—family, farm, and books. He had much with which to occupy himself at Monticello: remodeling his house, tending to his neglected land and the enslaved people on his plantation.

His recently married eldest daughter, Martha, whom he adored, was living with him, a good thing on one level, but an indication of a serious problem to which Jefferson, of course, does not allude. She and her husband, Thomas Mann Randolph, were at Monticello because they had no other suitable place to live. Randolph's father, for whom he was named, had just three years earlier, at age fifty, married the teenage Gabriella Harvie. He had a son with her, whom he also named after himself and would make the heir to the family's commodious plantation, Tuckahoe. Jefferson's daughter would never become the mistress of that place, as she had had every reason to expect when she married Tom Randolph that she would upon his father's death. The new stepmother, who seems to have bewitched her middle-aged husband, engaged in a series of blatant power moves that caused Randolph Jr.'s sisters, two of whom were around the same age or older than she, to flee their home. Father and son quarreled heatedly about property, and Randolph Sr. settled on his son the debt-encumbered and physical wreck of a homestead, Varina, with which to begin his married life.

Martha wrote to her father in despair about the situation with her father-in-law, but her letter is no longer extant. We can gauge the depths of her anguish from the letter Jefferson wrote in response. That letter is among his very best—beautifully composed and perfectly calibrated. We can hear Jefferson's voice as he counsels Martha to garner the strength to rise above her despair and carve a new path for herself, since there was really nothing else to be done. She should focus on what she could control by taking action—for example, attempting to make friends with Gabriella—to divert her thoughts from her emotional pain, rather than simply ruminating on her deflated hopes.[7]

This flintiness may not have been what Martha, barely out of her teens, wanted or needed to hear, but it was what Jefferson was prepared to offer, in keeping with the way he handled disappointments and setbacks in his life.

There was also, without question, a gender component to Jefferson's response. His daughter was a wife now. And he lived in a world in which wives were supposed to learn to sacrifice and bear the burdens of domestic life with as much aplomb as possible. For once they married, their individual personhood disappeared as a matter of law. Divorce, a scandalous thing, was near impossible to contemplate or obtain. Women of Martha Randolph's class did not go out into the work world to support themselves. She could return home permanently, which she would do eighteen years later, but that would be a mark of failure. Her father's advice was based on his own understanding of the way their world worked.

Randolph Sr. had died seven days earlier at his Tuckahoe plantation when Jefferson wrote to Church. Jefferson may not have known this, but he did know at the time from recent correspondence with his son-in-law that Randolph was at death's door. With this event the new Mrs. Randolph's property-based triumph over her stepchildren would become complete. In sum, Jefferson's daughter's new family was in great turmoil, a circumstance that could not have made him happy, but he concentrated on his son-in-law's positive attributes, instead of dwelling on all the ways he could have been disappointed about how things were turning out. And he counseled his daughter to attempt, as he had taught himself to do, to maintain control of herself and be forward thinking in her approach to the difficult circumstances in her life.[8]

It was in this willfully optimistic mind-set that Jefferson returned to Monticello in 1794. After some initial months when he was unwell, he dedicated himself as never before (and as he never would again) to being an active hands-on manager of his plantation affairs. He developed what he thought were great ideas for how to "form his feilds" and carry out the harvest in a more efficient way. He understood that farming tobacco, which quickly robbed soil of its nutrients, was a losing proposition for him, and he introduced methods of crop rotation to protect his land. By his own admission, however, not everything turned out as he hoped—as anyone who was familiar with farming in Virginia and saw his plan for bringing greater efficiency to his operations could have predicted. The historian Lucia Stanton has shown that the "patriarch" did not know very much about agricultural work as performed by enslaved people, or any people for that matter. His approach to the harvest betrayed his ignorance and/or lack of empathy with those whose "happiness" he was supposed to be watching for.

In Stanton's words, Jefferson "sought to achieve the clocklike regularity of a machine," which, of course, was impossible because he was dealing with human beings—men, women, and children. Jefferson wrote of the merits of his plan: "In this way, the whole machine would move in exact equilibrio, no part of the force could be lessened without retarding the whole nor increased without a waste of force." Naturally, in operation, "the force" was lessened, throwing the "machine" out of "equilibrio." As Stanton explains, it was the custom among some enslaved people who worked in the fields for the stronger to help out the weaker by slowing down. At Monticello, these were families working together. Husbands were not going to drive their wives, mothers, or children, simply because Jefferson had a blueprint in his head for how they were supposed to be working like some gigantic machine. The whiskey he provided for an incentive would not make them forget themselves to that extent. Three years after this experiment Jefferson lamented that he was "not fit to be a farmer with the kind of labour" they had in Virginia, meaning that he did not know how to make his farm productive under a regime in which work was forced.[9] By the time he wrote these words, he had abandoned his stint as the energetic farmer and was back in public life as vice-president. Now the head of what had become in the 1790s the Republican Party, he had his eye on the presidency of the United States. Farming would have to wait until he felt he was finally finished with his lifework: politics.

Jefferson's true feelings about matters cannot be discerned in the pronouncements he made while attempting to convince others, or himself, of his beliefs about a subject. They are much more likely to be found in the offhand comments he made as he discussed other issues, which is probably the case with all human beings. When writing to correspondents, during his first "retirement" in 1794, Jefferson gave the impression of one living an idyll as he threw himself into the daily rhythms of farming. Some years later, however, when he was back in the fray of political life, he wrote a deeply revealing letter to his daughter Maria. Concerned that she had become too isolated on her plantation at Bermuda Hundred, he encouraged her to be more outgoing, confiding that his years in retirement were, perhaps, the most depressing of his life.[10] This was the period when he was in the "bosom" of his family, but that did not suffice for him. It was not that he did not love his family and Monticello. There were just other things that he simply had to do—and he eventually went to do them, returning to politics as vice-president of the United States.

Madison Hemings summed up Jefferson's attitude about farming when he said that in contrast to George Washington, Jefferson "had but little taste or care for agricultural pursuits" and preferred to be among his "mechanics," by which Hemings meant the carpenters, joiners, and blacksmiths who worked on structures at Monticello.[11] Nevertheless, the image of Jefferson the passionate farmer has become emblazoned in the American historical imagination. There are many reasons for this. The caricature of the famous dispute between Hamilton, the champion of manufacturing, and Jefferson, the champion of agriculture, distorts both men's positions and exaggerates Jefferson's personal affection for and involvement in farming. Hamilton was not against farms, and Jefferson was not against all manufacturing. And it would be a non sequitur to say that Jefferson's enthusiasm for the agricultural stage of human development, his love for gardening and botany, or his invention of a type of plow necessarily translated into a desire to be intimately involved in the day-to-day aspects of being a farmer.

And then, Jefferson also often referred to himself as a "farmer"—a characterization that had cultural power at that time—and wrote romantically about "tilling" soil and all the trees and other things that he had the people enslaved on his plantations plant for him. That he kept a Farm Book detailing the operations of his plantation says nothing about his personal attachment to farming. Many other planters kept such books, and did so more diligently than he. Slavery was a business, and keeping track of inventory, which included human property, was simply part of the enterprise.

That his eldest daughter and her children came to live with him during his real and final retirement has also contributed to the view, in the public mind and in the minds of those who write about him, of Jefferson as an avid farmer. Their letters and, later in life, recollections fix him as he was around 1815. Thomas Jefferson the planter is always in his seventies at home on his plantation with a dozen grandchildren underfoot and visitors packed into every available space at Monticello almost all the time. The period of a complete set of grandchildren and hordes of visitors making pilgrimages up the mountain represented just seventeen of the fifty-four years that Jefferson was the master of Monticello. In the decades before his retirement, he was away from home more than half the time, and was not living the life of a farmer at all, leaving the task of running his plantations to various managers and overseers.

Writing in the months immediately after his death on July 4, 1826, his daughter Martha Randolph said that upon leaving office in 1809 her father was "broken in constitution with a load of debt contracted by his overseers, too old to learn and too feeble in health to give that attention to his affairs which a virginia slave estate requires."[12] Randolph wrote this letter to her daughter Ellen with the expressed intent of having portions of it shared to help explain, to people who mattered, just how her father had come to die bankrupt. This was her very direct—and calculated—attempt to draw sympathy for him and to prevent others from making negative judgments about the terrible circumstances in which the patriarch had left his family. Greater scrutiny of the letter is warranted, for it was not just a matter-of-fact, unself-conscious communication between mother and daughter. With that said, Randolph seems accurate in some ways, and in some ways she does not.

Randolph makes her father, described by many visitors to Monticello during his retirement as vibrant and quite energetic for one his age—one visitor encountering the eighty-one-year-old Jefferson thought he was in his early sixties—seem a near invalid immediately upon leaving the presidency. On the other hand, her half brother Madison Hemings echoed the sentiments of visitors, suggesting that it was not until the final years of his life that Jefferson's health began to fail to the point that he could have been described as "feeble." Certainly he was not so feeble in 1809 that he could not have learned how to manage his farm, which did not require him to actually go out into the fields and do manual labor. It just meant paying attention to detail and management. As a matter of fact, Jefferson in retirement remained very physical, spending time among the carpenters who worked at Monticello—including Hemings and his brothers Beverley and Eston working under the tutelage of their uncle John Hemings. He did not merely watch them. He even made furniture with his own hands during this period.

As for Jefferson's intellectual faculties, they remained sharp to the very end of his life, as evidenced by his lively and wide-ranging correspondence between 1809 and 1826, the energy he expended planning the University of Virginia, and the preparation of his last will in the final months of his life. Soon after his retirement, he took on the hugely challenging task of translating Destutt de Tracy's *Commentary on Book Two of Montesquieu's Espirit des Lois* from the original French. Surely, he could have concentrated enough to learn how to manage his farms had he put his mind to it. His daughter's suggestion that he had to learn such things as late as 1809 is, itself, quite telling. Madison Hemings, a farmer himself, was right: Jefferson had no real "taste" for applying himself to "agricultural pursuits."

SO IT WAS with great relief in 1815 that Jefferson transferred management of his farms to his grandson Jeff Randolph. The results were remarkable. Under Jeff's stewardship, Monticello produced three times more wheat than had been produced under Jefferson's supervision.[13] Jeff knew better what to do to make the plantation work, and he applied himself to the task in a way that his grandfather never did. What exactly did that entail? We do not have a firm answer, but the recollections of Jeff Randolph's nephew Thomas Jefferson Coolidge provide a clue about Randolph's plantation management style and attitude as a slaveholder that may account for some of the increased productivity under his regime as opposed to that of his grandfather's.

Coolidge described an event that occurred during a boyhood visit to his uncle Jeff's plantation, Edgehill. An enslaved man had been accused of stealing something on the farm. Randolph gathered all the slaves together to watch while he whipped the man. Something like this had happened before at Monticello—the gathering of the enslaved to watch a whipping, with James Hubbard as the victim. After Hubbard's repeated attempts at escape, in 1812, Jefferson decided that a whipping in front of other slaves would serve as a warning to all others not to try to follow Hubbard's example. He had already arranged for Hubbard's sale on favorable terms, because he was convinced that the determined man would never again "serve any man as a slave."[14] Although the end result was the same—an enslaved man was beaten—there was a very crucial difference: Jeff Randolph whipped the enslaved man himself, whereas Jefferson had his overseer mete out Hubbard's punishment. The willingness—and capacity—to do personal physical violence shows that Jeff Randolph had a very different personality from that of his grandfather. Jeff was more in the mold of his father, Thomas Mann Randolph, a mercurial man who got into violent scrapes even as an adult.

Did Jeff's greater personal ruthlessness play any part in the increase in productivity? The historian Edward Baptist has argued that whipping—torture, as he clarifies the activity—contributed to increases in productivity on slave plantations in the 1850s.[15] Using the lash made a difference. The incident that Coolidge described took place after Jefferson had died and after Jeff was running Monticello. There is no reason to think, however, that a propensity to violence grew stronger in him as he aged, as it has not been the typical pattern throughout history that men tend to get more aggressive and violent as they age. In his twenties, while Jefferson was still alive and Jeff was managing Monticello, Jeff threatened to "horsewhip" his brother-in-law Charles Bankhead after Bankhead made what Jeff thought were inappropriate comments to Jeff's wife. He actually struck Bankhead in the face with the handle of his whip, and the two men fought, with Jeff ultimately getting the worst of the altercation. Even if Jeff Randolph did not wield the whip himself all the time, his willingness to do so sent a message to all who witnessed it or knew of it.

Randolph experienced the plantation differently than his grandfather, and he was a different type of patriarch. He was protective of his blood family (though more effectively than his grandfather), and he could also be as sentimental about the family's favored slaves as Jefferson. In the days immediately following the auction of Monticello slaves—much to his wife's chagrin—Randolph bought back the wife and children of Wormley Hughes, a grandson of Elizabeth Hemings and the gardener at Monticello to whom Jefferson had been close. He later bought back even more. But, overall, he was a more hard-nosed plantation manager and businessman than Jefferson. Whatever motivated him—love of the process, the extreme desire to please his grandfather, a wish to avoid the fate of his father, who had been unsuccessful on his plantation—Randolph threw himself into the work of operating Monticello with great zeal. He could do this because, unlike his grandfather, he had no apparent passions that equaled or exceeded his desire to focus on farming on the mountain. He saw the plantation for what it was supposed to be—a venture in which enslaved people worked in the fields and the Jefferson-Randolph family profited from their labor.

As agricultural production at Monticello ramped up under the direction of Jeff's more intense and steady hand, Jefferson gave himself over to a new passion—what he would call "the hobby of [his] old age": the founding of the University of Virginia. Freed from having the primary responsibility for dealing with his farms, the task of building a curriculum, a faculty, and, finally, a structure itself engaged his energy for the rest of his life, as these things, too, went to the core of what Jefferson truly was: a builder, a "mechanic." He professed to

John Quincy Adams, at dinner at the President's House one evening in 1807, that "he had always been extremely fond of agriculture," acknowledging that "he knew nothing about it." James Madison, he said, was much better informed on the topic.[16] Fondness for a thing you know nothing about does not suggest a serious engagement with the thing. Although Jefferson obviously saw Monticello as an agricultural operation, he treated it more like an immense backdrop against which he played the role of statesman and participant in the republic of letters. It was a setting, the place where he also made entries into his various record books, read, played his violin (when he was younger), entertained guests when required, contemplated what to do about the plantation factories he built and operated for personal and commercial use, and planned his university. More than anything else, for Jefferson, Monticello was a place where he built things, most notably the house that was the centerpiece of his identity. He loved being at his plantations—both Monticello and Poplar Forest—but his passions and most sustained attentions were invariably directed toward the non-farm-related activities that went on in both places.

This was not just Jefferson's story in his final years. Even during his first retirement, when he pledged to devote himself to taking care of his farm, he allowed another venture at Monticello to capture his imagination—one that united his need for money, his interest in Enlightenment-driven projects, and his thoughts about slavery. As for slavery, we will explore in chapter 5 just how and why Jefferson's time in France transformed his attitude about the institution and shaped his view of himself as a slave owner for the next four decades. It was there that the antislavery advocate made his peace with slavery and, for the first time, expressed thoughts about what he called "ameliorating" it while floating agriculture-related schemes that he thought would achieve this aim.

Amelioration

Once Jefferson was home in the 1790s, his first real and most intense experiment with what he considered amelioration had nothing at all to do with agriculture—the botched harvest plan in which he sought to achieve machinelike efficiency among his field-workers owed more to his Enlightenment-based faith in technology than to his schemes to make slavery more humane for the enslaved. In 1796 he brought an industrial operation, albeit in miniature form, to his mountain: he opened a nail factory, staffed by young males aged ten to sixteen.

Jefferson took his example from England, where nail making was the province of women and children, though he left the enslaved women on his plantation out of this endeavor. He fixated on the nail factory to what might seem an excessive degree, checking on the boys' work at least twice daily and assiduously measuring the number of nails each boy produced. This was clearly not necessary, but this was a man who, under the influence of the Enlightenment era mania for measuring and quantifying everything, once individually counted garden peas to see how many would make a pint. What was the number? Two thousand and five hundred, he learned. Jefferson wanted to do this. And, most importantly, the nail factory (during this time period, at least) actually made money for him, providing much needed income to make ends almost meet, as he had been unable to make his farms profitable. In truth, Jefferson's nail factory brought to Monticello an odd mixture of what during his time were called the "stages" of development: the agricultural stage existing side by side with the final industrial stage—Jefferson the agriculturalist and Jefferson the factory owner. He thought this was progress.

In setting up the nail factory as he did, Jefferson made an early connection between plantations and prisons, places that held unfree people living under the control of others.[17] He knew well the distinction between prisoners held to service, except in extreme cases only for a time, because they had committed crimes, and the enslaved people on his plantation, who had done nothing but be born to mothers who were enslaved. In both cases, however, the law justified removing the freedom of a designated category of individuals and giving others the power to control them. In Notes on the State of Virginia Jefferson described the malign effects that power had on the manners of white slave owners. Slavery, he said, was a school for despotism, with attributes handed down from parent to child, thus ensuring that the basic characteristics of the system would roll forth from generation to generation.

> The whole commerce between master and slave is a perpetual exercise of the most boisterous passions, the most unremitting despotism on the one part, and degrading submissions on the other. Our children see this, and learn to imitate it; for man is an imitative animal. This quality is the germ of all education in him. From his cradle to his grave he is learning to do what he sees others do. If a parent could find no motive either in his philanthropy or his self-love, for restraining the intemperance of passion towards his slave, it should always be a sufficient one that his child is present. But generally it is not sufficient. The parent storms, the child looks on, catches the lineaments of wrath, puts on the same airs in the circle of smaller slaves, gives a loose to his worst of passions, and thus nursed, educated, and daily exercised in tyranny, cannot but be stamped by it with odious peculiarities. The man must be a prodigy who can retain his manners and morals undepraved by such circumstances.[18]

Jefferson writes in categorical terms about the corrosive attributes of slavery, considers the possibility that parents might conduct themselves in ways that would mitigate the damages, but immediately rejects this as likely insufficient. His approach to running the nail factory suggests how far removed he was from proclaiming to others that nothing could be done to stamp out the inherent corruption involved in enslaving people. Now, in his circumstances in the 1790s, a master like himself—a "prodigy"—*could* govern in a way that did not give vent to his "worst . . . passions" or stoke the "daily" exercises of "tyranny." In the midst of the age of revolution, Jefferson the revolutionary did not wish to see himself as a despot or tyrant—the names he had called George III. At the same time, he was not about to cease ownership of the people he enslaved. The solution was to find a way to make it emotionally easier for him to enslave people, given his professed values, and easier (in his mind) for the enslaved to endure their condition.

As historian Christa Dierksheide has shown, the ultimate effect of Jefferson's approach to amelioration, which manifested itself in different ways, was, in fact, to deepen his attachment to slavery as the years wore on, in ways that were probably imperceptible to him. To the very end of his life, he insisted that his position was well and long known—that he retained the strong antislavery position he had staked out as a young man that slavery was inherently evil. This sentiment had not started as mere posturing on Jefferson's part. At the age of twenty-eight, before he came onto the public stage, he copied into his commonplace book some lines from a William Shenstone poem, "An Inscription for an African Slave." The lines refer to an African who was torn from his "bless'd" homeland by "stern tyrant[s]" and compelled to work for others. This passage prefigures by five years his language in the Declaration of Independence, which was excised by the Continental Congress: "He has waged cruel war against human nature itself, violating its most sacred rights of life & liberty in the persons of a distant people who never offended him, captivating & carrying them into slavery in another hemisphere, or to incur miserable death in the transportation thither."[19] This idea was more to Jefferson than a spur-of-the-moment bogus charge against George III. Antislavery sentiment was part of the package of progressive thought at the time, like skepticism of the official church and support for scientific advances. These earlier statements and gestures were incompatible with the suggestion that slavery could be a happy state for the enslaved. But what if he could change the calculus and excise from the "whole" some of the worst parts of the "commerce" between masters and slaves? What if his passions were less boisterous, and he less despotic? Could he not institute connections to enslaved people (some, not all, for that would be too expensive) that did not require "degrading submissions," but instead rested (in his mind) on some degree of consent?

The phrase Jefferson used in writing to Angelica Church—"watching for the happiness of those who labored for" his happiness—imagines a reciprocal relationship. The enslaved did things for him. He, in turn, did things for them. In correspondence Jefferson pointedly noted that he acceded, when he could, to the requests of men and women who wished to have relatives bought so that they could live together as a nuclear family, or be sold so that they could do that on another plantation, as if this were evidence of his attention to slaves' happiness. He would offer this as an example of "commerce" with enslaved people that did not evince dangerous passion or despotism on his part, or of degrading submission by the enslaved. In fact, in a way that some modern readers might find striking, Jefferson's writing suggests that *he* was "submitting" by giving in to their requests, as if it were the most natural thing in the world that they should have to ask him.

The letter to Church shows Jefferson thought it possible to be a slaveholder and still have enslaved people's best interests at heart. It also shows that he believed that the enslaved actually could be made happy in their circumstances. If he did things to encourage that feeling, conflict could be minimized, or totally avoided—and work would proceed. Slavery was no longer, necessarily, a state of war, a Lockean formulation to which Jefferson adhered. An "enlightened" patriarch could make a difference, could make peace between the master and the enslaved. One is reminded of the words that the Roman historian Tacitus puts into the mouth of a Caledonian general, criticizing the Romans and their depredations in Scotland: *ubi solitudinem faciunt, pacem appellant*—"they make a desert, and they call it peace."

JEFFERSON, WHO ALWAYS wished to be in the forefront of progress, got his ideas about how to run his plantation's nail factory from what he had learned of enlightened penal practices from the Walnut Street prison in Philadelphia when he was living there as secretary of state. Proponents of prison reform deemed it a forward-thinking approach to use incentives rather than punishment to shape people's behavior. The nail factory was a moneymaking operation, but it was also an experiment, exactly the kind that played to Jefferson's scientific bent. In 1801, when he was away from Monticello serving as president, he wrote to his son-in-law Thomas Mann Randolph telling him to remind the overseers to eschew whipping except in extreme circumstances, hoping that the "stimulus of character" rather than the "degrading" whip would make the boys work harder.[20]

Jefferson described his plan to François Alexandre Frédéric, duc de La Rochefoucauld-Liancourt, a French aristocrat credited with correcting King Louis XVI when he insisted that disturbances just before the fall of the Bastille were merely a revolt, by saying, "No, your majesty, it is a revolution." The duc showed up unannounced for a week-long visit to Monticello in June of 1796 and took note of Jefferson's farm operations. The nailery made a distinct impression upon him, and he observed that Jefferson animated the boys with "rewards and distinctions."[21] What were they? Jefferson thought that making George Granger Jr. the foreman of the nailery, and allowing him to share in a percentage of the profits of the operation, was an incentive to Granger. It could also encourage the boys, who might aspire to become foremen themselves. Moreover, he paid the boys, including Granger's younger brother, Isaac, sometimes in cash, but mainly in double rations and clothing, depending upon how many nails they made.

Plantations were supposed to be as self-sufficient as possible. The enslaved at Shadwell and Monticello, for example, made clothes and shoes for other enslaved people. Monticello blacksmiths forged horseshoes and other iron products for the plantation. They often sold their services to the surrounding communities whose residents, evidently, found it convenient to come to this centrally located place. The Monticello nail factory, as it operated in the 1790s, was something different because the nails were not primarily for home consumption. Jefferson sent the products of this operation out into the market for a profit, competing with other nail makers. The young boys toiled away in closed quarters all day, doing repetitive work that almost certainly had an adverse effect upon their still growing bodies and their spirits.

As one easily could have anticipated, violence did not disappear from the nail factory, despite Jefferson's orders. One of his overseers during the years the factory was in operation, Gabriel Lilly, did whip the boys. In one instance, he gave a very violent whipping to a young member of the Hemings family, Critta Hemings's son James (not to be confused with his uncle James, Critta's older brother). Hemings ran away. When Jefferson found out where he was and ordered him to return, the young man—seventeen at the time—refused. He would come back, he said, only if Jefferson agreed to allow him to go to work for his uncle John Hemings, thus putting him out of Lilly's control. The overseer at Monticello did not have charge over the people who worked in the house, or over Jefferson's artisans. Jefferson agreed to Hemings's terms. No doubt traumatized by Lilly's abuse, and enjoying his rightful place in freedom, James Hemings never returned to Monticello, at least not as a slave. Jefferson took him, the grandson of John Wayles, half nephew of his late wife, cousin to his white daughters, and the nephew of Sally Hemings, off the slave rolls. That did not end Hemings's contact with Jefferson. There is a reference to Jefferson, then in retirement, having paid Hemings to find a part for a telescope.[22]

James Hemings's multiple connections to people Jefferson cared about provided ample reason for Jefferson to take this course of action, informally freeing the young man who defied his order, set conditions on his agreement to return to Monticello, and then, after those conditions were met, decided, nevertheless, to remain free. Members of the Hemings family had every reason to be angry about Lilly's treatment of their relative, and their unhappiness would affect those around them. Jefferson was not pleased with Lilly's actions either, for the overseer had brought into his household a thing that he abhorred: conflict. But he did not fire Lilly; he kept him on until Lilly did something else that really disturbed the peace: he began to agitate for a larger salary.

Jefferson resolved the conflict between Lilly and James Hemings— and one supposes the extended Hemings family—by letting Hemings go. Lilly remained, but Critta Hemings's son, who had run to Richmond, where his uncle Robert lived with his wife and children, could go his own way. This was another action that allowed Jefferson to see himself as a benevolent patriarch—doling out random acts of leniency as he thought the situation warranted without changing the basic nature of slavery or really weakening his position as a slave owner at all. The same was true of his operation of the nail factory. He enacted a modest reform that preserved the status quo, allowing him to think that he, too, was traveling on a road of progress that would be extended in increments toward the inevitable endpoint where slavery would disappear.

Of course, at Jefferson's place on the road to progress, an even more transformative move would have been to regularly pay, in money or other goods, the agricultural workers who made up his harvest "machine" and tended his crops in general—not just George Granger Sr., the overseer. What he gave them at harvest time—whiskey— was not, as he discovered unsurprisingly, a real incentive. Aside from being debilitating physically, it was not money, a thing that could be more easily exchanged for other things of value.

In Jefferson's oft-mentioned balance between humanity and self-interest, paying agricultural workers would have tipped the balance too far in one direction: weighing a bit too much on the cost-to-his-self-interest side—even though his "logic" and experiences suggested that giving people financial incentives would make them work more and do so more efficiently. But taking that logic to its most reasonable conclusion would have fundamentally altered the basis of the system of slavery. In the end, the enslaved people whom Jefferson more systematically "paid" at various points—in the form of wages, gratuities, or other incentives—were his house servants and artisans, the people who were closest to him physically and about whom he cared the most. This was a very small, easily managed group.

While in Paris with James and Sally Hemings, when he was as far away from plantation culture as he would ever be, Jefferson paid both siblings wages.[23] This began a practice that he continued after he returned to America. Whenever he was away from the plantation and living in a household that mixed free and enslaved workers, he paid all who worked for him. He did this in New York, Philadelphia, and Washington City when he became president, though none of the people there had as clear a shot for freedom as Sally and James Hemings did while they were in Paris. There was no doubt in Jefferson's mind that any slave who sought freedom in that city could obtain it. He had an incentive to try to keep the siblings from leaving him. Carrying this policy out in America was, in all likelihood, just Jefferson's way of keeping the peace within the confines of an urban household. On payday there would be no demoralizing spectacle of some workers in the house getting money while other workers looking on received nothing.

The gratuities and wages he paid to members of the Hemings and Granger families, the Grangers being the other enslaved family at Monticello who received the main share of Jefferson's attention and favor, can be seen as part of his effort at amelioration—no matter that the Grangers and Hemingses represented a mere fraction of the slaves he owned over the years. Unlike the Hemingses, who, in the main, provided personal and intimate comforts to Jefferson, the Grangers were in charge of two of Jefferson's important economic operations— Monticello and the nail factory. Over the years he paid a yearly gratuity to Burwell Colbert and John Hemings and gave them running accounts at the local store. Giving these men money (when he did not have to), buying or selling slaves to unite them with relatives (when he was of a mind to), and doing things like taking volunteers who would be paid to clean out Monticello's privies—because that was a disgusting job—helped mitigate Jefferson's sense that he was involved in inherently degraded encounters with the enslaved. Everything that he did, but did not *have* to do, could be seen as altering the law-based commerce between himself and those he held in bondage.

Mastery

It must be said that even before he went to France, Jefferson had ideas about how to conduct himself as the master of a plantation, and he developed those ideas in a singular context. He married a woman who had six enslaved siblings whom she brought to their marriage. Instead of hiding them away at one of their other plantations, Thomas and Martha brought the Hemingses to Monticello to work directly for them. As the males grew older, Jefferson gave the Hemings brothers Martin, Robert, James, and Peter an unusual amount of freedom. Martin was not a Wayles son, but his connection to the Wayles children and, probably, his status as the eldest son led Jefferson to treat him like his half brothers. The four traveled alone throughout Virginia, hired out their own time, and kept the money they made. Jefferson maintained loose tabs on them, and sometimes wrote to people in the towns where he thought they might be living to discover their whereabouts. The still young revolutionary critic of slavery put these men in a category that deemphasized their legal status and made them akin to "servants" in their day-to-day existences. Yet they were decidedly not free. They had to return when he summoned them, but he, and they, could think of themselves as different from other enslaved people.

By the time Jefferson reached the presidency, his understanding of how to play the role of the "good slave master" to the enslaved people closest to him had changed. The days of allowing favored slaves to travel about and to hire their own time were over. Nor were any Hemingses brought to Washington to serve in the President's House. In New York and Philadelphia, in the immediate aftermath of his time in Paris, Jefferson brought Robert and James Hemings with him to run his household. By the time he became president, these two men were free, Robert, as noted, living with his wife, Dolly, and their children, Martin and Elizabeth. When James Hemings, who spent the 1790s traveling in the United States and back to Europe, declined the job of chef in the President's House, Jefferson hired Honoré Julien. He also brought from Monticello young Ursula Granger—her mother, Ursula, had nursed the infant Martha Jefferson Randolph—to train under Julien. Ursula lasted only a brief time and was replaced by Edith Hern Fossett and Frances Gillette Hern.

In the eight years Jefferson was in office, Granger (for her brief time), Fossett, and Hern were the only slaves from his plantation who lived regularly at the President's House. They were there, not so much because they were needed in the kitchen, but to be trained to serve Jefferson's needs at Monticello once he returned there for good. In fact, Fossett went on to become Jefferson's favorite chef. This configuration of the presidential household was a far cry from the situation in 1779 when Governor Jefferson essentially transported his enslaved household staff, Hemingses and Grangers, to serve him in the governor's mansions in Williamsburg and then Richmond: why not reprise this setup?

The question why a man who had an overabundance of domestic enslaved men and women (living in "idleness at Monticello," as he described the women) chose to employ others was so obvious that Jefferson felt compelled to explain himself, though he did not do so very well. He said that he preferred to hire servants in Washington City because, unlike slaves, they could be fired if they "misbehaved," as if there was nothing to be done about misbehaving slaves. The more likely answer is that there was nothing he could think of doing to the enslaved people who would be the most probable candidates for positions in the President's House—the Hemingses and their children. There was no indication then that these individuals would have "misbehaved" or that if they did, they could not, like Ursula Granger, who it turned out was pregnant when she came to Washington, be sent home and replaced with hired labor if the situation warranted it.

The Jefferson of this era was not like the pre-1784 Jefferson. Upon his return to his country at the end of 1789, he performed "benevolence" in a completely different way than he had before, one in keeping with his greater comfort in the institution of slavery and with the people he held in bondage. He had also learned a great deal about the effects of having people exist in what could be termed a quasi-free status. Before his stay in France, subject to the gender conventions of the day, Jefferson signaled his attachment to particular enslaved people (the Hemingses, actually) by his willingness to put them in as near a state of freedom as they could be in without actually freeing them— attachment was associated with letting go. That is why the Hemings brothers could go off on their own until Jefferson called them back if he needed them for something. Other enslaved men—not attached to Jefferson by any affective ties—remained attached to the plantation and had to stay put. The Hemings sisters, Jefferson would naturally say, were different. No women, white or black, enslaved or free, were supposed to go wandering around Virginia by themselves. Elizabeth Hemings and her daughters *were* attached to Jefferson affectively because of the Martha Wayles Jefferson connection and to the farm because the farm was home, and that is where women belonged. Instead, Jefferson showed his attachment to them by limiting them to activities that the white wife of even a middling farmer might do—sewing, cooking, cleaning—tasks in keeping with his notions of femininity. They did not do fieldwork.

The relative freedom he had given the Hemingses, as it was bound to do, raised their expectations about how their lives should proceed. In the early 1790s all of the Hemings males, with the exception of Peter and John, who was still a little boy during this time, expressed the desire to leave Monticello. Martin Hemings and Jefferson quarreled—about what Jefferson would not say—and Hemings demanded to be sold. Jefferson agreed to do this, but there is no record of a sale and no mention of his death. It is possible that he, as his half nephew James Hemings would be, was simply let go. His brothers Robert and James Hemings were formally freed in the 1790s. Mary Hemings asked to be sold to the man with whom she had had children, and Thenia Hemings, Wayles's daughter, was apparently sold to James Monroe to be reunited with the father of her children. The raised expectations on the part of Sally Hemings began even before she and her brother returned to America. Living in Paris, receiving wages, and understanding that she had the opportunity for freedom in the country, she balked at the idea of returning to Monticello with Jefferson, until she and Jefferson came to an understanding about what her life would be like if she went back with him to Virginia.

Close as he became to Burwell Colbert, John Hemings, and Joseph Fossett, men he freed upon his death, the Jefferson devoted to amelioration signaled attachment to these men in a way that kept them firmly within the contours of the slave system. Everything they got would come from him and life at Monticello. There are no stories of these men traveling freely through Virginia to hire their time in order to make money, no sense that Jefferson did not know where

they were at given times. In fact, in 1806, when he learned that Joseph
Fossett had left Monticello to go to Washington City to see his wife,
Edith, whom Jefferson had left at the President's House when he came
home for a visit, he hired a slave catcher to find him. Jefferson was
nonplussed—why would Fossett leave "without the least word of difference with anybody, and indeed never in his life [having] recieved
a blow from anyone"?[24] Note Jefferson's focus on what had *not* happened to Fossett during his life as an enslaved man—Jefferson had not
allowed anyone to beat or hurt him. He had created an existence for
Fossett devoid of one of the signature aspect of slavery: whippings.
This restraint, once again what Jefferson thought of as softening the
commerce between master and slave, called for reciprocity on Fossett's part, a duty that he breached when he went off to see his wife.

Jefferson appeared similarly confused when Robert Hemings
arranged to have George Stras of Richmond, for whom he had
worked a number of years, purchase his freedom. At this time, 1793,
Hemings had a wife and child, Dolly and Elizabeth, respectively. The
couple would later add a son, Martin. Jefferson wrote petulantly to
his son-in-law Thomas Mann Randolph about concluding "Bob's
business"—the dealings with Stras—as if he saw Hemings's desire for
freedom as a betrayal. The close association between the two began
when Jefferson made Hemings his preteen valet after his marriage to
Hemings's half sister Martha. Hemings spent a good deal of his time
away from Monticello working on his own and for himself, facts
Jefferson noted in his complaining letter, as if this should have made
Hemings wish to maintain the status quo. In his mind he had been
"good" to Hemings. Jefferson also wrote as if he were powerless to
do anything other than go along with Hemings's proposal. This combination of being "good" to Hemings and being willing to submit to
Hemings's will, even when he did not have to, was a perfect example
of how Jefferson saw himself altering the commerce between master
and the enslaved.[25]

As is common among those who live under the power of others,
Hemings had every reason to pay attention to the man who had exer-

cised control over his life for two decades. His long association with Jefferson had given him great insight into the older man's personality. He knew what Jefferson wanted to hear. When he ran into Martha Randolph on a Richmond street shortly after the deal with Stras had been struck, he requested that she assure her father that he would never have left him for anyone other than his wife and child. It is not known whether this message placated Jefferson, but the two men did keep cordial relations with each other after Hemings's emancipation.[26]

ACROSS THE SPECTRUM of his relationships with the enslaved—from the bedroom to the fields, from his artisan shops to the backyard factories—Jefferson created connections on his plantation that promoted his self-satisfaction. Slavery worked well for the patriarch at all stages of his life, but particularly in the days after he left public service. It not only provided him with a basic livelihood, though not as good a one as he could have had; it also allowed him to "monopolize . . . [the] time, talents, and attention" of enslaved people in a way that "he could not do with the whites in his life."[27] There was no real incentive for him to do anything else, and he was willing to be a "prodigy" only within the confines of the institution. Slavery bounded his life from cradle to grave.

As previously noted, Jefferson family lore has Jefferson recalling that his earliest memory was of being handed up on a pillow to a slave when his family made the trip from Shadwell to Tuckahoe so that Peter Jefferson could fulfill his promise to act as guardian to the orphaned children of William and Mary Randolph. His grandson said that when Jefferson was on his deathbed, he spoke words that were unintelligible to anyone but his enslaved manservant, Burwell Colbert, a grandson of Elizabeth Hemings and nephew of Sally Hemings. He wished to be lifted higher on his pillows. Colbert made the adjustment. The old man closed his eyes. He went to sleep comforted, woke up to have a drink of water, then breathed his last breath. The first person he remembered and one of the last he saw was an enslaved Virginian. Jefferson traveled a great distance in his life, geographically, socially, and politically, as the colonial society in which he was born became a new nation. Through it all, however, he remained very much a product of Virginia's plantation society—the society that formed him and the place where he discovered what role he wanted to play in the world and how to position himself to play it.

... the particular customs and manners that may happen to be received ~~Manners~~ Manner in that state?

It is difficult to determine on the standard by which the manners of a nation may be tried, whether Catholic or Particular. it is more difficult for a native to ~~bring to their standard~~ the manners of his own nation, familiarised to him by habit. there must doubtless be an unhappy influence on the manners of ~~our~~ people, produced by the existence of slavery among us. the ~~whole~~ that tyranny in the daily ~~exercise~~ ~~of which we are~~ ~~ed & educated~~ from ~~our cradles~~ cannot fail to ~~stamp us with~~ odious peculiarities. the man must be a prodigy who can retain his manners & morals undepraved by such circumstances. and with what execration should the statesman be loaded, who permitting ~~one~~ half the citizens thus to trample on the rights of the other, transforms those into despots & these into enemies, destroys the morals of the one part, & the amor patriae of the other. for if a slave can have a country in this world, it must be any other in preference to that in which he is born to live & labour for another. or in which he must lock up the ~~most~~ faculties of his nature, contribute as far as depends on his individual endeavors to the evanishment of the human race, or entail his own miserable condition on the endless generations proceeding from him. with the morals of the people, their industry also is destroyed. for in a warm climate no man will labour for himself who can make another labour for him. this is so true, that of the proprietors of slaves a very small proportion indeed ~~are~~ ever seen to labour. and can the liberties of a nation be thought secure when we have removed their only firm basis, a conviction in the minds of the people that these liberties are ~~of~~ the gift of god? that they are ~~not~~ to be violated but with his wrath? ~~indeed I tremble for my country when I reflect that god is just: that his justice cannot sleep forever: that considering numbers, nature & natural means only, a revolution of the wheel of fortune, an exchange of situation is among possible events: that it may become probable by supernatural interference! the Almighty has no attribute which can take side with us in such a contest.~~ but it is impossible to be temperate and to pursue this subject through the various considerations of policy, of morals, of history natural & civil. we must be contented to hope they will force their way into every one's mind. I think a change already perceptible since the origin of the present revolution. the spirit of the master is abating, that of the slave rising from the dust, his condition mollifying, the way I hope ~~the way~~ preparing, under the auspices of heaven for a total emancipation, & that this is disposed, in the order of events, to be with the consent of the masters, rather than by their extirpation.

Manuscript Page, Query XIV, "Laws." (Massachusetts Historical Society)

CHAPTER 3

VIRGINIA

Jefferson's real journeys in life began when he left his plantation home to go to the then seat of power in Virginia: Williamsburg, the colonial capital. Matters were not always easy for him there. He experienced the normal range of frustrations common to young people trying to find their way in the world, most notably his unrequited and, apparently, unexpressed love for Rebecca Burwell. As a twenty-year-old, torn by what he saw as his competing desires to travel the world or to get married and settle down, he once spoke of submitting his fortunes to "divine will." It did not take him long to see that he could—and should—take matters into his own hands, for he had found a mission for his life: to protect, reform, and perfect Virginia, his "country." He began to prepare himself to do that at the College of William and Mary, where he very fortunately came under the influence of the Scottish professor William Small and the eminent lawyer George Wythe, and through them the larger world of the Enlightenment.

Jefferson admired what he called Small's "large and liberal mind" and credited his teacher, with whom he read natural philosophy and mathematics, as the source of his ideas about "the expansion of science & of the system of things of which we are placed."[1] He was even closer to George Wythe, whom he met through Professor Small.

Wythe, later a signer of the Declaration of Independence, taught other prominent lawyers in the eighteenth and early nineteenth centuries, among them Patrick Henry, John Marshall, and Henry Clay. He held the first chair in law in the United States at William and Mary and went on to become a prominent jurist. He had an enormous influence on Jefferson, who apprenticed with him for five years—much longer than was usual at that time—and the pair served together in the House of Burgesses, the Virginia legislature. Jefferson said of Wythe, "He was my antient master, my earliest & best friend; and to him I am indebted for first impressions which have had the most salutary influence on the course of my life."[2] Both Small and Wythe were prominent adherents to the Enlightenment and were considered progressive; over the years Wythe would become known for his anti-slavery sentiment. Jefferson was always very keen to be considered progressive and knowledgeable about the latest science and theories of government, while maintaining a healthy skepticism about organized religion. Through his association with these very influential men, particularly Wythe, young Jefferson soon found himself at the pinnacle of provincial society. That is how he came to be asked to dine and play his violin with Lieutenant Governor Francis Fauquier at the Governor's Palace. This rapid ascent to the upper reaches of elite society in Williamsburg while he was still a student confirmed Jefferson's high status, but it also testified to the limited opportunities the Old Dominion afforded its ambitious sons.

Situated between the James and York rivers, Williamsburg was not an impressive place when Jefferson arrived there in 1760. With a population of only a few thousand, more than half enslaved, the town's business was government. The Capitol and the Governor's Palace dominated Williamsburg's civic landscape. In later years Jefferson the accomplished architect had very little good to say about any building in Virginia, beyond noting that most private homes were built of wood and therefore not to last. "It is impossible," he wrote in *Notes on the State of Virginia*, "to devise things more ugly, uncomfortable, and happily more perishable." The brick public buildings of Williamsburg had pretensions to permanence, but were generally crude imitations of British metropolitan models. The Capitol was "a light and airy structure" and—notwithstanding lapses in taste ("the inter-colonnations [were] too large" and the pediment was "too high for its span")—it was "the most pleasing piece of architecture" Virginians had.[3] Perhaps Jefferson's retrospective view was colored by the stirring events he witnessed there, including Patrick Henry's famous speech of May 30, 1765, against the Stamp Act, or by his own career as a burgess in the run-up to the revolution, from 1769 to 1776.

The Governor's Palace was a particularly important place in the Williamsburg Jefferson remembered. During his school years Fau-quier had become the representative of royal authority in Virginia, after being deputized by the nonresident governors John Campbell, earl of Loudoun (1758–63), and Jeffery Amherst (1763–68), successive British commanders-in-chief in the great North American war for empire, or the French and Indian War. Fauquier's home was "not handsome without," Jefferson recalled in his *Notes*, "but it [was] spa-cious and commodious within, [was] prettily situated, and, with the grounds annexed to it, [was] capable of being made an elegant seat."[4] Jefferson had pleasant memories of the time he spent in the palace. The lieutenant governor's erudition and refined manner ingratiated him with enlightened and reform-minded Virginians, including the impressionable young Jefferson. Fauquier studiously avoided antag-onizing the thin-skinned, rights-conscious planter elite and thus proved an able manager of the provincial war effort.

Jefferson specifically credited George Wythe with introducing him "to the acquaintance and familiar table" of his "intimate friend" Fauquier at the palace. Jefferson remembered, "With him, and at his table, Dr. Small & Mr. Wythe, his *amici omnium horarum*, & myself, formed a partie quarree, & to the habitual conversations on these occa-sions I owed much instruction."[5] Jefferson's intimacy with Fauquier—and with Small before his return to Britain in 1764—showed how natural an affectionate union among like-minded Britons—or citizens of a cosmopolitan "republic of letters"—could and should have been, had Great Britain, in his view, not overstepped boundaries. Signifi-cantly, Jefferson's unfinished *Autobiography*, begun when he was in his late seventies, had Small returning "to Europe," not to Great Britain, thus separating his mentor, "a man profound in most of the useful branches of science," from the country Jefferson still disdained. Conversations at the palace constituted the young man's real education, modeling the edifying exchanges that would be central to his idealized conception of home as well as his vision of an enlightened republican future for Virginia and the new United States.

While the Governor's Palace held some semblance of grandeur, Williamsburg's other public buildings were, in Jefferson's memories, undistinguished at best. "The College and Hospital are rude, misshapen piles, which, but that they have roofs, would be taken for brick-kilns. There are no other public buildings but churches and courthouses in which no attempts are made at elegance."[6] The teenage Jefferson was hardly capable of forming such judgments when he first arrived in Williamsburg: the relevant comparisons for him then would have been with remote Albemarle, not with European metropolises, ancient or modern. He began to think deeply about architecture only when he traveled abroad and started to envision Virginia's future outside of the empire. Appearances mattered to the image and identity of a nation, and Virginians would have to do better with their architecture if they wished to be taken seriously. Additionally, they could not simply copy what Europeans had done. The public buildings in Richmond—after the state government moved there from Williamsburg in 1780—and throughout republican Virginia should, Jefferson thought, improve on Old World models. His indictment of Virginia architecture was part and parcel of his rejection of the provincial old regime. If the college was little better than a "brick-kiln" and was hopelessly compromised by its historic associations with the Church of England, perhaps those bricks could be reassembled, or new ones produced that would give rise to a structure befitting a new republican society.

Progress

Anglo-Americans were accustomed to comparisons between their semicivilized provinces and the great British metropolis across the

Atlantic: London was the province's real capital, and immersion in its literary culture only reinforced its attraction for serious students at the college. Williamsburg was an undeniably sorry replica of London, underscoring Virginians' dependency on a distant monarch. Provincial planters came together in the town and in their county courts as subjects of King George III: the corporate identity of the Old Dominion ultimately derived from allegiance to the crown and was grounded in royal charters. But the revolutionary crisis opened up exhilarating new vistas for young Virginians like Jefferson. Challenging imperial authority inspired him and other provincial Americans, eager to establish their cultural standards, to look beyond Britain. Instead, they went directly to the sources of modern European civilization found in ancient Greece and Rome, and looked forward to its future progress in their own part of the Western world. Differences between relatively primitive Virginia and sophisticated London were not necessarily markers of inferiority that could be overcome only by crossing the ocean.

Provincial patriots began to craft a narrative of their own, one that contrasted the supposed virtue of their countrymen with the luxury and vice of the British. They inveighed against a "venal and corrupt" ministry that sought to strip them of their rights. In this new climate the modest origins of Virginia's first settlers became a source of pride, rather than shame: "Our ancestors . . . were laborers, not lawyers," Jefferson wrote in the draft version of his *Summary View of the Rights of British America* (1774). Instead of "laborers," he had originally written "farmers," and that more inclusive term with its connotations of landownership and independence was restored in the published edition.[7] The lawyer Jefferson thus renounced his own profession—and his ambitions *within* an empire where "law" had become the tool of despotic rule—while he celebrated the productive labors of men like his father who had expanded the boundaries of Britain's North American empire.

From this new patriotic perspective, "Virginia" appeared more self-sufficient, more capable of improvement, and less dependent on Great Britain. After all, Virginia's surveyors who marked the way through the forests, and the farmers who followed, had contributed to the empire's wealth and power, tipping the balance of global dominance toward Britain. In light of this, Jefferson substituted a new conception of Americans as enterprising and forward-looking empire builders for less flattering images of provincial dependency and, even, degeneracy. He was able to effect this conceptual reversal because he had imbibed various tenets of Enlightenment thought from his wide reading and from his "habitual conversations" at the Governor's Palace.

During the mid-eighteenth century Adam Smith and other political economists emphasized the importance of population growth for state power, and identified economic development with unleashing the "natural" productivity of fertile landscapes. Agrarian theorists in the republican or "commonwealth" tradition lauded the virtue and independence of the freeholders who proliferated in the new settlements. Not coincidentally, these new ways of thinking about the history and progress of society, economy, and empire had a distinctively Scottish flavor. Beginning with its incorporation in the 1707 Act of Union, Scotland was both a site of imperial expansion—as British forces overcame powerful "native" resistance culminating in victory at Culloden in 1746 and the continuing progress of Highland clearance—and a seemingly inexhaustible source of the settlers, soldiers, bureaucrats, merchants, and investors who played a conspicuous role in the empire's extraordinary expansion. Embracing Enlightenment ideas about their place in a dynamic and growing empire, Jefferson and his fellow patriots thus could see themselves as true agents of empire at precisely the moment when shortsighted politicians in London launched a misguided assault on their most precious rights.

Very significantly, alienation from the British government encouraged Virginians to identify with fellow victims of imperial despotism across the continent, and thus to think of themselves as *Americans*. During the colonial period they compared themselves to their fellow Britons across the Atlantic and found reassuring points of commonality—"we might have been a free & a great people together," Jefferson wrote in his draft of the Declaration of Independence.[8] The imperial crisis exposed the differences between the two groups, suggesting that Americans and Britons were not truly one people. This realization transformed the colonists' conception of continental solidarity.

The idea that North America was a "continent," and that its destiny was to be British, had been deeply imbedded in the geographical thinking of policy-makers, merchants, and land speculators throughout the colonial period. The conclusive victory over the French in the Seven Years' War (the French and Indian War) confirmed this belief. Waging this war had been expensive, and Great Britain sought to use the tax power to recoup funds spent on the effort. The colonists, who had benefited greatly from the defeat of the French, balked. When British authorities took a hard view of Americans' recalcitrance and, among other things, threatened to unleash "indiscriminate ruin" on innocent Bostonians in retaliation for the Tea Party of December 1773, Americans in all regions snapped, almost in unison, to attention. A prospective community of suffering arose, binding Virginians to Bostonians.

Jefferson's Declaration tied together all of the colonists' grievances—some more serious than others—creating a united front. He commiserated with fellow Americans across the continent who had, like plantation and farm builders in Virginia, worked to promote the empire's prosperity and power. Bostonians were

> men who had spent their lives in extending the British commerce, who had invested in that place the wealth their honest endeavors had merited, [who now] found themselves and their families thrown at once on the world for subsistence by it's charities. Not the hundredth part of the inhabitants of that town had been concerned in the act complained of; many of them were in Great Britain and in other parts beyond sea; yet all were involved in one indiscriminate ruin, by a new executive power unheard of till then, that of a British parliament.[9]

The revolutionary crisis, having brought imperial and continental identities into sharp focus, also made plain America's wealth, population growth, and potential power. Links to the mother country could now be seen as restraints on development, badges of subjection and dependency, and even—in the hyperbolic, and highly ironic, language that came so easily to slave-owning planters like Jefferson—as chains of slavery. Looking away from Britain, and across American space, Virginians and Bostonians could not only recognize each other as fellow Americans but also begin to envision a common future in the conquest of the continent. This was the properly imperial project that the British had betrayed. As Jefferson insisted in his *Summary View*, "kings are the servants, not the proprietors of the people." Those people, the surveyors and settlers who improved the western landscape, were the true proprietors and ultimate source of authority in an expanding American empire. There was a logic and order to this process.

Scottish Enlightenment historians had posited that nations developed through stages, from primitive hunter-gatherers to the advanced commercial societies of the modern world. These stages of development were not simply learned conjectures about a distant past for Jefferson and his fellow revolutionaries. Successive generations of Americans seemed to be living out the predictions of Scottish theory, moving rapidly forward from the barbarous circumstances encountered by the first settlers. The "westward course of empire" mapped the progress of civilization onto the American landscape. Jefferson held fast to this vision. Late in life he asked a correspondent to reverse directions in an imaginary "journey from the savages of the Rocky Mountains, eastwardly towards our seacoast." "In his progress," the "philosophic observer" would "meet the gradual shades of improving man until he would reach his, as yet, most improved state in our seaport towns," the "equivalent to a survey, in time, of the progress of man from the infancy of creation to the present day." This was nothing less than the story of Jefferson's own life: "I am eighty-one years of age, born where I now live, in the first range of mountains in the interior of our country. And I have observed this march of civilization advancing from the seacoast, passing over us like a cloud of light, increasing our knowledge and improving our condition. . . ."[10]

As noted in chapter 2, Jefferson the agriculturalist is often mistakenly pitted against Alexander Hamilton the champion of industry, as if Jefferson believed that Americans should remain forever in the agricultural stage of development—a gross mischaracterization of his actual beliefs. Jefferson knew very well that the United States would not rest at one stage in perpetuity. He could not have been the progressive he was and think that. Jefferson knew that, eventually, the country would reach the final stage of development, a prospect he viewed with both anticipation and alarm. Progress would bring all the things he wished for—enlightened sensibilities, new inventions, and improvements in scientific and medical knowledge that would, overall, benefit mankind. It would, at the same time, disconnect individuals from family and true community as people poured into cities to work in dismal factories and to live in overcrowded and miserable slums breathing in bad air, as happened in the industrial cities of England. Since family and community were the basis of his vision of republican society, Jefferson saw as threats any social forces that put stress upon these institutions. As citizens became more pressured, less vigilant, and more dependent upon others for their livelihood, republicanism would suffer and corruption of the political system would set in. So Jefferson hoped that the United States, with its large landmass, could delay for as long as possible arriving at the final stage of development to allow ordinary people to maintain the independence they could achieve so long as they owned their own land, grew their own food, and made their own clothes without having to rely on wages provided by others. The whole inquiry about family, community, and government came home to Jefferson at the fixed point "in the first range of mountains" where his life's journey had begun and would soon end. Pulled eastward as an ambitious, young provincial and westward as a visionary proponent of America's great republican experiment, Jefferson would come home to rest at Monticello.

Notes on the State of Virginia

Jefferson's conception of Virginia emerged from the comparisons that he and other provincial patriots were forced to confront as they reconsidered their place in the empire. At first confident that Virginians could meet the challenges they would face upon separation from the mother country, Jefferson had become disillusioned with his countrymen by the end of his problematic stint as war governor of Virginia, which began when he succeeded Patrick Henry in the post in 1779. He had not wanted the position, but accepted it because there was really no way to turn it down. He took office in an uncharacteristically pessimistic mood, predicting (with great accuracy) that his "appointment would not likely . . . add to [his] happiness."[11]

There were mishaps in the Jefferson governorship almost from the beginning. Some of them grew out of mistakes Jefferson made; others were the result of forces not in his control. One of the most vexing, and serious, problems was the reluctance of many Virginia males to come forward and participate in the militia. And then Jefferson was forced to flee from the governor's residence in Richmond in 1779, and had an even closer brush with capture when Banastre Tarleton's troops came to Monticello in the summer of 1781. Jefferson's term had ended just days before this, and no successor had been named. He thought he was done with the post. Under the circumstances, however, it was not unreasonable to think that Jefferson was still at the head of Virginia's government. The British likely did not know precisely when the governor's term ended, and probably would not have cared. Jefferson would still have been an extremely attractive target. After watching through a telescope the beginning of the soldiers' ascent, he beat a hasty retreat to nearby Carter's Mountain, leaving Monticello to the enslaved, most notably Martin Hemings, the butler who got into a verbal altercation with the troops when they demanded to know where Jefferson had gone.[12]

In later years Jefferson's political opponents used his mad dash from his mountaintop home as proof of his weakness, adding physical timidity to the caricature of him as a head-in-the-sky philosopher. The criticism started early on. Jefferson was simply devastated when the legislature, spurred on by, among others, Patrick Henry (who had fled at the approach of the British, too), launched an investigation into his conduct as governor. In the end he was found not to have been derelict in his duties. But the pain of the charge never left him. In a patriarchal world that valued martial valor, this was an attack on Jefferson's masculinity. That he could not, in contrast to Washington, Hamilton, John Marshall, or Aaron Burr, point to any military service to counter the slurs on his manhood made matters worse. Even as an elderly man he was still trying to refute the allegation that he had acted in a cowardly fashion, suggesting that it would have been foolhardy for him to have attempted to fight Tarleton's troops single-handedly or to have allowed himself to be captured.

Jefferson's term as governor did, in fact, end with his ride from Monticello just ahead of the British army. He joined his family at his Bedford estate, some ninety miles away from Monticello. At this low point in his political career and personal life—he and his wife had lost their baby, Lucy, two months before Tarleton's raid—he began work on what would be the only book he ever wrote, *Notes on the State of Virginia*. Written in response to a set of queries from François Barbé-Marbois, secretary of the French legation to the United States, *Notes* is a compendium of data on Virginia's natural resources, population, institutions, and history. Jefferson also used the book, with chapters divided into numbered "queries," as an occasion to reflect systematically on his new state's "national character." If the French needed to know more about their American allies (Barbé-Marbois sent the same queries to other state governors), Jefferson had his own reasons to want to understand and explain his state and to shape its future.

As a man of the Enlightenment, Jefferson believed that it was possible to use reason and the patient accumulation of empirical data to explain why nations prospered or declined. The French philosopher Montesquieu and other students of "national character" emphasized the impact of climate and environment (a hot tropical environment gave rise to despotism and servility), or the size of a country (larger countries also tended toward despotic rule), on the character of the regime or government. These were all interdependent variables: the natural environment did not necessarily determine a nation's destiny, for nature could be "improved."

The idea of progress across space and time was particularly resonant for Jefferson and other provincial Anglo-Americans, anxious about cultural deficits in the inevitable comparisons with the mother country. *Notes on the State of Virginia* was Jefferson's ambitious blueprint for reform that would lay a solid foundation for a new republican superstructure for his state. The work betrays his profound anxieties about the commonwealth's future after the euphoria of the successful break with Great Britain. If, in their patriotic fervor, revolutionaries had countered the condescension and contempt of their fellow Britons across the Atlantic by repositioning themselves on the leading edge of the progress of civilization, they now faced the daunting task of living up to these exalted pretensions.

While the principles of republican self-government might be "self-evident," as Jefferson's Declaration proclaimed, his *Notes on Virginia* suggest that knowing these principles would never be sufficient. The success of the revolution and the republican experiment depended on the continuing strength of character of the people. Jefferson warned of the "germ of corruption and degeneracy" in "every government on earth," including republics. Vigilant citizens needed to be well armed against the mystifications of would-be rulers, recognizing "ambition under every disguise it may assume." Jefferson had no doubt about the natural capacity of individual Virginians for self-government as they embarked on the project of creating their own commonwealth. But when he began to think of Virginians collectively, he worried about the insidious ways in which their government—whatever its nominal form—could control the flow of information and impose its despotic will on a credulous people, who might think their interests were being attended to simply because they had voted representatives into office. As he famously wrote in 1816, during his late-life campaign to create the University of Virginia, "If a nation expects to be ignorant and free, in a state of civilization, it expects what never was and never will be."[13] Ignorance, the opposite of enlightenment, left ordinary people vulnerable to the designs of would-be aristocrats who would concentrate on ruling over others rather than exercising self-control.

Jefferson's concerns about popular ignorance reflected his growing ambivalence about his own class, the ruling elite of the former British province and now independent Commonwealth of Virginia. His identification with the enlightened republic of letters and his ambitious self-fashioning program gave him a critical perspective on the Virginia gentry and enabled him to identify with "the people." Provincial elites customarily looked down on, and sought to distance themselves from, their humble neighbors. Jefferson generally tacked in the opposite direction, though he never completely overcame his class's contempt for the vulgar herd, as is apparent in his derogatory comments about "the mobs of great cities" and immigrants who would "render" the commonwealth "a heterogeneous, incoherent, distracted mass," or in his references to "merciless savages" on the frontiers and rebellious slaves who threatened the racial order. But by displacing these negative characteristics of the lower orders onto "foreigners," Jefferson could give ordinary white folk a clean bill of civic health: "Those who labour in the earth are the chosen people of God, if ever he had a chosen people, whose breasts he has made his peculiar deposit for substantial and genuine virtue."[14]

Jefferson's agrarian celebration of "the mass of cultivators" constituted a radical leveling up, with "the people" now assuming the direct relation with God that kings traditionally claimed rendered their right to rule "divine." If this "chosen people" appears racially and culturally homogeneous in a way we now find offensive, Jefferson's animus was directed less against alien "others" than at their corrupt imperial masters who now deployed them as counterrevolutionary tools. These heterogeneous fragments should find homes with their own peoples in their own countries. They should struggle against the oppressive regimes that kept them in chains—and in the dark. Even the benighted inhabitants of South America, as yet unconscious of their collective identities as peoples and held down by "the accumulated pressure of slavery, superstition, and ignorance," might one distant day throw off this dead weight and gain their freedom.[15]

Compared with other peoples, Virginians were extraordinarily, even providentially, fortunate, Jefferson believed. This did not mean, however, that their hard-won liberties were secure against all risks, for people like Jefferson himself were well positioned to exploit their advantages and consolidate their power at the people's expense. It was this self-awareness that enabled Jefferson to identify with "the people" and achieve a critical perspective on his own class and, therefore, on himself. The reform he had in mind for Virginia focused primarily on the aristocracy: if Jefferson had his way, the people would be enlightened and empowered to monitor and control would-be aristocrats; "youths of genius from among the classes of the poor" would be "raked from the rubbish," as he rather indelicately put it, and take their rightful place in a meritocratic governing elite, mindful of their humble origins and grateful to the commonwealth that sponsored their ascent.[16]

Jefferson's solution for combatting the problem of latent, and potentially lethal, corruption was his proposed 1779 bill for universal public education. He fervently believed that education was a core requirement for empowered citizenship. As young Virginians learned to read, they would be immersed in history, "apprising them of the past" so that they "might judge of the future."[17] At the same time Jefferson took aim at government-imposed "mystifications," drafting his famous bill for disestablishing Virginia's state-supported church and guaranteeing religious freedom. When Jefferson wrote *Notes on Virginia*, neither of these key bills in his comprehensive revisal of the commonwealth's laws had been enacted, though James Madison would steer the Bill for Religious Freedom through the legislature in 1786.

Notes on Virginia was an extraordinarily personal text, much more revealing than the autobiography Jefferson started and quickly abandoned in old age to explain his public life away from home to his family at Monticello. He began by locating Virginia—and himself—in space, describing the new state's boundaries, rivers, mountains, and other physical features. In the "bad French translation" of 1785 and its more famous English successor, published by John Stockdale in London in 1787, Jefferson inserted a map adapted from the one his father and Joshua Fry had drafted in 1751, with additional details from maps of neighboring states.[18] Son Thomas thus memorialized the work of his surveyor father, Peter, in opening up Virginia's vast hinterland. The new map in *Notes* also showed how the Commonwealth of Virginia had very recently ceded (in 1784) "all the lands to which they had title on the North side of the Ohio" and thus provided for the future formation of self-governing new states. As early as 1776, when he added a provision to the first state constitution calling for new states, Jefferson linked the success of Virginia's experiment in republican government with fixed and manageable territorial limits. The homogeneity and coherence of Virginians as a people, capable of governing themselves, depended on their ability to come together— through representatives—in a central place. Jefferson was doubtless gratified to see that his own region of the Piedmont was centrally located in the geographical heart of the newly bounded common- wealth. Given the rapid westward spread of settlement, Albemarle eventually would be the center of Virginia's population as well, as Jefferson later claimed it was when he promoted Charlottesville as the site of the University of Virginia.

Jefferson filled in his cartographic and geographic frame with inven- tories of Virginia's natural resources in his longest "query," or chapter, "Productions Mineral, Vegetable and Animal." The message here was that Virginia was blessed by good fortune, with magnificent prospects for economic development. Jefferson triumphantly vindicated Amer- ican nature against the French naturalist Buffon's hypothesis that its supposedly colder and wetter environment produced smaller animals than Europe's and that "those which have domesticated in both, have degenerated in America."[19]

Humans also flourished in this bountiful environment. Indian populations were small and scattered for cultural reasons: native peo- ple were stuck at the first stage of historical development, not because of any diminution of their "generative" or sexual powers. Refuting the abbé Raynal's application of the degeneracy thesis "to the race of whites, transplanted from Europe," Jefferson invoked the examples of George Washington, Benjamin Franklin, and the astronomer David Rittenhouse: "America, though but a child of yesterday, has already given hopeful proofs of genius, as well of the nobler kinds, which arouse the best feelings of man, which call him into action, which substantiate his freedom, and conduct him to happiness, as of the sub-ordinate, which serve to amuse him only."[20]

The "genius" of Americans was most manifest in their revolution, though troubling questions remained about whether Virginians, par-ticularly, were capable of exploiting their natural advantages and ful-filling the revolution's promise. The chief problem lay with the state's constitution, whose imperfections were conspicuous to Jefferson, governor when the Revolutionary War came to Virginia in 1781. The most serious flaw was the failure of Virginia's revolutionary leaders to draft a constitution "unalterable by other legislatures" and through which Virginians could recognize and respect each other as fellow citizens. Instead, the revolutionary legislature had enacted the 1776 "constitution" as ordinary legislation, which could be changed at the whim of legislators. Like indeterminate boundaries, the absence of a duly authorized fundamental law or frame of government—that could be altered only after ratification by voters—made the very existence of Virginians as a people problematic. Procedural defects were com-pounded by legislative mal-apportionment that enabled "nineteen thousand" voters "living in one part of the country"—the Tidewater in the east—to "give law to upwards of thirty thousand" living to the west. The constitution was dangerously imbalanced. All powers were concentrated in the legislature, a concentration that was "precisely the definition of despotic government": "173 despots," Jefferson said, "would surely be as oppressive as one."[21]

The authors of the Virginia constitution had failed to defend the people against potential power grabs by either a legislative oligarchy or a single despot. During the British invasion legislators had even talked about passing "the reins of government" to an all-powerful "dictator" during the emergency, drawing on what had proved to be a "fatal" precedent in Roman history. Jefferson was appalled. The very idea of a dictatorship was not simply "treason against the people" of Virginia but "treason against mankind in general," for it would have been conclusive proof "of the imbecility of republican government . . . in times of pressing danger."[22] Throughout his life Jefferson used the word "treason" to describe serious betrayals of principles that he regarded as unassailable. Most famous was his description of the men he held responsible during the Missouri crisis between 1819 and 1821. They were committing "treason against the hopes of the world," for their actions threatened to destroy the American Union, which he was certain was indeed the hope "of the world." This usage takes the word beyond its legal definition, which refers to actions taken against an established government, of whatever form. For Jefferson, ideas could be as real as any established government, more real and enduring, in fact. The idea of the inherent rightness of republicanism transcended the boundaries of individual nations.

It should be recalled that Jefferson had even more personal reasons to question the legislators' judgments: the humiliation he felt at the official inquiry into the virtual collapse of the state government under his administration, despite being vindicated. Bruised by his failed efforts to meet the invasion threat, and the uncharitable assessments of the legislators, the ex-governor turned petulant and lashed out in the page of the *Notes*: perhaps, he suggested, Virginia's lawmakers *wanted* the republic to fail so that they could restore the old provincial regime, submit to imperial rule, and consolidate their dominant position.[23]

Retreating to Monticello in 1782 and temporarily renouncing public life, Jefferson used *Notes on Virginia* to diagnose Virginia's pathologies and prescribe appropriate solutions. In doing so, he charted his own growing alienation from Virginia's elite. The legislature's flirtation with dictatorship particularly offended him because it assumed that the people of Virginia—outside of the gentry—constituted a mindless "herd," gripped by fear—the animating principle of monarchical regimes, according to Montesquieu—and that they would "lay their necks on the block" as they submitted to despotic authority. Jefferson had more faith in the capacity of ordinary people; he believed that the proponents of this extreme measure (most of whom "meant well") grossly underestimated Virginians' virtue and "mistook their character." If the government had not been rescued by the changing fortunes of war, culminating in 1781 in the great victory at Yorktown (the French fleet arrived just in time to assure America's triumph),

Jefferson imagined that authority would have been "thrown back upon the bungling machinery of county committees for administration, till a convention could have been called, and its wheels again set into regular motion."[24] In this way Virginians would demonstrate their ultimate "attachment" to republican government, winding the clock back to 1776 and drafting a constitution that would establish a solid foundation and framework for self-government. A quarter century later, the newly elected President Jefferson imagined a similar scenario had the Federalists blocked his ascension to power, after his tie with Aaron Burr in the Electoral College threw the election into the House of Representatives. Jefferson did not expect chaos. Had the constitutional "clock or watch run down," the people would have responded and had a "convention . . . on the ground in 8. Weeks." They would "have repaired the constitution where it was defective & wound it up again."[25]

National Character

Through the years, Jefferson would apply the sociological analysis that he developed in *Notes on Virginia*—contrasting the mixed motives of "aristocrats" and "monocrats" with the virtuous character of the republican people—to the newly formed federal system. His focus on "the people" as a source of power grew out of his observation that without strong and serious checks, the "few" would always seek to dominate the "many"—even in a republic. The only hope for sustaining the republican form was to constitute the regime in a way that would sustain the people's virtuous character and enable citizens to repel any encroachments on their liberties. As Jefferson pondered these matters in response to Marbois's questions, he determined that the virtuous character Virginians supposedly displayed in the revolution was at least potentially mismatched with the character of their misbegotten constitution, which could be used by those hostile to true republicanism. A potentially fruitful moment had been wasted. As a result of his concerns, the Virginia that emerged from the analysis in Jefferson's book was unstable, a work in progress: prospects for a prosperous republican future for the state seemed boundless, but could be forfeited by the failure to have created a proper government.

It was not enough, however, to design the machinery of republican government according to the latest, most enlightened specifications. Students of national character understood that "manners" or *moeurs*—or what we might call "political culture"—were critical to a stable and enduring fit between the people and its governing regime. Climate, natural resources, soil fertility, the system of production, and the institutional legacy of the past all shaped the character of the people. In Virginia the most profound obstacle to the success of the republican experiment was not a defective constitution but rather the institution of slavery: here was an institutional continuity with the old provincial regime that made a mockery of patriots' claims to be launching a "new order for the ages."

Jefferson recognized that slavery was not simply an archaic vestige of British imperialism: it was the central institution in an unreformed and therefore imperfectly republican Virginia. Extraordinarily, in his *Notes on Virginia* he devoted an entire chapter—Query 18 ("Manners")—to the "unhappy influence on the manners of our people produced by the existence of slavery among us." Slavery was nothing less than a school for despotism that threatened to pervert and destroy whatever "virtue" revolutionary Virginians had demonstrated in making war against a British tyrant who threatened to "enslave" them. Only prodigies could "retain [their] manners and morals undepraved" in this type of society, the slaveholding Jefferson testified. "And with what execration should the statesman be loaded, who permitting one half the citizens thus to trample on the rights of the other, transforms those into despots, and these into enemies, destroys the morals of the one part, and the amor patriae of the other."[26]

Jefferson's eloquent testimony to the demoralizing effects of slavery brought him home to Monticello in a most discomfiting way. How, readers have long wondered, could he exempt himself, and his plantation, from this devastating indictment? His exchange with his granddaughter Ellen Coolidge referenced in the introduction—and the failed efforts of her father, Thomas Mann Randolph, and brother

Thomas Jefferson Randolph to initiate (very gradual) emancipation schemes—suggest that antislavery talk was never completely suppressed at Monticello. But Jefferson's attitude about slavery was not static. In the period in which he wrote *Notes on Virginia*, his conception of Monticello as the site of domestic happiness and refuge from the bitter conflicts of public life displaced the compelling need to do something immediately on his own plantation. Slavery appeared as a threat to Virginia's future. So, naturally, thoughts of restructuring his state overall were foremost in his mind. It was but one part, though an important one, of his hopes for reform. The demoralizing "circumstances" he invoked in his discussion of slavery affected *all* Virginians, white and black. Only a revolution of public opinion achieved through republican means could authorize a comprehensive solution that would redeem the commonwealth.

Jefferson could tell himself that *he* understood what had to be done even as the great majority of his fellow statesmen manifestly did not. He could also tell himself that history was on his side. Just as he "hoped" the people were virtuous enough to resist despotic designs against their liberties—his belief that chaos would not reign if the machinery of government were interrupted—so he hoped that a way would be prepared "under the auspices of heaven, for a total emancipation, and that this is disposed, in the order of events, to be with the consent of the masters, rather than by their extirpation."[27] Framed in these binary terms as a stark choice between "the consent of the masters" and their "extirpation," Jefferson was confident that enough people in Virginia would eventually see the light, for the stakes were high and clear.

In retrospect Jefferson's faith in the future seems absurdly misplaced. But he did, in fact, see a way forward, even in the dark moments when the death of his wife destroyed his dream of domestic happiness and when he contemplated the ignominious ruins of his political career. Focusing on slavery as the central challenge to republican Virginia—and to his own way of life—Jefferson could look to the "chosen people" of Query 19 ("Manufactures"): the independent "husbandmen" who escaped the "subservience and venality" that "dependance begets" and who were immune to market forces and "the casualties and caprice of customers." Here was an alternative vision of white Virginia, peopled by farmers who looked "to their own soil and industry," not by planters who exploited slave labor. Focusing on the opposition of virtuous farmers to would-be aristocrats in the gentry who owned the vast majority of Virginia's slaves and who were naturally reluctant to forfeit their political power and social preeminence, Jefferson could foresee the progress of an enlightened public opinion that would infuse the regime and its statesmen with the "substantial and genuine virtue" of the "mass of cultivators."[28] As society progressed, he and his kind would eventually disappear.

After mapping Virginia and assessing its prospects, Jefferson was prepared to take the great, long-delayed journey he had planned as a student in Williamsburg. There was no longer anything to keep him at home. Indeed, by the end of 1782 Monticello itself did not seem much like "home" to Jefferson. There was no longer a wife to be his companion and serve as mistress of the place. The house itself was an almost empty, half-built shell, situated on a plantation that exploited slave labor but generated little or no income, particularly in wartime. The most personal message in Notes on the State of Virginia, Jefferson's essay on the national character of his country, was that it was time for him to leave his home state.

James Madison, perhaps sensing that his grief-stricken friend needed a distraction, suggested to the Confederation Congress that Jefferson be sent to Paris to help John Adams and Benjamin Franklin negotiate a treaty of peace with Great Britain. Congress agreed. It was actually the third time it had asked Jefferson to go to Paris to represent America. He had declined the earlier requests because each coincided with periods in which his wife happened to be ill. Although this final commission was approved at the end of 1782, the press of legislative business kept him from leaving for France until 1784, after the peace treaty with Great Britain had been signed. His duties were changed. He would now focus on negotiating commercial agreements and, though he did not know it at the time, go on to succeed Benjamin Franklin as the American minister to France.

Jefferson arrived in Paris in the summer of 1784. As he looked homeward, he had misgivings about how Virginians would respond to his strictures should *Notes on the State of Virginia* be published: "there are sentiments on some subjects which I apprehend might be displeasing to the country," he told Madison, and particularly "to the assembly or to some who lead it." The extremely sensitive Jefferson did not "wish to be exposed to their censure," nor did he wish to forfeit a possible leading role in his state's politics.[29] In any case, Virginia would come to look much better at a distance—from the new comparative context Europe offered him.

Part Two

"TRAVELLER"

The Grille de Chaillot, view down the Champs-Élysées toward central Paris. The Hôtel de Langeac is on the left. (© The Thomas Jefferson Foundation at Monticello)

CHAPTER 4

FRANCE

Jefferson had an image of Europe before he set foot on the continent. Like many ambitious young American men of his station, he had dreamed of travel to the places he had encountered in his voracious and eclectic reading. The classics of Western literature, languages, and philosophy, books about architecture, law, and systems of government, created a vivid mental picture for him of the world across the Atlantic. Naturally, as a man of English and, he said, Welsh extraction—and an Anglophone—he had direct blood ties to the island that was part of Europe, but had always kept its insular distance from the continent. Different as the English and Americans had become—a cultural estrangement that contributed to the break between mother country and its colonies—the two peoples maintained enough points of commonality to be able to understand, and misunderstand, one another in critical ways.

France was a wholly different matter. First, there was the language barrier. Like most well-educated men of his cohort, Jefferson had studied French along with classical languages. Reading the language, and speaking it casually on occasion, however, could not have prepared him for the total immersion in French culture he experienced during his stay between 1784 and 1789. That rapidly became apparent the moment he set foot at Le Havre and, by his daughter

Martha's account, was promptly fleeced by porters carrying the family's bags. She recalled that her father "spoke very little french" and found himself at a disadvantage.[1] All the years of study in books were of little use when he was hit with what likely seemed to be rapid-fire conversation and interaction. This was an early lesson learned, a bracing immersion into what life would be like during his stay in France, at least until he got his bearings. Given who he was, this was undoubtedly frustrating. Jefferson loved words, lived by them, and wielded them with astonishing skill in both his public and his private lives to explain, persuade, and command. Now he was in a place where his words would often fail. Using his greatest talent would not come so easily.

There were other cold doses of reality. It was one thing for Jefferson to proclaim young America's superiority to decadent Europe, quite another to measure himself against the extraordinarily sophisticated and accomplished individuals he encountered in the upper reaches of Parisian society. Whatever the condition of its poor teeming masses on the verge of revolt, France had an established class of intellectuals whose talents and abilities often equaled or exceeded his own. Accomplished as Jefferson was, he could not count on being the smartest person in the room, as he nearly always would have been in the United States. Nor could he assume that the social preeminence he took for granted in Virginia would command respect, much less deference, in his new home with people who had aristocratic backgrounds cultivated over centuries.

Ellen Coolidge remembered Jefferson describing his first, and apparently only, foray into a chess club in Paris:

> He was, in his youth, a very good chess-player. There were not among his associates, many who could get the better of him. I have heard him speak of "four hour games" with Mr. Madison. Yet I have heard him say that when, on his arrival in Paris, he was introduced into a Chess Club, he was beaten at once, and that so rapidly and signally that he gave up all competition.

He felt that there was no disputing such a palm with men who
passed several hours of every evening in playing chess.[2]

Even if it were true that all who came to the chess club played for
hours every evening, playing them—or even just watching them
play—would have done Jefferson's game much good. It is an article of faith among chess players that the principal way of becoming
better at the game is to play against increasingly stronger opponents.
That Jefferson was unwilling to do this, to put himself at the mercy
of people who were better at something than he, even in service of
improving his skills, is telling. It would be different if chess had not
been so important to him. Then the continual losing might not have
been worth it. Jefferson, however, professed great love of and respect
for the game and continued to play it the rest of his life, teaching his
grandchildren, including Ellen Coolidge.

Coolidge's anecdote shows that she delighted in the memory of her
grandfather as a nearly unbeatable player, for it reinforced her view of
him as one who was usually the most powerful and impressive person
in any situation in which he found himself. But then there is the "yet"
preceding Coolidge's discussion of Jefferson's time in France. This
was a place where Jefferson played and was dispatched swiftly and
decisively. The granddaughter accepts his excuse as to why this happened, and offers it to posterity. By then Coolidge had seen enough
of the world—she was in her fifties—to feel comfortable revealing a
point of her grandfather's vulnerability—but with a suggestion that
the weakness could have been overcome if only Jefferson had cared
enough to try.

Compare Jefferson's attitude toward playing chess with his attitude
about another activity to which chess is often compared: mathematics. He loved mathematics from his student days and much valued his
study under Dr. William Small at William and Mary. He used it as an
architect, relished its utility for his design of a moldboard plow, and
for calculating America's likely rate of population growth. In his old
age he returned to it for recreation. As there are commonplaces about

the nature of playing chess, there are some about doing math as well. One is that learning the discipline depends on a willingness to accept failure. Making mistakes is integral to the process of problem solving; try one thing and, if it does not work, try another. Being able to recognize mistakes quickly and correct them is an important trait to possess. Mathematics, however, is most often a solitary activity. Jefferson could make his mistakes, "fail" in private with no one to witness his vulnerability. When he played a chess match and failed, there was always at least one witness: his opponent. Indeed, at the chess club in Paris, there may even have been multiple witnesses. That was something Jefferson apparently could not abide. The master had to appear to others as "master," even when he was at play.

It is easy to understand how Jefferson developed his will to mastery. Everything in his life pointed to it from birth onward. He was a first son at a time when that mattered far more than it would today. That he was a son at all—a male—automatically placed him above half the population in his patriarchal society. Then too, he was born at that top of his region's social stratum into a class that owned other human beings—he was the legal master of people. Members of his class learned habits of command at an early age, as Jefferson explained in the discussion of Virginian "manners" in his *Notes on Virginia*: countenancing any challenge to their authority—no matter how trivial—could prove fatal. Planters were quick to take offense at actions or words of their peers; their exalted sense of their own honor demanded immediate satisfaction, on the dueling ground if necessary. Social inferiors who failed to show due respect risked violent retaliation; slaves risked their lives.

The enlightened, peace-loving Jefferson saw the endemic violence of plantation society as a degrading mark of provincial barbarism. When his son-in-law Thomas Mann Randolph faced a possible duel with his kinsman John Randolph, Jefferson was incredulous and asked the young man whether he was really willing to risk leaving his wife and children unprotected in the world because of what another man had said about him.[3] But if he was averse to conflict, the personally thin-skinned Jefferson betrayed a southern planter's sensitivity to personal slights. The challenge was to develop personal attributes that would command respect: the "natural aristocrat" would seek to sustain his superior position through his recognized contributions to the people's welfare. The putatively grateful and deferential affection that was said to buttress the authority of republican fathers in family governance would take the place of fear and force in society at large.

Jefferson enjoyed extraordinary advantages in his quest for enlightened mastery. His keen intelligence was cultivated and nurtured in the best schools his provincial society had to offer. He was tall, an attribute in men that matters even today. And though there were differing opinions as to whether he was handsome, it was generally agreed that his intelligence, personal charm, passionate curiosity, and manner made it pleasant to be in his company. The other men to whom Jefferson is often compared—Washington, Hamilton, Franklin, Madison, and Burr—had some but not all of the attributes Jefferson so conspicuously displayed.

A powerful sense of self-worth and ambition propelled this very sensitive man into public life at perhaps the only period in American history—the very beginning—when he would have been comfortable being there. Jefferson did not have to campaign in the modern sense to enter the House of Burgesses, Continental Congress, House of Delegates, or the governorship of Virginia. Being a member of the gentry from certain families was the so-called ticket—another factor that contributed to his habit of mastery. Then he had been one of the leaders of a revolution that had wrested his provincial homeland from the control of the most powerful nation on earth and created a new country. Though his sensitivity never left him, by the time he entered national office and traveled to Europe, his determination to help set the course of that new country far outweighed his deep aversion to criticism and dislike of direct confrontation.

The opportunity to live in Paris, the great center of the enlightened and civilized world, in many ways represented the ultimate fulfillment of the ambitious young Virginian's long-held aspirations. Here he beheld a dazzling prospect of what he and his fellow Americans

might one day achieve—and transcend—in their new and improved
world; here too, the pathologies of the old regime—the vast, degrading extremes of wealth and privilege that marred European society
and justified America's republican revolution—were open for all to
see. Yet Jefferson's attraction to life in the French capital was complicated by troubling personal concerns that could not be reduced to the
exaggerated comparison between Old World and New that came so
easily to the republican ideologue.

A New Home

In Paris the Virginian patriarch quickly noticed the differences
between Virginian family life and French family life driven, mainly,
by the character of Frenchwomen. Although men dominated French
society, as they did nearly everywhere in the world, upper-class and
aristocratic Frenchwomen moved easily in what Jefferson considered
male domains. Gender relations in France troubled him deeply: the
"sexes have changed business," he wrote in a list of topic headings
on French manners he evidently planned to elaborate in an essay "on
sending American youth to Europe."[4] As the crisis that culminated in
the French Revolution deepened, gender lines blurred. The Parisian
air was "filled with political debates into which both sexes enter with
equal eagerness," he wrote to a French female friend, consoling himself with the fact that she was not there, for if she were she "would
be miserable"—as Jefferson was in beholding the spectacle. Female
politicians turned the world upside down, stripping men of the power
that Jefferson believed was rightfully theirs.[5]

In practically every way that mattered, France posed challenges
to Jefferson's sense of himself as the master of people, situations, and
things. The historian Winthrop Jordan describes the "disorientation" that English settlers felt upon coming to the New World. They
"were," he wrote, "isolated from the world as they had known it, cut
off from friends and family and the familiar sights and sounds and
smells which have always told men who and where they are."[6] Jefferson in Paris was not in a physical wilderness, nor was he surrounded

by actively hostile enemies. He was, however, "cut off" from many of the most familiar things of his daily life.

Unlike current-day Americans who travel to France and everywhere see examples of American influence—in commerce, popular culture, and the built environment—Jefferson had few other reminders of his native land. He lacked the comforting presence of familiar cultural markers and could not exploit them to promote a favorable image of his homeland to his French hosts. In the face of these challenges, he sought to control his world as much as he could, in some cases hoping that familiar things from home would bring some sense of order to his life.

The household Jefferson created for himself in Paris offered a measure of comfort. His daughter Martha was with him, along with James Hemings, his late wife's half brother, whom Jefferson had brought to Paris to train as a chef. William Short, a young Virginian whom Jefferson considered his "adoptive son," also joined him in Paris, as his secretary. While these people certainly served as forms of support, each one was also a very specific reminder of what Jefferson had left behind: his daughters (Mary and Lucy), an enslaved family with whom his wife and children shared blood ties and who catered to his every need, and the Virginia gentry of which he was a part.

Once permanently settled in Paris, Jefferson had a kitchen garden with vegetables native to the southern part of the United States planted for him, an effort that met with mixed success. He tried other things, indulging his penchant for expressing himself through architecture and construction. Indeed, he remodeled his first house in Paris, no. 5 cul de sac Taibout, despite having only a one-year lease for the place.[7] He made only minor changes to the Hôtel de Langeac, but while living there he began building in his head. He jettisoned his original plans for redesigning Monticello and reimagined his mountain home after having fallen in love with examples of French architecture, most notably the Hôtel de Salm—then under construction (completed in 1787), now the Palais de la Légion d'Honneur. If his first impulse was to make his Paris home more "Virginian," he now envisioned bringing Parisian refinement and civility to his distant mountaintop and its semisavage neighborhood. The consummate consumer acquired an extraordinary collection of furniture, furnishings, paintings, art objects, and, of course, books that would make Monticello a kind of museum that would educate all who entered. This is where Jefferson imagined he would exercise a more benevolent and public-spirited form of mastery, compatible with his revolutionary republican principles.

Americans were not unknown to eighteenth-century French society, and enthusiasm for the revolutionary republic guaranteed Jefferson a warm reception in enlightened quarters. He could deploy his personal attributes to good advantage: it is very likely that the very tall, strawberry blond, and fair-skinned Virginian stood out in what was to be his home for five years. Benjamin Franklin's enormous popularity also paved the way—and opened doors—for his successor. Still serving as minister to France when Jefferson arrived, Franklin was the most famous American of all, not only to the French but to all of Europe. He was the face of America: the eminent scientist and inventor, the supreme wit, the "Quaker" (he was not one but did not disabuse the French of this misimpression because of their admiration for the sect) in the beaver skin cap who became a cult figure during the nearly eight years he served as minister to France.

Jefferson earned the respect of his French hosts, but never attained the near-universal love and affection that Franklin enjoyed at all levels of French society. He did not seek it. Though they had much in common, Franklin and Jefferson were very different types of people. Franklin, the more cosmopolitan and adventuresome of the two, threw himself into France, joining French-speaking salons, establishing notoriously flirtatious relationships with Frenchwomen, befriending Frenchmen, and generally making himself into a real presence in French society. While he never attained proficiency in speaking French—he spoke it "badly"—he plunged ahead, because this was the best way to make the most of his diplomatic assignment. The historian Stacy Schiff observes of Franklin, "Rarely has a man so capably adapted to the rules of a foreign world, while at the same time playing that world to the benefit of his own."[8]

Jefferson took a different tack, managing to become a competent and effective representative of his country without going native. Gouverneur Morris, who succeeded him as minister to France and visited Jefferson toward the end of his stay in the country, noted the Virginian's preference for dining *en famille* over socializing outside of his spectacular home, the Hôtel de Langeac. It is not that Jefferson cloistered himself. He made the most of the great metropolis's rich cultural life, attending theaters, concert halls, and opera houses; he particularly admired the architecture, bringing the best he could find in Europe back home to America in the form of his own famous residence and, among other places, Richmond's state capitol building, which he designed.[9] He also made friends among the French, reacquainting himself with the marquis de Lafayette, and becoming a great favorite of Lafayette's aunt Madame de Tessé, whose salon he attended and with whom he shared a lively correspondence. Family and home, however, remained the center of his life. Jefferson made France his in his own way, a way consonant with his conception of himself as a Virginian and an American.

In fact, Jefferson's understanding of what it meant to be a Virginian and an American, newly strengthened by his time in the revolution, came into even sharper focus in a place that was so different from the world that had shaped him. The sense of new-arrival disorientation that Jordan describes also produces a clarity, or perceived clarity, about oneself and one's native land. The visitor compares the world she knows with the strange new one she encounters, and the comparison brings the known world into view—sometimes flattering, sometimes not, often both. Jefferson's correspondence shows that he set about playing the compare-and-contrast game almost as soon as he set foot in Europe, voicing his views on the relative merits of the United States and France to Americans and Europeans alike.

Jefferson came to his views about France from a mind-set that combined awe, envy, affection, respect, anxiety, and disdain. "Behold me at length on the vaunted scene of Europe!" he exclaimed in a famous letter to Charles Bellini, an Italian friend in Virginia.[10] Here was the denizen of the New World approaching the Old, acutely conscious of his nation's political, social, and cultural underdevelopment. Differences between American and European built environments and improved landscapes were particularly evident to the amateur architect, and Paris's superiority in music and the other fine arts was undeniable. Yet, he insisted, fundamental flaws in a dissipated, decadent, and overcivilized society offset these advantages. Europe might "dazzle" the Virginian, but Americans were, after all, closer to nature and thus to God. "The truth of Voltaire's observation offers itself perpetually," he told Bellini, that every man in Europe "must be either the hammer or the anvil." While the "great" and mighty strutted across the European stage, "the great mass of the people" suffered "under physical and moral oppression." The "bulk of spectators" might have their heads turned, but Jefferson could see clearly enough to count the cost, comparing European misery "with that degree of happiness which is enjoyed in America by every class of people."[11]

Jefferson's competitive spirit vis-à-vis Europeans was on full display in a very humorous (and actually quite touching) anecdote. To counter the charge by the French naturalist Georges-Louis Leclerc, comte de Buffon, that all living things in the New World inevitably degenerated, Jefferson wrote to New Hampshire's governor, John Sullivan, requesting that he send to him in Paris the "skin, the skeleton, and horns of the Moose, the Caribou, and the Orignal Elk." He was "most especially" keen to have the moose sent. If Buffon could see a fully grown male moose, he would know for a fact that animals could grow very large on the American continent. Jefferson was hoping for a majestic specimen that would look as imposing as a moose that was no longer living could look. What he received in Paris a year after his request was not so impressive. Sullivan had been unable to send all the bones in the head, but did send the skin of the head. The horns came from another moose. Very little of the hair on the rest of the carcass remained. But Jefferson professed to be satisfied with the effort because it was still possible to get a sense of the animal's size. He sent the moose, along with the horns of elks and deer that Sullivan had shipped. Those horns were smaller than he had wished, but in the letter he wrote sending the package of bones and horns to the

Jardin du Roi, out of which Buffon operated, he assured the comte that he had seen deer and elk that were much, much larger than the ones in the specimens that had made it to Paris. The comte was sick, and away from the Jardin, but he took note of Jefferson's gift and had his assistant send the Virginian a polite thank-you note.[12]

Jefferson's earliest statements about the differences between France and America suggest his basic framework for argument, one often employed by self-conscious and anxious individuals in developing societies, a variant of the character argument American patriots had made against the corrupt and decadent British. He took refuge in the intangible and the natural, asserting the superiority of the spirit and soul of the American people, and the country's physical landscape, over the concrete and visible accomplishments of the more civilized—and perhaps overcivilized—old world.

Ambivalence

As he approached his first-year anniversary in Europe, in the summer of 1785, Jefferson wrote to James Monroe, urging his younger Virginian colleague to join him in Europe. It was a strange invitation. "The pleasure of the trip will be less than you expect," he warned, "but the utility greater." Monroe, like Jefferson, would gain a new perspective on home. Living in Europe "will make you adore your own country, it's soil, it's climate, it's equality, liberty, laws, people and manners." Jefferson had not loved America enough before traveling abroad. "My god!," he exclaimed, "how little do my countrymen know what precious blessings they are in possession of, and which no other people on earth enjoy. I confess I had no idea of it myself." The picture Jefferson had recently sketched in *Notes on Virginia* took on a much brighter hue, most conspicuously in his new enthusiasm for the "manners" of his countrymen. No "thinking American" would come to Europe and want to stay there. Conscious of the new nation's advantages, American patriots abroad would instead join the growing numbers of Europeans who sought to escape oppressive conditions in their own countries and breathe America's free air.[13]

Unlike his more impressionable young compatriots, Monroe would not be likely to fall prey to Europe's seductive attractions. He would instead affirm what Jefferson wanted to believe about himself, that he set a much higher value on his own country's "precious blessings." But Jefferson's letter betrayed anxieties about his own vulnerability: was it possible that the apostle of reason himself would lose his bearings and go native? The company of mature, like-minded countrymen like Monroe might buttress his patriotism, preempting such an unthinkable outcome. Jefferson also reassured himself by invoking his understanding of psychological development through the life cycle. True self-mastery and independence came late, with attainment of the age of reason or "thinking." Moral development in childhood depended on the inculcation of good habits through unthinking submission to—and emulation of—revered authority figures; young adulthood was a stage of extraordinary danger, the time when boys began to exercise the prerogatives of men and formed the attachments that would shape their characters, for better or worse. Jefferson and Monroe were no longer at risk. But this was not the case with provincial young men who sought to complete their education abroad. Before the revolution a younger Jefferson had longed for this very experience. Now, in retrospect, it became clear to him that it was much better for young Americans to stay at home.

Jefferson was forty-one when he arrived in France. This was well beyond the age when young people of his class took the grand tour. The tour's purpose was educational, to allow young people to see and learn from the achievements of civilizations past. Encountering that world would have an impact upon their still-developing personalities. Jefferson was by no means too old to appreciate and learn from the glories of European civilization when he arrived in Paris—people who met him remarked upon his preternaturally youthful nature and demeanor until he was well into his final years. But he had lived a full life, seen many things to completion by the time he came to Paris. He had had a career as a lawyer, a legislator, a revolutionary, and a governor. He had been a husband and was a father, who had lost children and a wife. There were things he expected of the world and had grown used to. One detects in the didactic and moralistic tone he adopts as he surveys French society and finds it wanting in critical regards, the telltale signs of one who has grown set in his ways. He was already formed and was therefore leery of being *unformed*. He admitted as much to Bellini. "I am running on in an estimate of things infinitely better known to you than to me, and which will only serve to convince you that I have brought with me all the prejudices of country, habit and age."[14]

A psychological double standard came naturally to Jefferson, as he insisted that he was immune to risk, mature, reasonable, and set in his ways. He could benefit from the glories of European civilization without succumbing to its vices. Begrudgingly, if not disingenuously, acknowledging to Monroe that there might be "pleasure" in a European trip, Jefferson struck a more enthusiastic note in a less didactic letter to more intimate friends. There were things he loved about France. "I do love this *people* with all my heart," he exclaimed in June 1785 in an exuberant outburst to Abigail Adams, then living in London. Adams and Jefferson exchanged a series of letters comparing the virtues of the French character to the dour and gloomy English: the French "have as much happiness in one year as an Englishman in ten," Jefferson concluded.[15] He wrote to the Philadelphian Eliza Trist, who ran a boardinghouse in that city, in a similar vein. "I am much pleased" with the French people, he explained: "the roughnesses of the human mind are so thoroughly rubbed off with them that it seems as if one might glide thro' a whole life among them without a justle," and there is no reason to doubt his sincerity on that point.[16]

French manners made life smooth and easy. Conversation was a fine art, enabling participants to move playfully over a wide range of topics without giving offense. Yet if these exchanges were liberating and lively for the bookish provincial, they were also disturbing. Was there perhaps something artificial and inauthentic about these cultivated and witty people who betrayed no powerful emotions? Was there perhaps something to admire and protect in the "roughness" of uncultivated provincial minds? Jefferson fretted particularly about the negative effects that French society might have upon young American men who visited there: they would be led astray by sex, "the strongest passion of all the human passions."[17] The smooth manners that "pleased" Jefferson would seduce and corrupt his impressionable countrymen.

Responding to a query from a fellow Virginian about educational opportunities in Europe, Jefferson launched into an extended "sermon" on the "alarming . . . consequences of foreign education." He recognized that his moralizing response might seem disproportionate. After all, his friend John Banister Jr. had simply wanted to know where rustic young men from the United States might pursue the latest learning and perhaps acquire a bit of cosmopolitan polish. But the potential costs of such attainments, Jefferson warned, were far too high. The young American abroad "acquires a fondness for European luxury and dissipation, and a contempt for the simplicity of his own country." Living for the moment—as his use of the present tense suggests—the malleable young American becomes European; when he "returns to his own country," he does so as a "foreigner."

Jefferson focused on two major themes in his sermon to Banister, both crucially important for the success of America's republican experiment: young Americans abroad would fail to master the language of their countrymen, and therefore never achieve the persuasive "eloquence" so essential to leadership in a regime based on consent; infected by a "spirit of female intrigue," they would be drawn into illicit and fleeting sexual liaisons that spoiled them for the more enduring family bonds on which republican society depended. Conscious of his own lack of fluency in spoken French, Jefferson may have been alarmed by the ease with which William Short and other young men picked up the language. But he consoled himself with the thought that language acquisition was, in modern parlance, a zero-sum game: "thus no instance exists of a person writing"—much less speaking—"two languages perfectly." Jefferson's conclusion—offered as an "opinion" but asserted with dogmatic assurance—was "that there never was an instance of a man's writing or speaking his native tongue with elegance who passed from 15. to 20. years of age out of the country where it was spoken." These deracinated youth might return home, but no one would listen to them. "Cast your eye over America," he enjoined his correspondent: "who are the men of most learning, of most eloquence, most beloved by their country and most trusted and promoted by them? They are those who have been educated among them, and whose manners, morals and habits are perfectly homogeneous with those of the country."[18]

It is tempting to see Jefferson's bold assertions and hyperbolic language (he confessed to Banister that he sinned "through zeal") as a commentary on his own linguistic predicament. According to the logic of his sermon, his discomfiting lack of language mastery could be seen as a protective shield. The fully formed adult would never forget his homeland; his unease in French was a constant reminder of his fundamental attachments. Yet there is an undercurrent of ambiguity in Jefferson's protestations, for his invulnerability to insidious, antirepublican influences was at least partially a function of his own incapacity, not of the exercise of his reason—or the absence of desire. Jefferson found French society extraordinarily attractive. Why would he *not* want to be better assimilated and more at ease in this cosmopolitan world? After all, Franklin's career showed that cultural immersion could be an enormous diplomatic asset, simultaneously promoting the national interest and personal happiness.

Jefferson's admonitions to young Americans revealed compelling personal concerns. The ostensible subject of his sermon to Banister was the fragility of the republican experiment and the need to prepare the younger generation to assume a leading role in assuring its success. But the American minister was also, and more profoundly, speaking to his own anxieties and aspirations. Not surprisingly, the fraught question of sexual attachments and family formation elicited the preacher's most emotional and ambivalent language. Yet again invoking the radically reductive compare-and-contrast approach that enabled him to clarify his own loyalties and attachments, Jefferson sought to demonstrate that the French "happiness" he discussed with Abigail Adams was in fact a sham and delusion. Besotted by the dissolute pleasures of French society, the impressionable young American would not see beneath its glittering surface. Succumbing to "the spirit of female intrigue destructive of his own and others happiness, or a passion for whores destructive of his health," he would be unfitted for domestic life at home. Instead, he would learn "to consider fidelity to the marriage bed as an ungentlemanly practice and inconsistent with happiness."

The very definition of happiness was at stake, as Jefferson compared the instant gratifications of European society with the more enduring, simple joys of American domesticity. He was preoccupied with French sexual mores during his seasoning period in Paris, seeking to insulate his countrymen—and perhaps himself—from their seductive attractions. The challenge was to look beyond the immediate moment, to appreciate the solid satisfactions of "faithful and permanent" attachments. Most of all, the bereaved widower preached the transcendent virtues of the family life he had lost. It was almost as if his lost family was all he could see when he looked homeward. As the historian Brian Steele provocatively suggests, Jefferson conflated an idealized image of the patriarchal household—the little republic of the nuclear family—with "America."[19] The provincial defects that he cataloged at such great length in *Notes on Virginia* were washed away in a warm bath of domesticity. Americans did not know how happy they were. European society unleashed "all *our* bad passions" (Jefferson acknowledged he had them too) in vain pursuit of "moments of extasy" that punctuated "days and months of restlessness and torment." How much better, he insisted, the "tranquil permanent felicity with which domestic society in America blesses most of it's inhabitants." In America pursuits of pleasure gave way to those which "health and reason approve, and rendering truly delicious the intervals of these pursuits." Domestic happiness came from the "intervals," the reward for healthy and reasonable pursuits that promoted the prosperity and welfare of the new American republic.

Relations between the sexes were indicative of more fundamental questions about sex and family life, which, in Jefferson's way of seeing things, were tied to national character and, thus, had great implications for any nation. What happened when the family was disordered or, as Jefferson put it, when "domestic bonds . . . are absolutely done away," had profound implications for the civic health of the larger society.[20] Because family governance and the government of the whole nation were inextricably linked, it was little wonder that civic life in France was, in his estimation, such a mess. Jefferson thought that men and women bore a natural relationship to one another with their own distinct roles, and the way the French constructed that relationship and those roles was anything but "natural," as he understood the term.

Despite Jefferson's protestations, the temptations of Paris were all too real, all too close. His famous short-lived dalliance with Maria Cosway and his almost equally charged connection to Angelica Schuyler Church make clear that it was not just young men who could fall prey to the mores of French society. What was his liaison with Cosway—meeting without her husband, exchanging letters cloaked in ambiguity and flirtation—but the kind of "intrigue" that he criticized so strenuously in his letters to Banister and Bellini? It is highly unlikely that Jefferson, except in moments of private reverie, could have thought that his connection to Cosway could ever result in the kind of wholesome republican family that he saw as the foundation of society. Nothing in her background suggested she would have wanted that. Would she have lived with him without marriage, or married him after divorcing her husband, the ground for which would have been her adultery?

The way Jefferson pursued his own happiness in Paris—whether or not he indulged his "bad passions"—had little apparent connection with his prescriptions for his young countrymen. Jefferson might rhapsodize about conjugal bonds and the joys of family life when he warned young men to stay away from Europe. But because the widower did not see marriage in his own future, he could flirt with Cosway without compromising the family commitments that seemed to matter so little in French society. Jefferson was genuinely shocked by the ways men and women related to one another in France and thus anxious about the lessons that impressionable—and marriageable—young Americans might draw from French society. His aversion to forward and contentious Frenchwomen reflected both a principled commitment to republican domesticity and a personal predilection for harmonious, conflict-free social relations.

Fawn Brodie noted Jefferson family lore that Martha Jefferson had a "vivacity of temper" that could "border on tartness," which she curbed with her husband.[21] Perhaps she did not always succeed, a basic nature being difficult to stifle completely. Jefferson did assert that one of the worst things couples could do was to criticize one another in front of other people. The public appearance of harmony contributed to the all-important private harmony. Madison Hemings remembered that at home Jefferson was the "quietest of men," who was "hardly ever known to get angry, though sometimes he was irritated when matters went wrong, but even then he hardly ever allowed himself to be made unhappy any great length of time."[22] Jefferson himself confided that one of the most unpleasant experiences in life was encountering someone on the street with whom he had disagreements.

We can read personal anxiety into Jefferson's impassioned sermons about the sexual dangers of French society. The open display of prostitution and other evidence of licentiousness appalled him. He was talking about himself, of course, and the difficulties he was having maneuvering through all of this, as he often did in correspondence that touched on issues that were personally difficult for him to face. He did the same thing on the subject of slavery in France. Not long after his letter to Bellini, he engaged in correspondence with a man named Paul Bentalou, a Frenchman who had settled in Maryland after serving as an aide-de-camp to Casimir Pulaski during the American Revolution. Bentalou, on a visit to his home country, queried Jefferson about the status of slaves under French law. There was a danger that a young boy he brought from the United States might be freed or forcibly sent back home. Jefferson wrote a careful reply in which he was clearly speaking of himself when he said that he knew of "an instance where a person bringing in a slave, and saying nothing about it, [had] not been disturbed in his possession."[23]

Jefferson was referring to his situation with James Hemings. Displacement was the order of the day, on the question of slavery—as on so many other matters of profound personal importance.

"Domestic Society"

Family was very much on Jefferson's mind during his early years in Paris. It had been a long time since he had had a family situation that even approached the form he extolled in France, and he never had one again. He had arrived in Paris still devastated by the loss of his wife two years before. His eldest daughter, Martha, called Patsy at this time, had been his constant companion in the grief-stricken weeks after his wife's untimely death. Determined to sustain some connection to the family life he had so suddenly lost and the home he now abandoned, Jefferson had taken Patsy with him to Philadelphia while he prepared to undertake his French mission. His two younger daughters, Mary (Polly) and Lucy, stayed behind in Virginia with his in-laws, Elizabeth and Francis Eppes, at their home called Eppington: they needed the stable and loving home environment that the peripatetic widower could not now provide. Perhaps one day Jefferson would find some way to bring what remained of his family back together again. But the prospects were not good.

Despite Jefferson's best efforts, Patsy did not spend very much time with her father in Philadelphia. The transatlantic voyage was postponed, and in the interim Jefferson was reelected as a delegate to the Confederation Congress. When Congress moved to Princeton and then Annapolis, Jefferson followed, leaving Patsy to lodge with Mary Johnson Hopkinson in Philadelphia. The absent father sustained his presence in his daughter's life through a stream of letters, forging an epistolary relationship that would grow stronger through the years.[24] The domesticity that Jefferson loved thus flourished both in memory and in expectation of the reunions that punctuated sometimes extended separations. Father and daughter were reunited when the time finally came to travel to France, only to part again soon after they arrived in Paris and Jefferson decided to enroll his daughter in the prestigious Abbaye de Panthemont, a Catholic boarding school for girls. During their first two years in France, Patsy's biographer Cynthia Kierner writes, visits between the two were "sometimes frequent, but other times much less so, even when he was not traveling."[25]

Jefferson and Patsy might construct an enduring bond through letters, but her sisters were too young to be drawn into this imaginary, displaced domesticity. Polly could barely remember her father and transferred her affections to the Eppeses; Lucy had no memory of him at all, nor would she, for in January 1785, six months after he arrived in France, Jefferson learned that she had died at age three of whooping cough. The child whose birth had hastened the death of his wife would never be part of Jefferson's family, an irrevocable loss that aggravated a still raw wound. Jefferson was shattered. When he found out in May of that year that he would succeed Benjamin Franklin as minister to France, he became determined to reconstitute his family. For the next two years he engaged in a determined battle through letters to bring Polly back to him.

It was not just the Eppeses, who had grown to love Polly as their own, who resisted Jefferson's entreaties; Polly did not want to come to live with her father and sister. She was four years old when Jefferson took Patsy to Philadelphia and left Polly at Eppington. She really did not know her father. Jefferson must have understood this, but it would still have been hurtful to read letters in which his daughter forcefully asserted that she did not want to come live with him. Eventually Jefferson had his way. After staying in London with John and Abigail Adams, Polly finally arrived in Paris in July 1787. She was accompanied by Sally Hemings, the young enslaved girl who was both her designated companion and her half aunt.

Polly may have wondered at her reception—Abigail Adams certainly did. After pressing so hard to bring her to Paris, Jefferson could not find the time to cross the Channel to welcome her and take her to her new home, instead delegating that task to Adrien Petit, his maître d'hôtel. When Polly had been in the French capital about a week, Jefferson installed her at the elite Abbaye de Panthemont with Patsy. Some members of his family and friends were shocked that he would put his daughters under the control of Catholics. He had to reassure them that the nuns did no proselytizing. Cynthia Kierner suggests that Jefferson chose to have his daughter "in this most un-American environment" because he believed that being under the care of nuns was the best way to protect her from the "potentially dangerous excesses of Parisian life."[26] Although she could have gone to a day school or been educated at home, who would look after her once tuition ended? A governess was needed, but who could be trusted?

Kierner notes that Abigail Adams, one of Jefferson's dear friends at the time, shared his deep reservations about the supposed wanton character and behavior of Frenchwomen, and warned him. That seems likely. Jefferson and Patsy had dinner with Abigail and John Adams almost as soon as they had arrived in Paris and formed close friendships in subsequent months. Abigail Adams, never one to hold back, expressed very firm and negative opinions about Frenchwomen, saying she was more favorably impressed with the men. That Adams also had a negative reaction to Englishwomen suggests that she had quite fixed ideas about what constituted proper behavior for women. Encountering women from other countries who had different ideas about how to play the role of "woman" profoundly disturbed the New England matron, nor was she thrilled with the Abbaye de Panthemont, as she made clear to her Virginian friend.[27]

Jefferson faced a stark choice: take his chances with the nuns or put Patsy and Polly in the care of a secular Frenchwoman. By choosing the nuns, he chose *not* to keep his daughters with him as much as possible and so create some semblance of family life in his Paris home.[28] The widower did not enjoy the "domestic felicity" he preached with so much conviction to Banister and other correspondents. It might be tempting to conclude that the conspicuous gap between Jefferson's ideals and his living arrangements in Paris was yet another expression of his hypocrisy and leave it at that: he was looking after his own comfort and convenience, not the well-being of the daughters he professed to love. Yet there is another way to view his situation. Jefferson may have experienced the absence of his daughters as a sacrifice as he eagerly awaited their vacations from the Abbaye; and he was able to comfort himself with the thought that they were in the hands of pious and cultivated women who could offer them the nurturing care he knew he was unable to provide. At the Abbaye, Patsy and Polly were protected from the bad example of Frenchwomen and their forward and promiscuous ways, so remaining eligible for the domestic bonds they would one day form in their own country—with unspoiled young men who had not been contaminated by a miseducation abroad.

Jefferson's Parisian pronouncements about gender relations expressed his deep longing for the domestic happiness cut short by his wife's death. Looking beyond his daughters' remaining childhood and his brief enjoyment of their company, he imagined them in homes of their own—homes where he would be welcome to observe and participate in the "tender and tranquil amusements of domestic life." In early 1787 Jefferson explored this theme at great and revealing length in a letter to Anne Willing Bingham, the very attractive young American wife of a prominent English merchant then living in Paris. Jefferson could not preach a sermon to a married woman, nor could he lock her away in a convent. Assuming the playful and intimate voice appropriate to such a correspondence, he appealed to Bingham's reason, contrasting "the tranquil pleasures of America" to "the empty bustle of Paris."[29] Jefferson did not expect the young Philadelphian to renounce Paris's pleasures for the tranquil life of an American housewife. As a married woman, she had little choice regarding where she lived, in any case.

The playfulness of Jefferson's letter was disarming, enabling him to offer a devastating caricature of the empty life of a society matron without giving offense. He begins by identifying himself with his letter, as if he were physically present in it. The letter "will have the honour of being put into your hands," and through it Jefferson himself gains entry into her boudoir. Now he can "see" Bingham and imaginatively participate in her daily routine. The arch flirtatiousness of this conceit doubtless made Bingham smile. As he invites her to join him in observing the spectacle of her own empty life, Jefferson moves from addressing her in the second person to the third, from "you" to "Madame." Jefferson and Bingham were there together (presuming an intimacy between them) when his stylized Parisian woman finally awoke: "At eleven o'clock it is day chez Madame. The curtains are drawn. Propped on bolsters and pillows, and her head scratched into a little order, the bulletins of the sick are read, and the *billets* of the well." Everything is done for Madame, from pillow propping to head scratching. After writing a few billets of her own and receiving visitors, she ventures forth—if the brief morning hour is not too "thronged." She proceeds to "hobble round the cage of the Palais royal: but she must hobble quickly, for the Coeffeur's turn is come; and a tremendous turn it is! Happy, if he does not make her arrive when dinner is half over!" Overcoming the "torpitude of digestion," Madame then "flutters half an hour thro' the streets by way of paying visits, and then to the Spectacles." At this point "another half hour is devoted to dodging in and out of the doors of her very sincere friends, and away to supper." Jefferson quickly dispenses with the rest of Madame's empty day: "after supper cards; and after cards bed, to rise at noon the next day, and to tread, like a mill-horse, the same trodden circle over again."

By focusing on the endless repetition of Madame's daily routine, Jefferson could transform the heady spectacle of French social life into a kind of deluded, if not debauched, drudgery. Yet again, as in his depiction of the "restlessness and torment" of the young man's neverending pursuit of pleasure, he contrasted the immediate, sensual gratifications of a life "without an object beyond the present moment" with the genuine happiness of a purposeful life. Significantly, there were no "moments of extasy" to relieve the "ennui" of Madame's life, as there were for his young men—this was more than Jefferson could properly say to a young woman he liked and admired.

"In America," Jefferson reminded Bingham, "the society of your husband, the fond cares for the children, the arrangements of the house, the improvements of the grounds fill every moment with a healthy and an useful activity." This, of course, was the patriarch's idea of domestic felicity. Women fulfilled their true nature by sacrificing themselves for the comfort and well-being of their families. The kind of happiness available to men and women in Jefferson's America would not be found in Paris. American women might be forgiven for thinking of themselves as the real "mill-horses," subjected to the drudgery of endless domestic labor. Not surprisingly Bingham, who had returned to Philadelphia, objected strenuously to Jefferson's dismissal of her cultivated and accomplished French friends. "They have obtained that Rank and Consideration in society, which the Sex are intitled to, and which they in vain contend for in other Countries." Bingham celebrated the female politicians who so scandalized Jefferson. "We are therefore bound in Gratitude to admire and revere them, for asserting our Privileges," she boldly proclaimed, "as much as the Friends of the Liberties of Mankind reverence the successfull Struggles of the American Patriots."[30]

Bingham tactfully avoided challenging Jefferson's conception of "domestic happiness" in America, content to vindicate the achievements of French society women. "There is no part of the earth where so much of this is enjoyed as in America," Jefferson lectured Bingham from Paris. "You agree with me in this," he wrote (this was a bit of a stretch: she had agreed only "that many of the fashionable pursuits of the Parisian Ladies are rather frivolous"). But, he charged, "you think that the pleasures of Paris more than supply it's want: in other words that a Parisian is happier than an American." This was an intolerable conclusion, provoking Jefferson to abandon the playful tone of his earlier letter and reveal deeper sexual anxieties. "Recollect the women of this capital," he hectored Bingham. These were active women, moving purposefully around the city, "some on foot, some on horses, and some in carriages hunting pleasure in the streets, in routs and assemblies, and forgetting that they have left it behind them in their nurseries." Again, Jefferson, using such laden verbs as "hunting" to describe the women's activities, invoked the tired comparison with "our own countrywomen occupied in the tender and tranquil amusements of domestic life," imploring Bingham to "confess that it is a comparison of Amazons and Angels."[31] Bingham, a leading figure in the increasingly cosmopolitan society of America's first city, had nothing to say in response. There was nothing to be gained in pursuing this correspondence.

In his letters to Bingham, Jefferson conjured up an image of a married woman who turns away from domesticity, betraying her responsibility to her family and to the republic. She instead pursues a delusional and unnatural "happiness" in places where it would be almost impossible to find it. In taking to the streets and "hunting pleasure," respectable women compromised their reputations: the street was where prostitutes offered themselves for the pleasure of men. The "Amazons" of Paris were really miserable, unlike the happy and contented "Angels" of America who attend properly to their husbands and children. Of course, there was no "Angel" attending Jefferson or his daughters, and this was the real pathos of the letters he wrote in Paris about family life, gender roles, and sexuality. The Jeffersons had lost their Angel for good. And one should not take the word "nurseries" literally. Jefferson's daughters were still of an age where they needed a mother or a mother figure. That is, in all likelihood, one of the reasons he chose to place them in the convent, where they would be under the constant supervision of females. He would not be left to manage alone the tricky passages from girlhood to womanhood—among other things, puberty, menstruation, and a first interest in the opposite sex. Sally Hemings, the person sent to watch over his youngest daughter, was the same age as his eldest daughter and needed supervision herself. His construction of the ideal family life put a wife and mother at the center, with no mention of the duties of father and husband, except as a person to be attended to by his wife, the mother of his children. There is no wonder he missed this. His life in Paris did not approach that ideal. Jefferson therefore filled in the void in his and his daughters' lives with a vision of the perfect wife and mother.

According to Hemings family lore, Jefferson promised his wife on her deathbed that he would not remarry. She did not want her children to have a stepmother, perhaps reflecting her childhood experiences with two stepmothers after her own mother died not long after her birth. Whether owing to such a promise or not, Jefferson never remarried. He opted instead for a "substitute for a wife," his legal wife's half sister who because of her race and enslaved status could never be a legal or socially suitable wife. Whether he ever contemplated taking another wife will remain unknown. It was common for widowers to do so in Jefferson's time and may, indeed, have been expected. But what did it mean for him to have an ideal republican family in mind that he did not have in fact—but could have had if he had so wanted?

Faces of Slavery

There was another very important component to Jefferson's view of domesticity, and it was crucial to the way his experiences in France helped transform his personal life and his outlook on the world. It is often noted that after his return from France, Jefferson appeared to retreat on the subject of slavery. Though he continued to the end of his days to call it an evil, he declined to be an active agent for change. Instead, as an official of a new nation, Jefferson turned his attention elsewhere—to the development of the government of the United States along the lines he favored. He put the project of emancipation (a state matter) off onto later generations of Virginians and others who lived in slave states. As we will see, a number of things happened to Jefferson while he was in Europe that influenced his thinking on the question of slavery in the United States. One centered on the very nature of the domestic situation at the Hôtel de Langeac.

Jefferson grew up in the midst of, and ended his days in, a racially based slave society. Enslaved blacks were present in nearly all the important phases and events of his existence—childhood, leaving home for college, courtship, marriage, the birth of his children. There was no picture of family life without them. The institution particularly shaped the contours of his marriage because it not only brought him additional wealth—making him one of the largest slaveholders in Virginia—it also brought blood ties in the form of his wife's half siblings: Robert, James, Thenia, Critta, Peter, and Sarah (Sally) Hemings. The servants Jefferson encountered in France were, despite their low social status, free men and women. They could bargain for raises, quit and go to other employers or into other lines of work. Despite his servants' greater freedom, Jefferson lived a very good life in Paris. In fact, he enjoyed a much higher standard of living there than back home on his plantation, even though he was the "Master" of the Hôtel de Langeac in a much more limited sense than he was the Master of Monticello.

Jefferson, however, was not really free of slavery in his Parisian setting. James and Sally Hemings lived with him—Sally, arriving as Polly's companion, was not supposed to have come to France. Jefferson had requested that Polly be sent with an older enslaved woman, Isabel Hern, who would return to Virginia after sailing to France with the nine-year-old. Instead, the Eppeses (Elizabeth, or "Betsy," the daughter of John Wayles, was Sally and James's half sister) sent Sally, who remained in the country until the end of 1789. The siblings were reunited for what would be the time of their lives. They would also be the face of slavery for Jefferson during his Paris years, and their presence in his home would have great consequences for his attitude toward the institution.

One of the most elusive aspects of the South's slave society is the exact nature of the relationship between enslaved blacks and the white slave-owning families to whom they were linked by blood. This was not something white family members discussed openly and freely in letters, the kind of material that historians rely upon so heavily. The near absence of references to these connections in family papers was, for many years, taken as evidence that such mixtures were rare among upper-class whites. DNA testing on African Americans, which became possible only in the late twentieth century, makes clear that racial intermixture was endemic to southern plantation society and that it was not the province of any one class. Of course, African Americans had always said this was so. They were telling the stories of their families, without the same tradition of expressing hostility toward and anxiety about race-mixing that existed among so many white Americans (historians included)—during slavery and well into the twentieth century. The family histories of blacks were all too often ignored.

The bits of information we do possess about mixed families indicate, not surprisingly, that there was no one way to handle the situation. In some families blood ties made a difference. In the vast majority they did not. We are able to gauge what difference it made between the Jeffersons and the Hemingses only by drawing reasonable inferences from the way Jefferson treated his wife's enslaved half siblings, and the ways they responded to him, which can actually tell us much. He apparently took his cue from his wife, who, unlike many plantation mistresses, did not appear to resent the children her father had by an enslaved woman. They could have been placed out of sight and out of mind. Instead, Martha Jefferson put herself in the position to deal with Thenia, Critta, and Sally Hemings and their mother, Elizabeth, every day, bringing them to Monticello and making them her housemaids. As we have seen, once on the mountain, all of the Hemingses were marked early on for different treatment. The men were given the freedom to move about out of Jefferson's supervision, to take employment, and to keep their wages. The women were exempted from fieldwork and, instead, served in the household performing domestic tasks—sewing, baking, and minding children.

Law was the bedrock of the master and slave relationship, the master deriving power from the state's willingness to protect property in human beings. The Hemings-Wayles blood connection complicated matters for Jefferson, because that tie went beyond law and touched on his deep sense of the importance of blood and family. It led him to alter the terms of engagement with this particular set of enslaved individuals. He was able to play this flexible game back home, however, with the full force of Virginia law still in place, available to be called upon at a moment's notice if needed. France was different. The laws that tied the Hemingses to Jefferson did not operate there. In fact, French law gave brother and sister a way out of slavery. Both they and Jefferson knew this. His mastery over them, therefore, was of a different character from what it was at Monticello. The most telling indication of this is that both Hemingses were paid wages, indeed, very good wages by French standards.

Jefferson never explained why he paid wages to James and Sally Hemings, or why he did not differentiate between them and other comparable servants by paying them at a lesser rate. Was he signaling to the French servants, who would have noticed that their co-workers were not being paid, or being paid less, and then thought of him as a slave owner? Or was it about his French abolitionist friends who pressed him about slavery? They knew he had slaves at home in Virginia, where slavery was the norm, but seeing him play that role in Paris would have cast him in a particularly unflattering light. It is more likely that Jefferson paid the Hemingses to try to keep them happy and, perhaps, prevent them from leaving or protesting their circumstances in ways that would have drawn embarrassing attention to their legal status in France. As noted in chapter 2, once back in America, Jefferson continued the practice of paying all when he had free and enslaved labor in his homes away from Monticello—even at the President's House in Washington City, where slavery was legal. In addition to keeping the peace, this practice obscured his involvement in slavery. It was as if he were denying when in these places that he was really a slaveholder at all, but instead played the role only where the social circumstances required it, back at his plantations in Virginia.

Whatever his reasons for paying the Hemings siblings, living on a long-term basis with people who were slaves at Monticello, but treated as paid servants at the Hôtel de Langeac along with his staff of other servants, required Jefferson to think differently about his relationship to the pair and to the rest of their family. This also brought to the fore in the clearest way—for him and the Hemingses—the truth that slavery was not a natural state. It was a creature of law and, thus, a matter of policy. Jefferson's letter to the French expatriate Paul Bentalou revealed his anxiety about French law and the legally tenuous nature of his hold over the two African Americans living under his roof in Paris. Would he be able to keep the Hemings siblings under his control if they learned how to use French law to obtain their freedom? Madison Hemings said that his mother shared Jefferson's understanding about the ultimate meaning of French law and considered herself to be "free" in Paris, and it is likely that her brother, who had been there much longer than she, felt the same.

It is not clear how the Jeffersons presented the Hemingses, or how the Hemingses presented themselves, to people in Paris. From the relatively few facts that can be gleaned regarding their lives in the city, we can see that both siblings' interactions with the French were out of the ordinary. James, on his own accord, hired a tutor to help him improve his French. At one point the French tutor insulted James, who promptly beat him up. Hiring another's time was not a common thing for an enslaved person in America to do, nor was beating up a white man without apparent consequences. One of Patsy Jefferson's friends referred to Sally Hemings as "Mademoiselle Sally" in a letter she wrote to Patsy after the Jeffersons and Hemingses returned to America: that, too, was uncommon. Prerevolutionary France was rigidly hierarchical; the classes were separated by their titles and by the way they displayed their status, in manners and dress. Slaves were not given the honorifics monsieur, madame, or mademoiselle. This hints at a degree of familiarity between the Jefferson girls and Sally Hemings that the status-sensitive French picked up on when they observed them together and responded to accordingly.

In addition, their shared circumstances as Americans abroad provided an occasion for the Jeffersons and Hemingses to see that there was another dimension to their connection. One should not underestimate the importance of language to a sense of ease, security, and well-being. Jefferson read French well, but was always uncomfortable in conversation. James and Sally Hemings were, at one level, simply two more English-speaking people for him to talk to. Sally Hemings's arrival gave him an immediate conduit to home. Both she and Polly Jefferson could tell him about the people they both knew and events that had taken place back home during his absence.

Jefferson lived with the Hemings siblings in this curious state where his legal power to keep them in place was an ocean away and the legal power to transform their circumstances was within their immediate grasp. This was slavery without any certain societal support or legal protection, a slavery that was instead held in place by the habits and ties within this particular family. Even more than their family had been back in Virginia, the Hemings siblings represented slavery for Jefferson. How he interacted with them told him what kind of man he was. Despite the self-interest driving his decision to pay them wages, there is no reason to doubt that doing this, buying them clothes, and giving James Hemings, at least, free movement helped further Jefferson's sense of himself as a "good" master. While the Hemingses may have thought of themselves as free, there is little reason to believe that Jefferson ceased to view himself as their master. For him, their freedom was a potential fact that could be avoided—should be avoided—if he conducted himself the right way.

At some point an already confounding domestic situation grew even more complicated. Sally Hemings became what their son Madison called his father's "concubine," a term that in his time denoted a woman who lived with a man without being married to him.[32] This created another even more salient point of connection for Jefferson with the Hemings family, and it was a familiar circumstance. Brother and sister existed, and were in his household in Paris, because Jefferson's father-in-law had taken their mother, Elizabeth, as his concubine. This was but another aspect of the role of master—one that evidently meant enough to Jefferson for him to offer a vision of family life to sixteen-year-old Sally Hemings that made her, in the words of his great friend John Hartwell Cocke, his "substitute for a wife." Cocke, a cofounder of the University of Virginia with Jefferson, disdained slave owners' cohabiting with enslaved women; in his diary Cocke attributed the practice to widowers and bachelor slave owners who he said were following the example of "Mr. Jefferson."[33]

Cocke's formulation "substitute for a wife" suggests that he was addressing a specific type of circumstance that bothered him greatly: white men who opted for long-term liaisons with enslaved women instead of marrying white women and forming stable and respectable white families. Why have a substitute rather than a real wife? This question was posed directly to Jefferson in 1802 when James Callender, a Jefferson supporter turned enemy, published a story about Hemings and Jefferson in a Richmond newspaper. An extreme racist, Callender was, more than anything, incensed that Jefferson was involved with a woman who was not white. Others took up the complaint. "Why," one editor asked the then president Jefferson, "have you not married some worthy woman of your own color?"[34] That anyone thought it appropriate to ask this question, or complain about the choices of bachelor and widower slave owners, suggests that, for many, marriage was a public matter that implicated more than a man and woman's private affairs. This was, in their eyes, something other than the casual abuse of enslaved women—about which they cared little; actions that could more easily take place without drawing the specific attention of the community. Interestingly, while many commentators today insist that it was impossible for Jefferson to have loved Hemings, his early nineteenth-century critics wrote as if they assumed he did. In fact, it was his supposed affection for her that made the situation so awful, so worthy of ridicule, in their eyes. In fixating on one identifiable and totally inappropriate woman, and having a set of children with her over many years, Jefferson was setting a bad example for the community as a whole. It was too close to a marital situation for comfort and thus cheapened "real" marriages. Jefferson's detractors were making the same complaint about his way of ordering his life as he made about the French in the 1780s: Jefferson was, they charged, selfishly involved in a useless and unproductive relationship that threatened the health of the surrounding society.

As Jefferson spent time making plans for the house he would live in once he returned to the United States, a plan for how that household would be constituted came into view. The improved Monticello would not have a formal mistress in the form of his wife. He would not have been thinking in the 1780s that Patsy would marry and, nevertheless, come back to live with him as his hostess. That she did, because of financial troubles, eventually return to her childhood home with husband and brood in tow was the result of a series of misadventures that Jefferson would neither have contemplated nor wished for. Instead, he would remain a bachelor with a substitute wife, the half sister of the legal wife he had lost.

While we will never be able to get at the day-to-day nature of Jefferson's relationship with Hemings, we know that it was not a connection that could stand as a public example of republican family life. This would not, however, prevent the construction of a private connection along the lines that Jefferson favored and praised while in France. His comparison of French "Amazons" with American "Angels" displays his dreams about a woman who remained completely outside the public sphere, whose sole purpose was to take care of the man in her life, her children, and the home—a configuration that grew out of Jefferson's views about the natural roles of male and female, and the kind of woman he favored. From what we can determine from the few comments about her, Hemings fit this bill. First, it appears that Jefferson liked attractive women, and Hemings was that. Males—white and black—described her as beautiful. As for her personality, she was said to be "good naturd" and "industrious and orderly." As described by her son, her duties in life were to take care of Jefferson, look after their children, and sew occasionally. Unlike those of other enslaved women, Hemings's children always had unfettered access to their mother.[35]

This was not all about Jefferson's will. While still in Paris, Sally Hemings developed her own ideas about the direction her life would take, and they were based upon her understanding of the difference between slavery and freedom. The pair's respective visions came into conflict when Jefferson decided to request a leave of absence to take his daughters back home to Virginia. As Patsy approached marriageable age, and began attending balls and dancing with young men, Jefferson grew anxious. He most certainly did not wish for a French son-in-law, which in all likelihood would have required his daughter to remain in France with her husband. In fact, Patsy developed an attraction to Jefferson's secretary, William Short, and the feeling was, apparently, mutual. For much as Jefferson loved Short, the younger Virginian had already indicated by the end of the 1780s that he wished to stay in Europe. If he married Patsy, that would have kept her there, too—a circumstance that Jefferson would also have found unpalatable, for he longed to have family and friends as near as possible.[36]

When Jefferson spoke of going home, Sally Hemings at first refused to return with him. She did not want to be, in her son's word, "re-enslaved." That she would take this stance even after she became pregnant with Jefferson's child suggests how comfortable she felt in her new surroundings, and how adamant she was about not wishing to return to the status quo in Virginia. Hemings was not alone in this; all of the young people at the Hôtel de Langeac had become attached to Paris. She had learned French well enough to get by and, evidently, felt that she could function in the country, having spent nearly two and a half years there. That does not seem like a long time, but to a sixteen-year-old it could have appeared an eternity. Her brother James had been trained as a chef. His hiring of a tutor near the end of his stay in Paris suggests that he was also thinking of remaining in the country. He would have been a great support, along with William Short, who had his own connections to the Hemings family back in Virginia. His uncles had been married to James and Sally Hemings's half sisters Anne and Tabitha Wayles. The times could only have bolstered the brother's and sister's confidence. Matters at the Hôtel de Langeac were reaching a critical point just as the French Revolution exploded around the Hemingses and the Jeffersons. Patsy Jefferson recalled the demonstrators on the streets outside their home shouting for liberty and equality, and the mood influenced members of the household. Patsy wore a tricolor ribbon in support of the revolution. There is no reason to think that these sentiments would have been lost on the two people in the household who had the most to gain by revolutionary changes in the social order.

Jefferson had to use his powers of persuasion to change Hemings's mind about remaining in France. Even the barest hint of a public struggle over this—if she had decided to petition for her freedom—would have been an enormous embarrassment to him. He therefore suggested that her return to Virginia would not, in fact, be a return to slavery, as she knew it. He promised that she would lead a life of extraordinary privilege on the mountain and that their children would be free once they became adults. This was, apparently, a major concern for her. He would end the doctrine of *partus sequitur ventrem*, under which the status of children followed the status of their mother. That basic tenet of American slavery had kept generations of her family in bondage, despite their increasingly mixed racial heri-

tage. Hemings "implicitly relied" on Jefferson to keep the promises
he made to her.

Reports from the early 1800s indicate that, after she returned to
Virginia, Hemings was in fact treated as being "much above" other
enslaved people at Monticello.[37] When Jefferson was at home, taking
breaks from public life, and she had a newborn infant or a toddler,
a young enslaved girl would be moved into her household. Enslaved
children between the ages of six and ten were assigned to watch
the children of other enslaved women while they were in the fields,
but they did not move into the new mother's household. Hemings's
closeness to Jefferson made her singular in another way. Every adult
slave at Monticello save for Hemings, at one point or another, sold
vegetables or fruit to Jefferson and members of his household. When
he was a little boy, their son Beverley sold pints of strawberries that
he had picked. But a four-year-old selling strawberries to his relatives
makes more sense than a woman selling strawberries to the man with
whom she is sleeping. Given her connection to Jefferson, Hemings
did not have to sell him things in order to get money.[38] Of course,
the rules of slavery bound Hemings's life, for as an enslaved woman,
she was subsumed within Jefferson's legal personality. Significantly,
unlike a wife whose legal personality would disappear upon marriage, Hemings, once she returned to Virginia, could be sold, as
could her children—things that could not happen if she were a free
white woman to whom Jefferson proposed legal marriage. Convinc-
ing himself (and her) that neither he nor his family would ever do any
of those things fit perfectly with all the other rationalizations Jefferson was formulating about his behavior as a slave owner. He would
make sure things were done the "right" way, and all would be well.

Again, this was not to be an ideal republican family that set an
example for others to follow. It was, for Jefferson, an extralegal configuration that fit his understanding of the natural connections that
existed between men and women, and the children they produced.
The woman gave up her independence in return for the home and
protection that the man provided, along with a legacy that he would
give to their children. With no law to direct his behavior, everything

depended upon his character and Hemings's faith in his word. That Jefferson was able to pull this off—to have conducted himself in a way that allowed him to maintain his control over both siblings in the end—taught him how effectively he could manage himself as a slave owner with the enslaved people closest to him on a daily basis. It also helped him become much more comfortable in an institution that discomfited him, but from which he now was even less seriously inclined to escape.

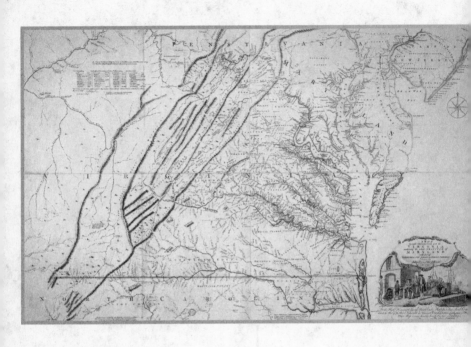

Joshua Fry–Peter Jefferson map. (© The Thomas Jefferson Foundation at Monticello)

CHAPTER 5

LOOKING HOMEWARD

Europe in the late eighteenth century proved to be a clarifying lens through which to view the newly formed American republic. As we have seen, Jefferson's encounters with the societies he visited there—especially during his time in Paris—deepened his appreciation for his native country and his countrymen. The New World may have been rough and unrefined compared with the Old World, but it had boundless potential. Because he located the fundamental difference between the Old World and the New in their respective political regimes, Jefferson's concerns about reforming Virginia faded from view.[1] Republican institutions promised to free Americans from the shackles of despotism that bound the mass of ordinary Europeans—the "anvil" that was subject to the unrelenting "hammer" blows of the entrenched aristocracy. The Virginia he now envisioned, as he looked westward from Paris, did not have to be reformed. Quite the contrary, the pure, uncorrupted institutions of the republican New World had to be protected against both the contamination of Old World influences and the efforts of homegrown "aristocrats" who might turn back the clock to the bad old days of provincial subjection and subservience.

This was a substantial change in attitude for Jefferson. Before he came to Europe, he had taken the opportunity presented, when Marbois asked him for information about Virginia, to sketch out a comprehensive indictment of his "country's" shortcomings in *Notes on the State of Virginia*. The success of the revolution depended on the *transformation* of Virginian and American society generally. Jefferson's powerful condemnation of the institution of slavery—an institution that he said brutalized masters and slaves alike—was a centerpiece of his indictment, as its placement in his query on manners made clear.[2] Jefferson was of Montesquieu's view that the manners, or *moeurs*, of a people were foundational to its politics. Certain conditions had to obtain before republicanism could take hold among the people and make them ready for self-governance. Many years later, during his retirement, Jefferson emphasized this point to his fellow Virginian Samuel Kercheval. "Where then is our republicanism to be found?" Jefferson asked. "Not in our constitution certainly, but merely in the spirit of our people. That would oblige even a despot to govern us republicanly."[3]

But what if that "spirit" waned, as Jefferson had feared it might after independence was won? "From the conclusion of this war we shall be going down hill," he warned: rights will be "disregarded," and Virginians will "forget themselves, but in the sole faculty of making money."[4] Jefferson, the governor in retreat from his bad experiences in office, had worked on *Notes*—his agenda for reform—with a sense of urgency. Now was the time to disestablish the Anglican Church to guarantee the religious liberty that would sustain the republican "spirit"; now was the time to do something about slavery, along lines that he had prescribed in his query on laws. Institutions shaped character, even as character shaped institutions. It was, Jefferson feared, a vicious circle, and one that could be broken and made virtuous only if an enlightened people—inspired by the same patriotic fervor that led them to break with the British Empire—proceeded to destroy the institutional legacy of the provincial old regime. Ending slavery, Jefferson believed, would be the ultimate test of Virginia's republican character. Would moneymaking Virginians like Jefferson himself overcome their self-interest in order to secure the commonwealth's republican future? Laws shaped manners, as their sequence in *Notes on Virginia* suggested, and educating, emancipating, and then expatriat-

ing Virginia's slaves was the only guarantee that the younger generation would not be "nursed, educated, and daily exercised in tyranny"
and so be "stamped" by the institution with its "odious peculiarities."[5]

Jefferson worked on revisions of the *Notes* during his Paris years. He
had originally hoped that the rising generation of Virginian statesmen
could draw inspiration from his reform agenda, though he understood that his sharp criticisms of slavery and the Virginia constitution
would offend many of them. But his actions, or inaction, by the time
he returned home show that the sense of urgency he had originally
brought to the reform agenda in the *Notes* was gone. He fell silent on
issues that had seemed of enormous import to him.

The efforts of his friend James Madison took off the table one of
the reforms about which Jefferson had been most passionate when he
shepherded through the Virginia legislature Jefferson's Bill for Religious Freedom in early 1786. The bill disestablished the Anglican
Church in Virginia and became a model for the First Amendment to
the Constitution of the United States. This momentous event provided some evidence of the spirit of Enlightenment in postrevolutionary Virginia, perhaps enough to allay his pessimism about the future
of republicanism in his home state. Passage of the bill restored his
faith in his countrymen and set a worthy example for others to follow: "it will produce considerable good even in these countries where
ignorance, superstition, poverty and oppression of body and mind and
in every form, are so firmly settled on the mass of the people, that
their redemption from them can never be hoped."[6]

And as the years wore on in Paris, there was greater distance from
the personal and political torments of the war years. This gave Jefferson a different perspective on American developments and prospects.
He was comfortable acting as minister to France. It suited him much
better than being war governor of Virginia. The role obliged him to
represent the United States in a positive light, by checking and correcting the ignorance and disdain so characteristic of metropolitan
attitudes—in France as well as Britain—toward people they considered semibarbarous provincials. The man who worried that after the
successful war everything would "go down hill" had to become a

vigorous defender and exponent of American virtues. This foreign venue was the perfect place to discover them.

New World Virtue, Old World Vice

Away from home Jefferson saw himself differently too. As a young man he had been eager to visit Europe, to revel in the glories of its high civilization and to become more enlightened, cultivated, and polite. Now that he was in Paris, his own essential character seemed much less malleable: the mature (then forty-two-year-old) Jefferson would not be so vulnerable to the attractions—and seductions—of the "vaunted scene." "I am now of an age which does not easily accomodate itself to new manners and new modes of living," he told a German correspondent in 1785, "and I am savage enough to prefer the woods, the wilds, and the independance of Monticello, to all the brilliant pleasures of this gay capital. I shall therefore rejoin myself to my native country with new attachments, with exaggerated esteem for it's advantages, for tho' there is less wealth there, there is more freedom, more ease and less misery."[7] Jefferson invoked a new calculus, with American "freedom" now easily offsetting Americans' lack of cultivation. The relation between New World and Old was thus reversed; political enlightenment now moved from west to east. With their new nation showing the way to the benighted and oppressed peoples of Europe, it was incumbent on revolutionary Americans to keep the "sacred fire of liberty" alight. Jefferson did not have to change. He had instead to remain true to the republican character that he discovered in himself and his countrymen in the great movement toward independence and national self-determination.

Jefferson's playful description of himself as a "savage of the mountains of Virginia" signaled a new self-confidence and willingness to embrace what had traditionally been seen as the markers of inferiority. Whether or not European creoles physically deteriorated in the New World, as Buffon and other leading natural historians claimed, provincial Anglo-Americans could hardly deny that, as their settlements penetrated the wilderness, they lived very much like the

Native Americans whom Europeans styled as "savage." But Jefferson countered this conventional view with a new anthropology of native peoples that celebrated their *potential* for development, emphasizing the potency of Indian men, the fertility of Indian women (if they stopped working in the fields and following the hunt), and the "natural" eloquence of their orators. Just as he positioned Indians at the threshold of historical time, poised to recapitulate the progress of European civilization across the millennia, so Jefferson and his countrymen could see themselves inaugurating a new era in the history of freedom. European civilization had bequeathed a rich legacy to this forward-looking, self-governing people, but Europe was no longer the measure of all things. Ambitious Americans insisted that they were no longer provincials, as they had escaped from cultural subservience as well as political dependence. Independence was transformational, initiating a fundamental revolution in morals and manners.

Jefferson was willing to grant that cultivated Europeans had the advantage in the fine arts, music, literature, and the higher learning. "With respect to what are termed polite manners," he told Charles Bellini, Europeans were ready to "make all those little sacrifices of self which . . . relieve society from the disagreeable scenes to which rudeness often exposes it." By contrast, crude, hard-drinking Americans were all too prone to transform "themselves into brutes." Jefferson could acknowledge these apparently unfavorable comparisons because they were so superficial and unimportant, disguising rather than revealing true national character. These were "manners" in the familiar, modern sense: rituals and conventions that facilitated social interactions among the leisured elite. As they grew more prosperous, Americans would become more refined, but this was not the key to the national character that was forged in the revolution. More telling for Jefferson was the comparison between the "happiness which is enjoyed in America by every class of people" and the "physical and moral oppression" of "the great mass of the people" in Europe. If politeness made social life more "amiable," it also provided a cover for the "intrigues of love" and "ambition" that subverted the morals and happiness of aristocratic society.[8]

It is not surprising that intimate encounters demolished his ideal-ized image of European civilization, or that American defects faded from view at a distance. Enlightenment values, which called for observation and comparison whenever appropriate, virtually com-pelled Jefferson's reevaluation of the two societies. His conception of "nature" was critical to his thinking. Nature was both the source of all value—in agriculture and other productive activities—and the end or ultimate purpose of civilized life, as men discovered and exploited its governing laws.[9] Of course, Americans were closer to nature than their overcivilized European counterparts and therefore better able to act in accord with its self-evident imperatives. In Europe man was alienated from nature, and "the mass of people" was "loaded with misery by kings, nobles and priests, and by them alone." The Amer-icans' advantage was *not* their superior environment: it was enough to stipulate its equal potential, as Jefferson did in his famous defense of New World fertility in his *Notes on Virginia*. Indeed, he found "the finest soil upon earth" and the "finest climate under heaven" in his travels in the south of France; moreover, as he told his old teacher George Wythe, the people he encountered there, "surrounded by so many blessings from nature," were "of the most benevolent, the most gay, and amiable character of which the human form is susceptible." Still, there were problems. The French peasantry was condemned to ignorance and misery by the character of a government that denied them equal access to the land and its fruits. The old regime was unnatural.[10]

Travels in the European countryside provoked Jefferson's most rad-ical statements about the need for an activist state that would take any measure short of an "agrarian"—or what we would call "socialist"—redistribution of property. The "enormous inequality" he observed produced "so much misery to the bulk of mankind," he told James Madison, that "legislators cannot invent too many devices for sub-dividing property" to remedy the problem. What could legislators do? One "means of silently lessening the inequality of property" Jefferson said, would be "to exempt all from taxation below a cer-tain point, and to tax the higher portions of property in geometrical

progression as they rise. Whenever there is in any country, uncultivated lands and unemployed poor, it is clear that the laws of property
have been so far extended as to violate natural right." Had there been
any European "legislators" who genuinely represented the people,
they could have looked to Virginia for inspiration and specifically
to the legislation Jefferson had sponsored abolishing primogeniture
and entail. The genius of republicanism was to enable Americans to
act in accord with nature, recognizing the need "to provide by every
possible means that as few as possible shall be without a little portion
of land." Echoing his celebration of yeoman farmers as the "chosen
people of God" in his *Notes on Virginia*, Jefferson reminded Madison
that "small landholders are the most precious part of a state." Immune
to the corrupting influence of "subservience and venality," they were
an ever-renewable source of moral virtue.[11]

Far from modeling the metropolitan refinement and civility that
Americans had so long sought to emulate, the rural landscapes Jefferson encountered in his European travels offered him a glimpse of
a future that Americans had to avoid at all costs. Whatever problems
he saw in his native society, he did not believe they were so deep and
extensive as those of French society—problems that were caused by
the extreme maldistribution of property. Jefferson may have owned
thousands of acres, but land was abundant and—thanks to his own
legislative initiatives—would never be concentrated in only a few
hands. National character was critical: once again Jefferson noted
that American families were different from European families, not
just in terms of gender relations but in their attitudes toward property. The attachments that made American families and connected
them to one another fulfilled nature's imperatives. To act in accord
with nature was Jefferson's definition of happiness—for individuals,
families, and society as a whole. Virginia's legislators had heeded his
call and wisely preempted the emergence of a European-style landed
aristocracy by abolishing primogeniture and entail. First sons would
no longer be favored in the inheritance of real property (primogeniture), and families would no longer be able to keep property within
their control by preventing fee simple sales outside of the family line

(entail). Americans took "care to let their subdivisions go hand in hand with the natural affections of the human mind," passing landed property on to *all* of their children. The equal distribution of property across the generations, evidence of solicitude for rising generations, would cement family feeling and strengthen the life of the family, the crucial foundation of American republicanism. This natural regime contrasted with the unnatural European system of aristocracy. The family was the incubator of moral sentiments in children, with "independent" patriarchs like Jefferson exercising their civic competence to protect and provide for all of their dependents. That women thereby enjoyed an exalted status in republican society was a measure of moral progress, for "it is civilization alone which replaces women in the enjoyment of their natural equality."

In France, Jefferson found a flattering place for American republicans between the oppressive old regime with its thin veneer of civilization and what he saw as the more primitive despotism Indian men exercised over women. Women worked in the fields in Europe and in Indian country, "a barbarous perversion of the natural destination of the two sexes." "Were we in equal barbarism" with the Indians, "our females would be equal drudges."[12] Only among white Americans were women kept in their proper place, at home, where they could perform their "natural" functions as wives and mothers. When societies reached a point where they no longer had to hunt and fend for food, women were brought into the home to do domestic chores while the men tilled the soil. The republican family, conforming to nature, fulfilled the needs of all families, not just the privileged few. This state of affairs could continue, and all could benefit so long as there was a guarantee of a broad distribution of property.

It was simply not true, however, that white women were always in the home and never worked in the fields in America. Jefferson was engaging in the common tendency (then and now) to confuse the behavior and norms of the upper class with those of society as a whole. Lower-class white women had worked in the fields of Virginia from the very beginning. And Indians aside, what of the enslaved women who labored in the fields of his own plantations? When Jefferson muses in the *Notes* and other writings on the differences between races and cultures, he avoids comparisons and analyses that would cause him, and other whites, discomfort or embarrassment. Not surprisingly, the problems Jefferson was willing to talk about openly were the ones that touched him the least personally and about which he was the least sensitive. For example, he was eager to note that white women and black women had more children than Native Americans, attributing the relative low fertility of Indian women to cultural practices that placed physical strain upon them—working arduously in the fields and living a nomadic life following the hunt. He was also willing to test the limits of propriety in comparing the organs of "generation" of white males and Native American males because the comparison did not put white males at a disadvantage. He said nothing, however, about black men's organs of generation, and the widespread belief that black males had larger penises than white males.

Jefferson's willingness to comment on the generative capacities of every category of person on the American continent—white men and women, Native American men and women, and black women—save for black men is telling. What stopped him? The answer lies, in part, in the workings of the patriarchal world that Jefferson inhabited. Patriarchy is not simply about male domination of women. It pits males against males, and white men's sense of competition with black men and their fear of them were fundamental to Jefferson's world-view. These deep feelings expressed themselves most often in fantasies of what black men *might* do if not controlled and in the spreading of canards about their basic nature. This was all very outwardly directed. Not much self-reflection was going on, and certainly no consideration that the problem might lie with white people's attitudes and their way of treating black men. Had Jefferson and other whites been willing to change, their relationship to black men would have changed, too.

Jefferson's belief that masters and slaves in America existed in a state of war almost inevitably led him to fixate upon black men and their potential as warriors. When he thought of slave rebellions, he thought of black men. Though whole families of enslaved people decamped to the British during the American Revolution, it was black men who bore arms and engaged in violent confrontations with their former masters. When musing to Jared Sparks about the prospect of blacks' future resistance to a scheme for emancipation that included expatriation, Jefferson thought of black men—"one million of these fighting men, will say 'we will not go.' "[13] In Jefferson's view, black women were not, as white women were not, potentially autonomous agents of change who could ignite his fears.

Seeing slavery as a state of war also fueled Jefferson's view of black men as potential sexual threats to his and other white males' ownership of white women's bodies. He was certainly not alone in this. White males' sexual anxieties also played an integral role in their competition with and fears about black men, though this was not something Jefferson could ever admit to in writing. He did, however, express his concerns in an indirect fashion. Perhaps the most infamous passage in *Notes on the State of Virginia* is the one in which he credulously accepts the notion, advanced in putatively scientific books he had read, that orangutans in Africa (an animal he had never seen, in a place where he had never been, a place where orangutans actually do not live) sought black women as sexual partners in preference "over those of their own species," just as black men preferred white women over black women.[14] This was but a crass variation on the male lament heard the world over from time immemorial: "They are after *our* women." This formulation is very often coupled with the idea that the women of the group have to be "protected" from the advances of men outside the group—whether the women really want protection or not. Such fears are not always fanciful, as capturing women in war and raiding villages to kidnap women are well-known phenomena. Still, the very designations "our" women or "their" women presume a form of male ownership that fit well within the framework of Anglo-American legal rules about marriage and family life that Jefferson knew so well.

Jefferson and his cohort evinced much more concern about black men having sex with white women than about white men having sex with black women. Virginia had codified this anxiety-ridden double standard in longstanding legal rules that punished black male–white female sex severely, while largely ignoring sex between white men and black women. In the rare cases in which a white man got into trouble for having sex with a black woman, it was a man from the lower classes. Neither John Wayles nor Jefferson needed to fear the law because of their liaisons with black women. Except in rare instances deemed to affect the public—a slave murdered someone or stole from someone other than his or her master, for example—patriarchs like Wayles and Jefferson were the law on their plantations. As Alexander Hamilton observed in his criticism of passages in *Notes on the State of Virginia* and of Jefferson's inaction on emancipation, Jefferson knew very well that the plantation was the perfect incubator for interracial sex. Hamilton saw Jefferson's expressed fears of "admixture" *after* slaves were freed as plainly bizarre. If the enslaved were freed, blacks and whites would not live so closely together and white men would not have as easy access to, or the same power over, enslaved women. He considered and commented on Jefferson's presentation of the matter:

> At one moment he [Jefferson] is anxious to emancipate the blacks to vindicate the liberty of the human race. At another he discovers that the blacks are of a different race from the human race and therefore, when emancipated, they must be instantly removed beyond the reach of mixture lest he (or she) should *stain the blood* of his (or her) master, not recollecting that from his situation and other circumstances he ought to have recollected—that this *mixture* may take place while the negro remains in slavery. He must have seen all around him sufficient marks of this *staining of blood* to have been convinced that retaining them in slavery would not prevent it.[15]

Hamilton might not have recognized that gender was at the heart of the matter. Southern white men gave themselves the right of access to the bodies of all types of women in their society—white, black, red—while denying less powerful nonwhite males access to "their" women, that is, white women. This has been the prerogative, and the way, of conquerors throughout the ages. Jefferson was not against racial admixture per se—he acknowledged the beauty and intelligence of its products, surrounded himself with them, and also facilitated and participated in the activity. He feared admixture on terms that gave black males the kind of access to white women that he and other white males had to black women. Hamilton was right: slavery created the perfect conditions for racial mixing, but that mixing was never an argument in Jefferson's brief against the institution, even though Monticello was filled with mixed-race enslaved people. He knew them at Shadwell, too, as a boy. The only runaway advertisement that Jefferson ever placed under his own name was for a man named Sandy, whom he described as a "Mulatto," with a "light-complexion." Sandy was one of the slaves Jefferson inherited from his father.

Just as Jefferson could not envision a multiracial society without conflict, he could not envision a successful republican society that contained a large class of people, that is to say, blacks—who would exist as second-class citizens in perpetuity. Over time these men would demand equal rights, and certainly one of those rights would be the right to form a family with whomever they chose and with whoever would have them as partners. Jefferson knew that the first interracial liaisons and marriages in Virginia were between black men and white women. There was no mechanism in the brains of white women that prevented them from accepting black partners. Indeed, historians have suggested that black men's success in competing for white women, during the period when there was an imbalance in the sex ratios in the white community and before large numbers of African females were being brought to North America, was a large part of the reason for outlawing interracial marriages. White women had freely accepted black men before. They could do it again in a new postrevolutionary republican society, if blacks were allowed to remain in the country.

If a frank discussion of white male insecurity was not possible for Jefferson in the *Notes*, or in his other writings, neither was he willing to talk specifically about what it meant to believe the things he said he believed about the "barbarous" nature of sending women to work in the fields and to be a man who did just that. Riding through Holland in 1788 and observing the figures of women hunched over crops, Jefferson purportedly turned his thoughts to Indian women in the fields of America. It is not possible that these were the women—or the *only* women—who came to his mind as he viewed these scenes. One doubts that Jefferson ever saw Indian women tending crops. We know for a fact that during his boyhood he saw groups of black women in the fields at Shadwell, as he did on an almost daily basis at Monticello and his other plantations when he was an adult and not away on the public's business.

Although he did not write about it as he reworked the *Notes on Virginia*, we also know that Jefferson did think about the enslaved women on his plantations while in Europe. Writing to William Drayton in 1787, he floated the idea of planting olive, fig, and mulberry trees in "countries" that had "slaves" in order to avoid "all temptation to misemploy" "women and children," who were "often employed in labours disproportioned to their sex and age."[16] Specializing in this type of cultivation would ensure that "the lot of this tender part of our species" would "be much softened." He acknowledged that black women were part of his "species" and were the "tender part" of it—as were white women. But he distanced himself from personal involvement (in much the same way as he wrote to Paul Bentalou about a "person" he knew who brought a slave to France) by referring to "countries where there are slaves," instead of naming his own "country"—Virginia. He thus avoided talking about his culpability in assigning the "tender part of [the] species" to tasks that he believed were "disproportioned to their sex."

Whatever Jefferson's mental evasions about the specific aspects of slavery, the institution's future in Virginia remained a problem with which he had to reckon while he was abroad. He was living among people whom he admired greatly, and who had taken the position that slavery was antithetical to the rights of man and of human progress—and he had claimed to agree with them. If Virginians had shown evidence of Enlightenment values by doing away with an established

religion and feudal elements in their system of property, there had
been very little movement on the slavery question. The Virginia legislature had, in 1782, made it easier to emancipate slaves by allowing
for private manumissions. Before this legislation slave owners who
wished to free enslaved people had to receive permission from the
government, because it was seen as an act that affected the public welfare. The logic of the revolution, and Jefferson's words in the Declaration particularly, highlighted the problem of holding human beings
in actual, as opposed to metaphorical, bondage. It opened the door for
northern states to adopt gradual emancipation statutes. But white Virginians showed no sign whatsoever of any inclination to end slavery.
Jefferson came to believe that there would be no republican solution
to this question in his time, and, as we now know, none ever arose.

Slavery was undoubtedly a major flaw in Virginia society, but as
time passed in France, Jefferson no longer regarded it as the demoralizing and degrading foundation of his country's way of life. The
homesick Virginian—an official in a newly constituted government
whose interests he had to promote—shifted his focus to an idealized
domesticity and to a republican regime that would foster civic competence and moral development. In the *Notes* Jefferson described his
plan for emancipation that never made it to a discussion in the House
of Delegates, quashed by opposition forces before it could be raised.
This effort would have required action and sacrifice on the part of
white society as a whole. Although he still spoke of his desire to see
slavery eradicated in the United States, Jefferson began to adjust his
thinking to concentrate instead upon his conduct as the master of
Monticello. In France slavery became fully domesticated in his mind.

Jefferson wrote to a friend in 1788, telling of an experiment that he
planned to conduct upon his "final return to America":

> I shall endeavor to import as many Germans as I have grown
> slaves. I will settle them and my slaves, on farms of 50. acres
> each, intermingled, and place all on the footing of the Metayers
> [Medietarii] of Europe. Their children shall be brought up, as
> others are, in habits of property and foresight, and I have no

doubt but that they will be good citizens. Some of their fathers
will be so: others I suppose will need government. With these,
all that can be done is to oblige them to labour as the labouring
poor of Europe do, and to apply to their comfortable subsistence
the produce of their labour, retaining such a moderate portion of
it as may be a just equivalent for the use of the lands they labour
and the stocks and other necessary advances.[17]

For this brief time, Jefferson had the idea that he could improve
upon other "experiments" with emancipation by having his slaves
mingle with, presumptively, industrious Germans, whose example
would help them become "good citizens." It is odd to see Jefferson
speak of African Americans' becoming "citizens," "good" or otherwise—odder still to see him suggest that he had any thought of
freeing slaves on his plantation without a plan to have them leave the
country. But he was in a frame of mind geared toward transforming
life at Monticello, and this encompassed restructuring not only his
house but the grounds and all who lived there—including himself.

As Jefferson floated ideas about turning slaves into a form of serfs
and planting olive and fig trees so that the enslaved women on his
plantations would not have to work so hard, the statuses of James and
Sally Hemings—slaves back in Virginia, potentially free in France,
blood relatives to his wife, and Sally, at some point, his mistress—fit
perfectly into Jefferson's evolving conception of the institution. As
far as the record indicates, thoughts of turning slaves into serfs to
prepare them for eventual freedom disappeared. Instead, slaves were
to be incorporated into plantation households where self-governing
citizen-householders like himself would spur the new nation's forward progress. They would be part of the "family" in the manner of
Roman notions of household governance with patriarchs presiding
over all the dependents in their domains. By focusing on measures to
ameliorate slavery, instead of immediately abolishing the institution,
Jefferson would seek to disarm what he had described in the *Notes*
as the captive nation of enslaved Africans that had during the revolution seemed to pose such a dire threat to Virginia's security and

civic health. And by blending Virginian families into a broader image of *American* domestic life, Jefferson could envision the ultimate outcome of family-centered moral development in the slave-free farming regions to the North coming to fruition in the South. As planters became farmers, enlightened public opinion would prepare the way for emancipation.

Jefferson's strange marriage of eighteenth-century revolutionary antislavery sentiment to nineteenth-century antebellum proslavery fantasies of happy relations between masters and slaves on southern plantations is confusing to modern sensibilities. They rested comfortably, however, in the mind of a man who fervently, and some might say, naïvely, believed in the notion of inevitable human progress. Significantly, Jefferson was considering these matters while in a country that was the very seat of Enlightenment thought, French philosophers and scientists having virtually defined the age. But it had taken France a thousand years to come to a true reckoning about the degraded state of its peasantry in the countryside and starving workers crowded into its metropolitan areas. Jefferson was ecstatic to be in Paris when the ferment began, and he viewed the rumblings of discontent—the rising of "the people"—with great enthusiasm. In the end, he would hold on to his enthusiasm far longer than he should have, well into the period in which the mass killings, even of some people he knew, began. Progress had a price, he felt.

Jefferson could never have truly accepted that he and his fellow white Virginians should pay such a high price in order to transform their slave society. As a matter of fact, the likelihood that the "wheel of fortune" would soon turn and Virginia's slaves would rise up in rebellion seemed increasingly remote to Jefferson in Paris. The end of the war and the retreat of the British had deprived them of armed allies and, thus, severely diminished any large-scale security threat. White Virginians had time. They could now, if they were of a mind, take a longer, more enlightened view of their self-interest in ameliorating and eventually abolishing slavery.

The comparisons Jefferson made between the revolution-prone masses of Europe and their American counterparts encouraged this more optimistic perspective. Landless Europeans had no recourse but to follow the American lead and overthrow the aristocratic and monarchical regimes that oppressed them; self-governing Americans had the power—and the means through the workings of their new governments—to redress the injustices done to an enslaved minority. But with no legislative solution to the problem on the horizon, Jefferson contented himself with the dream of a slavery domesticated, with emancipation to come—someday.

The juxtaposition of Old World vices and New World virtues had a critical personal dimension for Jefferson. Fascinated and repelled by French sexual mores and gender relations, the homesick Jefferson conjured up an idealized domesticity in republican America that was, he repeatedly insisted, the only source of true and lasting happiness. His identification with the American people grew out of a conception of family life that evoked his own sense of loss and longing. What he had lost—the "domestic felicity" that his wife's death shattered—is what he had once shared and hoped to share again with his countrymen. But Jefferson did not plan to marry again. Instead, the widower focused on his obligations to future generations, beginning with his surviving daughters, and to the attachments they would form with other families. A well-ordered republic was predicated on these obligations and attachments, within and across generations.

Jefferson's idea of the American people had once been something of an abstraction: Americans were no longer English, he wrote in the Declaration of Independence; endowed with natural rights, they were entitled to exercise sovereignty in their own name. But the republic Jefferson imagined from Paris was far more than the opportunistic negation of monarchy and aristocracy. America's republican regime enabled citizens to recognize their true interests. "In science," Jefferson wrote Charles Bellini, "the mass of people" in Europe "is two centuries behind ours, their literati half a dozen years before us."[18] This was Jefferson's way of reversing Eurocentric conceptions of the progress of civilization, for the future surely belonged to the masses, not their erstwhile masters. The two centuries' gap roughly equated to the time elapsed since the first American settlement and the subsequent history of cultivating and improving the New World's natural endowments. While Americans moved forward, making their own history and becoming progressively more enlightened, the European masses remained fixed in time and place. European civilization could not progress because—unlike Jefferson and his fellow American patriots—the aristocratic "literati," using Jefferson's term, did not identify with the people: their privilege, power, and wealth depended on exploiting the labor of the people and keeping them in their place.

Aristocrats appeared blind to the misery that was so conspicuous to Jefferson in France. He was appalled by "the numberless instances of wretchedness" he observed on his travels, telling Madison about a typical encounter in the vicinity of Fontainebleau. "As soon as I had got clear of the town I fell in with a poor woman walking at the same rate with myself and going the same course." He questioned her about "her vocation, condition and circumstances," learning that "she was a day labourer" with two children to support who earned "8. sous or 4 d. sterling the day"—when she could find work. But the poor woman was often unemployed and of course "without bread"; because she was landless, a good portion of what she did earn went for rent. "As we had walked together near a mile and she had so far served me as a guide, I gave her, on parting 24 sous.," Jefferson concluded. "She burst into tears of a gratitude which I could perceive was unfeigned, because she was unable to utter a word. She had probably never before received so great an aid."[19] Such an encounter, Jefferson believed, was inconceivable in America.

Liberated from the chains of old regime despotism and the ignorance it imposed on its subjects, the American people both benefited from and contributed to the progress of useful knowledge. Their republican regime was an engine of Enlightenment. European civilization could make no further progress, Jefferson was convinced, until the old regime collapsed—or was destroyed. "If all the sovereigns of Europe were to set themselves to work to emancipate the minds of their subjects from their present ignorance and prejudices, and that as zealously as they now endeavor the contrary," Jefferson wrote George Wythe, "a thousand years would not place them on that high ground on which our common people are now setting out." The great distance between Europe and America—a distance that Jefferson and other provincial Anglo-Americans had once sought to overcome—now could be seen as a protective barrier. Republican governments would never have been established in the United States had the people "not been separated from their parent stock and been kept from contamination, either from them, or the other people of the old world, by the intervention of so wide an ocean."[20]

And for all their glorious attainments, the highly educated Europeans Jefferson so admired had only a scant six years' advantage over their counterparts in America. "Books, really good, acquire just reputation in that time, and so become known to us and communicate to us all their advances in knowlege." Of course, Jefferson in Paris did not have to wait that long for the best books, nor would Madison and his other correspondents in the republic of letters. And the gap would narrow as Americans made their own contributions to the general stock of learning, most notably in the "science" of politics, where they had already taken the lead.

The condemnation of American slavery in the most enlightened European circles was one persisting marker of the Old World's supposed superiority over the New. But Jefferson equated his own advanced views on the subject with the progress of public opinion; using himself and several of his friends like James Madison as a barometer, he could say that even slave owners who were deeply invested in the institution could see that it had to go. It was only a matter of time before the "mass of people," eager for education and enlightenment, would catch up with his cohort. A free people, vigilant in defense of its rights, must be able to see threats to its liberties clearly. As Jefferson wrote in his Bill for the More General Diffusion of Knowledge in 1779, "the most effectual means" of securing the "free exercise of natural rights" was "to illuminate, as far as practicable, the minds of the people at large," so "that they may be enabled to know ambition under all its shapes, and prompt to exert their natural powers to defeat its purposes."[21] Sensitivity to potential encroachments on their own rights would in turn make better-educated Virginians more keenly aware of the "unremitting despotism" they exercised over their own slaves.[22]

Natural Philosopher

The glaring inequalities that were so obvious in France reinforced Jefferson's tendency to see the world in black-and-white, binary terms. Drawing inspiration from the work—and conversation—of enlightened political economists, he could only conclude that the oppressed "mass of the people" that produced the nation's wealth paid an unacceptably steep price for the luxury and leisure of the privileged few. Yet it was also true that the New World had much to learn from the civilization of the Old, even as the mass of Americans became progressively more enlightened and the civility gap diminished. Jefferson's challenge was to separate the achievements of modern European civilization from the decadent excesses that inevitably flowed from its corrupt foundation. Republicanism was his shield, enabling the awestruck Virginian to distance himself from the dazzling life of the wealthy and wellborn even as he partook of its splendid offerings. Virtue intact, the New World ambassador could move freely in the highest circles of French society, while other Americans remained at risk. Impressionable young American men were vulnerable to the seductive charms of promiscuous Parisian women; American women would be all too easily tempted to follow the lead of their French counterparts and betray their sacred domestic obligations.

Jefferson's anxieties about his insufficiently republican countrymen and women doubtless reveal another of his characteristic tendencies: to project misgivings about himself onto others. But they also testify to the success of Jefferson's self-fashioning project. Holding his own in Paris, particularly in English-speaking salons and with a widening circle of intimate friends, women as well as men, Jefferson's self-confidence grew. Americans enjoyed a certain cachet in the French capital. A playful Jefferson could call himself a "savage" because there was no danger that anyone would ever see him as such, even in the increasingly fashionable image of the "noble savage" that he had helped promote. Jefferson situated himself in American "nature" without fearing the taint of degeneracy or degradation. He took his cue from the French military officer François Jean de Beauvoir, marquis de Chastellux, who visited Monticello in 1782, and later published his impressions of the house and its owner. Chastellux emphasized Monticello's unusual, mountaintop location: possessing "considerable property in the neighbourhood, there was nothing to prevent him from fixing his residence where-ever he thought proper." But Jefferson chose this location for exalted reasons, because of its—and his—relation to nature. "It was a debt Nature owed to a philosopher and a man of taste," Chastellux wrote, "that in his own possessions he should find a spot, where he might best study and enjoy her."[23]

Chastellux recognized a soul mate in Jefferson, a "philosopher" and "man of taste," whose relationship to the natural world epitomized rather than compromised his civility. He sent this tribute to his friend in manuscript form, well in advance of its publication in English. Jefferson was overwhelmed, confessing that he read Chastellux's description of his visit to Monticello "with a continued blush from beginning to end, as it presented me a lively picture of what I wish to be, but am not."[24] Most gratifyingly, Chastellux was suggesting that other enlightened Europeans—whose good opinion Jefferson most hoped to cultivate—would agree with his French friend. Blushes notwithstanding, Jefferson eagerly embraced Chastellux's flattering portrait. When he proceeded to call himself a "savage" shortly after receiving Chastellux's letter, he was exulting in his status as a "philosopher" with a privileged—American—perspective on nature. Indeed, he could describe nature itself, in all its positive, protean connotations as "savage."[25]

Chastellux's image of the philosopher in nature captured Jefferson's new sense of himself and of his country. Overcoming the provincial's sense of inferiority, Jefferson found himself moving comfortably in the highest circles of French society. The republican patriot disdained the pomp and circumstance of the French court, where his occasional appearances signified recognition of the United States as a nominally equal member of the family of nations. Recognition as an equal cit-

izen of the enlightened republic of letters was much more important to Jefferson. His ascent promised to erase the cultural deficit that
Anglo-Americans felt so acutely within the empire, pointing the way
toward a more inclusive, democratic enlightenment that would sustain the new nation's bold experiment in republican self-government.

Monticello

Jefferson's sojourn in Paris was the belated fulfillment of his adolescent fantasy of encountering the great world beyond provincial Virginia and making something of himself there. The death of his wife,
Martha, and disruption of his family life added a powerful impetus to
his decision to leave Virginia. Paris reawakened his deadened senses,
turning the Virginian homeward. The new household he constructed
there reminded him of home, with James and Sally Hemings, William Short, and locally hired servants all tending to his needs. Jefferson's "family" was unconventional: his staff filled the place of
the missing plantation mistress, and his daughters Patsy and Maria
boarded out at the Panthemont convent school. But it was a comfortable arrangement, cobbled together with familiar materials. And as
family, friends, and a stream of visitors filled his rented quarters with
life, Monticello came back to life in Jefferson's imagination.

Jefferson first described the view from Monticello in *Notes on Virginia* in terms that would appeal to his fellow natural philosophers.
Following a discussion of meteorological readings, he described
the phenomenon of "looming." Early in the day, he reported, distant mountain peaks in the Blue Ridge seemed to change their natural shape, rising and sinking below the horizon and assuming "at
times the most whimsical shapes, and all those perhaps successively
in the same morning."[26] It was as if, from his elevated perch, Jefferson were surveying the wide seas and could experience what sailors
called looming, a perceptual phenomenon that defied the rules of
optics and that philosophers had yet to understand. When he was in
Europe, Monticello loomed large for Jefferson, growing ever larger
in his mind's eye as he looked across the ocean. Now he envisioned

Monticello in more intimate, aesthetic terms that reflected his longing to be home; a showcase that he hoped would attract his newfound
European attachments.

Jefferson evoked the natural wonders of the New World most eloquently in the famous Head and Heart letter to Maria Cosway, the
beautiful (and married) English artist with whom he had just spent
some frenzied, deliriously happy days in Paris. Seeking to entice the
artistic Cosway to visit him there, Jefferson played aesthetic variations
on Chastellux's themes. Nature was ostensibly the chief attraction,
but Jefferson himself was clearly the focal point of the verbal vista he
conjured up for Cosway. In Paris, Jefferson saw himself at Monticello,
the place and the house that would preoccupy him for the rest of his
life. It would not be too much to say that he identified himself so
closely with Monticello that the house and the man blended into a
single image.

Jefferson wrote to Cosway that it was "worth a voyage across
the Atlantic" to see Niagara Falls, the "Passage of the Potowmac"
through the mountains to the sea, and Jefferson's very own Natural
Bridge, located near his Poplar Forest plantation in Bedford County.
By painting "these objects," Cosway would "make them, & thereby
ourselves, known to all ages." The chief attraction, however, was "our
own dear Monticello," where Cosway could join Jefferson in surveying nature's works. "With what majesty do we there ride above the
storms! How sublime to look down into the workhouse of nature, to
see her clouds, hail, snow, rain, thunder, all fabricated at our feet! and
the glorious sun when rising as if out of a distant water, just gilding
the tops of the mountains, & giving life to all nature!"[27]

Jefferson's relationship with Cosway has fascinated and puzzled
his biographers. Almost always portrayed, rather improbably, as a
supremely romantic love letter (what lover truly wishes to hear "I
love you, but I really have to think hard about that"?), the "Dialogue
between My Head and Heart," written in the fall of 1786, is far more
akin to a "Dear Jane" letter as Jefferson began the process of extri-
cating himself from a relationship that had no chance of survival.
Cosway herself was confused by the letter. The dialogue form com-

plicated any clear message, even though the Heart's claims seemed to prevail in the end, as Jefferson eloquently testified to the value of the heartfelt attachments that had enabled Americans to win their independence. This pairing of the personal with the political—as if to say, "my love for you is like the love the patriots expressed for one another when joining together to throw off the British yoke"—should have alerted Cosway to Jefferson's mind-set. He was not looking to cement a romantic connection to her, or to serve as a diversion from her unhappy marriage.[28] The attachment he offered to Cosway—or rather to *both* Cosways, Maria and her husband, Richard—was one of deep and sincere friendship that might survive his return to the United States. "Perhaps you flatter yourself," Head teased Heart, "that *they* may come to America?"[29] The mention of "they" reminded Cosway that their Parisian dalliance had no real future unless they were willing to do substantial damage to their families, Jefferson's career, and his reputation. At most Jefferson was willing to consider Cosway as just one of a select cast of characters to enliven the scene at Monticello; intimate attachments could appreciate what he and "nature offered," "subjects of immortality to make her pencil immortal."[30] But this was mere playacting. Whatever Maria's attractions, Jefferson had no interest in spending time with her husband. It is doubtful that he expected either to show up at Monticello.

Jefferson was not looking for a wife, nor could he contemplate returning to Monticello with Maria Cosway—what on earth would the urbane Cosway of that period do on his mountain? And, of course, she already had a husband. Any kind of public and permanent connection to her would be in complete contravention of the wholesome image of American domesticity that he cherished. Disorderly females who breached the barriers of domesticity constituted the greatest threat to the "tranquility" and happiness of republican family life. Yet despite his subtle disengagement from Cosway, Jefferson did not imagine Monticello as a lonely, isolated outpost of civility in the American wilderness. He instead imagined a marriage of American virtue and European civilization that would enable him—and the nation he represented—to reconcile the claims of head and heart. In more modest terms, Jefferson would transport the glamorous life he came to love in Paris—and the attachments he formed there—to the wilds of Virginia.

Jeffersonian dreams of the future began at Monticello. The home he had abandoned—and the family life that his wife's death had shattered—came back into view when he was in Paris, in a new frame that gave him a fresh perspective on his own life story. "I consider myself here as a traveller only," he told his Virginia neighbor George Gilmer, "and not a resident." "All my wishes end, where I hope my days will end, at Monticello. Too many scenes of happiness mingle themselves with all the recollections of my native woods and feilds, to suffer them to be supplanted in my affection by any other."[31] His most captivating vision centered on the house itself, a place that he hoped would epitomize the new nation's prospects. Situated on a mountaintop, in the sky, Monticello was well suited to the visionary philosopher. Augustus Foster, a dyspeptic British diplomat, made fun of the far-seeing Jefferson, "a visionary" who "loved to dream, eyes open, or, as the Germans say, 'zu schwärmen.'" But "America is the paradise for 'Schwärmers,'" Foster admitted, for "futurity there offer[ed] a wide frame for all that the imagination can put into it."[32] If Monticello's vistas spurred Jefferson's imagination, they also evoked memories. When Jefferson was a boy, growing up at nearby Shadwell, "the top of this mountain was his favorite retreat," his daughter Martha reported him saying. "Here he would bring his books to study, here would pass his holiday and leisure hours: that he never wearied of gazing on the sublime and beautiful scenery that spread around, bounded only by the horizon, or the far off mountains." The "indescribable delight" he experienced on his boyhood rambles "attached him to this spot" and he then decided that he would one day "here build his family mansion."[33]

Jefferson was "attached" to his "own dear Monticello" before he gave the small mountain its Italian name and hired slaves to level the mountaintop, at great effort and expense. He and Dabney Carr, his closest childhood friend, wandered the Monticello woods and dreamed with their "eyes open." When Carr, who later married Jefferson's sister Martha, died a tragic early death in 1773, Jefferson had his remains removed to the mountain. Over the next decade Carr was followed to the grave by Jefferson's daughters Jane and Lucy, an unnamed son, and his wife, Martha, all buried at Monticello (a second Lucy died at Eppington, the home of Martha's sister, in 1784 when Jefferson was in Paris).[34] By the time of Martha's death in 1782, the sentimental associations of Jefferson's "storied mountain" were so overwhelming that he could no longer bear to live there with them.[35]

Four years after his wife's death, when Jefferson evoked the aesthetic delights of Monticello to Maria Cosway, inviting the beautiful young artist to come to the mountain and capture the scene, his invitation and manner with Cosway suggested that he was in the process of moving beyond his emotional pain. His invitation, however, also struck darker notes, returning obsessively to the themes of death, loss, and grief that shadowed memories of Monticello. After summoning up a bright and beautiful picture of his mountaintop home, his tone shifted suddenly, offering the Cosways "an asylum from grief!" "With what sincere sympathy I would open every cell of my composition to receive the effusion of their woes! I would pour my tears into their wounds: and if a drop of balm could be found at the top of the Cordilleras, or at the remotest sources of the Missouri, I would go thither myself to seek and to bring it." This extravagantly worded offer, gushing from Jefferson's pen, had no discernible pretext or purpose. But Jefferson did have something important to say—and it is worth recalling that he was talking to himself in this dialogue, so often styled as a love letter to another person. "Deeply practised in the school of affliction," he could now deal with his own losses. "The human heart knows no joy which I have not lost," he exclaimed, "no sorrow of which I have not drank! Fortune can present no grief of unknown form to me!" Now he understood that grief was *not*, as Head would have it, the price paid for forming attachments that death eventually, inevitably would rupture. Quite to the contrary, the experience of grief gave rise to the deepest and most enduring attachments. Returning to his theme later in his letter—and no longer pretending to address Cosway—Jefferson insisted that grief and joy were inextricable, perhaps even indistinguishable. Was there any "delight" more "sublime . . . than to mingle tears with one whom the hand of heaven hath smitten!" "When heaven has taken from us some object of our love," as had happened so often to Jefferson, "how sweet is it to have a bosom whereon to recline our heads, & into which we may pour the torrent of our tears! Grief, with such a comfort, is almost a luxury!"[36]

Jefferson's morbid effusions baffled Cosway. After all, "the greater part of life is sunshine," as he proceeded to tell her, and the sun had never shone more brightly than during their recent days together in Paris. Why not simply live for more such moments? But Jefferson imagined a deeper intimacy when he conjured up his portrait of Monticello for Cosway. This is where so many of his loved ones had died and he had experienced the "sublime delight" of grief: "to watch over the bed of sickness, & to beguile it's tedious & it's painful moments! to share our bread with one to whom misfortune has left none! This world abounds indeed with misery: to lighten it's burthen we must divide it with one another." Jefferson knew this "story," with its exclamatory punctuation, made sense only in retrospect, at a great distance. His eldest daughter, Martha, just then turning twelve years old, would have understood what Jefferson was saying. She and other relatives had sought to share his grief when his wife died, but Jefferson—by Martha's account—was inconsolable, nearly dead to the world. Sally Hemings also would have understood, for she and her sisters were with Jefferson at Martha's bedside as she lay dying; they knew that the broken man who had been led from the room in the moments before his wife died had lain in his chamber at Monticello for days prostrate with grief. Yet when Jefferson in Paris looked back to Monticello, as if through a sentimental haze, the inexplicable effects of "looming" seemed to operate. Incomplete and virtually abandoned, a mere shell of what the younger Jefferson imagined, Monticello now emerged as the site and object of his most profound attachments. Here is where Jefferson shed his tears and sacred memories could be kept alive, when the "traveller" finally returned home and where he hoped his days would end.[37]

Monticello was a sacred space where Jefferson's loved ones died and where he eventually planned to join them. But, of course, he was by no means ready to die, and his brief affair with Maria Cosway was a powerful reminder of the more fleeting joys that flowed from passionate attachments. Chastellux's visit in 1782, just before his wife's death, produced another such moment, as the two savants discussed the poetry of the great Celtic bard "Ossian" (a literary hoax perpetrated by the Scot James Macpherson) and "a spark of electricity . . . passed rapidly from one to the other."[38] Unsurprisingly, few of these intense encounters have left traces in the historical record, for Jefferson closely guarded his privacy. Note the contrast between his treatment of the "Dialogue between my Head and Heart" and other letters to and from Maria Cosway and his treatment of his letters to his wife. Jefferson preserved the letters to Cosway, fully expecting that posterity would view them and see him in a playful, carefully bounded trifle with a pretty and talented young married woman. The letters would give evidence that he, as a middle-aged widower, was still able to attract a racially suitable woman. On the other hand, he apparently destroyed the letters that passed between him and Martha Jefferson and was, even as an elderly man, seeking to find any that might still be extant in others' hands, with the apparent aim of destroying them too. For obvious reasons, his private life with Martha's half sister Sally was left unrecorded.

Charming and friendly, Jefferson could nevertheless preserve a distance between himself and those who were not in his family. Margaret Bayard Smith, one of his greatest admirers, noted that his "affability" precluded "familiarity." "On the contrary," she reminisced, "there was a natural and quiet dignity in his demeanour that often produced a degree of restraint in those who conversed with him, unfavorable to that free interchange of thoughts and feelings which constitute the greatest charm of social life."[39]

Yet Jefferson breached these conventional restraints when he was in Paris, most notably with Cosway, the Americans Angelica Schuyler Church (another married woman Jefferson sought to lure to Monticello) and Anne Willing Bingham, Lafayette's aunt Madame de

Tessé, and others. Jefferson's education in Europe taught him both how to transgress the boundaries that were central to his idealized construction of American domesticity and how to secure his privacy by projecting a dignified, self-protective "demeanour" that somehow seemed "natural." He successfully cultivated the kind of "manners" that enabled his aristocratic and enlightened European friends to distance themselves from the sordid realities of old regime France. Having to operate in this setting, he condemned the artificiality of European social life in theory, even as he emulated it in practice. Manners provided him with a protective shield. The "real" Jefferson remained hidden from view. He employed this shield for the rest of his life, not always to good effect. Many years later he told his grand-daughter Ellen Coolidge that his political enemies "had never known *him*. They had created an imaginary being clothed with odious attributes, to whom they had given his name; and it was against that creature of their imaginations they had levelled their anathemas."[40]

Jefferson brought European manners back to Monticello and to his temporary homes away from home in America. Chastellux, Cosway, and other sophisticated Europeans played a crucial role in Jefferson's self-fashioning, reassuring him that he belonged in their cosmopolitan world. Through correspondence with European friends, he could claim membership in the Enlightenment republic of letters, creating a flattering image of himself as philosopher and "Friend of Nature."[41] The self-portrait he presented to Cosway in the form of his Head and Heart dialogue signaled the "traveller's" imaginative return to his mountaintop home: Cosway did not figure in this picture. Of course, the patriarch would not live alone when he returned to Virginia. He would reassemble his Parisian household there, including his daughters Patsy and Maria (while they remained unmarried), Sally Hemings, her brother James, now trained as a French chef, and various other dependents. Jefferson had created an unusual and extraordinarily comfortable version of plantation domesticity in the French capital, experimenting with the kind of life he hoped to re-create at home. Yet he would also live with—and draw sustenance from—memories of lost loved ones that would bind him to his surviving daughters, wherever they lived. This was not the kind of family life he envisioned for them, and for future generations. But it was a transcendent, idealized conception of family that linked past and future, made sense out of the joys and grief of his personal life, and animated his political career.

Coda

Jefferson had no illusions about the rudeness and monotony of social life in rural Virginia, and he took steps in Paris to do something about this. His nearly compulsive shopping, accumulating the latest and best products of European high civilization, shows that he anticipated the cultural deficit he would find upon his return. It also reveals how he hoped to play a role in educating his countrymen. He had other plans along these lines. In order to elevate the tone of neighborhood life, he sought to persuade a coterie of enlightened younger men to settle near Monticello. Throughout his stay in France, Jefferson pressed James Monroe to establish himself "near Monticello," "that spot of ultimate repose" for Jefferson; he also hoped to recruit another protégé, William Short, his secretary in France, and he did "not despair of [James] Madison."[42] This quartet of worthies may have evoked memories of the young Jefferson's Williamsburg days, when he was the junior member of the "partie quarree" that gathered at the Governor's Palace.[43] Jefferson would set the tone, orchestrating conversations that would reaffirm shared values and strengthen bonds of friendship.

Jefferson's campaign was only partly successful. In 1799 Monroe eventually settled at his Ash Lawn–Highland estate near Monticello; Madison remained in Orange, thirty miles away, at Montpelier, the family plantation, but visited frequently; though Short bought property that Jefferson would manage at nearby "Indian Camp," he also resisted the call, remaining in France for many years before returning to Philadelphia instead of his native Virginia. Yet Jefferson's designs for the neighborhood did anticipate the kinds of visitors who would be drawn to him and Monticello in future years as a new family configuration emerged there, centered on Martha and her husband, Thomas Mann Randolph, and their children.

When Jefferson retired from the Washington administration in 1793, he could imagine himself a "benevolent patriarch," happily presiding over his extended family and many dependents. Perhaps Maria would one day marry away, the French visitor La Rochefoucauld-Liancourt speculated in 1796. But "Mr. Jefferson's philosophic turn of mind, his love of study, his excellent library, which supplies him with the means of satisfying it, and his friends, will undoubtedly help him to endure this loss." And Jefferson could (and did) hope that "the second son-in-law of Mr. Jefferson may, like Mr. Randolph, reside in the vicinity of Monticello, and, if he be worthy of Miss Maria, will not be able to find any company more desirable than that of Mr. Jefferson."[44] Jefferson's magnetism was apparent in his conversation.

The Monticello that Jefferson redesigned in Paris (and spent the rest of his life building), its contents, and the good people who gathered there and in the neighborhood would embody and enact the progress of civilization, freed from European-style tyranny. Jefferson thus imagined a kind of dialogue between nature and civility—heart and head—that expressed his own sense of endless possibility. He also looked beyond home, to the bonds of "friendship" that attached him to the like-minded republicans of his generation who struggled to secure American independence and redeem the revolution's promise. He always insisted on the fundamental and inviolable distinction between his private life and the public commitments that subjected him to the misery of politics and public life. Those two worlds, however, could never be kept separate. Indeed, they made sense only in relation to each other. Jefferson sacrificed the tranquillity and happiness he identified with life at home in order to work with his friends—the republicans who became Jeffersonian Republicans—to defend home and family against internal and external threats. The attachments that he forged with these friends were critically important to the self-understanding that first crystallized for him in Paris.

On his deathbed Jefferson described himself to his granddaughter Ellen as an "old watch" that had run down and was now irreparable.[45] Life at Monticello had something of a clockwork character, too, and its master something of the character of the deists' clock-maker god. Jefferson managed conversation masterfully, La Roche-foucauld observed, and "his superior mind directs the management of his domestic concerns with the same abilities, activity, and regularity."[46] In the wake of an 1816 visit, Richard Rush, son of Benjamin Rush, Jefferson's revolutionary colleague, playfully likened him to another god. If his house "had not been called Monticello, I would call it Olympus, and Jove its occupant. In genius, in elevation, in the habits and enjoyments of his life, he is wonderfully lifted above most mortals."[47]

Many visitors ascended to Monticello after Jefferson returned to the United States. They encountered there a republican patriarch who fashioned his mature sense of himself when he was in Paris, designing and decorating a mansion house that would accentuate his mastery. At Monticello, Jefferson dominated the landscape, and the men and women who lived there—and visited there—were most assuredly not created equal.

High Street, from Ninth Street, Philadelphia, Engraving by William Birch, 1799.

(© The Thomas Jefferson Foundation at Monticello)

CHAPTER 6

POLITICS

Over the course of his political career, Jefferson complained repeatedly about the "miseries" of public life, and spoke often of wishing to be home with his family, the consoling counterpoint to the tumultuous "changes & chances" of public life. Family was, he said, "the only soil on which it is worthwhile to bestow much culture."[1] Even after ascending to the highest political office in the land, he told his daughter Maria in October of 1801, "It is in the love of one's family only that heartfelt happiness is known," insisting that nothing could "repay" him for the loss of family "society, the only one founded in affection and bosom confidence."[2]

Yet for all his protestations, Jefferson found the pull of politics irresistible. As time passed, he was able to link the idea of a much treasured home and family life to all he might be able to achieve in his political career. Though he spoke of the vast differences between public life and private life, the two were forever intertwined for him. In the revolutionary crisis the patriarch saw himself venturing forth to protect home and country against a corrupt ministry and despotic monarch; then the republican statesman sought to redeem the revolution's promise in his home state by purging all traces of the provincial old regime and securing the rights of future generations of Virginians; in Paris the American diplomat struggled to vindicate the new nation's independence and vital interests against "the powers of the earth" that might threaten the nascent country and, thus, his family and home.

By the time he came back to Virginia in November of 1789, Jefferson's political commitments had come into sharp focus. His return to the United States was to have been temporary. He left furniture, clothing, and his secretary, William Short, at the Hôtel de Langeac, fully expecting to resume his diplomatic career abroad after dropping off Patsy and Polly Jefferson and Sally Hemings with his in-laws, the Eppeses, and tending to pressing financial business. An urgent invitation to serve as secretary of state in the new administration President George Washington was organizing in New York under the recently ratified federal Constitution changed his plans. There had been hints that he might be asked to serve in some capacity before he set sail, but he was determined to finish his diplomatic appointment. He had no intention of meeting or besting Franklin's term as minister to France—almost eight years—but he did think another year or so was in order. Back on American soil with the request in hand, he wavered; framing this momentous choice in familiar terms: would he retire to domestic bliss in the bosom of his family or, yet again, sacrifice everything on the altar of public service? There was more than a little posturing in what was, during this period, an utterly conventional dilemma. Many men all over the new Union had similar choices to make. It was in the very nature of having fought a revolution and started a new country. Offices had to be filled, some local, some in the new country's capital. These matters were complicated a bit because in Jefferson's day open ambition was suspect. No good republican patriot could be seen displaying too intense a desire to hold public office. Great passion—enthusiasm, generally—was suspect, and to be subject to those emotions called into question one's qualification for public service.

George Washington demonstrated better than anyone else how to manage this tricky business with great finesse when he presented himself as reluctantly bowing to the will of the people as he assumed the presidency. He had already given many years of service as a British provincial soldier and then as the head of the Continental army. Known as a wealthy man—he had married into one of the richest families in Virginia—with a great plantation where many enslaved people labored, he was clearly making a personal sacrifice in not returning immediately to Mount Vernon. This sacrifice was the chief evidence of his selfless virtue, indicating a good republican's pledge not to exploit power and privilege for personal advantage. Jefferson's case was a bit different. He was wealthy, but not so wealthy as Washington. He was also more of a political animal—public service was *already* a career choice that made his life meaningful and, coincidentally, at various times, provided him with critical financial support: his choice was really about where and in what capacity he would serve the public. In any case, the future of Virginia's debt-ridden plantation economy remained uncertain in the wake of wartime disruptions and postwar depression. For as much as Jefferson idealized his home, as he thought of what to do next in his life, the prospects for his plantation at Monticello and his other holdings were particularly bleak.

It would be a mistake, however, to completely dismiss Jefferson's concerns as he pondered Washington's offer. If his personal situation was uncertain, the future of the federal republican experiment was impossible to predict, even with Washington at the helm. Many prominent Virginians, including the revered patriot George Mason and Jefferson's nemesis Patrick Henry, had opposed ratifying the Constitution, convinced that it would give rise to an overly powerful, "consolidated" central government that would destroy American liberty. Virginia, they argued—the largest and most prosperous state—would be better off under a renegotiated federal pact that recognized and secured its leading role in the Union; perhaps it would be better off with no Union at all. But Jefferson was no disunionist, whatever his later reputation as a states' rights advocate. Despite some serious reservations about the new frame of government that his friend and colleague James Madison had helped to craft, he knew that disunion would be disastrous for Virginia and for the viability of the American experiment in republican self-government and the possibilities for world peace.

While he was concerned about domestic matters, Jefferson always had his eye on the world. The United States existed *among* nations. How the government was constituted within the country affected the country's fortunes without, in the world at large. In the absence of a union, the American states might become fertile ground for European-inspired mischief as the great powers used individual American states—perhaps pitting one against another—as pawns in European balance of power politics. This was Jefferson's nightmare scenario. One of the clear purposes he saw for creating the United States was to remove the country from this sort of entanglement, and prove to the world that republican societies, trading freely and openly with other nations, could exist and be forces for peace. On the other hand, it was not clear to Jefferson how he should chart his course forward in his home state, and he was not yet ready to give up on having influence there. His traumatic experience as Virginia's war governor, and the continuing prominence of Henry and other political enemies in state politics, made holding office in Virginia an unattractive prospect for the foreseeable future. If he moved on to New York, he would still have to find a way to secure his home base in Virginia by reviving and strengthening ties with old political "friends" and recruiting new allies.

Washington's offer gave Jefferson a new framework within which to view his life and career. While in Paris, he had fixated on Monticello as his home—a specific place—rich with personal associations. At the same time, he became aware that there was another home to which he had become attached: the new country, the United States of America. This attachment grew deeper as he took to celebrating the virtues of the American people compared with those of their counterparts in Europe, and thinking about the new country's imperial destiny. Returning to the United States forced a radical reorientation. He could no longer simply dream about his house in the sky. There were grim realities to confront: that house for which he held such hopes was situated on an unproductive plantation with uncertain prospects. He had to establish a new labor regime and reorganize a working household economy; he had to provide for his daughters' futures and renew relations with his neighbors. This was the critical moment in his career as a plantation patriarch and republican statesman: in both inextricably related roles, he needed to know exactly where he stood. Atop his little mountain and looking outward, he began to think of home in a new way.

Jefferson's career as a national politician, begun in the 1790s, was thus predicated both on his fundamental attachment to Virginia and on an ever-strengthening identification with America and the American people. He came to this position, however, from a somewhat problematic route. His identification with his new country would be shaped by his role as the reluctant leader of the emerging opposition to the administration he ostensibly served. He joined Washington's cabinet, but soon had serious misgivings about how matters were proceeding. Not long into his time in office, Jefferson, Madison, and their Republican allies began to mobilize liberty-loving men across the continent against what Jefferson, in particular, saw as counterrevolutionary domestic enemies: the would-be "aristocrats" and "monocrats" who he thought dominated the ranks of the Federalists in the Washington administration. These enemies were "domestic" in a double sense: Treasury Secretary Alexander Hamilton and his followers pretended to be good republicans, but secretly conspired to re-create a form of aristocratic and monarchical government on the ruins of American liberty. They wanted the United States to be as much like Great Britain as it could be without returning to the British Empire. To do so, these "aristocrats" threatened to subvert and destroy American families, assaulting the sacred precincts of republican domesticity. Jefferson and fellow tribunes of the people preached vigilance against assaults on the independence and autonomy of republican patriarchs; they preached their own version of family values.

Jefferson's republicanism, and hostility toward those in the Washington administration who admired aspects of the British constitution, was animated by his profound hostility to monarchy and aristocracy and by his hatred of nearly all things British (with the conspicuous exception of their gardens). Anything that smacked of the British political system raised his ire, for it reminded him of the decadent Old

World against which he defined the United States. American virtues stood in sharp contrast to the vice, corruption, and empty show that so appalled him at Louis XVI's Versailles; it was at George III's court that wicked ministers had conspired against American liberties. The moralistic thrust of republican revolutionaries was to expose the corruption in European courts: if unthinking subjects opened their eyes, they would discern the false pretenses and evil intentions of their would-be rulers. True citizens, on the other hand, had no need of the kind of "courts" that grew up around monarchs. They governed themselves through their elected leaders, and no one else. The success of America's republican experiment thus depended on transparency and responsibility: politicians were the people's "servants," not their masters, and they should certainly not allow themselves to be influenced by would-be courtiers.

Under the revolutionary republican dispensation, citizens were secure in their rights, free from the interference and oversight of supposedly superior authorities. Citizens with equal rights claimed autonomy and independence within the limits of their household domains: patriarchal household heads governed, or exercised mastery over, wives, children, and other dependents—including the people whom they enslaved. That the term "servant" could describe both those who served the public interest and enslaved people who labored for the "happiness" of Jefferson and other masters captures the paradoxical character of his new republican world. Even as revolutionaries demolished old regime hierarchies of privilege and power, they secured and reinforced the "natural" authority of republican patriarchs. Although "home" was a refuge from politics, as a weary Jefferson repeatedly testified, it was also the elemental building block of the new republican edifice—and a defensive bulwark against any interference in citizen-patriarchs' private affairs.

Home and family could only take on new meanings for Jefferson when he returned from France and then prepared to move on to New York. The welcome he received from the people of Norfolk when he landed there in November of 1789, from the enslaved people at Monticello when he made it to the mountain and also from his white neighbors after he arrived in Charlottesville at the end of December, helped tell him what he was supposed to do, and set the course he would follow. Identifying with his fellow white Virginians who were also now citizens of the United States, he embraced them in this now more capacious conception of "home." At this point he could have no idea who, beyond the enslaved African Americans, would live with him on the mountain—when he did live there. But he now knew, more clearly than ever, where he came from.

Homecoming

Jefferson's return to America had not gone unnoticed. His friend James Madison evidently took a leading role in arranging a meeting between Jefferson and his prominent Albemarle neighbors in February 1790, and more was on their minds than just social niceties. It was not only Patrick Henry and other prominent Virginians who had concerns about the new government. Opposition to the federal Constitution still ran high among all strata of Virginia society. In truth, Jefferson needed to overcome his own misgivings about the new government while reassuring himself of his neighbors' ongoing political support.[3] Just as the Declaration of Independence invoked unanimity on fundamental principles in the face of broad and deep divisions over the break with Britain, Jefferson's address to his neighbors amounted to an affirmation of his Virginian identity designed to allay concerns about the consolidationist tendencies of the new federal regime. His very presence in an administration headed by the revered patriot and fellow Virginian George Washington refuted the dire warnings of Henry and other Antifederalists. Yet more was at stake in this exchange than mere calculation, for Jefferson was now self-consciously crafting a political persona as a Virginian nationalist who always kept the best interests of "the people" at heart.

There was something more. The reception Jefferson received from his neighbors helped him overcome the bitterness he had felt about the way members of the legislature had treated him in the wake of his unsuccessful governorship. Even as he reluctantly agreed to leave his "native country" once more to join the new federal government, Jefferson pledged himself to his Albemarle neighbors, thanking them for their "testimony of esteem" and exclaiming that their "affection [was] the source of [his] purest happiness." "We have been fellow-labourers and fellow-sufferers," he told his fellow citizens, "and heaven has rewarded us with a happy issue from our struggles." Jefferson drew strength from this shared identity—the "we" that bound him to family members, friends, and neighbors—and that identity in turn led him to invoke the "self-evident" truths he had so eloquently articulated in the Declaration of Independence.[4]

Victorious "in the holy cause of freedom," Jefferson and his neighbors had finally achieved what the American people had aspired to in 1776. He told them, "It rests now with ourselves alone to enjoy in peace and concord the blessings of self-government, so long denied to mankind: to shew by example the sufficiency of human reason for the care of human affairs and that the will of the majority, the Natural law of every society, is the only sure guardian of the rights of man." These were universal truths, but they had a deep personal meaning for Jefferson. The "will of the majority" was no abstraction, and it certainly did *not* include the enslaved people Jefferson and his neighbors kept in bondage. Excluded from Virginian "society," they could not claim the benefit of this "Natural *law*," notwithstanding the natural *rights* Jefferson acknowledged that "all men," even the enslaved, possessed. Jefferson, then, could assure his neighbors that his opposition to slavery—no matter how deeply felt—was beyond the reach of practical politics as matters stood in 1790. He and his fellow Virginians were not prepared to give up on an institution that sustained their way of life: for his generation at least, the project of abolishing slavery was effectively closed. He could not know—though it must have become clear to him in subsequent years—that the republican principle of majority rule virtually guaranteed that the slavery question in his native region would remain closed. Republicanism was *not* inevitably an engine of moral progress.

Jefferson would represent his neighbors, submitting to their will; he would defend his and their homes in order to serve those he loved.

"In the general tide of happiness," he was delighted to see "that yours too flows on in just place and measure." Jefferson reciprocated the testimony of his countrymen in testifying to his faith in them. He thus offered his "fervent prayer to heaven" that the progress of enlightenment "may flow thro' all times, gathering strength as it goes, and spreading the happy influence of reason and liberty over the face of the earth." This was a consoling thought, for God would in the fullness of time show white Virginians the way forward out of backward beliefs and practices, including slavery. In the meantime Jefferson could turn inward, contemplating slavery's injustice and praying for enlightenment in the privacy of his study. Of course, this was the same sacred domestic sphere—Jefferson's plantation world—that slave-owning citizens defended so vigorously against outside interference.

In 1816, during his final retirement, Jefferson drew out the implications of his republican faith in a letter to Samuel Kercheval, a fellow advocate of constitutional reform in Virginia. Patriot homes were castles, he assured his reform-minded correspondent, fortified against the prying eyes of corrupt despots. "The true foundation of republican government," Jefferson wrote, "is the equal right of every citizen, in his person and property, and in their management."[5] Because slaves were incorporated into plantation households, slavery was a domestic institution, not an "interest" subject to public scrutiny. Holding slaves did not compromise the independence and integrity of republican representatives. To the contrary, the slaveholding patriarch could exercise authority over his extensive "black and white family" only *if* he were truly independent. Jefferson's awareness of slavery's injustice may have made him more conscious of his responsibility for his slaves' "happiness," as he had told Angelica Schuyler Church in 1793, but it also—and, for us, paradoxically—heightened his awareness of his rights as a master.[6]

What it meant to be a master came into clearer focus for Jefferson when he returned to Virginia in 1789. In France the only contact he had with the people he enslaved was with James and Sally Hemings. Their unique status in France, however, and their intimate connections with him (especially Sally's) distinguished them from every other enslaved person in his life. Jefferson's thinking about the vast majority of the slaves on his plantations centered on them not as individuals but on how in the aggregate they could be used to help him deal with his deceased father-in-law's debts, for which he, through his own poor judgment and bad luck, had become personally liable. His slaves' status as property—abstracted from their human particularity—was their most salient attribute. Monticello had also been something of an abstraction during these years. But both the house, in its present deserted and dilapidated condition, and the people who worked the estate came vividly before Jefferson when he arrived at Monticello on December 23, 1789. In subsequent recollections recorded many years later by the biographer Henry Randall, Jefferson's daughter Martha Jefferson Randolph and Wormley Hughes, an enslaved man at Monticello and a grandson of Elizabeth Hemings, described a tumultuous homecoming scene. Their accounts offer clues to the significance of a critical moment in the lives of the returning patriarch and the people he enslaved.

Anticipating the traditional Christmas holiday, the enslaved community asked for another day off in order to greet Jefferson upon his arrival. Given permission, all assembled to wait for the carriage at the foot of the mountain. As time passed, they moved farther on the road leading to Monticello. The carriage, almost certainly driven by James Hemings, finally appeared. Randolph and Hughes differed on what happened next: Hughes said the slaves unhitched the horses and pulled the carriage up the mountain; Randolph recollected that they simply ran alongside. The two agreed that once the door of the carriage opened, Jefferson was hoisted in the air until he was inside his house. Randolph said they "received him in their arms and bore him to the house, crowding round and kissing his hands and feet—some blubbering and crying—others laughing."

Jefferson never wrote about what he took all of this to mean, but Martha Randolph was firm in her opinion: those enslaved at Monticello "were *at all times* very devoted in their attachment to" her father.[7] Retrospectively filling in the lines after decades had passed, Martha translated the slaves' collective "attachment" to Jefferson, "the kindest of masters," into countless, and utterly fanciful, transactions with a man few, if any of them, had ever met: "they spoke to him freely, and applied confidingly to him in all their difficulties and distresses"; in return, Jefferson "watched over them in sickness and in health— interested himself in all their concerns—advising them, showing esteem and confidence in the good, and indulgence to all." Martha's description suggests that Jefferson performed the role of "master" that was in keeping with the understanding he had come to in France about how he would be able to live comfortably with slavery for the rest of his life.

If Jefferson could enact the role of the "kindest of masters," he never lost sight of what the human beings he enslaved meant to him as property. For their part, the enslaved could make a show of devotion to Jefferson with a clear understanding of the precariousness of their position under a brutal and immoral institution. They could not possibly have loved him in any meaningful sense. Any attachment they may have felt to him was born of an obvious and harsh reality. Given the rules of property that they had every reason to understand, if anything happened to Jefferson, their lives could be made worse, almost instantly. In fact, when he died thirty-six years later, Israel (Gillette) Jefferson, who had been enslaved at Monticello, recalled in 1873, "His death was an affair of great moment and uncertainty to us slaves."[8] Dozens of people on his farms had been uprooted—if not sold away—from the homes, families, and friends they had known because of property settlements after the death of John Wayles, Jefferson's father-in-law. At the very least, they could have been happy to see Jefferson alive. This was a bid for the future, one that grew out of a straightforward exchange: the slaves' "ebullitions of joy" promised at least a plausible performance of devotion in future years—and Jefferson would play the role he scripted for himself, as a benevolent master.

Jefferson had to become resituated to Albemarle County, rebuild Monticello, and manage his plantation profitably in order to make the home to which family members would gravitate. The enslaved community—the people who had stayed at Monticello and its neighborhood through Jefferson's protracted absence—represented con-

tinuity from the first Monticello and its plantation regime to the
redesigned and rebuilt second Monticello and the new, more productive regime Jefferson now envisioned. The returning master knew
that he could not take the presence of the enslaved for granted: thirty
of them had fled from his plantations (mostly from Elk Hill) during
Lord Cornwallis's invasion of Virginia in 1781, and future wartime
disruptions might be even more devastating. The enslaved were
potential enemies, a captive nation held in chains: "if a slave can
have a country in this world," Jefferson had written in *Notes on Virginia*, "it must be any other in preference to that in which he is born
to live and labour for another."[9]

The enslaved people Jefferson encountered that December day
reconnected him to Virginia, grounding him in his home soil and the
peculiarities of his culture and community. Knowing that he would
soon leave again, he made home and family his touchstones. He could
tell himself that he was sacrificing for family and community, even
if members of his family would rather he had stayed close to them.
Whether he was in New York, Philadelphia, or Washington, Jefferson kept up a steady stream of correspondence with family members,
friends, neighbors, contractors, overseers, and other collaborators
in his ongoing, never-ending home and family building campaign.
Far from the static, idealized place the homesick Virginian imagined
and told people about in Paris, Monticello now became the vital and
dynamic center of his world—a world whose physical structures he
would transform armed with all the knowledge and tastes he had
acquired in his travels across Europe. The community of Monticello,
driven by slavery, would proceed according to his new plan for ameliorating an institution that he once thought incapable of amelioration. Over the years this new Monticello would exercise a powerful
gravitational pull that dictated the rhythms of Jefferson's life as public
servant until he returned home permanently in 1809.

The homecoming that the enslaved at Monticello staged coincided
with Patsy's whirlwind courtship and marriage to her distant cousin
Thomas Mann Randolph—the couple became engaged mere weeks

after she returned from Paris. This would prove to be another foundational relationship in the reconstruction of Jefferson's home and patriarchal domain. If Jefferson seemed precipitately eager to sanction the marriage of his seventeen-year-old daughter, the choice of mate guaranteed that she would not stray too far from the paternal orbit: the patriarch could not have predicted that Patsy and her family would one day live permanently at Monticello, but he did not hesitate to use his influence over a loving and impressionable daughter to keep her as close as possible to home or to persuade her young husband—through property transactions and political patronage—to settle in the neighborhood.

Jefferson had anticipated the day when Martha and Maria would marry and leave home. The redesigned Monticello that he envisioned in Paris was not intended to house his daughters, their husbands, and all of their children, nor is there any reason to suppose he would have wanted either of his daughters to marry a man who would be effectively disinherited by his father, fail financially, and be required to move his family into Jefferson's house. The second Monticello was made for the comfort of a widower who would have many visitors, sometimes long-term, as was then customary. Monticello's famous narrow staircases and small upper rooms were not designed for the maximum comfort of other permanent residents. Jefferson configured his personal living quarters, however, to provide him both the comfort and the privacy that were the hallmarks of privilege among European aristocrats. This was yet another way in which his years abroad shaped his thinking and preferences about how to live. Here was the place to retreat from the world to write, think, and plan, emerging to greet relatives and visitors on his terms. It was a place where Sally Hemings could, as a matter of course, spend her time when she was not taking care of their children.

Jefferson ventured forth into public life as a self-sacrificing patriot, determined to defend his country's liberties and promote the happiness and well-being of his fellow citizens. The self-governing patriarch looked homeward. Holding fast to his independence, he fulfilled himself through the mastery he exercised over his plantation and his extended family, white and black. His home was his castle, and his private life was nobody's business but his own.

Family Values

Jefferson's disdain for politics, most insistently expressed in family correspondence, disguised his extraordinary political gifts. Sensitive to his own patriarchal prerogatives, he was careful not to challenge those of his colleagues. The equality principle operated most effectively among honorable men who were sticklers for their own rights and reluctant to submit to anyone else's authority. Jefferson and his allies combined this manly self-regard with an aversion to conflict that Alexander Hamilton and other partisan foes described as "womanish," but which enabled men of feeling to forge enduring bonds with each other. Moral philosophers argued that sociable impulses were universal, not only characteristic of women—or of "womanish" men, or of men who had served as soldiers together and become a band of brothers, the sort of connections that Hamilton had made with Washington and John Laurens, for example.

Jefferson had a different definition of masculinity, one that was unmoored from both the worship of martial glory and a concept of honor that led some men to engage in duels, an activity he found "barbarous" and even ridiculous. When he was inaugurated as president, he did not—as his predecessors had done—wear a sword. He did not want to automatically associate the office of the presidency with war. Upon learning that his son-in-law Thomas Mann Randolph was on the verge of dueling with their kinsman, John Randolph, Jefferson was aghast and offered a heartfelt plea to Thomas to avoid the encounter. He noted the vastly "different" stakes the two men "would bring to the field," and in the process gave a devastating assessment of John Randolph's personal life, a state of existence that Jefferson considered a nightmare. John Randolph, he said, was "unentangled in the affections of the world, a single life, of no value to himself or others." Because no one loved John Randolph, he had nothing to lose, nothing to live for. Thomas, on the other hand, had "a wife, & family of children" who were "depending, for all their happiness & protection in this world" on him. Were he to die in the duel, Jefferson said, he could offer his support to Martha and their children, but it would be fleeting due to his age. Thomas's death would leave "seven children, all under the age of discretion & down to infancy . . . without guide or guardian but a poor broken-hearted woman doomed to misery the rest of her life." And what if something happened to Martha, if "her frail frame" were to sink under the weight of her grief? What would become of their children? "Is it possible," Jefferson asked, "that your duties to these dear objects can weigh more lightly than those to a gladiator?" Most "thinking" people did not believe they should. "Duelling" was made "for lives of no consequences to others, not for father of families, or for those charged with great moral concerns." Such men were to have the discipline and courage to deal with insults in ways that did not put them in danger of abandoning their families.[10]

Family feeling could bind ever-widening circles of friends; devotion to higher principles sanctified the friendship of patriots, giving birth to an expansive national family that transcended particular families and their rivalries. With their sights set on a greater good than their own fame, glory, and dynastic ambitions, revolutionaries ideally aspired to a virtuous self-sacrifice that transcended traditional notions of manliness. Perhaps, as sentimental moralists now argued, it was women—in their willingness to sacrifice everything for their families—who modeled the kind of virtue that nation making required.[11]

Jefferson elaborated his conception of the republic as family writ large when, on the eve of his return to America, he told his friend and fellow patriot James Madison that "the earth belongs in usufruct to the living."[12] His idea of generational sovereignty had a patriotic pedigree, evoking the "sons of liberty" who had mobilized against the king who had betrayed his paternal responsibilities to his loyal American subjects and culminating in the self-recognition of Americans as a single people in his Declaration of Independence. Of course, the revolutionaries who pledged their "sacred honor" to each other at Philadelphia in 1776 were men, but they took the pledge with an acute consciousness of family obligations: to the wives, children, and future generations whose liberty and happiness depended on their success. "Generation" proved to be a protean concept. On the one hand, it incorporated or "covered" women, effectively denying them civil existence and thus reinforcing patriarchal power; yet it also "softened" men, incorporating them in a domestic sphere, where family values reigned supreme—and republican wives and mothers shared in household governance. Most importantly, the term "generation" itself underscored women's indispensable role in perpetuating and perfecting the new nation.[13]

A separate sphere for women, even—and perhaps especially—when elevated to semidivine status in republican celebrations of domesticity, did not translate into equal rights or a conspicuous role in public life. Party politics was a man's world, the antithesis of family life and the values that inspired virtuous republicans. Jefferson and his friends sought to protect women and children by keeping the nastiness of partisan combat from invading the sacred precincts of home. At the same time, however, Jeffersonian Republicans adapted family values to public life, fashioning bonds of friendship that made their "party" into something far more than an alliance of interest groups and ambitious politicians—or so they liked to think.

Jefferson periodically retreated to the home and family he so ardently protected from outside interference. Yet he was also at home in the world, forging friendships with fellow patriots in the common cause of liberty and enlightenment. As he meticulously fashioned his political persona over the years, Jefferson promoted a progressively more expansive conception of nation and homeland, suppressing and transcending the peculiarities of particular families and household regimes in his vision of the self-governing "living generation." The successful defense of individual homes—and the sense of self that was nurtured by family attachments—depended on recognizing and resisting counterrevolutionary tendencies. Would-be aristocrats were everywhere, assuming pseudo-republican masks as they sought to dominate others and perpetuate power and privilege across the generations. In response Jefferson and his political friends sought to rekindle the "sacred fire of liberty" and create a continental coalition of patriots that could save the revolution.

The republican patriarch's moral sense and natural sociability drew him outward, from family feeling to love of country and ultimately to "universal philanthropy, not only to kindred and friends, to neighbors and countrymen, but to all mankind." Looking homeward, as he did in 1803 when summarizing Jesus's teachings for Dr. Benjamin Rush of Pennsylvania, an old friend and fellow signer of the Declaration of Independence, Jefferson could envision all mankind as "one family, under the bonds of love, charity, peace, common wants and common aids."[14] So, family was an expansive concept, shaped both by the planter's nostalgic longings for home and by the philosopher's dreams of universal peace and harmony. The family home was a refuge, a place where the patriarch could be secure in the love of those who depended on him.

Retreating behind the protective barriers of cool civility, bureaucratic procedure, and endless official correspondence, the embattled politician stole moments to write to family members, evoking images of domestic felicity and eliciting declarations of love. He exaggerated his misery. Everywhere he served, Jefferson established a home away from home, providing—sometimes extravagantly, and at great expense—for his own privacy and comfort. And like-minded political "friends" gravitated to him, affirming his values and sustaining his hopes for the future.[15]

At War with Federalists

When he left Monticello for New York in 1790, Jefferson could not have foreseen that he was launching a political career of nearly two decades on the national stage. Nor could he possibly have imagined that he would become the leader of the first great national political party. That he would spearhead opposition to presidential administrations he was supposed to serve—as George Washington's secretary of state (1790–93) and as John Adams's vice president (1797–1801)—was simply unthinkable. Republican virtue required subsuming personal interests. Factious combinations betrayed a corrupt and self-interested lust for power; an opposition party could not possibly be "loyal." The great mobilization that had culminated in American independence in 1776 had been a "party" to end all parties.

Jefferson expected that the new national government would rise above partisanship. But even Washington's first administration was riven by conflict. Never doubting his own motives, Jefferson did not hesitate to question those of his antagonists, beginning with his archrival Hamilton. As a revolutionary patriot, Jefferson drew deeply on the critique of prerogative power that had animated the radical republican tradition. He believed that Hamilton exploited the resources and patronage of the Treasury in ways that seemed all too reminiscent of Robert Walpole's reign as First Lord of the Treasury and "prime minister" in Britain (1721–42).[16] Very importantly, Hamilton did not reject the comparison to his notorious exemplar.

And then there were the optics of the new administration. The emergence of a kind of court life around the president heightened Jefferson's anxieties about monarchical tendencies in the nascent federal regime as the new ruling class awkwardly performed unfamiliar and unscripted roles on the national political stage. Unsure of what else to do, they resorted to the familiar, taking as models and inspiration the provincial courts of royal governors in America, themselves pathetic imitations of the metropolitan Court of Saint James.[17] Washington's "republican court," with its quasi-monarchical rituals—the president and first lady ("Lady Washington") hosted weekly "levees" aping the kind of court life that surrounded monarchs—set Jefferson's teeth on edge. William Maclay, a senator from Pennsylvania, pronounced these events "certainly anti-republican."[18] The sycophants and place seekers who surrounded Washington and his official "family" had nothing to do with republican domesticity. In fact, connections formed at "court" among those gravitating toward power and seduced by wealth, luxury, and the lure of illicit sexual relationships threatened to subvert the republic. Jefferson contrasted the ties that bound true republicans with the corrupt machinations of Alexander

Hamilton and his crew of followers. In his view, Hamilton had put all of this in motion.

Jefferson's Anglophobia heightened his profound personal antipathy to Hamilton, for the New Yorker's pronounced Anglophilia simply shocked him and his allies. The British constitution was "the most perfect government which ever existed," an appalled Jefferson heard his nemesis say, *because* it was corrupt. Hamilton was "so bewitched and perverted by the British example," Jefferson recollected in his *Anas*, "as to be under thorough conviction that corruption was essential to the government of a nation."[19] This notion of top-down governance was the very opposite of Jefferson's bottom-up conception of popular self-government. Failing to recognize that Hamilton was most likely having a bit of fun at his expense, the super-earnest Jefferson concluded that the secretary of the treasury sought to turn the clock back to 1776 and restore monarchical rule in America. This was no joking matter. The 1790s was political wartime for Jefferson. Hamilton's efforts to create a more "energetic," British-style fiscal-military state raised the alarm among revolutionary patriots who—with Jefferson—envisioned America as monarchical Britain's republican antithesis.

Jefferson and his followers insisted that Hamilton and his allies had initiated partisan combat by forming a covert and corrupt party within the new federal government; so too, an outraged Jefferson accused his cabinet colleague of starting an unseemly exchange of personal attacks. As he began planning to resign as secretary of state—and thus resolve the cognitive dissonance of opposing the policies of the administration he was serving—Jefferson drafted an intemperate, self-exculpatory letter to President Washington. The secretary of state charged the treasury secretary with systematically assaulting his character. "I will not suffer my retirement to be clouded by [Hamilton's] slanders," he fumed.[20] Alluding to his rival's illegitimate birth, Jefferson contemptuously dismissed him as "a man whose history, from the moment at which history can stoop to notice him, is a tissue of machinations against the liberty of the country which has not only recieved and given him bread, but heaped it's honors on his head."

Jefferson and his fellow revolutionaries had made America; coming from nowhere, the opportunistic Hamilton seized the revolutionary moment to make himself. Hamilton lacked character because he lacked the local attachments—to family, friends, and neighbors—that defined the true patriot. Without such attachments, he could not act disinterestedly on behalf of others.

Jefferson's letter was the unintentional confession of a partisan masquerading as a disinterested observer of a public official. Hamilton, he said, had slanderously accused him of politicking "among the members of the legislature" to obstruct Hamilton's financial plan. But this was "contrary to all truth." Jefferson neither "had the desire to influence the members," nor had he "any other means than [his] friendships" to do so. Jefferson wrote as if the contrast between his disinterested approach to politics and Hamiltonian corruption would be obvious to a virtuous fellow Virginian. Hamilton dominated Congress by distributing favors: "his system flowed from principles adverse to liberty, and was calculated to undermine and demolish the republic," Jefferson told Washington, "by creating an influence of his department over the members of the legislature." The treasury secretary thus created a faction or party in the federal legislature that compromised members' character as genuine representatives of the people and gave rise to a "monied aristocracy." Jefferson did not hesitate to "acknolege and avow" his disapproval of Hamilton's system in "private conversations" with congressmen. But he valued the independent judgment of his "friends" too highly to interfere with "the conscientious pursuit of their own sense of duty." Liberty-loving congressmen gravitated to Jefferson and Madison because of their commitment to republican principles. Patriots recognized each other as "friends" of incorruptible character grounded in—and confirmed by—the kinds of attachments to home and family that self-interested Hamiltonians conspicuously lacked.

Jefferson may have misunderstood Hamilton, and he failed to convince an exasperated Washington of his enemy's supposed designs against American liberty and independence. The caricature of Hamilton, nevertheless, had a crucial effect in valorizing Jefferson's

self-image as a virtuous republican and in justifying the "private conversations" among political friends that were widely disseminated
through correspondence and the emerging opposition press. Republican friends rallied in defense of the liberties that Federalists threatened, reviving the slumbering Spirit of '76. Projecting self-interested
partisan intentions onto their political enemies, Jefferson and his followers were oblivious to their own persistent provincialism. Jefferson's identification with Virginia never seemed problematic to him.
Protecting home and family was the patriot's sacred responsibility,
transcending the sordid pursuits of selfish partisans.

Party conflict in a supposedly nonpartisan age inevitably descended
into "personalities," and into vicious exchanges of charges that called
into question the good faith and motives of antagonists. Jefferson kept
his sights focused on potential abuses of power, seeking to discern
corrupt, self-interested motives of officers who would betray the public trust. This fixation led him to a campaign waged through his
congressional ally and fellow Virginian William Branch Giles against
Hamilton's management of the Treasury, in February 1793, seeking to
expose congressmen's holdings in Bank of the United States stock.[21]
Popular sovereignty was not simply an abstraction, substituting an
invented "people" for a deposed monarch. Every citizen was a sovereign or "patriarch" within his own household, Jefferson insisted, and
public servants were responsible to their citizen masters. The people
had a right to examine the financial portfolios—and interrogate the
character—of public officials. Private citizens, on the other hand, had
the right to mind their own business, free from oversight unless they
violated duly enacted laws.

Congressman Giles's initiative turned up no damning revelations,
but it did unleash the succession of charges and countercharges that
blurred the distinction between privacy and publicity that Jefferson
claimed to uphold. In the heat of party conflict, nothing was sacred,
certainly not the private lives of the combatants, including Jefferson.
Focusing on individuals, their personal foibles and personalities, and
their families seemed more fitting for a monarchy than a republic where
virtuous citizens sought to promote the common good under a govern-

ment of laws and not men. Professions of patriotism and disinterested virtue, however, invited skepticism. Defenders of the administration doubted that what looked suspiciously like organized opposition to its policies was really the spontaneous expression of the "people's" will. Could it be that Jefferson and his most prominent allies cloaked their own self-interested agenda in the mantle of patriotism?

There could be no secrets in a well-governed republic. Citizens might be equal under the law, but they all—in their distinctive, *unequal* ways—had an interest in shaping the laws to serve their own particular purposes. In policy terms, it was worth noting that Jefferson owned vast acres of land and myriad enslaved people to cultivate them, and that he and his fellow southern planters sought overseas markets for their crops. In personal terms, it was worth asking whether he had the "character" to look beyond self-interest toward the public good. Did it matter, as Jefferson confessed it did in his *Notes on Virginia*, that the institution of slavery was a school for despots? Did it matter that Jefferson and his fellow slave owners forged illicit liaisons with enslaved women?

Jefferson always insisted that vigilant citizens had the right and responsibility to monitor the performance of public servants. But he never understood why anyone could be—or had any right to be—interested in his private life. He assumed that republican patriarchs had a "natural" right to govern their dependents—and that all of *these* men were "created equal": their domestic domains were the site and source of virtuous family life and therefore inviolable. In later years, when an aspiring biographer asked Jefferson for the names of his grandchildren, he was surprised. Why on earth, he wondered, would a biography of him contain their names? Surely only his public actions should be the focus of any book written about him. Personal matters would "produce fatigue and disgust to . . . readers."[22] But much more was at stake. If curious outsiders looked too deeply into life at Monticello and other plantations, they might uncover the unsettling secrets—about blended families and about the everyday brutality and injustice of slavery—which the young, reform-minded Jefferson had revealed to the world in his *Notes on Virginia*.

The very distinction Jefferson insistently and self-servingly drew between private life and public service made him into a partisan. His exchange with his Albemarle neighbors in February 1790 sealed his commitment to slavery as a purely domestic institution, beyond the ambit of national politics. This was the dark "secret" that could not be disclosed or discussed and was hidden from view by the family values that animated Jefferson's politics. But all *other* interests were fair game for the disinterested patriot. Jefferson's conviction that Hamilton and his coadjutors were secretly conspiring to reverse the revolution's outcome drove him and like-minded republicans into the patriotic opposition.

The antitype of the good republican was the predatory "politician," the man who made a living out of politics at the expense of productive fellow citizens. This was in fact a reasonably accurate description of Jefferson himself: without the generous subsidy of his official salary, the planter would have been hard-pressed to support his gracious lifestyle at his showplace home. Given this discomfiting reality, it was vitally important for Jefferson's self-image to conflate public service with private sacrifice: every plaintive letter he wrote about the "miseries" of political life was a testimonial to his own virtue; every invocation of the Spirit of '76 reaffirmed his patriotism. What was true for the virtuous man must also be true for the "people" collectively. Citizens, Jefferson insisted, were not politicians who pursued selfish interests in the conflict-ridden arenas of public life. They instead understood that they could be happy only at home, as Jefferson claimed to be, with their families. Good citizens participated in public life only in order to secure their rights and protect their homes.

This patriotic devotion to home—and homeland—inspired the greatest sacrifices. The good republican, Jefferson wrote his friend and ally Joseph C. Cabell in 1816, "will let the heart be torn out of his body sooner than his power be wrested from him by a Caesar or a Bonaparte."[23] Thomas Paine and other republican theorists drew a similarly sharp distinction between "society"—the natural expression of human sociability and interdependence—and "government," the coercive imposition of order on an unruly people.[24] Under a self-governing republican regime, a virtuous and vigilant people would hold on to the reins of power, entrusting its servants to promote common interests—and dismissing them from service when they failed to do so.

Jefferson could never acknowledge that he was a partisan, much less a party leader. The great challenge for Jeffersonian Republicans in the 1790s was to rationalize and justify opposing a government that had been duly elected by the American people, according to procedures set forth in the federal Constitution. The ultimate solution was to don the mantle of patriotism and project partisan intentions onto Treasury Secretary Hamilton and his allies—even after Hamilton left the government. Jefferson and his friends claimed to speak for a people whose voice was distorted and suppressed by the "Anglomen," "aristocrats," and "monocrats" who infested the administration. These "Tories" constituted a secret, corrupt, and corrupting party, the direct descendants of the advocates of unbridled prerogative power who had threatened to undermine the people's liberties throughout English—and now American—history.

In retrospect, Jeffersonian rhetoric seems hyperbolic and hypocritical, a transparently self-exonerating way to cope with the cognitive dissonance of party building in a nonpartisan age. Hamilton and his allies reversed the charges, gleefully exposing the Republicans' interested motives and dubious methods. But Jefferson's claims to republican probity were not simply opportunistic or instrumental. Insisting that he was drawn into public life at great personal sacrifice and in compliance with the will of his countrymen (or the new president's importunities), Jefferson never doubted his own pure intentions—or those of the people. His sense of himself reflected his powerful and enduring identification with the nation-making generation of 1776. The fellow feeling that enabled the break with Britain could not be reduced to the head's rational calculations but instead expressed the heartfelt solidarity of family and friends.

Franco-American

Jefferson's political persona was forged in the crucible of a revolutionary age. As they mobilized a continental coalition against Federalist "aristocrats" and "monocrats," Jeffersonian Republicans evoked the Spirit of '76 and celebrated their iconic leader's authorship of the Declaration of Independence. The Francophile Jefferson was also a sympathetic witness to the outbreak of the French Revolution. With most of his grateful countrymen, he celebrated France's crucial role in the American Revolutionary War and eagerly awaited its revolutionary transformation. And for their part, French revolutionaries drew inspiration from their "sister republic." Some of them, including Jefferson's great friend the marquis de Lafayette, had risked their lives in the American struggle for independence.[25]

Jefferson's years in France came to shape the vision of the new nation's destiny that he would so eloquently express in his first inaugural address. Though the French Revolution's notorious excesses—and its ultimate descent into Napoleonic autocracy—tempered his hopes for Europe's imminent transformation, Jefferson's faith in the world-historical significance of the American Revolution only grew stronger. Political opponents might mock him as a Frenchified philosopher, in his kinsman Supreme Court Justice John Marshall's characterization the "great lama of the mountains,"[26] a mysterious figure hopelessly out of touch with the real world, but Jefferson was confident. Distance from home had given him a new perspective, which enabled him to appreciate the homegrown virtues of his countrymen and how they might maintain the new nation's republican experiment. His observations of French society led him to believe that the obstacles to change in the Old World were so formidable that "rivers of blood" would have to flow—and centuries pass—before its shackled nations could gain the freedom that Americans already enjoyed.[27] Early in 1793 Jefferson told his former secretary and protégé William Short in one of his most famous letters that he "would have seen half the earth desolated" rather than see the French Revolution fail: "were there but an Adam and an Eve left in every country, and left free, it would be better than as it now is."[28] His message was that the American Revolution had succeeded, patriots' blood had stopped flowing, and the nation was "left free." In America, unlike Europe, radical reforms were no longer needed. Under the new nation's republican governments, reform would inevitably, irresistibly proceed in tandem with the progress of popular enlightenment.

FRANCE ON THE EVE of its great revolution—the France Jefferson knew and loved—without question left an indelible imprint on his mind and manners. Despite the claims of his enemies, however, Jefferson eschewed the "philosophical" radicalism they imputed to him. If engaged fellow citizens preserved their rights and thus vindicated the revolution's promise, successive generations of Americans would enjoy the peace, prosperity, and happiness Jefferson envisioned for them in the Declaration and reaffirmed in his first inaugural address. This was a vision of American exceptionalism, and a beacon to oppressed peoples everywhere. The French had struck the first bloody blow in their own struggle for national self-determination. One day, Jefferson prayed, they too would enjoy the great boon of republican self-government.

In the meantime Jefferson acknowledged his debts to France. When he returned to America, he fashioned himself as an emissary from the French Enlightenment, attracting admirers and followers as he performed the role of learned savant and cultured man of the world. No American could match his cosmopolitan sophistication, and he quickly grasped the advantages he had gained from his years abroad. When he served in the Continental Congress, Jefferson was known for his literary skills and dedication to the republican principles he articulated in the Declaration. But otherwise, John Adams recalled, Jefferson did not make much of an impression: modest in manner and a poor public speaker, although he was said to have been good in a courtroom, he did not make a show of himself in those days. The cosmopolitan Jefferson who returned from Paris stood out much more conspicuously, shaping a new self-image by exploiting the cultural capital now at his command.

Jefferson's manner was distinctive; so were the ways he dressed and the settings he created for himself in his homes away from home.[29] The many crates of furniture, furnishings, tableware, paintings, and art objects that he had shipped from Paris to New York provided props for his stylish performances. Jefferson simultaneously became more self-consciously "American" and more "French," eagerly adapting the ethos of the great French metropolis to life in the new nation's temporary capitals and introducing his countrymen to the best French wines and cuisine. He even ate in the European style. "He would have his plate changed several times during dinner, a habit not observed, in those days, by country gentlemen generally," Ellen Coolidge said, remembering that a cousin who had lived for a time in Europe told her that Jefferson's was "the only table in the country where [he] would dare ask for a clean plate." As for what was on his plate, Jefferson was partial to French fare and French-style cooking. Coolidge said of her grandfather's tastes, he "liked boiled Beef, Bouilli [a form of stewed beef], better than roast. He ate a great many vegetables and little meat, contrary to the custom of his countrymen." There is no doubt about his preferences for wine. Coolidge stated firmly, and additional evidence bears this out, that Jefferson "preferred french wines to Madeira or Sherry." His characteristically Franco-American self-presentation still struck at least one observer as Jefferson approached his eighties. The book peddler Samuel Whitcomb showed up at Monticello one afternoon in 1822 and reported that Jefferson "shrugs his shoulders when talking, has much of the Frenchman, is rapid, varying, volatile, eloquent, amusing."[30]

In the early 1790s when Secretary of State Jefferson rented a house in Philadelphia, he proceeded to make it as much akin to his Paris residence, the Hôtel de Langeac, as it could be. He filled it with the furniture he had purchased while there, and he lured Adrien Petit away from the turbulence of revolutionary France to reprise the role he played at the Hôtel as maître d', with James Hemings once again serving as chef de cuisine of Jefferson's kitchen. His younger daughter,

Maria, soon rejoined the household. The only people missing from France were the newly married Martha, William Short, who had remained in Paris, and Sally Hemings, who had given birth at some point in 1790.

Jefferson modeled a cosmopolitan alternative to the dominant Anglo-American provincial style of postcolonial elites who remained in thrall to British cultural traditions. He showed himself and his fellow Americans that they could have it both ways, combining fealty to simple native virtues with metropolitan polish: civility could flourish on the far periphery of European civilization. Jefferson's Franco-American synthesis blended nature and civilization. In what would become his characteristically didactic manner, he would transcend the "homespun" aesthetic of his humble neighbors and model a more refined "authenticity."[31] For the Jefferson who hated England, Paris represented a superior, more "civilized" alternative to London, enabling him to break out of a neocolonial cultural dynamic that perpetuated a sense of inferiority and dependency long after independence. The superiority of the French was reflected in the progress of enlightenment and their apparent readiness to learn from the Americans as they launched their world-changing revolution.

Jefferson was most profoundly affected by the reception he received from the enlightened intelligentsia, the fraternity of like-minded liberals who celebrated the American Revolution and the new states' republican constitutions and lionized his predecessor Benjamin Franklin. For the bedazzled Virginian, this was the republic of letters come to life; in salons and other refined settings, the cognoscenti of Europe combined civility and enlightenment with an enthusiasm for the American republican experiment. If the French court at Versailles epitomized monarchical decadence for Jefferson, the social world of the intelligentsia was a kind of "anti-court," populated by monarchy's most trenchant critics. This was an implicitly oppositional space where like-minded friends deconstructed the old regime and imagined the new. "Public opinion" took shape in the circulation of ideas through face-to-face encounters as well as in print. Here, perhaps, was what Jefferson had in mind as his political friends spontaneously coalesced in opposition to George Washington's "republican court." This was no "faction" or "party" in the conventional sense. It was instead a meeting of hearts and minds.

Jefferson's time abroad prepared him for his subsequent career in American national politics. Admirers gravitated to the Virginian's French-inflected cosmopolitan persona. Conversation in private, intimate settings was his distinctive métier: he proved adept at drawing colleagues and acquaintances into his personal orbit and thus making "friends" who shared his fundamental values and commitments. His immersion in the culture of the French intelligentsia validated the radical republican principles he so eloquently articulated on his return to Virginia. But if these principles were oppositional in France, challenging the legitimacy of its ancien régime, they were consensual in America, where the republican revolution was an accomplished fact. Jefferson's neighbors recognized that his republicanism did not call their way of life into question. Quite to the contrary, his affirmation of home virtues reflected his appreciation of the exceptional circumstances that enabled the republican revolution to succeed in America—and the more formidable obstacles to its success in France. "The happy influence of reason and liberty," he told his fellow citizens, would spread from America, from their home in Albemarle County, "over the face of the earth."

Jefferson's bedrock conviction that his countrymen—in Virginia and across the continent—were united in their dedication to revolutionary republican principles shaped his subsequent political career. He was surprised and appalled by the factious, self-interested combinations that he soon discovered within the Washington administration. Disagreements over Hamilton's financial plan and other administration policies that threatened to concentrate power in the federal government at the expense of the states confirmed Jefferson's longstanding suspicion that the greatest internal threat to the republic came from aspiring "aristocrats" who would betray the people's trust. A rapidly deteriorating international situation in the waning years of the eighteenth century showed that the new nation was equally vulnerable to external threats, and the combination raised Jefferson's anxieties to a fever pitch.

The French Revolution's radical turn unleashed "the dogs of war," with Britain in the vanguard of a reactionary "Conspiracy of Kings."[32] Americans' gratitude for French support in their own revolution, fealty to the 1778 alliance, and enthusiasm for the worldwide cause of republicanism were increasingly at odds with the commercial connections and common interests that tied the new nation to the old mother country. Given Britain's maritime supremacy, even Francophiles recognized the compelling need to stay neutral in the war between Britain and France. But neutrality could be defined in different ways, more or less friendly to each of the warring powers. And when the British, without prior warning and in violation of the law of nations, launched devastating assaults on American shipping in the French West Indian trade beginning in late 1793, the possibility of any sort of neutrality evaporated. The overmatched United States could not go to war yet again with Britain (as France's ally), but it resisted a peace that would effectively draw the new nation into an anti-French alliance.

President Washington sent Supreme Court Chief Justice John Jay to London to seek a diplomatic solution to the crisis. The resulting Jay Treaty, ratified by a single vote in the Senate in August 1795, kept the country out of harm's way—and subsequently enabled American producers and merchants to prosper under what amounted to a British protectorate. Jefferson and his allies were unimpressed. They were convinced that Jay should have negotiated a much better treaty. Britain depended on trade with its former colonies and could not afford to open up another front in what was becoming a world war. Jeffersonians were most incensed by the administration's allegedly gratuitous betrayal of the "sister republic." Popular revulsion against the Jay Treaty polarized the incipient parties, offering militant oppositionists an unprecedented opportunity to shape and exploit public opinion. The treaty may have kept the peace, but it brought the European war home to Americans in powerful and frightening ways. Hysterical partisan rhetoric was suffused with threats of imminent violence: Federalists dwelled on the anarchy and terror of the French revolutionary assault on Christian civilization; Republicans, on the administration's betrayal of the American Revolution's republican legacy.[33]

In the wake of the Jay Treaty, the great struggle between Federalists and the Republicans seemed like war to anxious participants who shared a pervasive sense that the future of the republic hung in the balance. As the French Revolution broadened into a wider European conflict—pitting revolutionary republicanism (or the forces of "democracy") against the "conspiracy of kings" (or "aristocracy")—Americans saw their party conflict through a new, more portentous lens. The European conflict spurred party political mobilization in America, evoking memories of 1776 for increasingly hard-pressed Republicans. Partisan conflict in America in turn encouraged foreign interference in American politics. Republicans characterized Federalists as the "English party," accusing their enemies of making the United States into a satellite of the former mother country and refashioning the federal government along counterrevolutionary, antirepublican lines. Federalists replied in kind: the Republicans were intent on revolutionizing America into yet another French puppet state; their disloyal opposition brought on French retaliation against American shipping in the undeclared "Quasi-War" of 1798–1800. That war led to efforts by the Adams administration to shut down opposition newspapers and deport dangerous foreigners under the ill-advised Alien and Sedition Acts of 1798. This was the Federalist-imposed darkness, or what Jefferson called a "reign of witches," before a new day dawned for Republicans in 1800.[34]

It was in this era of intense partisan rancor that Jefferson's Franco-American persona grew so polarizing. The conflict-averse gentleman from Virginia became a lightning rod for political conflict: for his supporters, the iconic author of the Declaration of Independence; for his enemies, a dangerous democratic ideologue who pandered to the people. Controversial in spite of his own predilections, Jefferson was a reluctant warrior whose democratic persona was fashioned by his followers to lead them out of the political wilderness and back to the promised land. His authorship of the Declaration enabled Republicans to counter Federalist claims to the aura of moral authority that surrounded Washington, the "father of his country." However much the people revered Washington (and Republicans began to question his exalted status in his second administration), the voice of the people—speaking through Jefferson's Declaration—commanded a still higher authority. Perhaps, Republicans suggested, it was more appropriate to celebrate the people's birthday on the Fourth of July than to honor the "father," Washington, on *his* birthday, as if he were a semidivine figure and something like a king.

American Exceptionalism

By distinguishing the virtuous American people from the supposedly corrupt, counterrevolutionary Federalists in power, Jeffersonians could justify a mass mobilization against the government. Invoking the Spirit of '76, these antipartisan partisans sought to save the revolution. In retrospect this is precisely what Jefferson thought had happened when he was elected president, in the happily peaceful "Revolution of 1800."[35] This was, as he saw it, the people's triumph, as they took their government back from conspirators against their liberties, not the triumph of a political party for, as Jefferson later told the radical Republican editor William Duane, "the republicans are the nation."[36] It was certainly *not* a triumph for Jefferson himself. The people's humble servant was filled with "anxious and awful presentiments" as he assumed the reins of presidential power at his inauguration on March 4, 1801, duly conscious of the "greatness of the charge and the weakness of [his] powers." Torn from the comforts of home and family and subject to the constant surveillance of vigilant citizens, Jefferson could not expect to be happy. He could only hope "to be instrumental to the happiness and freedom" of his countrymen.[37]

Jefferson sought to craft a presidential persona that would lift him above the partisan fray. His victory was narrow, the outcome finally determined by the vote of state delegations in Congress after he and Aaron Burr (the Republicans' presumed vice-presidential candidate) received the same number of votes in the Electoral College. The exultant new president nonetheless claimed a popular mandate. A "mighty wave of public opinion" had swept him into office, Jefferson wrote his friend Joseph Priestley: springing from the people, this irresistible natural force expressed their deep and fundamental identification with republican principles. Now that the storm was "subsiding & the horison becoming serene," the success of America's bold experiment in republican government seemed assured. The happy resolution of "the momentous crisis which lately arose" revealed "a strength of character in our nation which augurs well for the duration of our republic, & I am much better satisfied now of it's stability, than I was before it was tried."[38] Wary Federalists were understandably skeptical, though Jefferson's conciliatory language helped defuse a widely shared sense of crisis.

The inaugural address was a prayer for peace. "Let us . . . unite with one heart and one mind," he exhorted his fellow citizens. "Let us restore to social intercourse that harmony and affection without which liberty, and even life itself, are but dreary things." The reluctant partisan claimed that he had been misrepresented and misunderstood: "we have called by different names brethren of the same principle." With his election, he hoped, harmony would again prevail in the great American family: "we are all republicans: we are all federalists." Jefferson projected a palpable sense of relief. Rising above the "miseries" of partisan combat, he would dedicate himself to the service of the whole American people. Victorious Republicans would no longer be mobilized against the Federalist administration, and their embattled leader could reach out in a conciliatory spirit to his erstwhile enemies. The "voice of the nation, announced according to the rules of the constitution," had spoken, and patriotic Americans "will of course arrange themselves under the will of the law, and unite in common efforts for the common good."

In his inaugural address Jefferson juxtaposed his own modest self-image as the people's humble servant, conscious of his limitations, to the illimitable power and prospects of the American people. "Sometimes it is said that man cannot be trusted with the government of himself. Can he then be trusted with the government of others? Or have we found angels, in the form of kings, to govern him?" Jefferson did not set himself up as an angel, identifying instead with fellow citizens who sacrificed everything in defense of the republic. All citizens were equal in the great republic, and this made their government "the strongest government on earth." Jefferson thus testified to his faith in a republican regime "where every man, at the call of the law, would fly to the standard of the law, and would meet invasions of the public order as his own personal concern." In responding to the call of an aroused and enlightened electorate, Jefferson claimed he was following the lead of the citizen-soldiers whose sacrifices had secured American independence. Their patriotism dissolved the distinction between private and public, home and homeland, giving the government of the people extraordinary, unprecedented power.

Patriotism was a great leveler, rendering all good Americans equal in the sacrifices they made—or were prepared to make—for each other. There was one who stood above all others, however. The "pre-eminent services" of George Washington, "our first and greatest revolutionary character," entitled him "to the first place in his country's love." Jefferson told his fellow Americans that he had no "pretensions to that high confidence you reposed" in the great commander in chief. Ever since George Washington's death on December 14, 1799, formerly skeptical Republicans had joined Federalists in adulation of the "father of his country." But the newly sanctified image of Washington was purged of the controversial partisan associations Federalists had so assiduously cultivated. He was no longer the dupe or pawn of corrupt ministers. Jefferson instead aligned the great general with the Spirit of '76, emphasizing his key role in eliciting sacrifices from a willing people in the war for independence. Washington demonstrated his greatness by resisting the temptations of power. By relinquishing his command at the end of the war—and later by retiring from the presidency—he demonstrated his faith in the capacity of the people to govern themselves.

Looking back to the revolution, Jefferson and his fellow Americans acknowledged their indebtedness to their father, the immortal

Washington. But the future belonged to a rising generation. "Kindly separated by nature and a wide ocean from the exterminating havoc of one quarter of the globe" and "too high minded to endure the degradations of the others," the new nation possessed "a chosen country, with room enough for our descendants to the thousandth and thousandth generation." This succession of generations, spreading across the continent, constituted Jefferson's vision of American nationhood. With "a due sense of our equal right to the use of our own faculties, to the acquisitions of our own industry, to honor and confidence from our fellow citizens, resulting not from birth, but from our actions and their sense of them, enlightened by a benign religion," Americans would conquer the continent. A "wise and frugal government" would "close the circle of our felicities," making us "a happy and prosperous people."

Jefferson's inaugural address was a paean to American exceptionalism. In discounting the significance of the party battles in which he had played such an important, if sometimes unwilling, role, he insisted on the moral as well as geographical distance between New World and Old. It was not surprising, he explained, that "the throes and convulsions of the ancient world" should wash up even on "this distant and peaceful shore." Nor was it surprising that Americans could hold different "opinions" about the danger that the war in Europe posed for the United States. Fortunately, Americans had already secured their liberty and understood that they were far removed from "the agonising spasms of infuriated man, seeking through blood and slaughter his long lost liberty." However much they sympathized with their European counterparts, Americans should steer clear of foreign conflicts.

Jefferson was not alone in recognizing the danger of foreign entanglements. Washington's Farewell Address, originally drafted by James Madison in anticipation of an earlier retirement, had taught the same great lesson. But whereas Federalists—fearful of frontier separatism, Indian wars, and conflicts with imperial rivals—saw danger in the West, Jefferson saw redemption. Portraying the vast hinterland as a blank slate (and imaginatively banishing all those threats), Jefferson envisioned the continuing expansion of a boundless American "empire of liberty" through the creation of new self-governing state-republics. This was a conception of the nation's future that captivated future generations as they contemplated their "manifest destiny."

An expanding union was the promise. Yet that promise would be fulfilled only so long as Americans remained united "with one heart and one mind." Mankind elsewhere has "long bled and suffered" from "religious intolerance," and the never-ending wars in Europe showed that "political intolerance" could be "as despotic, as wicked, and capable of as bitter and bloody persecutions." Equal in their dedication to the fundamental principles of republican self-government, patriotic Americans were also "enlightened by a benign religion, professed indeed and practised in various forms, yet all of them inculcating honesty, truth, temperance, gratitude and the love of man, acknowledging and adoring an overruling providence." There would be no persecution of defeated Federalists, even of those few who favored a return to monarchical government. "If there be any among us who would wish to dissolve this Union, or to change its republican form," Jefferson concluded, "let them stand undisturbed as monuments of the safety with which error of opinion may be tolerated, where reason is left free to combat it."

President Jefferson's America would hardly be free of political conflict, despite these lofty and inspiring sentiments. Federalists continued to dominate in many parts of the country, ascendant Republicans quarreled with each other over policies and principles, and the world would become a very dangerous place for the United States when war resumed between Britain and France. Through it all, Jefferson ran a smooth administration, keeping a tight rein on his cabinet and avoiding the contentious meetings that characterized earlier administrations; he enjoyed comfortable majorities in Congress and maintained civil, sometimes even congenial relations with his partisan opponents. Aspiring to be a "president above parties," Jefferson kept a low, republican profile.[39] Unlike his predecessors, he did not make personal appearances before Congress, nor did he promote the stilted rituals and ceremonies of European-style courts. The president instead presided over countless dinners at the White House, sharing good food and wine and edifying and amusing conversation with his guests. Like the man himself, the tone and cuisine were gracious and elegant, with distinctive Franco-Virginian accents. Jefferson knew how to set his companions at ease, exercising his influence through his engaging manner and extraordinary stock of information.

Of course, the president could not avoid the business of politics, but Jefferson discovered that the persona he developed as a reluctant partisan, bringing political allies together in casual, intimate, and quasi-familial settings, worked well in his new Washington home. He displayed extraordinary gifts as a politician both within the government and among the legion of "friends" who affirmed their support for him at the polls and validated his presidential persona. His sensitive, sympathetic, and approachable self-presentation ingratiated him with the many people he encountered in person or through a voluminous correspondence. These encounters in turn reinforced the conception of his relationship with the "people" more generally that he articulated in his inaugural addresses and other state papers.

An extraordinarily self-confident President Jefferson claimed to draw his authority from the sovereign people: they would judge whether he had acted according to their will when they returned to the polls. His authority was always theirs, he insisted, never his own independently. The president was not a patriarch, for the country was *not* his exclusive domain; unlike the master's actions in the privacy of his household, the public servant's performance was always subject to a vigilant people's surveillance. These constraints sustained his legitimacy, enabling him to tap into the collective power of the people in his service to them. Later presidents invoked this direct connection with the people as a "mandate"; the political scientist Jeremy Bailey provocatively calls it Jefferson's "democratic prerogative," foregrounding its source in the executive discretion of the king.[40] Paradoxically, that authority was available to a democratic leader precisely because he was *not* a king: his interests were completely subsumed in and subordinate to those of the people. When Jefferson told Americans that they constituted a great nation, enjoining them to "unite with one heart and one mind," he wrote the script for a successful presidency.

JUST OVER A YEAR before his death on July 4, 1826, Jefferson wrote a famous letter to Henry Lee, son of the revolutionary general (and prominent Jefferson critic) Henry "Light Horse Harry" Lee, disclaiming authorship of the Declaration of Independence. "Neither aiming at originality of principle or sentiment, nor yet copied from any particular and previous writing," Jefferson told Lee, the Declaration "was intended to be an expression of the American mind, and to give to that expression the proper tone and spirit called for by the occasion." Commentators on the Declaration have noted that it was the Declaration itself that "invented" the people that declared itself independent. But Jefferson had no doubt such a people already existed. "With respect to *our* rights," he insisted, "there was but one opinion on this side of the water. All American whigs thought alike."[41] Of course, the assertion was tautological: some colonists were Tories, not Whigs, and therefore not "American." The unanimity he posited in his first inaugural address depended on similar rhetorical moves. In both cases, however, Jefferson expressed the deeper logic of patriotism and national identity. The nation's existence depended on patriots' fundamental attachments to their country and to each other.

Jefferson's conception of family love animated and justified his political commitments. For Jefferson patriotism began at home. The affectionate bonds that sustained family life constituted the only stable and enduring foundation for republican self-government. In defending his patriarchal domain against foreign threats, he sustained the Spirit of '76. Like that of the great Roman hero Cincinnatus, the Virginian's only ambition was to return home to cultivate his lands and manage his household. Keeping home in mind throughout his political career, Jefferson could tell himself that politics was a dreary business, that he had no interests to pursue in public life, that he never sought power as an end in itself. The reluctant statesman was before all else a devoted patriarch, determined to vindicate his rights and protect his dependents. "Who can limit the extent to which the federative principle may operate effectively?" Jefferson asked in his second inaugural address.[42] The patriarch was a patriot, envisioning young patriarchs in future generations starting families and making farms as they extended the boundaries of a great "empire of liberty" across the continent. For Jefferson self-fashioning and nation making were inextricably, intimately linked.

Part Three

———

ENTHUSIAST

Photograph of Monticello parlor with harpsichord at right. (© The Thomas Jefferson Foundation at Monticello)

CHAPTER 7

MUSIC

"When he was not talking, he was nearly always humming some tune, or singing in a low tone to himself," the Monticello overseer Edmund Bacon said of Jefferson.[1] It was a habit that anyone who spent a great deal of time around Jefferson at Monticello would have noticed. Isaac Granger, the former nail boy, tinsmith, and blacksmith, who often accompanied Jefferson on hunting trips, agreed with Bacon. Jefferson was "always singing when riding or walking; hardly see him anywhere outdoors but what he was a-singing."[2] Granger, who could be quite frank in his assessment of the people discussed in his recollections—Jefferson was not nearly so handsome as one of his portraits made him out to be—nevertheless praised Jefferson's singing abilities, saying that he had a "fine clear voice" and typically sang "minuets and such." He sang when he was alone, too. Ellen Randolph Coolidge, whose bedroom, for a time, was above Jefferson's rooms at Monticello, recalled hearing her grandfather's voice wafting upward as he sang Italian airs and Scottish hymns and songs, particular favorites of his. He sang for people. "His singing," as he "journeyed" to his retreat at Poplar Forest, entertained his traveling companions and "made the time pass pleasantly."[3]

Not content with using his own singing voice, Jefferson even turned to the animal kingdom—mockingbirds—to provide him with daily song. Some of his earliest mentions of the Hemings family were the notations in his Memorandum Books of paying Martin, aged twelve in 1772, and then James Hemings, aged eight in 1773, to capture mockingbirds for him. Over the years Jefferson bought mockingbirds that did what they usually do—imitate the songs of other birds—but that had also been trained to sing specific tunes from America, Scotland, and France. He did whatever he could to have music around him at all times.[4]

Music was in Jefferson's life from the beginning. Peter and Jane Jefferson made sure that their children were given music and dancing lessons, and when young Thomas was not practicing or playing himself, he would have heard his sisters and brother practicing and playing. When he contemplated becoming the head of his own household, his vision of domestic happiness with his wife and future children focused on making music with them—playing instruments and singing. Martha Wayles Jefferson, whom her husband called by her girlhood nickname "Patty," was a talented musician, who sang well herself. Family lore has it that two of Martha's suitors knew at once that things were hopeless when they both arrived at her doorstep one day and overheard Thomas and Martha singing a duet in the parlor—she on the harpsichord, he playing his violin. After listening to the blending voices of the pair for a brief while, they left with no attempt to interrupt the couple.[5] Anticipating his musical marriage, the victorious suitor ordered a fortepiano from London as a wedding gift for his wife.[6]

The Jeffersons began their marriage in 1772 during America's revolutionary crisis. Even in the midst of the turmoil, the young husband and father looked for ways to bring music to the mountain, engaging the talent of Europeans. As the war dragged on, he corresponded with Giovanni Fabbroni, a young Florentine friend of his neighbor Philip Mazzei, about coming to Virginia to give music lessons. When the war ended "one two or three years hence" and it was safe to travel, Fabbroni might recruit some of his countrymen "proficient in singing and on the harpsichord" to join him in the long journey to Albemarle County. Jefferson lamented his circumstances.

"Fortune has cast my lot in a country where" music "is in a state of deplorable barbarism," he confessed. But with the return of peace that cultural deficit would be offset by opportunities for European immigrants to make new and better lives for themselves in America. Fabbroni's musically inclined countrymen could come to work for Jefferson at Monticello in dual roles as workers and musicians. Surely this was possible. "In a country where, like yours, music is cultivated and practised by every class of men," there must be gardeners, weavers, carpenters, stone masons, and "vignerons" (cultivators of grapes for wine) who could be employed at Monticello and who could also "perform on the French horn, clarinet or hautboy and bassoon, so that one might have a band of two French horns, two clarinets and hautboys and a bassoon" without exceeding "the bounds of an American fortune."[7] Jefferson would have, without spending too much, his own small orchestra from among his workmen. This seems a fanciful idea, particularly given the instruments Jefferson sought. Decades later, however, his own sons Beverley, Madison, and Eston Hemings grew up at Monticello trained to be carpenters and musicians—the kind of men Jefferson imagined in his correspondence with Fabbroni.

Music, Jefferson told his Italian correspondent, "is the favorite passion of my soul." It was a "passion" that connected him with the most important people in his life, linking soul to soul and defining domestic happiness. Indeed, it was a metaphor for life itself. When his eldest daughter complained about difficulties with her father-in-law and his new wife, Jefferson invoked musical performance to suggest how she should deal with the trials and tribulations human beings inevitably face. Consider the tough moments, he told her, "as a bad stop in your harpsichord. Do not touch on it, but make yourself happy with the good ones."[8]

Jefferson's use of the word "passion"—and other comments he made over the years—show that music was certainly about joy and exaltation for him. The sheer pleasure of hearing sounds called forth deep feelings and put him into contact with beauty and a sense of fun. He danced, and he played his violin to watch his grandchildren dance. But his letter to his daughter suggesting that she use what she knew of musicianship to help her solve problems makes clear that music had other properties that were also very important to him: music satisfied Jefferson's love of order and desire for control. The mastery of a violin—playing songs on it in just the right way—fit well with his basic inclinations about how to go through life. Passion would always be present, but it had to be kept under control. Jefferson's instrument of choice required its master to strike the perfect balance between the two.

Not surprisingly, Jefferson believed that his ideas about family radiated out to the community at large. Music not only bound families together; it also had a profound role to play in shaping societies, enabling even rustic provincials far removed from the centers of metropolitan civilization to redeem themselves from the "deplorable barbarism" he had mentioned to Fabbroni. Making music epitomized the refined and enlightened sociability that was crucial to the success of the new nation's republican experiment. The moral philosophers the young Jefferson so admired taught him that although men and women were naturally sociable and were endowed with a "moral sense," they were prone to misunderstanding and conflict because they failed to communicate effectively with each other or to anticipate the remote consequences of their actions. The stages of human development, as Jefferson saw them, also had to be considered. Before a young student could discern patterns and laws in nature through the exercise of reason, his or her moral character had to be shaped and refined at home and at school. "Time is not lost which is employed in providing tools for future operation," he wrote in *Notes on the State of Virginia*. If the critical adolescent years "be suffered to pass in idleness, the mind becomes lethargic and impotent, as would the body it inhabits if unexercised during the same time."[9] Jefferson, who described himself as having been a "hard student" in his youth, understood that rigorous self-discipline was essential to cultivating an individual's natural gifts.[10] Mastering languages and making music were crucial to forging strong attachments within the family and beyond.

Practice made perfect: endless, seemingly mindless, ultimately effortless repetition left lasting impressions on developing minds. One had to be serious and, preferably, under the direction of more experienced teachers and mentors. Not long after he married Martha, Jefferson persuaded Francis Alberti, a native of Italy who was teaching the violin, harpsichord, and dance in Williamsburg, to become his violin instructor. Alberti relocated to Charlottesville and gave lessons to both Thomas and Martha, as well as other prominent people in the area. The historian of music Sandor Salgo has speculated that the Italian violin master, "a product of a tradition of violin performance as practiced in Italy," almost certainly "attempted to communicate Italian performance practice to Jefferson."[11] As the musicologist Candida Felici has noted, "The Italian style of playing was characterized by the brilliance and rapidity of passages in the *Allegros*, the expressiveness of the *Adagios*, the rich ornamentation, the agility in the use of the bow, the melodic skips of more than two octaves and the improvisation of cadenzas [and] new techniques like double stops and the use of natural harmonies."[12]

Jefferson took his role as student musician very seriously. "During at least a dozen years" of his early life, he said, he "played no less than *three hours* a day" on his violin, though Salgo wisely cautions against accepting Jefferson's late in life description of his daily practice regime, suggesting the hours be "discounted by half."[13] But his disciplined approach to study showed itself in other parts of his life. Through equally long hours of strenuous study, he mastered mathematics and learned ancient and modern languages. By his adult years Jefferson was so habituated to sustained study that it no longer seemed "hard" or tedious. To the contrary, reading Latin or Greek or puzzling his way through math problems became a recreational pursuit, an escape from the pointless, noisy, life-sapping tedium of public life. "Music is invaluable," Jefferson reflected in 1818, furnishing "a delightful recreation for the hours of respite from the cares of the day, and lasts us through life." But this was true only "where a person has an ear." The cultivated ear could hear the sense in sounds and thus distinguish them from "discordant noises."[14]

Isaac Granger remembered that in "his early time" Jefferson "kept three fiddles; played in the afternoons and sometimes after supper."[15]

The "early time" was cut short in 1786 when a crippling accident in Paris transformed Jefferson's relationship to the violin. The exact origins of the mishap remain mysterious because Jefferson never revealed how it happened, even when asked directly. According to a contemporary report, he "dislocated his right wrist when attempting to jump over a fence in the Petit Cour." Jefferson was not alone when this happened. He was with Maria Cosway, and there is a hint that he may have been acting on her behalf in some way when he injured himself. Not long after his records show his payment to the doctor who attended him, she wrote to Jefferson and apologized for "having been the cause of his pain." Had he tried to impress her by leaping a fence? Did he try to leap a fence to retrieve something for her? Or was she taking the blame for having been the occasion for him to be outside walking? Jefferson never, in any letter that is extant, said, though he described the event as "one of those follies from which good cannot come, but ill may."[16]

Although Jefferson refers to the injury as a "dislocation" of his wrist, his daughter Martha in later years said that while walking with "some friend," her father "fell and fractured his wrist." It was, she said, actually a "compound" fracture. Martha's assessment fits with the enormous pain Jefferson felt, and the long time it took for him to recover. More accurately, one should say partially recover, for the surgeon who attended Jefferson set the bones improperly, and Jefferson never recovered the full strength and use of his right hand. For months afterwards he wrote letters—tolerably well—with his left hand, including the famous "Dialogue" letter to Maria Cosway.

Jefferson was eventually able to regain the use of his hand to write, but there is no question that the arthritis that set in after the injury limited his ability and, likely, his willingness to play the violin regularly. The injury and his career in public life, which greatly magnified the extent of his responsibilities, gave him ample reason to limit playing the instrument that had been so important to him. He played less and focused more on fostering music among others at Monticello, providing his daughters and, later, his grandchildren with pianos, harpsichords, guitars, and sheet music that he collected for family members.

Long hours of practice in childhood enabled Jefferson's children and their families to make music with each other and to revel in the performances of expert players in Philadelphia, Paris, or wherever they might be found. This applied to the Hemings-Jefferson children, as well. Before he left Monticello to enter the white world in 1822, young Beverley Hemings played the violin at Jefferson's granddaughters' parties. Isaac Granger remembered Madison Hemings as a "fine" violin player. Practice and talent allowed Eston Hemings to make a living as a musician. He played the violin and fronted his own musical group, which performed at society events throughout Ohio in the mid-nineteenth century. Hemings was said to have "always officiated at the 'swell' entertainments of Chillicothe." He was described as a "master of the violin, and an accomplished 'caller' of dances."[17] Although the Hemings children were known to Jefferson's neighbors—as a little boy, Beverley was said to be "well-known" in the area—they were not to be "known" in the Jefferson-Randolph family's epistolary record, the chief means through which the family would convey its image to posterity. As a result we do not know how the Hemings brothers learned to play the violin.[18]

Practicing and performing music was, actually, playful work for Jefferson. In sentimental retrospect the music he made with loved ones remained vivid in his memory. The point of all that practice was not a showy virtuosity, but rather developing a voice that could communicate in a language that was at once natural and refined, speaking from heart to heart while achieving ever higher levels of harmonious communion. Jefferson achieved this kind of communion early in his life. He and his boyhood friend Dabney Carr "were inseparable companions" who not only roamed Monticello (the mountain) together but also "practiced their music, and formed their plans together."[19] Jefferson and his beloved older sister, Jane, the namesake of their mother, forged an even more powerful musical bond. "She had been a singer of uncommon skill and sweetness," the biographer Henry Randall learned from Jefferson's granddaughters, "and both were particularly fond of the solemn music used by the Church of England in the Psalms." "More than half a century afterwards," Jefferson expressed his "admiration and love" for Jane "as if the grave had just closed over her." Hearing settings for the psalms and other "solemn music" of the old Church of England most often triggered these memories. Jefferson dissented from the doctrines of his childhood church and from the other denominations that proliferated in republican Virginia: "I am of a sect by myself," he declared in 1819.[20] But family and community ties—and the music that evoked them—kept calling him back to worship with his neighbors.

Jefferson's relentless insistence on disciplined practice—whether in language, dance, drawing, or music—was the hallmark of his approach to educating the daughters he had with his wife. Jefferson was determined to supervise their education, and music was critical to his hopes for them. Of course, he had a different plan of action for his children with Sally Hemings. We do not know about his other siblings, but Jefferson's grandchildren taught Madison Hemings how to read and write. The Hemings siblings' education was vocational. Jefferson arranged to have the Hemings brothers trained by their uncle John Hemings, who was, in turn, under Jefferson's supervision. Little is known about Harriet Hemings's childhood beyond the fact that she did not do any hard work, but learned to spin and sew—skills that prepared her to be a wife and mother. Significantly, none of the Hemings children worked as actual servants at Monticello, beyond running errands, a task that children black and white, enslaved and free, often performed.

Practicing, performing, and listening to music would sustain Jefferson's small family in years to come. Before departing for France in 1784, Jefferson made his expectations clear to eleven-year-old Patsy, then living in Philadelphia with Elizabeth House Trist. "The acquirements which I hope you will make under the tutors I have provided for you will render you more worthy of my love," Jefferson admonished Patsy, "and if they cannot increase it they will prevent it's diminution." Modern readers are hard-pressed to forgive Jefferson for expecting perfection or for suggesting that his love for his daughter depended on how close she came to that state: "Inform me what books you read, what tunes you learn, and inclose me your best copy of every lesson in drawing," write weekly to your aunts, taking "care that you never spell a word wrong." Jefferson laid out a daily schedule for Patsy that would guarantee her success, including three hours of music practice and shorter periods for French, dancing, and drawing. "If you love me then," he concluded, "strive to be good under every situation and to all living creatures, and to acquire those accomplishments which I have put in your power, and which will go far towards ensuring you the warmest love of your affectionate father."[21]

Jefferson clearly expected Patsy to invest the same number of hours in daily music practice that he had during his younger years. To be sure, he would always "love" her, but he was impelled to suggest that the quality of their relationship would depend on her—and his— "accomplishments" and their ability to express that love through music. This was, apparently, the best, during this phase of his life, that the recently widowed father of prepubescent daughters could do. By the time he had granddaughters, he had discovered more nuanced ways to exhort young people to strive for excellence.

A Family Passion

Jefferson's efforts to recruit an Italian music teacher or, even better, a band of Italian musicians-workmen to Monticello demonstrate his acute awareness of the enormous culture gap between European metropolitan civilization and relatively primitive rural Virginia. He struggled to bridge the gap by claiming membership in the Enlightenment republic of letters, imagining the sights and sounds of European civilization by reading the best books and playing the best published music, as if he were experiencing these things on behalf of his country. With his extraordinary "stock of information," he would hold "a distinguished rank among men of letters" in Europe. In central Virginia, however—if not in all of the United States—there was simply no one quite like him. Still, his limited and largely mediated exposure to the fine arts could not have prepared him for the overwhelming experience of "the vaunted scene of Europe."

In late 1784 the widower Jefferson, his daughter Martha (Patsy), and James Hemings arrived in a city that was at the very heart of European high culture. As Patsy grew to maturity in her Paris years, she and her father experienced together the sublime joy of hearing what they considered to be the best music in the world. Jefferson's "enjoiment" of Paris evoked a deeply felt lament: America lacked a music scene, "the deprivation of which with us cannot be calculated." The rational "head" was at a loss, for music was a matter of the "heart." "I am almost ready to say," Jefferson wrote to his correspondent Charles Bellini, that music "is the only thing which from my heart I envy them, and which in spight of all the authority of the decalogue I do covet." Jefferson knew that he and Patsy would feel an acute sense of "deprivation" when they returned to Virginia. He also knew that they would cherish their musical memories forever. So while he had the chance, Jefferson was determined to make the most of what Paris had to offer him in the way of music.[22]

Considering that he traveled during his time in France, and had much to do as minister to the country, Jefferson did manage to go a long way toward satisfying his musical tastes, understanding that he would never be able to replicate these experiences at home. He was a frequent attendee at the Concert Spirituel, a yearly series of orchestra performances held at the Salle des Machines. When the twelve-year-old mixed-race violin prodigy George Bridgetower performed in Paris, Jefferson went to see him, and he also attended numerous benefit concerts at the Panthéon. He loved going to the opera as well. Notes in his Memorandum Books show that in one two-year period he bought tickets for three performances at the Paris Opéra, *La Caravane du Caire*, *Didon*, and *Penelope*, but this probably does not tell the entire story of his engagement with opera and concerts while he was in the city. Lucia Stanton and James A. Bear have pointed out that several of his closest friends in Paris had boxes at the Paris Opéra, and often took their dinner guests to performances there.

Jefferson also kept up his interest in lighter fare. He was devoted to musical theater, a passion he developed while a student in Williamsburg, where he went often to performances by the Virginia

Company of Comedians and the American Theater Company. His tastes for "theatrical performances" was eclectic, but he particularly loved what were called English ballad operas, "exemplified by such works as Thomas Arne's *Thomas and Sally*, *Love in the Village*, and the more famous *The Beggar's Opera*." In these productions the player-singers alternated between speaking dialogue and singing, as distinguished from opera in which all lines of dialogue are sung. He sought out similar fare in Paris, attending eleven performances of the Comédie-Italienne.[23]

Jefferson also sampled musical offerings outside of Paris. He went to the opera during his travels through southern France and Italy and was especially impressed with one young prima donna. Her voice, he said, was mercifully free "of that dreadful wheeze or rather whistle in respiration which resembles the agonizing struggles for breath of a dying person" that he observed when watching some singers in Paris. Visiting the Adamses in London, he attended several plays and operas, including, ironically enough, a "royal command performance" of Antonio Salieri's *La scuola de' gelosi* when the Prince of Wales was in the audience.[24]

Jefferson's "passion" for music was a spur for self-improvement, refined sociability, and the progress of the new nation's culture. Family life, where loving bonds were so carefully nourished, provided the most intimate and important context for fulfilling all these aspirations, and Jefferson's relationship with his daughter Martha epitomized the ideal, harmonizing attachment. His overseer Edmund Bacon remembered that "she always had her father's pleasant smile" and, like him, "was nearly always humming some tune." Smile and song projected a happy disposition, putting others at ease. They also offered a protective shield against unpleasant encounters.

Maria Jefferson was understandably less comfortable with her father than was her older sister. Separated from him during crucial early childhood years, she formed a deep and lasting attachment to the family at Eppington and eventually married her first cousin Jack Eppes. Monticello did not exercise the powerful attraction for her that Martha felt, nor did she attain the "accomplishments" that put her older sister at such ease with their father. The girls' different physical appearances may have influenced matters, as well. Physically, Martha was described as a "female version of her father," who when reporting from Paris to his in-laws on both daughters' progress noted that Martha "inherits stature from her father, and that you know is inheriting no trifle."[25] Maria, on the other hand, was said to have been the image of her mother, both facially and in terms of her stature. Isaac Granger described her as pretty and "low," meaning that she was not tall or, at least, not nearly so tall as Martha. Unfortunately, in addition to her looks, she also inherited her mother's more fragile body and constitution, unlike her older sister, who bore twelve children with no reported serious complications. By the consensus of those who commented on the sisters, Maria was the more beautiful of the two. Descriptions of her border on rapturous. One person who knew her when she was a married woman recalled one occasion: "The singular beauty of Mrs. Eppes caused all eyes to be riveted on her when her lovely face and graceful form appeared in the doorway." To another "her face . . . was divine. Her complexion was exquisite; her features all good, and so arranged as to produce an expression such as I never beheld in any other countenance: sweetness, intelligence, tenderness, beauty were exquisitely blended in her countenance. Her eye, fine blue, had an expression that cannot I think be described."[26]

Jefferson demanded, with little success, that young Maria correspond regularly when they were apart, but over the years adjusted his expectations downward. She took harpsichord lessons in Paris with her sister and later in Philadelphia, where she lived with Jefferson after their return to the United States, though she was never as disciplined a musician as Martha was. In early 1791 her newly married sister tattled from Monticello, where she and her husband, Thomas Mann Randolph, temporarily made their home, that Maria avoided the harpsichord during an extended visit there. The "remarkably docile" Maria was eager to please, but had to "surmount her Laziness of which she has an astonishing degree and which makes her neglect what ever she thinks will not be imediately discovered."[27]

Martha's disapproving report echoed Jefferson's admonitions to her at a similar age, attesting to the closeness between Martha and their father and to the seemingly more distant and tenuous attachment that would lead an older Maria to question his love for her. In the midst of the protracted crisis over Jefferson's elevation to the presidency in February 1801, Maria, now Mrs. John Wayles "Jack" Eppes, wrote her father that her "tender love" for him was unsurpassed, but acknowledged her sister's special bond. Maria was "sensible of the distance which Nature has placed between" her sister and herself, adding, "I rejoice that you have in her so great a source of comfort & one who is in every way so worthy of you."[28] She made these comments after having dropped hints about her insecurities in some of the letters she had written to him just before this one. Jefferson had not noticed the hints, but this letter made clear what Maria was saying. He then responded quickly, as his concern about family harmony displaced anxiety about his political future, resolved two days later by the vote in the House of Representatives that made him president. "Never imagine that there can be a difference with me between yourself & your sister," Jefferson protested: "you have both such dispositions as engross my whole love, and each so entirely that there can be no greater degree of it than each possesses."[29] The exchange of declarations continued for the rest of Maria's life, cut short by childbirth complications in April 1804, when she was just twenty-four years old. In the year before her final illness, Maria poignantly expressed her dilemma: "I feel my inability to express how much I love and revere you"—an inability that Martha never felt.[30]

Despite their differences, the bond between Patsy and Maria was strong and loving—Martha nursed Maria's child when Maria was unable to do so—and, in the final analysis, both adored and were adored by their father. Whatever the supposed defects of Maria's approach to practicing music, she participated happily in the family's musical life. Jefferson reported one revealing musical moment in his small family's last months in Paris in a letter thanking Francis Hopkinson—lawyer, composer, and a fellow signer of the Declaration of Independence—for a "book of songs" the Philadelphian had composed and sent to him. While Martha was playing one of these songs on the harpsichord, Jefferson "happened to look towards the fire" and noticed that Maria was "all in tears." Jefferson "asked her if she was sick? She said 'no; but the tune was so mournful.'"[31] That Martha's expressive playing so effectively captured the "pathos" of Hopkinson's composition was a tribute to her disciplined and "worthy" character. But Maria was exquisitely tuned to the music, perhaps hearing something in it that her performing sister and preoccupied father had missed. Music, after all, spoke to the heart and fostered natural attachments, even among the less gifted and less well trained.

There were undoubtedly many such moments in Jefferson's life, evanescent and unrecorded but resonating in enduring memories of family happiness. Surely Jefferson recalled making music with his wife, Martha, whose premature death in 1782 destroyed the family they had made together. Before then the Jeffersons had already lost three of their six children, and the birth of Lucy Elizabeth, the third briefly surviving daughter, brought on her mother's death. Jefferson, almost inconsolable at his wife's death, mourned Lucy's strongly as well, bemoaning the transatlantic distance that had prevented their true acquaintance. But every loss left an echo, a musical trace that continued to resonate with and in Jefferson.

Lucy, approaching three years old, "was too frail and too intensely susceptible to last long," according to family legend. "Her sensibilities were so precociously acute, that she listened with exquisite pleasure to music—and *wept* on hearing a false note!"[32] Many "mournful" notes marked the passing of loved ones and strengthened attachments among survivors. In his love-letter dialogue to Maria Cosway, written two and a half years after Lucy's death, Jefferson expressed the paradoxical combination of joy and grief that heartfelt love sustained. "What more sublime delight than to mingle tears with one whom the hand of heaven hath smitten!"[33]

Letters and Songs

Letters were resonant tokens of absent friends and loved ones, echoing across space and time. When accompanied by music and poetry, they enabled correspondents to experience and share emotions that eluded conventional literary expression. Francis Hopkinson, Maria Cosway, and many other correspondents sent songs to Jefferson, while Jefferson collected music for his Monticello library, anticipating future performances that reinforced sentimental attachments among performers and with appreciative audiences.[34] During his presidency he found time, despite the consuming duties of his office, to clip hundreds of songs and poems from newspapers and magazines, assembling them in scrapbooks for his own and the family's amusement and edification; he also clipped, copied, and composed poems for his grandchildren as he initiated them into the family life of letters.[35] "I congratulate you," he wrote his nine-year-old granddaughter Cornelia Randolph, "on having acquired the valuable art of writing. How delightful to be enabled by it to converse with an absent friend, as if present!"[36]

Another granddaughter, Virginia Randolph Trist, later recalled that Jefferson "never saw a little story or piece of poetry in a newspaper, suited to our ages and tastes, that he did not preserve it and send it to us," prompting the imitative girls to start scrapbooks of their own.[37] A tantalizing hint of the nature of Jefferson's connection to the Hemings children comes in the form of his treatment of a popular song. One of the few items of popular music he liked enough to copy out in his own hand was a tune called "Money Musk." Later on, in a nineteenth-century article about Chillicothe, Ohio, an Ohian would recollect that "Money Musk" was one of the signature tunes of Eston Hemings and his musical group as they performed throughout southern parts of the state.[38]

Letters, stories, poems, songs, and tunes all fostered sociability among family and friends. They also connected Jefferson's domestic circle with the larger community. The provincial planter was thrilled to hear the best music beautifully performed in Paris, but he also came to value the popular ballads and familiar tunes of his own country. This greater appreciation for American music grew out of his overall reassessment of the cultures of France and the United States.[39] Jefferson's respect for European high civilization never diminished, and it remained central to his self-fashioning project as well as his pedagogical aspirations for his children and grandchildren. After his return from France, however, he became increasingly attuned to the language and music of the people—and of his childhood home. He and fellow Enlightenment observers recognized that the sounds a "people" made—its language, poetry, and music—reflected its distinctive character. Jefferson would no longer describe the culture of the new American citizenry as barbaric.

Measured by metropolitan standards, music might be in a state of "deplorable barbarism" in Virginia, as Jefferson told Fabbroni in 1778. But those standards might not be the appropriate ones for his new country. The author of the Declaration of Independence who gave voice to the "people" now listened to them; the ambitious young provincial who sought to distance himself from his humble neighbors now identified with them. Jefferson still loved the music that he had enjoyed so much in Paris, but now took equal pleasure in the music made by the ordinary folk of his own country as well as the productions of enterprising and patriotic American songsmiths. As Jefferson added a growing number of "national" songs and poems to his library, family members and visitors who performed them affirmed a broader national identity. Popular music sometimes pushed the conventional boundaries of good taste, but Monticello music makers apparently were unfazed. The historian Bonnie Gordon has noted, "Contrary to received notions of Jefferson the prude, some of the music in his collection feature lyrics that might make a UVA frat boy blush":

When first I saw Betty and made my complaint
I whined like a fool and she sighed like a Saint.[40]

The boundary between "high" and "low" became less sharply defined in Jefferson's musical world. A burgeoning music publishing business provided access to an expanding repertoire of popular songs as publishers in London tapped a growing market for the poetry and music of Scotland, Ireland, and other regions of the British Isles. Americans could hear the distinctive rhythms and accents of the places they or their ancestors came from. The music that untutored country fiddlers passed on from generation to generation thus resonated in more refined spaces, like Monticello's parlor, as young performers mastered the simple tunes that rolled off metropolitan presses and new lyrics were fashioned for old tunes. The world of print did not mark a clear sonic boundary between the refined and learned elite and the cacophony of the vulgar crowd. Certainly thick walls and doubled-paned windows segregated Monticello soundscapes, distinguishing inside from out and buffering quiet spaces for reading, conversation, and musical performance. But family and friends moved easily through these spaces, and the music they made in the parlor could connect them with their countrymen even as it transported them to distant centers of high culture.

The Enlightenment fostered a cosmopolitan sensibility that enabled Virginians to imagine themselves fully equal citizens of a larger world and to express a love for their own "country" that valorized their claims as a distinct, even "chosen" people. Their vision of the new nation inspired patriots to give themselves a history and pedigree. For Jefferson that nation-building project focused on language and music and took him back to the British Isles. He was an enthusiastic exponent of the myth of ancient Saxon liberties. He created an imaginative narrative that traced the American revolutionaries' love of liberty back to the self-governing ethos or "character" of free peoples in the forests of Germany.

Our "Saxon ancestors . . . left their native wilds and woods in the north of Europe" to form self-governing colonies in Britain, Jefferson wrote in *A Summary View of the Rights of British America* in 1774, and their descendants in turn exercised their natural right to seek "new habitations" and establish "new societies" in the American wilderness.[41] American settlers could thus trace their roots to regions that had been conquered and oppressed by the same corrupt and tyrannical regime that now sought to deprive them of their freedom. Before the Norman Conquest extinguished Saxon liberties and established the feudal institutions that gave rise to the modern British monarchy and aristocracy, England itself had been a free country. The great transatlantic migration that peopled America was set in motion by systematic assaults on the liberties of the free peoples of the British Isles. Some of these peoples fled to America; others remained in their native homes and dreamed of regaining their freedom. This same logic led Jefferson to identify with the Irish and Scots, Celtic peoples, and the Welsh, his father's people. It also led him to emphasize the importance of recovering the ancient languages of liberty, for the spirit of free peoples survived in the words that expressed their common sentiments. Uncorrupted, authentic language sustained communities. For romantic nation makers like Jefferson, the history of a people's poetry, song, and music was the vital source of their collective identity.

Jefferson's ecstatic response to the poems of "Ossian," the "rude bard of the North" and "the greatest Poet that has ever existed," anticipated the young patriot's quest for a usable, national past. As noted, Ossian was a fraud, conjured up by the gifted antiquarian James Macpherson in the midst of a literary revival that celebrated the spirit of Scottish liberty. Eager to learn Gaelic, "the language in which he [Ossian] sung and of possessing his songs in their original form," Jefferson wrote Macpherson's brother Charles to thank James for his "translations." They were the "source of daily and exalted pleasure" for Jefferson, evoking "the tender, and the sublime emotions of the mind were never before so finely wrought up by human hand."[42] In 1782 the marquis de Chastellux visited Monticello and communed with his passionately enthusiastic host over Ossian's poetry. They sat up reading verses aloud to one another.[43] The "rude bard" spoke to Jefferson's "heart" even after it became clear that Ossian was a product of Macpherson's imagination, for his ballads expressed deeper truths, striking "sublime" and authentic chords that continued to resonate for Jefferson.

As he grew older, Jefferson claimed to have outgrown Ossian, though his realization that he and other readers had been duped may have colored his view on the matter. "In earlier life," the new president wrote in June 1801, "I was fond of it, & easily pleased," but if his "powers of fancy . . . declined," his appetite for poetry quickly revived, as his poetry scrapbooks testify, and the uneven quality of the pasted poems demonstrates that he was still "easily pleased."⁴⁴ Perhaps "the mighty wave of public opinion" that made him president signaled that the Spirit of '76 had revived, reassuring him about "the strength of character in our nation."⁴⁵ Or perhaps Jefferson was now more attuned to the unpretentious poems and songs that he regularly harvested in the popular press. The first song that he pasted in his scrapbooks was about him: it enjoined patriotic Americans to "join with heart, and soul, and voice, for JEFFERSON AND LIBERTY," and was followed by three other celebratory songs, including Thomas Paine's "The Land of Love and Liberty" (sung to the tune of "Rule Britannia").

> HAIL great Republic of the world,
> Which rear'd her empire in the west,
> Where fam'd Columbus' flag unfurl'd,
> Gave tortured Europe scenes of rest;
> Be thou forever great and free,
> The land of Love, and Liberty!⁴⁶

Subsequent clippings covered a wider range of patriotic, domestic, and romantic themes that—in conjunction with his massive correspondence—enabled him to listen and hear his constituents' voices.⁴⁷

What did not make it into Jefferson's scrapbooks were the numerous songs, poems, and ballads that ridiculed him and Sally Hemings. Even before James Callender's exposé, and afterward, Jefferson's political opponents targeted the pair with crude verses in black dialect, others done in the style of patriotic songs of the day, and some efforts aspired to classical styles of poetry. John Quincy Adams took time from his duties as senator to make contributions to the repertoire. The offerings mixed political messaging with sexual and racial panic, and used Jefferson's words in the Declaration and *Notes on the State of Virginia* against him. When he wrote that all men were created equal, this meant that black men could have white wives and, in the words of one song, "Massa Jefferson shall hab de black." In 1802 the

Boston Gazette published a long—nine stanzas—ballad to a tune that Jefferson would have known: *Yankee Doodle*.

> When press'd by loads of state affairs
> I seek to sport and dally
> The sweetest solace of my cares
> Is in the lap of Sally

Another, more didactic, poem admonished the patriarch:

> Cease, cease old man, for soon you must,
> Your faithless cunning, pride, and lust. . . .
> Thy tricks with *sooty Sal* give o'er:
> Indulge thy body, Tom, no more;
> But try to save thy *soul*.

Thomas Paine, in America and visiting Jefferson in the early 1800s, was drawn into the fray through the medium of another very long ballad that imagined a love triangle between Jefferson, Hemings, and Paine. The mania for American song and verse bolstered Jefferson's image and, sometimes, it hurt.[48]

Not many volumes of poetry made their way into Jefferson's library, and those that did were largely by his beloved classical poets. The poetry and songs that circulated within the Jefferson-Randolph clan and contributed to Monticello's musical sociability were popular, reflecting and shaping the new nation's emerging character. When he sent his "Jefferson and Liberty" to the new president, the song-ster Michael Fortune emphasized the civic logic of patriotic tunes: "the popular Song has sometimes produced greater effects than the sublimer flights of Poetry" in encouraging good citizens "to support a wise and virtuous Administration, by conciliating the minds of the people." If Jefferson's task was to strengthen the bonds of union through enlightened policies, it was "the Province of the Poet to promote Union by Means of harmony."[49] Familiar tunes with less didactic purpose undoubtedly did more to conciliate and harmonize public opinion, appealing across party battle lines and reminding countrymen of their common history. Jefferson did not look down on "Yankee Doodle" and other folk ditties: according to the literary scholar Jonathan Gross, he "saw such songs as the beginning of a national literature."[50]

Jefferson identified not only with the ancient traditions of the British Isles; he appreciated modern British poetry and music as well. The enthusiastic nation maker pasted poems by Robert Burns, the national poet of Scotland, Walter Scott, and Thomas Campbell, another Scottish poet with Virginia connections, into his scrapbooks. According to Ellen Randolph Coolidge, Jefferson also "sympathized keenly with the Irish patriots." With some trepidation, while she was still living at Monticello, she presented a copy of Thomas Moore's *Irish Melodies* to her grandfather after their American publication in 1815.[51] Moore and Jefferson had encountered each other before, but Jefferson did not realize it. During a visit to the United States in 1803, Moore went to the President's House. As he stood in the foyer, President Jefferson walked past him without speaking to him, thinking the diminutive Irishman—then twenty-four years old—was a boy, perhaps the child of a servant or one sent on an errand. Moore was deeply offended. Later he had some disparaging things to say about the much taller American in the widely reprinted poetic "Epistle to Thomas Hume, Esq., M.D.":

> The patriot, fresh from Freedom's councils come,
> Now pleased retires to lash his slaves at home;
> Or woo, perhaps, some black Aspasia's charms,
> And dream of freedom in his bondsmaid's arms.[52]

The family was upset by Moore's reference to Jefferson's relationship with Sally Hemings, but Jefferson appeared to be unfazed. During his presidency he had pasted a large number of the Irishman's poems in his scrapbook. Now the *Irish Melodies*, Moore's lyrics to old Irish tunes, captivated Jefferson: "the delightful rhythm fell like music on a susceptible ear."[53]

These were the rhythms of the British Isles that gave the founder settlers of Virginia and their descendants a common history and culture. This was the sentimental, patriotic, popular music that Jefferson welcomed into his parlor and that connected him to his neighbors. Significantly, this sentimental conception of the nation did not include the people he enslaved. They did not have a history worth tracing back across the Atlantic. The ever curious man who wanted to follow the truth wherever it led did not, in this case, wish to pursue lines of inquiry that might cause discomfort. Black people, he wrote, had "accurate ears for tune and time, and they have been found capable of imagining a small catch." He also felt that blacks had a better sense of rhythm than whites, but it was an open question "whether they will be equal to the composition of a more extensive run of melody, or of complicated harmony."

Jefferson knew quite well that his slaves and other African Americans could make music. He greatly admired the work of the Scotts, a mixed-race family of musicians, whom he hired to play at his daughter Martha's wedding and again—many decades later—to play for the marquis de Lafayette when he came to visit Monticello in 1824. He could hear the echoes of his ancestors' poetry and music, and imaginatively share the pain and misery of *their* struggles for freedom, but he could not open himself to feel or express this empathy across the color line. When he touched on the subject of blacks and music in *Notes on the State of Virginia*, he proceeded, as he did with other comments about blacks, to recite a form of the catechism of white supremacy: these are the things we are going to say we believe, whether we will actually live by those beliefs or not.

The philosophical Jefferson claimed that blacks could not employ reason, and he spoke patronizingly of his hopes for their intelligence, observing at the age of eighty-one that he had not yet seen a "genius" among the race. Yet the plantation owner Jefferson gave black people tasks that he knew required reason and that he fully expected them to complete—which they did. Of his negative comments about interracial mixture, no more need be said here. He also claimed blacks could not be poets: "Misery is often the parent of the most affecting touches in poetry," the sentimentalist asserted: "Among the blacks is misery enough, God knows, but no poetry." One wonders how people who he later insisted had the "best hearts of any people in the world"[54] would be unable to master a form so famously associated with the heart. As is now well known, the enslaved certainly did master the form and showed their mastery in the development of spirituals or, as W. E. B. Dubois termed them, their "Sorrow Songs." This form of music came after Jefferson's time on earth. If he acted true to form, however, one suspects that, upon hearing such music, he would have stuck with his catechism and denied that they offered any "affecting touches" at all—whether he actually believed this to be true or not.

It was the revolutionary moment that gave rise to a new and inclusive conception of the sovereign people, leveling old regime distinctions and celebrating the common folks' history and culture. Jefferson's passion for music, song, poetry, and language itself took a profound, democratic, vernacular turn, enabling him to imagine the nation in affective and sensual terms. But as he turned toward white folk, he turned away from his slaves. They did not belong in Virginia: it was not their "country." They could never learn to love it (how could they when they had been enslaved there?), and whites could never learn to truly accept blacks. His expatriation scheme imagined them away, across the ocean, severing the transatlantic connections that his romantic nationalism fostered with European ancestors.

Sounds

Music, of course, consists of sounds. Jefferson's near-unbounded enthusiasm for music, his apparent incapacity to live without it, invites consideration of other sounds that were in his life and his reaction to them. Jefferson spent a good amount of his adult life in cities—Philadelphia, Paris, New York, and Washington City. He loved what these cities had to offer—the shops, markets, and forms of entertainment. At the same time, he disliked their basic aspects—the crowds, the noise—all things "pestilential to the morals, the health and liberties of man."[55] Both discordant notes and cacophonous noises

disturbed Jefferson's tranquillity, and they were akin to raw, unre-
strained emotions and destructive conflict. Sonorous music and intelligent conversation restored his equilibrium, fostering the bonds of
sympathy, love, and like-mindedness that made life worth living. It
was a constant struggle to keep noise at bay when he plunged into
the narrow and crowded streets of late eighteenth-century cities. In
the bustle of life in Philadelphia, the new nation's capital for a time,
Jefferson would "lose" himself in "reveries" about his harmonious
life at Monticello in the company of his beloved daughters. "The
discordant noises, the oppressive heats and other disagrement of this
place awaken me through the channel of every sense to very different
scenes." He longed to be home, to exchange "useless debate, and rhetorical declamation" for sweet conversation and beautiful music.[56] The
low, intermittent hum of country sounds—birds singing, dogs bark-
ing, the distant voices of men and women at work along Mulberry
Row, in Monticello mansion, and in the fields down the mountain
were much more to his liking.

For the planter and mapmaker's son, well-chosen vistas revealed
and imposed order on the land, appealing to "Jefferson, the man of
Reason," by inspiring contemplation, reflection, and calculation.
Sounds instead spoke to his feelings, evoking the passage of time,
movement through space, and the transitory experience of life itself.
Jefferson knew the world by using his head, exercising his formidable reasoning powers; he knew himself and identified with other
selves, in joy and sorrow, by listening to his heart. As he told Maria
Cosway, he would exchange all the head's "frigid speculations" for
"the solid pleasure of one generous spasm of the heart." Where would
"our country" be, he asked, if the patriots of 1776 had "calculated"
the new nation's chances by comparing "wealth and numbers" and
not risked everything by following their hearts and being led by the
"pulsations of our warmest blood"?[57]

The day the United States declared its independence, July 4, 1776,
was the most transformative day of Jefferson's life. He remembered
it by the impression it made on his heart, by the "pulsations" he and
his countrymen felt and shared. When drafting the Declaration, the

Virginian—only thirty-three years old—was so concerned with how the text would sound that he offered directions for its oral delivery. He hoped that Americans would hear its resonant phrases—and imagine themselves part of this newborn people—when it was read aloud to them and by them, over and over. The Declaration was like a musical score, enabling Americans to translate abstract principles—the counsels of reason—into heartfelt commitments.[58] The document's "authority," Jefferson insisted late in life, rested on "the harmonizing sentiments of the day." He disclaimed any "originality of principle or sentiment." His modest, self-effacing goal as chief draftsman was to give this "expression of the American mind" the "proper tone and spirit called for by the occasion." Americans, he hoped, could hear themselves speak in the Declaration, and echoes of the people's voice would resound across the generations, keeping the Spirit of '76 alive.[59] Americans would come to experience the passionate meaning of liberty through the sound of his words.

Second Monticello, ca. 1825. (Art Resource)

CHAPTER 8

VISITORS

While Jefferson was in France contemplating his eventual return to Virginia, he imagined rebuilding his mountaintop home according to the highest Parisian standards and filling it with the most fashionable furnishings. He would build a new house free from the unhappy memories associated with its partially built but already deteriorating predecessor at a site resonant with emotional associations. A model of the best the Old World had to offer, this new Monticello would overlook a New World of limitless natural potential. Jefferson himself, standing at the nexus of old and new, would embody both the transit and renewal of civilization in the figure of the "Philosopher" and the "patriot" who, in the words of his eulogist William Wirt, could "look down, with uninterrupted vision, upon the wide expanse of the world around, for which he considered himself born."[1] Wirt's eulogy, given in the House of Representatives on October 19, 1826, three months after Jefferson's death, drew on the accounts of many visitors whose images of Jefferson and of his home were inextricably blended, visitors who came to share the patriarch's view of the world below and beyond. Jefferson built the second Monticello with them in mind.

There were skeptics. Some visitors found Monticello's remote location inaccessible and disagreeable; others noted the disarray of a house and grounds under apparently endless construction. A few political conservatives chided the visionary philosopher, questioning the liberal bona fides of Jefferson and the slaveholding "gentleman Jacobins" who dominated his Republican party. His acerbic kinsman John Randolph mocked "that prince of projectors, St. Thomas of Cantingbury," and the "pilgrims" who came to his shrine.[2] Yet whatever their misgivings—and however bored they might grow during long, quiet intervals in the daily routine—most visitors found both the surrounding landscape and the conversation at Monticello captivating. The patriarch set the tone, replicating the harmonious and refined civility he admired so much in France. The organization of space in and around Monticello, the predictable schedule of daily activities, and the customs and rituals of the house set the stage and provided the cues for everyone's performances. As family members, friends, visitors, and enslaved people played their respective roles, a benevolent harmony seemed to reign. Of course, this was the powerful patriarch's vision of harmony: dissenting views were muted, and controversy, if not suppressed altogether, was certainly not encouraged. As they joined him on his mountaintop, visitors rose above the rudeness and contentiousness of the world below, enacting their better natures by following the scripts Jefferson prepared for them. A visit to Monticello was meant to evoke the progress of civilization itself. The visitor would be "improved" by the refined company and conversation there, even by the house itself and the furnishings and artwork he brought back from Paris.

Visitors came to see Jefferson for many reasons, and he was intensely concerned with, and self-conscious about, the way he was seen. As many commentators across the centuries have observed, Monticello was a kind of self-portrait, Jefferson's lifelong effort to represent himself to the world; it was also, as we have suggested, designed to be a stage for the performances that constituted his ongoing self-construction project. The paradox of selfhood is that it is profoundly social, defining a domain of privacy and autonomy through interactions with others. In terms of contemporaneous social theory, the isolated, uncivilized individual without social connections was a mere barbarian; true autonomy or "independence"—the capacity for reason, forecast, and self-determination—was the ultimate product of the civilizing process. Indeed, Jefferson was convinced that his countrymen had achieved an advanced state of political civilization by breaking from the British Empire. Patriots' claims to liberty and rights authorized an increasingly expansive conception of the citizen and his claims against the state, or any other external authority, and even against society itself. This lofty conception of self was on open display at Monticello; indeed, it depended on that very display.

Jefferson's decision to build his home on a mountaintop lifted him above his Albemarle and Charlottesville neighbors. From the perspective of his fellow planters, this was an irrationally expensive and inconvenient site that complicated plantation management. How does one get water up a mountain? It was a conspicuous way for Jefferson to distance himself from his fellow planters, suggesting that maximizing crops and profits was not his highest priority. His concerns and tastes were loftier than theirs.

This sense of being above worldly concerns showed itself in other aspects of Jefferson's personal presentation. Commenting on the way he dressed, his granddaughter Ellen recalled that her grandfather "did nothing to be in conformity with the fashion of the day." Sometimes to the notice and ridicule of observers, he mixed styles of differing eras, wearing "long waistcoats, when the mode was for very short, white cambric stocks fastened behind with a buckle, when cravats were universal." He kept wearing "red breeches," a style of earlier times, longer than fashion allowed. Though she saw him as "careless" with his clothes, Margaret Smith noted that the material used to make them was always of fine quality.[3] In other words, Jefferson did what he wanted to do. By the time of his presidency, he was so comfortable with, and sure about, his position in the world that he did not have to be "in style." He was beyond that.

Despite his physical remoteness from other dwellings, Jefferson was no recluse. Aspirations for a more cultivated way of life presupposed the appreciation and emulation of his countrymen: the performance of gentility demanded an audience. Yet if the distinctive character he impressed on Monticello attracted a steady stream of visitors from distant locations, particularly during his retirement, Jefferson assiduously guarded his privacy. Visitors were drawn to him but were at the same time kept at some remove. The sage would maintain a seemingly impenetrable "wall of separation" around his own most personal and deeply held beliefs.

Approaching Jefferson

In setting the design of Monticello and its grounds, Jefferson self-consciously shaped visitors' experience of the place, beginning with the circuitous approach to the house. Margaret Bayard Smith thought she would never get there on her visit in 1809.[4] Leaving all traces of civilization behind, Smith and her party at first "could discern nothing but untamed woodland." Jefferson said he intentionally left the "majestic . . . native woods" standing, and the wildness of the scene was accentuated by "the close undergrowth, which [he had] not suffered to be touched." Smith and other visitors gradually ascended, with vistas opening up on the world below. "Of prospect I have a rich profusion and offering itself at every point of the compass," Jefferson told the prominent horticulturist William Hamilton of Philadelphia, with "mountains distant & near, smooth & shaggy, single & in ridges, a little river hiding itself among the hills so as to shew in lagoons only, cultivated grounds under the eye and two small villages." Because all this might be "a satiety"—too much for the untutored visitor to absorb at once—Jefferson composed a series of landscape views, deploying thickets to frame "the scenes as you advance on your way."[5] Moving upward, the progress of civilization came into view, from distant mountains to the villages of Charlottesville and Milton and culminating in Jefferson's Monticello. For the Bostonian George Ticknor, the first professor of Spanish and French at Harvard, "the ascent of this steep, savage hill, was as pensive and slow as Satan's ascent to Paradise."[6]

Jefferson's landscape aesthetic framed visitors' views of the man himself. Rising to his level, visitors could see how far they had come, through nature to new heights of civility. The British visitor Adam Hodgson "had traced man through every successive stage of civilization" in his travels across the United States, "from the roaming savage, whose ideas scarcely extend beyond the narrow circle of his daily wants," to the "statesman" and "philosopher" at Monticello "who has learnt to grasp the complicated interests of society" and "contemplate the system of the universe."[7] Signs of improvement in the landscape below were auguries of the enlightened and prosperous future that Jefferson had envisioned in *Notes on the State of Virginia*, with his inventories of abundant natural resources sketching the booster's aesthetic of development. When the duc de La Rochefoucauld-Liancourt visited in 1796, the view from Monticello did not yet match Jefferson's vision. "The disproportion existing between the cultivated lands and those which are still covered with forests as ancient as the globe" was too great, the French visitor wrote, and "the aid of fancy" was still "required to complete the enjoyment of this magnificent view." Only by seeing this wild scenery through Jefferson's eyes would it be possible to "picture to us those plains and mountains such as population and culture will render them in a greater or smaller number of years."[8] In later times visitors needed less assistance from "fancy" as they ascended the mountain, looked out on an improved landscape, and looked toward Monticello and its patriarch.

The winding, roundabout approach to Monticello, rising through old forest on a rough track, accentuated the juxtaposition of nature and civilization. Mrs. Smith remarked on the striking "contrast" between "the sides of the mountain covered with wood, with scarcely a speck of cultivation" and Monticello's "summit, crowned with a noble pile of building, surrounded by an immence lawn, & shaded here & there with some fine trees."[9] This was not the usual approach to a great plantation house, typically sited by a river and convenient to the neighborhood it dominated. Prosperous Virginia planters displayed their wealth and power in grand houses that Jefferson thought in lamentably bad taste. "The genius of architecture seems to have shed its maledictions over this land," he complained in *Notes on Virginia*, before he had seen any good buildings in person and when he drew his own inspiration from the books of the architect Andreas Palladio and his followers.[10] Jefferson's fellow planters were clearly insecure about their recently achieved and often tenuous status. They signaled their social preeminence by directing traffic through domesticated, productive landscapes—perhaps along ceremonial, tree-lined avenues—toward the imposing façades of their big houses and their village-like dependencies.

Jefferson's Monticello made a far different statement. The house was *not* meant to be seen from a distance; it was separated from its neighborhood by a "wilderness" buffer; and most of the productive activities that sustained the plantation household were scattered in semi-autonomous quarter farms across his 5,000-acre domain and in distant, disconnected plantations. Visitors might wonder why Jefferson had chosen this inaccessible, far-from-central site. As they ascended, they were not looking toward the house. Instead, he directed their attention toward the horizon, arranging "thickets as that they may have the effect of vista in various directions," and framing a succession of landscape views that led Mrs. Smith and other impressionable visitors to "sublime" transports: "Below me extended for above 60 miles round, a country cover'd with woods, plantations & houses; beyond arose the blue mountains, in all their grandeur!"[11] Visitors came to see Jefferson, the builder of his seemingly modest mountaintop retreat, not a great aristocratic estate house that inspired awestruck deference. Joining Jefferson on his mountain, visitors would look away, sharing his perspective on the "grandeur" of nature, "wonderfully lifted above most mortals."[12]

The most striking thing about Monticello was the enormous cost of preparing an inaccessible site and building the house to the architect's high and ever-rising standard. Only a great planter with ample resources could afford to make this anti-aristocratic gesture, and only someone with the most refined taste could so self-consciously and openly assert his social and cultural superiority over his fellow planters. In 1796, as Jefferson began to reconstruct Monticello, La Rochefoucauld-Liancourt offered an astute commentary on his host's cultural ambitions. "According to its first plan," the noble French visitor reported, Monticello was "infinitely superior to all other houses in America, in point of taste and convenience." Yet that plan, formulated before the provincial planter had traveled abroad, was derived from exemplars of "taste and the fine arts in books only." Now that Jefferson had seen "models" of refined architecture in his European travels, the plans for the second Monticello that he shared with his aristocratic guest promised something much better. At its completion (optimistically predicted "before the end of next year") "his house will certainly deserve to be ranked with the most pleasant mansions in France and England."[13]

Monticello was an ambitious project, which was still in progress many years after La Rochefoucauld-Liancourt's visit. Columns on the original, dismantled west façade were not reinstalled until 1822, by which time the house seemed "rather old and going to decay."[14] By that time, visitors had been remarking on the dilapidation and decay for years. After Jefferson's death it almost seemed as if the house itself had died. "The first thing" that struck John H. Latrobe, son of the renowned architect Benjamin Latrobe, was "the utter ruin and desolation of everything."[15] If visitors at this time were predisposed to Romantic hyperbole, they had ample material with which to work, for the place seemed haunted by its departed "genius." But while Jefferson lived, it was his vision of what Monticello might *eventually* look like that captivated visitors, not the noise and confusion of construction or intimations of mortality in his Sisyphean struggle against decay. The visionary looked forward, and visitors shared his perspective.

Jefferson's conception of "natural aristocracy," freed from ties to the old regime and lighting the way forward for a self-governing people was eloquently articulated in his building project. Monticello was a private home situated in nature, modeling the higher levels of civilization to which true aristocrats aspired.[16] Nature was a protean concept for Jefferson, at once signifying the original source of his inspiration while illuminating the ultimate destination of human development. "The natural aristocracy," he wrote his old revolutionary comrade John Adams in 1813, "I consider as the most precious gift of nature for the instruction, the trusts, and government in society." The revolution had demolished the pretensions of "an artificial aristocracy founded on wealth and birth," enabling the virtuous and talented—worthy people like Jefferson and Adams—to rise to the top.[17]

The comparison of "natural" and "artificial" resonated with a younger Jefferson's vaulting ambitions. That Jefferson, setting his and the new nation's sights on promoting the progress of civilization, was no leveler. Quite to the contrary, his conception of nature enabled him both to transcend his provincial origins and to assert his equality with metropolitan counterparts as citizens of the great republic of letters. Jefferson recognized that many of the privileged and wellborn aristocrats with whom he mixed on such familiar terms in Europe could also legitimately claim a place in the "first class" of natural aristocrats. After all, their privilege enabled them to cultivate the "virtues and talents" with which nature had endowed them; they had seized the opportunity that so many of their class squandered as they reveled in ill-gotten wealth and illegitimate power. Titled aristocrats redeemed themselves by recognizing nature's gifts in their fellow men of merit, wherever they might be found—even atop a mountain in provincial Virginia. Jefferson thus overcame the stereotype that consigned provincials to a supposed inferior status.

William Wirt's eulogy of Jefferson presented a stylized image of first encounters with the natural aristocrat, the philosopher and statesman who had played such an important role in overthrowing the British imperial regime. The visitor would "be met by the tall, and animated, and stately figure of the patriot himself—his countenance beaming with intelligence and benignity, and his outstretched hand, with its strong and cordial pressure, confirming the courteous welcome of his lips."[18] In truth, Jefferson might not have been there to greet the visitor, given his faithful adherence to his daily routine, and he might not have been smiling. Many visitors, beginning with his great friend the marquis de Chastellux in 1782, found Jefferson at "first appearance serious, nay even cold."[19]

As the years wore on, others would note that Jefferson's initial coldness would transform itself to warmth as he got to know more about the person to whom he was speaking. When points of connection were made, he could be an extremely amiable companion. Isaac Granger said that Jefferson "bowed to" everyone he met, thus prefacing every encounter with a polite performance of good manners that seemed increasingly archaic in his later years.[20] According to his grandson Jeff Randolph, Jefferson's "manners were of that polished school of the Colonial Government," though others marked their foreignness as "French." "Under no circumstances" would he violate "any of those minor conventional observances which constitute the well-bred gentleman, courteous and considerate to all persons." This included African Americans. "On riding out with [his grandfather] when a lad," Jeff recalled, "we met with a negro who bowed to us; he returned his bow, I did not; turning to me he asked, 'do you permit a negro to be more of a gentleman than yourself?' "[21]

Good manners had an equalizing effect, facilitating cross-class and even cross-race exchanges, yet they simultaneously reinforced social distinctions: the "condescending" slave owner, looking down from his horse, and the "negro"—probably a slave—looking up at a member of the master class, both knew how to act their appropriate parts. Jefferson's conception of mastery was predicated on self-regulation as well as social domination. Isaac Granger was an astute observer of how Jefferson regulated himself in encounters with white fellow citizens, maintaining his distance with a preemptive bow. He conversed "with his arms folded," perhaps an additional method of social defense. Alternatively, the very active long-limbed statesman, who was used to writing, holding the reins of a horse, playing the violin, or just tinkering, may simply have needed to find something to do with his hands and arms when they were not in active use.[22]

Enlightenment conceptions of the progress of civilization emphasized the role of politeness and refinement—or artifice—in subduing violent impulses. Refined manners were certainly artificial, but this was artifice that was true to—and improved on—human nature, not the luxurious, corrupting, and *unnatural* artificiality of court life in the ancien régime. If good manners were by definition artificial, the gracious host's challenge was to use them to put his guests at ease. As a younger master of Monticello, Jefferson may have gone too far in accommodating a guest. When Archibald Cary, a prominent member of the Virginia gentry, visited Jefferson and his wife, he took liberties that one could not imagine anyone's taking after Jefferson came into his own as an established figure. In addition to hitting slaves at Monticello at will, Cary would go into the kitchen and inquire about the dinner menu. If it was not to his liking, he would demand a change, requiring the Jeffersons, and any other guests, to wait for dinner until the new meal was cooked. Whether Jefferson was employing what he considered good manners—or wisely appeasing a madman who happened to be higher on the social pecking order—is an open question, though Isaac Granger's apparent shock at these events suggests that Cary was unusual among the people who visited the mountain; the very opposite of artificial, he was all too real. To avoid a confrontation Jefferson, not yet the renowned patriarch, simply gave way to Cary's deplorable lack of manners.[23]

Many years later the White House confidant John Bernard described his "good friend" Jefferson as a "citizen of the world" who understood that "manners have no general standard" and "that an excess of artificiality is as opposed to human happiness as utter barbarity." An exaggerated manner betrayed local attachments and thus underscored national differences: "refinement in France is frivolity in Holland, and frankness in Holland is boorishness in France." The cosmopolitan Jefferson passed the crucial "test of general consideration of others," recognizing and cultivating a common standard of civility.[24] Jefferson's manner set the tone for exchanges that would secure the integrity and self-respect of conversing guests, keeping them at a civil distance from each other, and thus preventing a descent into "utter barbarity." The civil society over which the benevolent patriarch presided constituted an idealized image of the emerging republican order that the American Revolution had initiated. Ascending the mountain, visitors recapitulated the stages of historical development the Scottish philosophers described, rising out of a state of nature in order to fulfill their own better natures.

As visitors looked up, Jefferson looked down. The patriarch's ability to *condescend* to his many visitors—kin, friends, political allies, admiring countrymen, strangers, and opportunists—was critical to his mastery. Safe behind the ramparts of good manners and armed with his unequaled store of knowledge about the world of nature and the affairs of men, Jefferson demonstrated an extraordinary genius for pleasing others. "His countenance was always mild and pleasant," his former overseer Edmund Bacon recollected, long after Jefferson's death: "you never saw it ruffled."[25] He was "so condescending and naturally pleasing in his manners and address," the visitor John Edwards Caldwell remarked, "that no person, at all acquainted with him, can feel in his presence perplexity and embarrassment."[26]

The magic of condescension was that it simultaneously dissolved and reinforced distinctions, enabling social superiors to engage with those beneath them in affective, or what we would call "human," terms. In the time of the "Colonial Government" when Jefferson's old-fashioned manners were formed, condescension was a conventional lubricant of social relations: the complementary ethos of what the upper class would have considered to be voluntary, unforced deference to the "better sort." This social arrangement facilitated cross-class mobilization during the imperial crisis. In the new republican era, however, condescension and deference could no longer be assumed. Jefferson and other radical republicans railed against the assumption that a privileged few were born to rule the masses: the artificial "aristocracy" of the old regime had to be uprooted and demolished. This did not mean, however, that all distinctions should be abolished and that all men were in fact equal: Jefferson, Adams, and their fellow revolutionaries had earned the deference that succeeding generations owed to their fathers. "I belonged to" the revolutionary generation, Jefferson wrote in 1816, "and labored with it. It deserved well of its country."[27]

Self-described aristocrats like Jefferson (who was really a member of the gentry class) played a crucial role in founding and sustaining the new republican order. The great man deserved deference for many reasons: his knowledge was so comprehensive—"from the details of the humblest mechanic art, up to the highest summit of

science"—that he could, by a process of synecdoche, be identified
with nature itself. Grateful Americans revered the "Philosopher"
who helped them grasp their country's potential: for visitors who had
basked in his knowledge, "the *terra incognita* of the human understanding" was now illuminated, made "familiar" like a "garden walk"
on the mountaintop. So too, Americans honored "the patriot" who
"could—literally and figuratively—look down, with uninterrupted
vision, upon the wide expanse of the world around," serving as "sen-
tinel, over the rights and liberties of man."[28] Wirt and his patriotic
countrymen could look up to Jefferson without diminishing themselves. Encounters with the man were uplifting, raising visitors in
their own estimation.

Monticello

The end result of the ascent up the mountain was the view of the
house. From the outside, Monticello was ostentatiously modest, with
window treatments that disguised its upper stories and created the
illusion of a single-story building. Jefferson adapted his fenestration
from the much more imposing Hôtel de Salm in Paris, the residence
of a German prince designed by the prominent architect Pierre
Rousseau and completed in 1787, as the smitten American looked
on. Monticello's façade signaled that the house was a refined gentleman's private retreat, a site of domesticity where visitors would be
treated like family members. Though the entire complex would grow
to contain forty-three rooms, thirty-three in the house itself, it did
not give the impression of a big house where the master reaffirmed
his exalted position in a hierarchy of orders among whites by staging
rituals of deference and subordination at odds with the new republic's
egalitarian ethos. Monticello was not meant to diminish awestruck
visitors, but rather to arouse their interest in what interested Jefferson,
preparing them for encounters with the great man.

The absence of a grand staircase reinforced the leveling message
of Monticello's fenestration. The great man would not descend to his
visitors, nor would they be reminded of his superior status as they

ascended to him. If Jefferson was not physically present to do the honors, the Indian Hall, or entry room, introduced guests to their host through the display of art, artifacts, and natural objects that signaled the extraordinary range of his interests. This was a "cabinet of curiosities" that complemented an aristocrat's private library, displaying the erudition that gained the cognoscenti citizenship in the republic of letters. Jefferson thus leveled himself upward, claiming an equal status with fellow citizens of this virtual republic, regardless of their exalted rank or superior genealogy. What was most remarkable about Jefferson's Indian Hall was its accessibility to so many ordinary, often uninvited visitors. "The concourse of strangers which continually crouded the house" nearly drove his daughter Martha, the mistress of the house, to despair. Her father assured her, these visitors were *not* the "loungers" or hangers-on who infested "the houses of the wealthy in general." Monticello pilgrims were worthy fellow citizens who respected Jefferson and aspired, as he did, to improve themselves. Their presence validated his status as a natural aristocrat, showing "the general esteem which we have been all our lives trying to merit."[29] In return for the people's esteem, Jefferson offered enlightenment, beginning with the Indian Hall. Maps and clocks, Indian artifacts, natural history specimens, busts and portraits of heroes and villains situated attentive visitors in time and place, inviting them into Jefferson's world.

Jefferson eschewed the hierarchical organization of great aristocratic homes, with the status of a visitor signified by progressive access, through a succession of rooms, to the semisacred person of the great man himself.[30] Visitors who arrived without letters of introduction or plausible equivalents might not penetrate beyond the Indian Hall and had to be satisfied with poking about the grounds and peeping through windows. Meanwhile, their more fortunate counterparts proceeded through ingeniously designed double doors into the parlor, dining room, and tearoom. The movement of one door was synchronized with the other by an invisible mechanism, making passage into the parlor seem effortless. The public rooms were all on the same level. The intimate scale of these rooms and their openness to each other encouraged familiar conversation. At the same time, thanks to a placement of windows that maximized natural light and the generous distribution of artificial lighting, the company could withdraw into silent reading and other more solitary pursuits without withdrawing from each other. Being alone together was a hallmark of the new regime of bourgeois "comfort" that the historian Jack Crowley has brilliantly delineated.[31]

For the duration of their stays, visitors virtually became members of the family. Domesticity did not necessarily connote intimacy, however, for visitors and family members alike were subject to Jefferson's daily routines and rituals, and their movement in the house was strictly regulated. "Everything is done with such regularity," George Ticknor ruefully noted, "when you know how one day is filled, . . . you know how it is with the others." The family gathered at fixed times for meals: "At eight o'clock the first bell is rung in the great hall, and at nine the second summons you to the breakfast-room, where you find everything ready"; then, "at half past three the great bell rings, and those who are disposed resort to the drawing-room, and the rest go to the dining-room at the second call of the bell, which is at four o'clock." After a "choice" dinner "served in the French style," the cloth was removed and "wine was set on the table." "The ladies sat until about six, then retired, but returned with the tea-tray a little before seven, and spent the evening with the gentlemen; which was always pleasant, for they are obviously accustomed to join in the conversation, however high the topic might be."[32]

The spaces where domestic life was staged and performed were designed to facilitate agreeable interactions, at table or in the parlor, making conversation or music. Jefferson was the central figure in these domestic ensembles (though the wrist injury he suffered in Paris kept him on the musical sidelines). But the maestro had a gift for flattering his "familiar friends" and beloved family members, acknowledging and respecting their equality and autonomy. "His cheerfulness and affection were the warm sun in which his family all basked and were invigorated," his granddaughter Virginia Randolph Trist recalled: "cheerfulness, love, benevolence, wisdom, seemed to animate his whole form. His face beamed with them."[33] Everything was supposed to run smoothly and harmoniously at Monticello, following familiar scripts and scores. The apparent absence of enslaved people in visitors' accounts was also comforting: the "servants" were offstage, in the wings, as the players in these domestic scenes well knew. Dumb waiters and revolving service doors spared visitors the experience of dissonant rituals of rank and servility, a function they would have served, as they did in France, even if Jefferson employed free labor. Jefferson often dished out the food himself.

It would be a mistake to think that visitors to Monticello did not know they were on a full-fledged slave plantation. Jefferson's fields were scattered down the mountain in areas that have now been reclaimed by the forest, but the evidence of slavery was all around. As his visitors strolled the grounds around the house, they would have seen people coming from and going to their labors, perhaps heard the sounds of work. Mulberry Row, where Monticello's enslaved domestics and artisans lived in small cabins, was adjacent to Jefferson's rooms on the south side of the mansion, as were some of his workshops. Indeed, Jefferson took visitors to look at his plantation factories. And enslaved people moved through the house doing various tasks for Jefferson's family and the visitors themselves. Jefferson could not have hidden slavery if he tried.

There were also supposed "mysteries." The most famous had to do with the person who connected Jefferson to enslaved people in the closest possible way. Although no letters of visitors mentioning encounters with Sally Hemings have yet surfaced, letters do refer to her and the situation at Monticello, which should not be a surprise. It is safe to say that after Callender's exposé in 1802, and the fallout from it, anyone who had been paying attention to Jefferson's life would have heard of her. Margaret Smith, who perished the thought that Jefferson could have had an enslaved mistress, had heard about Sally Hemings when she visited Monticello in 1809. It seems unlikely that Smith or any of his visitors would have asked Jefferson about Hemings outright, or that he would have brought up the subject. And then there was the question of Jefferson's marital status. He was widowed at thirty-nine, was thought of as rich, powerful, charming, intelligent, and—by some—handsome; why had not the white women of Virginia swarmed?

Jared Sparks, a New Englander who had entertained hopes of writing a life of Jefferson, but ended up authoring a life of George Washington, wrote to Henry Randall in 1859 about the time he "passed a day" at Monticello in 1820. Sparks referred to the Jefferson and Hemings story, saying that he "was a good deal taken by certain resemblances among some of the members of the household." In 1820 Beverley Hemings was twenty-two years old; Harriet, seventeen; Madison and Eston, fifteen and twelve, respectively. They were all said to resemble Jefferson, one of the brothers so much so that if seen from a short distance, he could be mistaken for the patriarch. Visitors other than Sparks who saw the siblings no doubt wondered about this matter, too. The question hung in the air during Sparks's visit and stayed with him for many years. Sparks said he was "exceedingly glad to see it [the 'mystery'] explained," telling Randall that his "explanation seems to [have] put that matter on the right footing." He was referring to Randall's discussion of why Sally Hemings's children looked like Thomas Jefferson. Randall had accepted and, apparently, spread the story Jeff Randolph had told him about the Hemings children's paternity. Randolph, while admitting that all of the Hemings children looked like Jefferson, explained the phenomenon by saying that they were the children of Jefferson's nephew Peter Carr. Sparks's expression of his great joy upon finally getting an answer shows the level of his concern about the matter.[34]

Elijah Fletcher, a New Englander on his way to Lynchburg—and on his way to slaveholding himself—visited Monticello in 1811. Jefferson's neighbors in Charlottesville told him a number of negative "anecdotes" about Jefferson, and he raised the issue of Hemings:

> The story of black Sal is no farce—That he cohabits with her and has a number of children by her is a sacred truth—and the worst of it is, he keeps the same children slaves—an unnatural crime which is very common in these parts—This conduct may

receive a little palliation when we consider that such proceed-
ings are so common that they cease here to be disgraceful.

Northerners like Sparks and Fletcher knew that men in families who
had servants sometimes impregnated servant girls. Those girls would
usually be sent away. Certainly they and their children would not
remain on the premises with the father of their child, or children,
living among his "legitimate" family. Southerners who visited Monticello would have found the interracial mixing there familiar, for
it was one of the features of slavery. But even they were surprised
by Jefferson's failure to be more circumspect. He could have moved
Hemings and their children off Monticello, putting them out of sight
of his legal family and visitors. It is doubtful he ever thought to do so.
He built his house on a mountain to suit himself.[35]

In his famous indictment of Virginians' "manners" in his *Notes*,
Jefferson condemned the "perpetual exercise of the most boisterous
passions" that characterized "the whole commerce between master and slave."[36] But he was sensitive to more subtle, less passionate,
though nonetheless discordant manifestations of mastery and servility
in the rituals of domestic life. One of the few comments by visitors
on the way Jefferson dealt with the enslaved testifies to the seriousness
with which he approached the task of attempting to wear down the
inevitable rough edges of relations between the enslaved and those
who enslaved them. "How gentle, how humble, how kind," were
the master's "manners," Margaret Bayard Smith exclaimed: "His
meanest slave must feel; as if it were a father instead of a master who
addressed him, when he speaks."[37] For modern readers, Smith's con-
flation of "father" and "master" points toward proslavery paternalism; for Smith, it was comforting to imagine that Jefferson's mastery
was predicated on the same good—and far from boisterous—manners
that governed domestic life at Monticello, and to which she and other
friends and family members so willingly submitted.

We see all that was behind this—the legally enforced labor of the
enslaved and the culturally imposed domestic labor of white female
family members that made it all possible. Visitors, on the other hand,

experienced a seemingly effortless, spontaneous harmony that enabled them to imagine (and perform) an idealized republican, consensual community. Visitors and family members were equally accessible to each other in shared domestic spaces; in his sanctum sanctorum Jefferson was accessible to no one. His daughter Martha used the first room to the left of the Indian Hall, in the private wing of the house, as a schoolroom to teach her children and as an office, buffering Jefferson's library, study, and bedroom from family as well as guests. His privacy was not perfect: louvered blinds and ornamental "porticles" on the promenade outside his windows did not completely block the view of curious interlopers; slaves discreetly went about their housekeeping; and urgent business might bring a family member or overseer into his bedroom or study. And though the library was generally off limits, Jefferson occasionally invited honored guests to join him there in examining choice volumes. All the while it was universally understood that he was not to be bothered. "We would not speak out of a whisper," Virginia recalled, "lest we should disturb him."[38]

Conversation

The courteous welcome set the tone as visiting "pilgrims" gravitated to the hospitable host. Jefferson's conversation "was as simple and unpretending as nature itself," Wirt marveled: "and then came that charm of manner and conversation that passes all description—so cheerful, so unassuming—so free, and easy, and frank, and kind, and gay—that even the young, and overawed, and embarrassed visiter at once forgot his fears, and felt himself by the side of an old and familiar friend."[39] Wirt was far from alone in attesting to Jefferson's power as a conversationalist in intimate settings and on a one-to-one basis. He had the gift of being able to speak to people at whatever level he found them, a feat achieved, in part, by expressing interest in what others were doing. This was effective whether he was talking to a workingman, fellow member of the gentry, an enslaved person, or a politician. Conversational exchanges at the dinner table at Monticello were, of course, more exclusive, assuming the equality of participants:

the enslaved were either absent or they receded, ever so discreetly, into the background. While the philosopher poured "out instruction, like light from an inexhaustible solar fountain, he seemed continually to be asking, instead of giving information." Visitors were more likely to reveal themselves than to discover anything about their host, with his genius for deflecting controversial—and therefore revealing—topics of conversation. Jefferson managed to dispense lots of information without being particularly informative about himself.[40]

Unlike Parisian salons before the French Revolution, Jefferson's parlor would not be the arena for the various forms of "excessive artificiality," the dazzling displays of wit, subversive sallies against the established order, and malicious, reputation-destroying gossip that barely disguised and inevitably provoked competition and conflict. Jefferson would have none of this. His drawing useful information from his guests and keeping to certain topics enabled them to contribute to the common store of practical knowledge. Jefferson and his guests were not simply modeling higher standards of civility in a still relatively backward new country; they were also glimpsing the complementary and interdependent pursuits of happiness that propelled a dynamic and improving political economy. Commerce among equals was "sweet," enlightened savants taught. For revolutionary republicans, the market offered a liberating alternative to the coercion and command of hierarchical regimes in which one's status determined one's rights—including, of course, the institution of slavery, the old regime's most vicious legacy in Jefferson's Virginia.[41] The exchanges among guests at Monticello were devoid of strenuous argumentation and strife, making the home an ideal model for the world at large.

Jefferson projected an image of self-mastery to visitors that was most conducive to free and civil exchanges. "In conversation," the great lawyer and then congressman Daniel Webster reported in 1824, "Mr. Jefferson is easy and natural, and apparently not ambitious." He was "not loud" and did not seek to command the "general attention," instead usually addressing "the person next to him" on topics suited to "the character and feelings of the auditor."[42] Thomas Jefferson Randolph recalled that his grandfather "never indulged in controversial conversation." He was, rather, a good "listener": the closer a visitor came, the more Jefferson would seek to draw him or her out, deflecting conversation away from himself. "If any one expressed a decided opinion differing from his own," Jeff wrote, his grandfather "made no reply, but changed the subject."[43] Direct argument, Jefferson believed, too rarely changed people's minds. Instead, it tended to make the combatants ever more set in their opinions. Thus it was a waste of time that simply fomented deeper discord.

Jefferson's aversion to conflict compelled him not only to direct conversation into safe channels; it helped check the impulse to dominate that Jefferson believed was universal—and which he therefore recognized in himself. "Differences of opinion, and party differences" reflected irrepressible divisions into the "many" and the "few" that characterized human history "from the first establishment of governments, to the present day," Jefferson wrote John Adams in 1813: "the terms of whig and tory belong to natural, as well as civil history."[44] A still greater threat was that power would be concentrated in the hands of a single tyrant, for "timid men" notoriously preferred "the calm of despotism to the boisterous sea of liberty."[45] There would be no party strife at Monticello, nor would the master exercise his prerogative to command the same submission from visitors that he demanded of his enslaved dependents. Paradoxically, men could fulfill their better natures—gender is significant here—only if they submitted to an internalized self-discipline and a highly refined regime of politeness and civility. What a "curiosity" Monticello was, Richard Rush, then James Madison's attorney general, exclaimed in 1816: set in nature, it was "artificial in a high degree; in many respects superb."[46] Jefferson imagined Monticello to be a place where the "natural aristocrat," the living embodiment of civilization's progress, would hold court, showing how enlightened republicans could overcome their barbarous natures and transcend conflict. Self-mastery was the predicate of this progress.

If Jefferson rarely participated in contentious and divisive arguments about politics or other topics that might lead him to express controversial opinions or principles, and his gracious manner undoubtedly discouraged others from doing so, he certainly did not bare his soul, even to family members or close friends. "To a disposition ardent, affectionate & communicative," reported Margaret Bayard Smith, "he joins manners timid, even to bashfulness & reserved even to coldness."[47] He certainly would never have revealed any self-doubt or inner conflict to those who came to see him and enjoy his hospitality. If acting true to form, he was more likely to rebuff overtures to intimacy that would have revealed any turmoil, and instead concentrated on orchestrating conversations that made visitors feel good about themselves. "Above all men," Mrs. Smith wrote, Jefferson had "the art of pleasing, by making each pleased with himself."[48] Yet she confessed that there were limits to this pleasure: "there was a natural and quiet dignity in his demeanour that often produced a degree of restraint in those who conversed with him, unfavorable to that free interchange of thoughts and feelings which constitute the greatest charm of social life."[49] Jefferson was warm and friendly with those outside of his family—up to a point. The reflections on Patrick Henry that he wrote in 1814 are deeply revelatory of his mind-set on these matters:

> whenever the courts were closed for the winter season, he [Henry] would make up a party of poor hunters of his neighborhood, would go off with them to the piney woods of Fluvanna, & pass weeks in hunting deer, of which he was passionately fond, sleeping under a tent, before a fire, wearing the same shirt the whole time, & covering all the dirt of his dress with a hunting shirt.[50]

Jefferson's language makes this type of activity—this kind of closeness with "poor hunters" for weeks at a time, "wearing the same shirt" every day—seem almost hellish. It might be one thing to converse with such people, give them the right to vote, but this sort of intimacy would be out of the question. While Jefferson did go fox hunting with his wife, there is no reason to think that he would have engaged in Henry's style of hunting even with members of his own class. Gouverneur Morris, who observed Jefferson when they were in Paris, was right: Jefferson much preferred the intimacy of family.

THERE IS EVIDENCE that, as close as Jefferson was to them, members of his own family were unable, at times, to read his emotions effectively. He was, apparently, very good at keeping his feelings for enslaved people carefully hidden from his white family and, perhaps, from everyone. While on a visit to Poplar Forest during his retirement, his valet Burwell Colbert, a grandson of Elizabeth Hemings and nephew of Sally Hemings, became gravely ill. His granddaughters Ellen and Virginia Randolph reported to their mother that they had never seen Jefferson so frantic and upset. He who did not trust physicians waited nervously for the doctor to come and attend to the stricken Colbert. The girls seriously worried about what would happen to their grandfather should he wake up and find that Colbert had died during the night. The depth of the feelings he showed during these days utterly shocked them. Ellen said she had known he cared for Colbert, but she had no idea how much.

Far more interesting than Jefferson's attachment to Colbert is the fact that his granddaughters, particularly Ellen, who watched him like a hawk, were taken aback by Jefferson's response to Colbert's illness. Eighteenth-century males were not regularly given to showing their emotions, as society placed a premium on self-control. And one certainly did not wish to be seen as controlled by feelings for one's supposed inferiors. This defied the natural order of things. Indeed, when the danger had passed and Jefferson was back in control of himself, he reported to Martha Randolph on Colbert's ordeal in a fashion more in keeping with that of a gentleman speaking of a subordinate. He was terse: "We have been near losing Burwell . . . but he has got about again and is now only very weak." He retreated to a zone that shielded his most intimate thoughts and feelings.[51]

Madison Hemings described Jefferson's affect by saying he was "uniformly kind" to everyone, noting that "he was not in the habit of showing" him and his siblings "partiality or fatherly affection," though he did openly show affection toward his legal white grand-children who were part of the same age cohort as Hemings and his siblings. Then Hemings goes on to mention all the ways that his and his siblings' lives were different from those of other enslaved children, different in ways that allowed them to be "measurably happy" as they grew up. It is very likely that Jefferson went as far as his sense of social propriety and loyalty to his legal white family would allow in showing "partiality" and, perhaps, his understanding of "fatherly affection" to the Hemings siblings. Placing his sons under the tutelage of his best enslaved artisan, John Hemings, and then spending a good deal of his free time with them was certainly evidence of a sense of connection to the brothers that Jefferson would not let himself express in more conventional ways.

Hemings, quite naturally, was speaking comparatively—contrasting the playful grandfather with the "kind" but impartial father. Though he clearly understood the rules of nineteenth-century law, and the rules of race on the question of family, Hemings would not be human if he (and his siblings) never once wished that things could be different. As Lucia Stanton has noted, Hemings mentioned that the man he called "father" kept the promise he made to his mother in France to free all of their children, even as he disparaged other white people who failed to keep their promises to black people.[52]

IF JEFFERSON'S CONVERSATIONAL exchanges did not elicit strong statements of principle or encourage intimacy, his interest in the expertise and accomplishments of his guests was "pleasing." Visitors were flattered to be so singled out. This individual attention set them apart from each other, preempting "party formation" in Jefferson's parlor. Assuming, of course, that everyone was a good and principled republican, inconsequential differences of opinion were muted. No matter how crowded Monticello might be, Jefferson would not see the citizens who gathered in his home as akin to the sycophantic dependents and hangers-on who gravitated to great houses and county courts: they were not a "mob" in which individual identity was obliterated.

Visitors were drawn to Monticello to share in the phenomenon of the place and in the prestige of having conversed with Jefferson and having him tell them things. Most agreed that his erudition was remarkable. The author Joseph Delaplaine celebrated the "freedom" with which Jefferson shared "his stores of knowledge," similar to the way "nature unfolds her bounties."[53] As the end of his life neared, Margaret Bayard Smith echoed these encomia, marveling at "a store of intellectual wealth . . . which falls to the lot of so few." How many of those who possessed this "treasure," she wondered, could claim Jefferson's "faculty of imparting it to others?"[54] These characteristic comments all emphasized the *value* of what Jefferson gave to fellow conversationalists. As Mrs. Smith explained, "Mr. J. has not only the sterling gold, but has the baser coins, which afford an easy currency of thought, and are so important in social intercourse."[55] The topics that circulated among his guests were often inspired by the commodities on display in Monticello's public spaces. The man and his house opened up new vistas for aspirational consumers as well as eager students of all ages. Furniture and furnishings modeled good taste (though as the years passed they might have seemed increasingly unfashionable and a bit faded); conversation pieces—paintings and prints, art objects and artifacts—spurred interesting exchanges. Monticello brought people together, but conversational exchanges at the same time defined them apart, in relation to each other, reaffirming their autonomy and independence.

Jefferson drew on a wealth of knowledge in conversation. He also deployed an array of sometimes playful rhetorical techniques that belie his reputation as a humorless, self-serious "philosopher." "Mr. Jefferson tells large stories," a skeptical John Quincy Adams told his diary in 1804, and "you never can be an hour in this man's company without something of the marvellous, like these stories,"[56] though at other times Adams was bored with what he thought were Jefferson's too frequent disquisitions on wine. George Ticknor was struck, after visiting Monticello in 1815, with the way his host combined an "appearance of sobriety and cool reason" with a love of paradox. Clearly, many visitors found him amusing if not playful—though some may have wondered whether they always got the joke. Jefferson's storytelling and mastery of the language were engaging, enabling him to draw listeners into his orbit. But, as was the case with his manner, he also used language as a self-protective shield. Exactly what this great exponent of transparency and "natural language" meant to say was not necessarily "self-evident."[57] His growing disenchantment with novels—whose didactic value he had emphasized in his earlier years—and his insistence on the superiority of well-documented historical writing reflected a skilled practitioner's awareness of the potential dangers of language. In the privacy of their homes, women might read sentimental novels without risking their virtue. But on the other, public side of the gender boundary, men had to be able to secure themselves against the seductive wiles of subjectivity and relativity.

Yet if Jefferson was acutely aware of the boundaries between female and male domains, Monticello's civil society blurred them in practice. In a domestic sphere in which accomplished women—his daughter Martha and her daughters—were very much present, Jefferson gave free rein to a sensibility that transcended gender differences. Thomas Jefferson Randolph recalled his grandfather's indulging "in all fervor and delicacy of feminine feeling." "Soft and feminine in his affections to his family, he entered into and sympathized with all their feelings, winning them to paths of virtue by the soothing gentleness of his manner."[58] Characterizations of Jefferson as feminine were not always so complimentary, of course, as when Alexander Hamilton famously castigated him for his *womanish attachment to France.*[59] "Attachment" was a key word for Jefferson, for it connoted the indissoluble bonds that tied family members to each other, across the gender barrier. Domesticity was a source of strength for Jefferson, not simply a refuge from the "miseries" of his conflict-ridden public life. It was in the confines of the family that Jefferson thought he could achieve the self-control, sublimating and overcoming the barbarous impulse to dominate fellow males and exploit females. The solicitude for others and aversion to conflict that Jefferson taught his grandson and that Jeff Randolph in turn called "feminine" constituted bulwarks against encroachments on—and violations of—Monticello's domestic world.

But what Jeff called "feminine" represented an aggressive assertion of privacy and the sovereignty of the self. As the "most blessed
of the patriarchs" staked out the boundaries of his plantation world
and secured the autonomy of his domestic domain, he tried to exercise an oblique, benign, seemingly effortless mastery of himself, his
family members, and the people he enslaved. For Jefferson, mastery
was the predicate of good citizenship, engendering the capacity to
consent—and sacrifice—for the family and the family of families that
constituted the commonwealth. Monticello was the stage on which
Jefferson performed this mastery, modeling "natural" aristocracy and
eliciting the deference of equals. This is where he orchestrated the
harmonious assent of fellow citizens in conversation, or in musical
performance, thus glimpsing the possibility of transcending political
conflict and fulfilling the American Revolution's ultimate potential.

Apotheosis

At first the appearance of guests paying homage was gratifying,
but by the end of Jefferson's life, Monticello was inundated with an
"immense influx of visitors," some invited, many not. "The pilgrimage to Monticello" had become obligatory for the aspiring "patriot"
and "philanthropist," Jefferson's attending physician Robley Dunglison wryly remarked. For too many of these visitors, concluded
Dunglison, the first professor of medicine at the new university in
Charlottesville, the transparent motive was "idle," if understandable,
"curiosity."[60] Jefferson was a public figure, and the people thought
they had a right to know him personally. When he was still in office,
he might have imagined a tranquil retirement, freed from the need
to entertain the stream of political "friends" and supplicants for office
that too often spoiled periodic retreats to his mountaintop refuge. In
Jefferson's retirement years the stream of visitors became a flood.

The pilgrimage became an act of civic piety. The former president
had "filled a seat higher than that of kings," the visitor Francis Hall
reported, and he now succeeded "with a graceful dignity to that of
the good neighbor, and [became] the friendly adviser, lawyer, physi-

cian, and even gardener of his vicinity."⁶¹ In this ultimate act of condescension, Jefferson relinquished the power the people had bestowed
on him and returned to private life in his old neighborhood. As he did
so, the man of the people became the people's man. When pilgrims
trekked up the mountain, the "neighborhood" expanded to include
the whole nation: Jefferson turned into an iconic figure and Monticello a shrine. Jeff Randolph recalled that Jefferson wanted "to live
like his neighbors, in the plain hospitality of a Virginia gentleman,"
but that "the number of strangers who visited him, kept his neighbors from him."⁶² The "Virginia gentleman" had been supplanted by
the republican icon. Pilgrims who ascended the mountain assumed a
degree of familiarity that rank-conscious commentators found disorienting, but were at the same time awestruck by the larger-than-life
figure they encountered there, a veritable "Jove" who, in Richard
Rush's playful formulation, presided over an American "Olympus."⁶³

The role Jefferson came to play in his retirement was costly, in
more ways than one. In the "evening of life" when "embarrassed
circumstances" demanded retrenchment, "the immense influx of visitors could not fail to be attended with much inconvenience." Dr.
Dunglison asked Martha Randolph "what was the largest number of
persons for whom she had been called upon unexpectedly to prepare
accommodations for the night, and she replied fifty."⁶⁴ The overseer
Bacon recalled that his wife lent bedding to Mrs. Randolph in order
to accommodate the overflowing crowd. Bacon sought to contain
costs by putting visitors' horses on "half allowance." "Somehow or
other," he said, "Mr. Jefferson heard of this" and "countermanded my
orders."⁶⁵

Jefferson's hospitality, however, bore little resemblance to that of
the "Virginia gentleman" of colonial days. Many fewer visitors had
passed through his father's Shadwell plantation, and they usually could
claim some connection through kinship, friendship, or business. By
contrast, the promiscuous and undiscriminating flow of visitors made
Jefferson's Monticello more like a tourist site than a plantation house.
Jefferson "returned in his old age," his grandson Jeff told the biographer Henry Randall, "to be hunted down by the reputation he had

won in the service of his country." This was his reward for devoting his life to his country: to be victimized by a predatory public that would not leave him or his family alone. In 1814, Jeff recollected, his grandfather had predicted "that if he lived long enough he would beggar his family—that the number of persons he was compelled to entertain would devour his estate."[66]

Jefferson, however, was by no means the passive victim of public adulation. He *chose* to be hospitable, to people and horses alike. Jefferson solved a problem of his own creation when he sought to protect his privacy from visitors' prying eyes by escaping to his Poplar Forest plantation. Visitors had a right to come to Monticello, whether or not they could produce letters of introduction from old friends or acquaintances. And Jefferson understood that hospitality had its own rewards. If his generosity sometimes bordered on profligacy, it was after all "so much pleasanter to *give* than to *refuse*."[67] Indebted throughout his adult life to British creditors and their agents, American bankers and merchants, and prosperous fellow planters, Jefferson had an acute understanding of the psychology of credit and debt. In its most extreme form, indebtedness meant a loss of the mastery that was fundamental to his sense of himself. If Jefferson could imagine himself "enslaved" by the compounding debts he owed British merchant houses, the incalculable and irredeemable debts his countrymen owed him redressed the balance.[68] Indebted planters in colonial Virginia had extended credit to one another and to their humble neighbors, reinforcing communal bonds and their own claims to superior status. Jefferson now "accommodated" visitors as the gentry traditionally accommodated their countrymen, but these were debts that could be repaid only in the currency of devoted veneration.

His daughter Martha and grandson Jeff conspired to shield the patriarch from the costs of his late-life hospitality to them and to the family estate. They instead enabled him to experience an exalted form of mastery in which the patriarch *gave* everything—and *refused* nothing—to a grateful nation. The aging sage of Monticello could fashion an image for and of himself that survived him. Monticello was the "patriarchal seat," a eulogist exclaimed, "whose just celebrity has attracted the wayfarer of every land, and left him to wonder on retiring from it."[69] Jefferson and the pilgrims he drew up the mountain together made Monticello "a monument to his memory." "There remained a halo lingering around" this "noble spot," John H. B. Latrobe wrote a few years after Jefferson's death, despite "the utter ruin and desolation of everything."[70] The place, a veritable diorama blown up to scale, had a "genius" that echoed past times when the "old philosopher" had entertained countless visitors, performing the role of patriarch as a supporting cast of family members and enslaved people orchestrated scenes of domestic tranquillity. To the last, Jefferson carefully regulated his own appearances, periodically retreating to his suite of private rooms and the rarefied company of his own books and thoughts. Yet it was at this intersection of private and public that Jefferson constructed an enduring image of himself that was so intimately linked with Monticello.

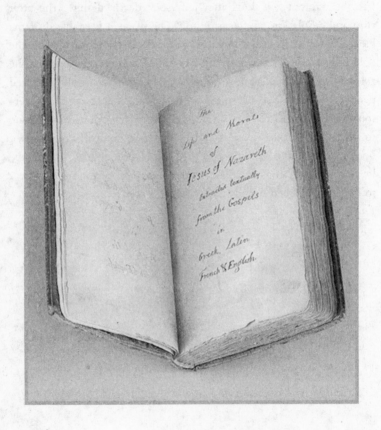

The Jefferson Bible, *opened to title page.* (Division of Political History, National Museum of American History, Smithsonian Institution.)

CHAPTER 9

PRIVACY AND PRAYERS

The very public man insisted on having a zone of privacy, a place where he could be alone to think, plan, and write. And, for the most part, wherever he was, Jefferson had the resources and the power to have the privacy he so craved. Building a house virtually hidden atop a mountain certainly made intrusions more difficult, though as we have seen, this was not enough to deter the many people who visited despite the extreme effort it took to reach Monticello. More had to be done. Jefferson's design of the house itself threw up further barriers of access to him. The doors to his private compartment opened out into the entrance hall, giving him entrée to the rest of the house. But those doors, Anna Maria Thornton noticed on her visit to Monticello in 1802, were always locked. Jefferson could go out, but no one who did not have a key—which he would have had to give them—could get in. That the doors were "always" locked may be an exaggeration; there is no question, however, that Jefferson's private living quarters were his "sanctum sanctorum."[1]

Closed off as his rooms would have appeared looking from the entrance hall and other rooms on the first floor, Jefferson would not have felt restricted in his private quarters, because there were, in fact, multiple ways to go in and out of them. He configured his rooms so that he could stroll out onto the south terrace when he was of a mind to, or into the greenhouse that was situated between his bedroom and sitting room. In the early 1800s he decided to build "two small private porches on the western and eastern flanks" of his private chamber. Each "porticle" was enclosed, with "louvered blinds" that prevented anyone from seeing inside when he did not want them to. He could sit on either porch and have the feeling of being outside. He could actually get outside from the porticles because each had a door and steps that allowed him to come from and go out onto the grounds at Monticello as he pleased. This feature of the house's architecture gave Jefferson another form of privacy—this, from the people inside the house. At times they might not have known whether he was inside his rooms or not.[2]

For most of the day, when he was at Monticello, Jefferson was at work. Madison Hemings's description of his father's daily regimen states it plainly: Jefferson, he said, "occupied much of the time in his office engaged in correspondence and reading and writing."[3] The telling word is "office." An upper-class man of the eighteenth century, living in a rural environment, Jefferson had no separate work space to go to. Rather than being a mark of mere eccentricity, or an effort to hide Sally Hemings, Jefferson's quest for privacy grew from his engagement with what was essentially the writing life, a life that requires great discipline and as much solitude as possible for contemplation and composition.

Jefferson's way of life also required organization, and he was, if he was anything, an organizer. He organized the spaces within the house to secure his privacy, but he maximized the function of his design by instituting an undeviating daily schedule that helped guard him from intrusions almost as effectively as the design of his rooms. He joined family and friends for meals in the dining room and sociable evening hours in the parlor. Rising early, every morning he rode about his estate to superintend work and survey the progress of his crops and inspect his mills. During his retirement, he added gardening to the menu of activities, and the avid gardener began to spend short periods of time with his vegetables and flowers, usually assisted by Wormley

Hughes, an enslaved grandson of Elizabeth Hemings, or an eager granddaughter. More frequently, he retreated after his morning ride to the protected space of his "office."[4]

The retirement years were particularly tough for Jefferson's quest to be left alone, so much so that he decided not long after the end of his presidency to build a retreat at Poplar Forest. There was a precedent for this. While in Paris, and living at the Hôtel de Langeac, he also had a getaway on the outskirts of Paris. Mon Valerian was a complex of apartments run by monks. He took rooms there "whenever," as his daughter Martha put it, "he had a press of business" and wanted to get away from people in order to write.[5] That was but a temporary situation in Paris. By the time he was in the "elder statesman" phase of his life, attracting hordes of visitors, it became clear that he had to take drastic action. Rather than discourage visitors to Monticello—and be thought inhospitable, which would never do—Jefferson effectively decided to leave his mountaintop home, for long stretches of time, to the sometimes dozens of people who came to call.

Even when Jefferson was at Monticello, he was often conspicuously absent from his company for much of the day. People had to wait until he finished what he was doing before they had any contact with him, though especially favored visitors were sometimes given a tour of his compartment. Margaret Bayard Smith and her husband, Samuel, felt profoundly flattered to be admitted to Jefferson's private space. Margaret Smith described what she found inside: this was a place "where any other foot than his own seldom intrudes." Welcomed through a "door . . . which is never opened but by himself," the Smiths were introduced to a "suite of apartments" consisting "of 3 rooms for the library, one for his cabinet one for his chamber, & a green house, divided from the other by glass compartments & doors; so that the view of the plants it contains, is unobstructed."[6] This was no perfunctory walk-through. Jefferson "shewed us every thing he thought would please or interest us," including "his most valuable & curious books" containing "fine prints" and maps, and his collection of garden seeds, with "every thing labeled and in the neatest order."

"More than two hours passed most charmingly away" in Jefferson's company, after which "he bade us take whatever books we wished, which we did & then retired to our own room."[7]

Jefferson opened his quarters to others on a more limited basis. On occasion he gave access to his library to fellow bibliophiles, but it was decidedly not a public space. At least one visitor suggested that this limitation had a negative effect on the experience of visiting Monti-cello and staying there for any period of time. "If the library had been thrown open to his guests," remarked the British diplomat Augustus J. Foster, who visited in 1804, "the president's country-house would have been as agreeable a place to stay as any I know." But this was where Jef-ferson "sat and wrote, and he did not like, of course, to be disturbed by visitors, who in this part of the world are rather disposed to be indis-creet."[8] Monticello was not the kind of "country house" Foster would have visited in Britain. Though it had over thirty rooms, it was not so large or grand as one could have found in the English countryside.

It could well have been that Jefferson did not feel as warmly dis-posed toward Foster as toward others, or that he grew more willing to give his guests access to his books as time wore on, because George Ticknor, who visited in 1815, recalled spending more than one after-noon leisurely reading in Jefferson's library. He estimated that the for-mer president had seven thousand books in his collection, "arranged in the catalogue, and on the shelves, according to the divisions and subdivisions of human learning by Lord Bacon."[9]

If visitors were impressed with Jefferson's erudition and with the books he delighted in showing them, the library's visual presentation made less than a grand impression. This arrangement suited Jefferson, an active and extensive reader, but disappointed the casual visitor. "I do not think with its numerous divisions & arches," Margaret Bayard Smith concluded, "it is as impressive as one large room would have been."[10] The same might well have been said of Monticello itself, a house that presented an ostentatiously modest façade to the world. It was the contents of the house and of the library that mattered, for they offered tantalizing glimpses of the world beyond Monticello, as seen through Jefferson's eyes. Smith herself sensed this when she

described Jefferson's "retirement" from the world and into his sanctum sanctorum as somehow "sacred."

The Smiths' obvious delight in being allowed into Jefferson's rooms
shows that he managed to convey to observers just how obsessively
and self-consciously determined he was to protect his privacy, and
safeguard his ability to work. There was an aura of mystery about the
sanctum sanctorum as workspace. Family members followed strict
rules about approaching Jefferson in his intimate space, visiting only
when business called, though one suspects that his beloved daughter,
Martha, who had her own office adjacent to his rooms on the first
floor, visited her father's chambers as needed. Affectionate and easy
as his relationships with his children and grandchildren seemed to be,
one does not get the sense that Jefferson's rooms were places for casually dropping in just to chat with "Papa," "father," or "Grand-Papa."
Ellen Coolidge spoke of the enormous pride she felt when she was
asked to enter his rooms and carry messages to him there, as if it were
a special favor to be allowed to do so.

Plantation business also justified routine interruptions of Jefferson's privacy. Many years after Jefferson's death, his overseer Edmund
Bacon boasted that he had "had full permission to visit" his employer's private quarters "whenever [he] thought it necessary to see him
on any business."[11] And when Jeff Randolph assumed managerial
responsibilities at Monticello, his grandfather's "private apartments
were open to [him] at all times," and he saw his grandfather "under
all circumstances." That Randolph felt compelled to say this is further evidence that Jefferson's rooms were considered special territory.
"Being fifteen years older than my brothers," Jeff proudly recalled,
"the duty devolved on me to place myself in the breach" of his grandfather's dire "pecuniary embarrassments" and to shield him "living
and dead, from their practical effects." This access enabled Jeff to
know Jefferson well: "I was more intimate with him than any man I
have ever known," and his character "invited such intimacy."[12]

It may seem a paradox—though it really is not—that the people
who had the most contact with Jefferson's intimate space were the
enslaved. Their duties and roles required them to have daily access

to his rooms, likely more access than his white family. They would have seen him, over the years, in ways that others would never have had occasion to see him. During the final days of his life, he allowed no one but enslaved people in his rooms after dark. Not wanting to be alone, he had them make pallets and stay with him to assist if he needed anything, or wished to talk. Members of his white family who sat with him and watched him during the day wanted desperately to remain inside. He would not allow it. They were, instead, reduced to furtively sneaking into his living quarters periodically to see for themselves how he was doing.

A number of enslaved people came in and out of Jefferson's chambers, and their reports reveal his less formal side. Isaac Granger provided a vivid picture of Jefferson's quarters that seems just right, describing the "abundance of books" stacked on the floor that Jefferson would consult if asked a question that he could not readily answer. Granger saw the casual Jefferson, in his most comfortable space. For some years Israel (Gillette) Jefferson "made the fire in [Jefferson's] bedroom and private chamber, cleaned his office, dusted his books, run of (sic) errands and attended him about home." Gillette identified Sally Hemings as Jefferson's "chamber-maid." He also said that he knew from his "intimacy with both parties" that Jefferson was "on the most intimate terms with" Hemings. Madison Hemings recalled, "It was [mother's] duty, all her life which I can remember, up to the time of father's death, to take care of his chamber and wardrobe, look after us children and do such light work as sewing."[13]

When Gillette, a teenager during Jefferson's retirement, said that he knew from his "intimacy" with Jefferson and Hemings about the nature of their connection, he was not saying that he had talked with either one of them about it. His mentioning that he came into Jefferson's rooms to carry out specific functions, and that Hemings was the actual chambermaid, suggests that he was connecting the two duties and had observed the two of them together in Jefferson's private space. Gillette did not necessarily witness anything salacious, but it is often possible to tell whether a man and woman are in an intimate relationship by the way they address each other, how close they stand to each other, what they say. Of course, Gillette would have known about the connection because it was part of the social knowledge of the plantation and the surrounding community. In any event, slavery required breaching barriers of privacy, as the enslaved saw their owners in all states and conditions of their lives. It was not for nothing that Burwell Colbert, Jefferson's last valet, was referred to as Jefferson's "confidential servant." He and his aunt Sally Hemings knew things about Jefferson that others did not know, not even Jefferson's immediate legal family members.

For most of his adult life, Jefferson took advantage of the privacy that he was able to achieve in order to work effectively in every role he played as he made his way up the hierarchy of public life in Virginia and the United States. This was work that needed to be done in the ordinary course of business. It was also work that looked to the future, to his legacy, for Jefferson had a clear understanding of his role in the American Revolution and the beginning of the early American republic. He knew he would go down in history. The historian Francis D. Cogliano has written of Jefferson's determination to use his vast epistolary record to shape how history would view him. The long hours "drudging," as he called it, in his office would be the record of his life—a public life that was worth the attention of history. He went so far as to arrange his letters in the way he wished them to be read, an effort that, in the end, was for naught. When his grandchildren sold large swaths of his letters to help raise funds to pay off his debts, Jefferson's careful system for ordering his letters was effectively destroyed.[14]

A Religious Quest

The time Jefferson spent working in his chambers was not all about drudging and crafting his legacy away from prying eyes. In later life he appears to have embarked upon a genuine spiritual quest, which he managed to keep hidden even from his immediate family. Whether this was spurred by the relentless attacks based on his alleged lack of religious faith, or by impending mortality, Jefferson took religion seriously. He preferred, however, to remain solitary and undisturbed as he contemplated the metaphysical questions that he had so impatiently dismissed when he was an active young man seeking answers from the ethical teachings of ancient authors in their original language. Reading widely in sacred texts and commentaries in many traditions doubtless inspired sustained reflection. But Jefferson's engagement with the Christian gospel was particularly intense; by his own idiosyncratic lights, it justified his calling himself a "primitive Christian." He drew inspiration from Jesus's life and authentic teachings, but rejected the concept of Jesus "Christ," a divine being who performed miracles and was resurrected from the dead. Indeed, he rejected all the miracles in the Bible, seeing them as distractions from the real messages that the philosopher, whom he deliberately called "Jesus of Nazareth," brought to the world.

From 1819 to 1820 Jefferson completed work on his "Life and Morals of Jesus of Nazareth," popularly known as *The Jefferson Bible*, a laborious collation of parallel texts excerpted from the four Gospels in Greek, Latin, French, and English, languages all known to him.[15] The culmination of many years of reading and planning, dating back to the early years of his presidency, "Life and Morals" famously excluded accounts of the miracles and mystifications that Jefferson thought had corrupted the gospel through the millennia. Jefferson's cutting and pasting from multiple testaments required an extraordinarily intensive close reading—focusing on textual variations and inconsistencies and seeking to establish a coherent life of the historical Jesus. The contrast between Jefferson's Bible reading and the omnivorous and extensive reading that enabled him to master the other titles in his vast and constantly expanding library is striking. He kept returning to scripture, seeking meaning in an edited text that—for most faithful Christians—would seem to have been drained of mystery and stripped of purpose.

It was only after his grandfather's death that Jeff Randolph learned from a letter Jefferson had written to a friend that "before going to bed . . . he was in the habit of reading nightly" from his own "Life and Morals."[16] Perhaps, with the very small, edited testament—measuring approximately eight by five inches—in hand, Jefferson no longer read the "large Bible" that Edmund Bacon recalled "nearly always lay at the head of his sofa." Bacon may have exaggerated Jefferson's Bible reading and his access to his employer's private rooms: "Many and many a time I have gone into his room and found him reading that Bible." He would have had good reason. Writing in an era of pervasive piety at the onset of the Civil War, Bacon evidently felt it important to establish his former employer's Christian credentials and refute the scandalous charge that he was a deist or, worse, an atheist. If Jefferson had been an atheist, Bacon asked, "what did he want with all those religious books, and why did he spend so much of his time reading his Bible?" On the other hand, it is clear that Jefferson *was* deeply interested in the Bible.[17]

One could argue that Jefferson followed a similar logic as Bacon on the question of his status as a Christian. As this was a matter of individual conscience and experience, he could say that he did consider himself to be a Christian *by his own definition*, "a sect by myself," because of the way he, in the privacy of his home, engaged with—and even improved on—the earliest Christian traditions. Thus, he was not simply, minimally, or "culturally" a Christian out of respect for his neighbors' faith. Jefferson's identity as a Christian signified much more than that. By his retirement years, if not long before, the separation of church and state was serving the higher purpose of protecting the sacred domain of conscience. This was not freedom *from* religion, as it might well have been for the young revolutionary and politician as he sought to demolish a corrupt church establishment that preyed on people's credulity and ignorance. This was instead the freedom that enabled enlightened, self-governing republicans to pursue their own quest for religious truths.

From the time he entered public life, religion was a delicate matter for Jefferson. During his early career in Virginia politics, his reputation as a progressive and his desire to disestablish the Anglican Church in Virginia caused some to wonder about his faith. When he came onto the national stage in the 1790s, even more and louder questions were raised after his ardent support for the French Revolution became well known. The revolutionaries had, after all, attacked the Catholic Church, wishing to force the secularization of French society. This, combined with his earlier history in Virginia, was treated as proof of his hostility to religious faith. Sensing a political opportunity, Federalists seized on Jefferson's religious ambiguity and promoted hysteria among their followers. By the time they were finished, a number of Americans believed before the election of 1800 that if Jefferson became president bibles would be burned and incest would become a norm.

There is little wonder that Jefferson had no interest in allowing his skepticism about the miracles portrayed in the Bible and his lack of belief in the divinity of Jesus to become topics of conversation. He was not an atheist, but how to explain to the general public his unorthodox beliefs, in the cultural context in which he operated? Why should he have to explain to the public, or to anyone? Close though Jefferson was to his family, evidently no one at Monticello knew about his painstaking cutting and pasting of the New Testament. Jeff Randolph told Jefferson's biographer Henry Randall that "his codification of the Morals of Jesus was not known to his family before his death."[18] Astoundingly, Randolph acknowledged that of his grandfather's "peculiar religious opinions, his family knew no more than the world."[19] Jefferson demanded freedom of conscience for himself beyond the "wall of separation" between his sanctum sanctorum and the spaces he shared with family and friends in Monticello. If any family member pressed him on his beliefs, "his uniform reply was, that it was a subject each was bound to study assiduously for himself, unbiased by the opinion of others—it was a matter solely of conscience."[20]

Jefferson believed that the greatest threat to religious and political freedom was the overreaching of rulers who sought to indoctrinate dependent subjects in their supposed duties. In his own domain Jefferson was careful not to breach the barriers of conscience that secured the spiritual autonomy and independence of his family members. And it was that independence that made their voluntary consent to Jefferson's authority meaningful, binding them to him with love, not force.

He hoped his children and grandchildren would struggle with their own faith as he still struggled with his in his retirement years. Interestingly enough, when Madison and Eston Hemings settled in the black community in Chillicothe, Ohio, after leaving Virginia, neither man formally joined a church, though Madison was known to attend services. This was a curious omission considering the very important role the church played in the religious and social life of the African American community. During the first quarter of the nineteenth century, some Virginia slaveholders who experienced their own religious awakenings became directly involved in the religious life of enslaved people, sometimes preaching to them. This was not anything Jefferson would ever do. For him there were no "right" answers to the ultimate questions, only a "righteous" approach to them. He enjoined his family members to seek their own truths: "they were responsible for the righteousness, but not the rightfulness of their opinions." If he expressed "his opinion," he might "influence theirs," and thus compromise and subvert their "responsibility."[21]

There was, however, one group upon whom Jefferson was more than willing to impose his opinions: the young men who would attend the University of Virginia. If he saw his role in founding the university as proof of his undying commitment to the "illimitable freedom of the human mind," his firm views about the impressionability of young people, and his sense of responsibility for bringing them to this place to be taught, led him to lay down some fundamental rules. There were limits to what the young men of Virginia would study at the new university, and their proper education would enable them to draw the line and defend the state's vital interests against its enemies, among them, any Federalists who still existed in the North. The university would have no professor of theology, for his presumptively bigoted teachings might corrupt the pure spring of republican enlightenment that he wanted his university to be. Jefferson was determined that the new law professor be an orthodox republican, if not a Republican, and that students read the right, canonical texts. One of his strongest arguments for creating the university was that it would keep Virginia boys at home: too many were matriculating at Princeton and other northern schools where they were at risk of imbibing northern (read "anti-republican") values. The university itself would constitute an institutional buttress against foreign encroachments. In the early years the rowdy young men often disappointed Jefferson, moving him to public tears on one occasion when he was present and they were particularly out of hand, but he continued to believe that eventually the university would rival the great ones in the North and in the world.

Prayers

Freed from the demands of office and of intense scrutiny, Jefferson was at leisure to reflect on the meaning of a life dedicated to public service. The religious quest he embarked upon was inextricably connected to his political philosophy, which emphasized the importance of individual autonomy and self-determination; his engagement with the ultimate questions of life underscored the deeply personal implications of his commitment to the separation of church and state and the "illimitable" nature of free inquiry."[22] As the aging revolutionary generation left the stage of public life, he prayed for the progressive enlightenment of those who followed.

The "general spread of the light of science" was opening eyes everywhere to "the rights of man," Jefferson wrote on the eve of the fiftieth anniversary of the American Declaration of Independence, even as his own eyesight flickered and death approached. The United States would be a beacon of light in a benighted world if Americans remained faithful to the legacy of 1776, upholding "the free right to the unbounded exercise of reason and freedom of opinion."[23] If, as Jefferson repeatedly asserted, republican self-government was predicated on the principle of majority rule, it also depended on the individual citizen's freedom from the tyranny of public opinion. The same freedom that enabled Jefferson to search for his own religious truth, and to "question with boldness even the very existence of a god," was vitally important to the new republic's progressive moral development.[24] Republican self-government depended on citizens' capacity to consent and contract, equally free from the influence and control

of supposedly superior authorities and from the tyranny of the ignorant and unreasoning mob. Because the "mass of mankind" could not
yet see far or clearly, however, it was crucial that a visionary vanguard
remain free to chart an enlightened future course.

The former president vigorously promoted constitutional and
institutional reforms that would foster the enlightenment of his fellow
citizens, with the founding of the University of Virginia as the centerpiece. Though the private man avoided publishing his opinions, as
he had throughout his public career, Jefferson did not hesitate to exercise his own considerable influence on behalf of various measures.
And he did continue to speak within the confines of his home. Family members occasionally heard him hold forth on political issues in
conversations at Monticello. Visitors present at those rare times when
he gave his opinion were sometimes surprised at his vehemence: "He
is more positive, decided and passionate than I had expected," an itin-
erant book peddler recalled from an 1824 visit, and "I should think
him less of a philosopher than a partizan."[25] But if Jefferson was passionate about promoting a more democratic and representative state
constitution, establishing the university, or holding the line against
the nationalizing agenda of John Marshall's Supreme Court, which he
believed was taking too much power from citizens and their representatives, he remained mute about the truths he sought in the privacy
of his study. Jefferson's political creed, set forth in the Declaration and
other state papers, was America's, an oft-repeated catechism that every
good patriot took to heart; his private beliefs about ultimate questions
were nobody's business but his own.

Jefferson's late-life meditations grew out of an epiphany, noted in
an earlier chapter, that he first elaborated to James Madison when he
was in Paris in 1789 that *"the earth belongs in usufruct to the living."* Using
the civil law term "usufruct," he suggested to Madison that no living
generation of any era has total ownership over land. It merely had the
right to use the land, and to do so in a way that did not negatively
affect the future generations who eventually would own the land. In
the flush of the fall of the Bastille, which stoked his mounting excite-
ment about the spread of revolutionary republican principles from the

New World to the Old, Jefferson sought to generalize and institution-alize the liberating spirit of change and progress that was breaking all around. If every generation was understood to be "an indepen-dant nation" with respect to every other generation, as he thought it was "by the law of nature," then it should exercise its sovereignty to reconstitute itself every nineteen years. This was the duration of a generation according to Jefferson's calculations from mortality tables, or the interval between its original constitution and the moment when "a majority of those of full age at that date shall be dead."[26] Madison threw as much cold water as he could on his friend's poten-tially incendiary doctrine: he and his fellow constitution drafters who had gathered at Philadelphia hoped that the recently adopted federal Constitution would establish a new order for the ages, not for a single generation, earning the kind of time-out-of-mind "veneration" that Americans had once had for their monarch.[27] Madison's prudent res-ervations notwithstanding, Jefferson was not to be dissuaded from the principle of generational sovereignty. It was central to the full elabo-ration of his democratic political theory in his retirement.

When he first discovered the generational sovereignty principle, Jefferson looked to the future, seeking to curb public indebtedness, the temptations of debt-fueled militarism, and the dangerous "con-solidation" of power in the central government. Looking backward in his retirement, he found deeper, more personal implications in the generational idea. Most importantly, he understood retirement itself as the passing of his own generation, as if he himself were in some civic, public sense now dead. "There is a ripeness of time for death, regarding others as well as ourselves," Jefferson wrote his old revolu-tionary colleague John Adams, "when it is reasonable we should drop off, and make room for another growth." His renewed connection to and correspondence with Adams affirmed this notion of a genera-tional identity, invoking their shared labors in the Revolution while contemplating their shared fate. "When we have lived our generation out, we should not wish to encroach on another," Jefferson enjoined. This was not a morbid or gloomy line of thought. He appeared relieved to be a spectator, to be suspended between an active, history-making life and death's obliteration. "I enjoy good health; I am happy in what is around me," he told his old comrade, "yet I assure you I am ripe for leaving all, this year, this day, this hour."[28]

Thus, Jefferson began to style himself as an "old man" in his retirement, no longer fit to act on the world's stage and ready to die at any moment. He marked this momentous transition by substituting prayer for action. "The only succour from the old must be in their prayers," he told the Republican editor William Duane.[29] "I leave public cares to younger and more vigorous minds," he wrote John Melish after his retirement, "and repose my personal well being under their guardianship." Confident that his successor James Madison, whose administration was in the midst of the War of 1812, would guide the ship of state into a "safe port," Jefferson offered "to heaven [his] daily prayers, the proper function of age."[30] For Jefferson prayer signified a posture of patient and hopeful expectancy. The aging patriot could glimpse the immanent fulfillment of God's design in the actions of the coming generation.

In his retirement correspondence Jefferson referred to "*daily* prayers" for the first time, though many earlier letters included conventionally "sincere" or "earnest prayers" for the recipient's health and well-being. These daily prayers were evidently a distinct activity, *not* simply and formulaically performed in the very act of writing a letter. What actually constituted prayer for Jefferson cannot be known. It is doubtful that he would have followed the conventional script of appeals to God's intercession familiar to him from childhood in the Anglican Church or public worship services he attended in Charlottesville. Nor was he likely to have sought some personal benefit or outcome that would have brought God down to earth, to take part capriciously in the affairs of men. God did, however, reveal providential purposes to enlightened observers who discerned the lawful properties and intelligent design of his creation. "When we take a view of the Universe, in it's parts, general or particular," Jefferson told his old friend Adams, "it is impossible for the human mind not to perceive and feel a conviction of design, consummate skill, and indefinite power in every atom of it's composition."[31]

The new meaning of prayer that Jefferson discovered in his retirement was apparent in the occasions that provoked it. Confident in the ultimate triumph of republicanism, he prayed "daily" that his former "fellow laborers" in the Republican Party would continue to "love one another, as I love you."[32] Many Republicans, fearful that their party would fall apart, had urged him to stay on for a third term. But no single individual—not even Jefferson himself—was indispensable, for it was the love that bound the "living generation" to one another that guaranteed the nation's glorious future. The "*nation* will be undone" if the party does not remain united, Jefferson warned William Duane, "for the republicans are the *nation*."[33]

Slavery, Prayers, and the Living Generation

Jefferson had expressed the view in stark terms: If his God were just, He surely would judge Americans for the sin of slavery. "The Almighty has no attribute which can take side with us" if slaves followed their masters' example and struck for their own freedom. In this case there would be an intercession. To deny the slaves' rightful aspirations for emancipation would provoke God's "wrath," Jefferson asserted in his *Notes on Virginia*, for "his justice cannot sleep for ever." Even when he was not putting this matter in religious terms, Jefferson believed that Virginians' failure to free their slaves betrayed the republican revolution's progressive promise. A much younger Jefferson had believed that it would be possible to find a solution to this problem: the Virginia legislature could end slavery. The General Assembly's rejection of his proposal for a gradual, compensated emancipation scheme in 1779 convinced him that his own generation was not yet ready to act. His belief was reinforced in 1796 when the much respected St. George Tucker presented a detailed plan for gradual emancipation to the Virginia assembly, only to have it thoroughly and summarily rejected. The only hope lay in the coming generations. They, under the influence of the progress that Enlightenment-based thought would surely bring, would have very different values.[34]

Jefferson had originally intended that the limited circulation of

Notes on Virginia should include students at the College of William and Mary, the commonwealth's future leaders. The principle of generational sovereignty was implicit in his hopes that the rising generation would complete the great reforms that his generation had initiated, but failed to complete. Rather than praying for the intercession of the Almighty, Jefferson hoped instead that enlightened students would preempt God's righteous judgment and so keep the master designer and lawgiver at His proper distance. By following their teacher's path "through the various considerations of policy, of morals, of history natural and civil," young Virginians would come to conclude that it was *their* responsibility to dismantle an unjust institution that jeopardized the liberties of their own and succeeding generations.[35]

As the years passed and slavery became more deeply entrenched, the likelihood of a legislated emancipation receded into an ever more distant future. The same was true of the cataclysmic judgment that seemed so close at hand when Jefferson first engaged with the slavery problem during the revolution. No doubt the chaos of the time, when some of the people he enslaved ran away to join the British and white Virginians feared servile insurrection, moved him in 1782 to think in such prophetic terms. By the time of his retirement, the threatened "revolution of the wheel of fortune" that would lead to "an exchange of situation" between masters and slaves was no longer a credible enough threat to spur complacent white Virginians to action. Events in another part of the world, however, cast a different light on matters in the Old Dominion.

Reverberations from the great revolution in Saint Domingue (Haiti) in the early 1790s caused Jefferson to fret about what it meant for his beloved France. Upon first hearing of the revolt, he sounded sanguine about events. In a letter to his daughter Martha Randolph in 1793, he wrote as if the rebellion were simply an inevitable part of the tide of revolution sweeping the world. "St. Domingo has expelled all it's whites, has given freedom to all it's blacks, has established a regular government of the blacks and coloured people, and seems now to have taken it's ultimate form, and that to which all of the West India islands must come."[36] By

1797, after a flood of refugees from the island—black and white—
came to the United States bringing news of black people killing
white people, Jefferson snapped to attention. He and other Virginians, conscious of their large slave populations, feared the possibility that what happened on the Caribbean island might happen
in their state. The enslaved would take their freedom rather than
wait for whites to confer it. While British Americans had declared
their own independence, Jefferson's vision of the emancipation of
African Americans had white Americans *declaring blacks* a "free and
independant people" through the republican processes of the new
state governments.

The self-determination, fierceness, and resolution of Saint
Domingue's blacks frightened the patriarch and his cohort. Indeed,
it was the events in Saint Domingue that spurred St. George Tucker
to formulate his ill-fated emancipation plan. The disappointed jurist
wrote to Jefferson in 1797 complaining about his treatment in the
legislature. Jefferson wrote back, "The sooner we put some plan under
way, the greater hope there is that it may be permitted to proceed
peaceably to it's ultimate effect." He went on, "If something is not
done, and soon done, we shall be the murderers of our own children."[37]

Legislators in Virginia did nothing after the revolution in Saint
Domingue except enact more restrictive measures against the enslaved
and free black people. In truth, solving the slavery problem was
nowhere near the forefront of Jefferson's mind. Once he returned to
politics in the 1790s, he became obsessed with vanquishing the Federalist Party and therefore, he thought, saving the American Revolution.
During his presidency, global politics did require some focus on the
new Republic of Haiti. The Haitians' defeat of French forces prompted
Napoleon to make the deal that led to the Louisiana Purchase. The
tiny struggling island had helped pave the way for the doubling of the
landmass of the United States. The black republic nevertheless frightened Jefferson and other white southerners. His administration, and
the following ones headed by southerners, was hostile to the new government, denying it recognition and limiting trade, fearful that the
example of a successful slave revolt would influence enslaved people

in Virginia and other southern states. Later in life, at eighty-one, Jefferson professed to personally support recognition of Haiti, but trade with the island should be limited because "the nation"—by which he meant the majority of white people—was too prejudiced against black people to engage with them on an equal basis.[38]

Presenting himself as civically "dead" after leaving public life and therefore a "spectator," not an "actor," Jefferson was only willing to pray that justice would ultimately be done to enslaved Virginians. He offered his most famous prayer on slavery to his neighbor Edward Coles in a letter that he wrote on August 25, 1814, the day after British invaders put the torch to public buildings in Washington, DC. Coles sought Jefferson's public endorsement for a plan to liberate his own slaves and take them to the free soil of Illinois Territory. Lauding Coles for sentiments that did "honor to both the head and heart of the writer," Jefferson, whose original draft of the Northwest Ordinance in 1784, which covered Illinois, sought to prohibit the expansion of slavery into the territory, nonetheless demurred. He urged Coles to remain in Virginia. Jefferson reminded the young man that his own antislavery sentiments had been public knowledge for many years, insisting that every useful thing he could say about it was in *Notes on the State of Virginia*, and his words and thoughts would live forever in that work. He cautioned Coles that were he to leave Virginia, his voice would no longer be heard there. Coles, then twenty-eight years old, was exactly the kind of young person Jefferson had been counting on to do something about slavery. The old Jefferson's voice was stilled; he would not act. That glorious "enterprise . . . [would] have all [his] prayers," he assured Coles, "and these [were] the only weapons of an old man."[39]

Jefferson's prayer to Coles was a testament to his faith in progress. "The hour of emancipation is advancing in the march of time," he told his young neighbor. If Coles and his generation worked toward voluntary emancipation, they would avert "the bloody process of St. Domingo" and so answer Jefferson's prayers. Coles was unmoved. He emphatically rejected Jefferson's distinction between praying and acting, impatiently dismissing the old man's conceit that he was in some sense dead and that his voice therefore should *not* be heard, and that he was beyond the point of taking action to deal with this urgent moral problem. People might listen to Jefferson. "Your prayers I trust will not only be heard with indulgence in Heaven, but with influence on earth." Coles could see what was happening. As eastern planters moved west to cultivate new land, the price of slaves was rising. In Virginia, the state with the largest number of slaves and with the most to benefit from the rising prices, the peculiar institution was becoming more deeply entrenched.

Time and progress were not, as Jefferson assumed they would be, marching forward in unison—at least not toward the place in the future he predicted. His later-life support for diffusion—spreading the enslaved across the opening territories in the West—reflected his intuitive (and correct) understanding that white people's behavior toward blacks depended upon the numbers of blacks at issue. Here, Jefferson's New England fixation—his belief that the world would eventually adopt the most progressive characteristics of that region— was in effect. Those states with small black populations had, for the most part, ended slavery relatively easily. Whites in New England had no reason to fear a large population of blacks living outside of their control, because the large populations did not exist. In the end, of course, Coles's understanding of the economics of slavery gave him much better insight into this question than Jefferson's near-total focus on politics through the lens of his Enlightenment philosophy. Coles was adamant: as the most eminent remaining member of the revolutionary generation, Jefferson had the moral authority and duty to break the silence and be heard—to "awaken" his fellow white Virginians to "the true interest of their country."[40]

Jefferson's conception of generational sovereignty reinforced the wall of separation he constructed around himself. He withdrew from the noisy and contentious world of the "living generation" into the "tranquillity" of retirement. But even as he defined a generational boundary in his letter to Coles that justified his refusal to make another public statement against slavery, it was still important to him to identify with his young neighbor's antislavery principles. The commitment to justice that inspired Jefferson and the revolutionary generation had now inspired Coles, thus vindicating the old man's faith in the future. He could not know this, but as things turned out, Jefferson's faith was not entirely justified. Coles did accomplish his original mission, but over the years he, like St. George Tucker, lost his own faith, and turned on African Americans, expressing views about their innate inferiority and supporting their expatriation to Africa.

Jefferson did not expect his prayers to be answered soon; Coles would also have to be patient, speaking "softly," barely louder than the praying Jefferson. "The revolution in public opinion which this cause requires, is not to be expected in a day, or perhaps in an age," Jefferson told another correspondent. But he could die with the consoling thought that "time, which outlives all things, will outlive this evil also." Jefferson continued to insist, whenever approached about the matter, that his commitment to the cause had never wavered. The "sentiments" set forth in his *Notes on Virginia* "have been forty years before the public," he told James Heaton shortly before his death. "Had I repeated them forty times, they would only have become the more stale and threadbare." Yet it was the repetitions, not the sentiments themselves that would have been "stale and threadbare," for "they will not die with me." With only a short time to live, Jefferson knew he would "not live to see them consummated." Yet just as his antislavery sentiments survived, he himself would gain a kind of immortality through the continuing progress of republican self-government. "Living or dying," the end of slavery "will ever be in my most fervent prayer."[41] Jefferson in prayer glimpsed the eternal life of the immortal mind.

Jefferson's prayers were double-edged. The patriarch's solicitude for the welfare of future generations was shadowed by his lingering fear that the sons might betray him. Heedless of the future and mindlessly indulging their "vices" and "passions," pseudo-republican sons would beggar their own children, thus replicating the degenerate histories of monarchs and aristocrats as they became "all body & no mind." Jefferson never blamed himself or his generation for failing to set the new nation on a proper course, as ungrateful children are so tempted to do in the intergenerational accounting we call "history." The "generation of 1776" had done its part by breaking away from Great Britain and founding a republic. They had sacrificed everything *for* the children, Jefferson lamented in 1820 during the controversy over Missouri statehood, when the Union seemed destined to collapse. "I regret that I am now to die in the belief," he wrote the former Massachusetts congressman John Holmes, that these sacrifices had been "useless." The fathers' republican legacy was "to be thrown away by the unwise and unworthy passions of their sons." Jefferson's only consolation was that he might die *before* they committed "this act of suicide on themselves, and of treason against the hopes of the world."[42] Of course, this was no true consolation to Jefferson, for all the available evidence called into question his abiding vision of the republican millennium. Yet, as he clung to life in his waning years, he reaffirmed his faith, praying for a future that the all-too-passionate sons threatened to "throw away."

The issue of slavery, freedom, and the living generation came home to Jefferson in an even more personal way in January of 1818 when he learned of the death in Switzerland of an old friend, the Polish patriot and American Revolutionary War colonel Tadeusz Kościuszko. Kościuszko had written a will in 1798 leaving funds to educate and emancipate slaves. Jefferson, then vice-president, had helped Kościuszko draft the will, and he became its executor. Kościuszko lived, in part, on the interest of the money, which Jefferson distributed to him over the years. He later gave Jefferson power of attorney over his affairs in the United States. What he never told Jefferson was that he had in 1806 written a second will, which gave nearly one-third of the funds to the son of a friend, and then, in 1816, yet another one, distributing property in Europe. That will contained the following provision: "I revoke all the wills and codicils which I may have made previous to the present, to which alone I confine myself, as containing my last wishes." In the year he died, 1817, Kościuszko wrote a letter to Jefferson referencing the 1798 bequest but not mentioning the subsequently drawn wills. And there was one more will to come, written just before he died.

Upon hearing of his friend's death, Jefferson, who had every reason to be enraged but said nothing about his friend's bizarre behavior, immediately voiced reservations about remaining executor of the will. He cited his age (seventy-five) and the likelihood that it would be too difficult for one his age to effectively handle. Had he known about the 1816 will, which effectively revoked all previous wills, including the 1798 bequest, he would have been even more adamant. Only hesitant at first, Jefferson bowed out upon learning of Kościuszko's other wills and of people's making claims to Kościuszko's funds under them. This complicated matter, he said, would take longer to resolve than he had to live. Seventeen thousand dollars, the amount at issue, was in 1818 a great deal of money, by the most conservative estimate, worth almost half a million dollars today. The beneficiaries of the other wills were not simply going to walk away from that without fighting, and they did not. Jefferson was right about the inherently litigious nature of this situation. The case, started in the early 1820s, dragged on for decades, going all the way up to the U.S. Supreme Court, which decided in 1852, not surprisingly, that the 1816 bequest had revoked the 1798 bequest.[43]

This matter was all very public, and people waited for the well-known antislavery advocate to execute the will. It would have been an incredibly important and symbolic moment. Many were sorely disappointed when Jefferson did not follow through. What the general public likely did not know, and he did not wish to be known, is that Jefferson in 1818 was in dire financial straits and had only recently suffered a grievous legal setback that left him with no stomach for another legal battle. For over a decade Jefferson had been in litigation with his neighbors the Henderson family concerning land in nearby Milton that he thought he had purchased from them in 1801. After having sunk a considerable amount of money and hopes for development into the property, and fighting over it, he lost the case, and was told that he had to repurchase the land. It was a devastating blow. The historian Robert Haggard correctly describes this loss as a "monumental disappointment" to Jefferson, whose "purchases in and around Milton . . . represent[ed]" the squandering of one of his last chances at solvency.[44]

Acting as an executor of an estate then, as now, is no small thing. The law in Maryland, where the Kościuszko will was probated, required executors of wills to post a bond and find two sureties in case there were any problems with the administration of the estate. Any mistake that entailed costs would make the executor and sureties liable for repayment. Though Jefferson believed the 1798 will might stand (again not knowing about the 1816 will that contained revocation language), there would still be a fight. Being an executor to a contested will, with a large amount of money at stake, was not a duty for one in personal financial distress to undertake. Could people who knew him well enough to be asked to stand as a surety for him under these conditions be confident in Jefferson's financial circumstances? His fame had not helped him win the Henderson case. There was no reason to assume it would have mattered in the inevitable Kościuszko litigation.

Jefferson wanted the will executed, and he took action to see that it would be. He turned to a member of the younger generation in whom he had great trust, John Hartwell Cocke, thirty-nine, to undertake the task. The freed slaves would benefit just as much if Cocke were successful as if Jefferson had been. Cocke, six years older than Coles, was a part of the "living generation" for whom Jefferson had high hopes. Having become something of a right-hand man to Jefferson, he was helping him found the University of Virginia. There, too, Jefferson's fame was no assurance of success, for Virginians were skeptical about, if not in many cases downright hostile toward, the proposed university because of his determination to make it a secular institution that would be built with public funds. Cocke tried, but determined that the will's provisions were in contravention of Virginia law. Jefferson then turned to William Wirt, who asked the Orphan's Court in Maryland to appoint an executor. Benjamin Lear, a local attorney, took on the matter. Jefferson kept track of the progress of this case until his death, and afterward his grandson continued to correspond with Lear. In the end, no slaves were freed from the bequest. Kościuszko's inexplicable decisions to write four wills, one with a revocation clause, doomed the effort. It would have been better had the Polish patriot forgone the interest on the investment of the money, and instead used the funds to free slaves when he was alive.

Ward Republics

Unlike the slavery question, the workings of politics and the government, a true passion for Jefferson, never totally receded from view. He continued to think about Virginia's future, setting forth his mature conception of federalism and democracy and building on his notion of generational sovereignty that would perpetuate the republic. In 1816, in the midst of a debate over whether Virginians should replace their 1776 constitution, Jefferson renewed his familiar call for each generation to draft its own fundamental law, adding a new, spatial dimension to the temporal boundaries of generational self-determination. As he explained to Joseph C. Cabell, "dividing and subdividing these republics from the great national one down through all its subordinations, until it ends in the administration of every man's farm by himself," would best secure the legacy of the revolution. The problem in Virginia was that the process of subdivision had not been completed: this was Jefferson's agenda for constitutional reform. The commonwealth itself had a democratically elected republican government (though representation was unequally distributed), but counties were still ruled by irresponsible, effectively self-appointed oligarchies, as they had been in colonial days, and there was nothing in Virginia equivalent to the New England town meeting, with its array of local elected officials. Jefferson's mission was to bring republican government down to the level of the people, where they lived, and his reformist mantra now was "Divide the counties into wards."[45]

Jefferson's campaign to democratize Virginia spoke to a variety of compelling late-life obsessions. Most critical, perhaps, was his anxiety that the Spirit of '76 would gradually diminish as younger generations busied themselves with more selfish and immediate concerns.

Continuous political participation would foster patriotic attachments. "Where every man is a sharer in the direction of his ward-republic, or of some of the higher ones, and feels that he is a participator in the government of affairs, not merely at an election one day in the year, but every day," then he would be prepared to sacrifice everything in the republic's defense. "When there shall not be a man in the State who will not be a member of some one of its councils, great or small," Jefferson told Cabell, "he will let the heart be torn out of his body sooner than his power be wrested from him by a Caesar or a Bonaparte." A fully elaborated federal regime would connect each citizen to his neighbors and, through ever more inclusive spheres of jurisdiction and communal identification, to the "great national" republic. Each citizen would feel a sense of ownership over his own government; the citizen-soldier, ever ready to fight and die, embodied the patriotic commitment that would perpetuate the republic. He was the republic's "heart," and his blood sacrifices cemented the ties that bound generation to generation.

It is no accident that Jefferson's thinking about "ward republics" drew him back to his earlier advocacy of universal public education. His 1779 proposal for primary schools in the Bill for the More General Diffusion of Knowledge would constitute the base of a pedagogical pyramid, rising through a system of selective secondary or "grammar" schools to its collegiate apex in a renovated and republicanized College of William and Mary.[46] Jefferson's scheme would require new jurisdictions that could mobilize the fathers and property owners of each neighborhood to locate, support, and manage the local school. Convinced that oligarchs who dominated the county courts balked at universal primary education "as a plan to educate the poor at the expense of the rich," Jefferson still promoted a comprehensive system in 1816 as he mobilized support for Central College and what would become the University of Virginia.[47] But Cabell and other local informants made it clear that wary taxpayers more generally, not just the county gentry, were unwilling to pay taxes to support local public schools.

Jefferson came to accept the fact that Virginia was not ready for his idea of a statewide system of primary and secondary education, and decided to go for what he could get. He focused his energies on gaining state support for his college, but kept the overall idea of dividing Virginia into the "wards" that would have put in place and administered the local schools. Whether or not neighbors wanted to invest in schools, he believed that they knew their own interests better than unelected county officials. Creating ward governments would give citizens an authoritative voice in what concerned them most intimately, yielding administrative efficiencies as it engaged and attached them to government. "Divide the counties into wards of such size as that every citizen can attend, when called on, and act in person," Jefferson urged Samuel Kercheval, and "ascribe to them the government of . . . all things relating to themselves exclusively," including the election of county officials. Not surprisingly, New England was his model. "These wards, called townships in New England," he concluded, "are the vital principle of their governments, and have proved themselves the wisest invention ever devised by the wit of man for the perfect exercise of self-government, and for its preservation."[48] Jefferson envisioned a perfected republican polity that was "divided and subdivided" along both vertical and horizontal lines: successive jurisdictional levels, rising up from the solid foundation of the ward republic along a vertical axis. This configuration would secure the great "national republic" against "a Caesar or a Bonaparte" or any other external threat; meanwhile, Americans would be protected from each other—along a horizontal axis—by a federal division of authority that secured the equal rights of citizens, wards, counties, and states.

The apparently paradoxical theme of dividing to unite was foundational to Jefferson's republican thought, beginning with his defense of individual and corporate rights in the revolution. Only when citizens were equally secure in their rights could they identify with their fellow citizens, thus seeing each other collectively as a generation, and freely consent to sacrifices on behalf of future generations. What would happen to the republic if rights were *not* secure, and vigilant citizens detected bad faith in their supposed "countrymen"? In that case, the "gradations" of government would serve as "a system of fundamental balances and checks" or, perhaps more accurately, a series of defensive barriers *against* any level of government that overstepped its boundaries.[49] This was no mere hypothetical possibility to Jefferson. He grew anxious throughout his retirement years about encroachments by the federal judiciary. And he saw the Missouri crisis as a conspiracy of northern neo-Federalists to recapture the federal government and deprive Missourians of their right to establish a republican government for themselves, even if that meant they voted to maintain slavery. "Altho' I had laid down as a law to myself, never to write, talk or even think of politics, to know nothing of public affairs & therefore had ceased to read newspapers," Jefferson wrote his old protégé William Short, "the Missourie question aroused and filled me with alarm."[50]

The ambiguous character of Jeffersonian federalism, simultaneously connecting citizens to and defending them from the larger world, mapped neatly onto Monticello's ambiguous moral geography. Jefferson's retreat into his private compartment allowed him to sustain relations with the larger world through his correspondence, renewing himself for engagement with the world at home. The final stage of the subdivision he outlined to Cabell in 1816 underscored the parallel between his constitutional theorizing and his personal circumstances. The "secret" of good government, Jefferson told his loyal lieutenant, was that each citizen must be made "himself the depository of the powers respecting himself." The genius of federalism was to be found "in the administration of every man's farm by himself." "All will be done for the best," he concluded, "by placing under every one what his own eye may superintend."[51]

The patriarch was the sovereign in his own plantation domain, and therefore free from the control—and prying eyes—of his neighbors, or of any supposedly higher authority. Jeffersonian democracy was grounded in the sovereignty of the citizen, secure in his rights. What Jefferson wanted for himself—and had in his own life—was conflated with the desires and capacities of all other free white American men. Jefferson's envisioned a country of such people who would live and be just like him, albeit on a smaller scale. These men would not only be sovereigns in their own homes; they would be able to move freely in the larger world, forging the solidarities—among citizens, in families, across generations—that enabled human beings to flourish. What man would not wish to be a patriarch after this fashion?

Morality and Faith

"I am old, and tranquillity is now my summum bonum," Jefferson told Dr. Benjamin Waterhouse, his Unitarian correspondent in Cambridge, Massachusetts, in 1822. As an old man, he could take comfort "in the prospect of a restoration of primitive Christianity," stripped of the mystifications and distortions "engrafted into it by the mythologists of the middle and modern ages." Yet again, this reformation would be the work of the "younger Athletes" of the living generation.[52] Jefferson thought he could discern history's progressive trajectory as his time on earth was coming to a close. "I rejoice that in this blessed country of free inquiry and belief, which has surrendered its creed and conscience to neither kings nor priests, the genuine doctrine of one only God is reviving," he wrote Waterhouse, concluding with the wildly mistaken prediction "that there is not a *young man* now living in the United States who will not die an Unitarian."[53]

Jefferson's prayers and predictions connected him with the world of the living, offering him the consoling prospect that his republican faith would be redeemed in the fullness of time. It might take more than an "age," but Americans would eventually recognize the injustice of slavery and work toward emancipation; perhaps the religious reformation would come sooner, even in the next generation. Jefferson could thus look forward to a time, sooner or later, when his vision of an enlightened future would be fulfilled. He and his fellow Americans would then speak with a single voice, as they had in 1776 when he set forth the self-evident principles that justified American independence. On his gravestone Jefferson thus commemorated his authorship of the Declaration, for this marked the epochal moment— the beginning of American time—that would live on in the memory of future generations. So, too, he identified himself as the author of the "Statute of Virginia for religious freedom." Free to think for themselves and to worship accordingly, Jefferson told Adams, Americans inevitably would recover "the primitive and genuine doctrines" of Jesus, "the most venerated reformer of human errors."[54] Recovering the tenets of "primitive Christianity" and keeping faith with the principles of 1776 would guarantee the republic's perpetuity.

The people's progress, however, depended on their enlightenment, and this is where his role as "Father of the University of Virginia" was crucial to Jefferson's legacy. He could die in the comforting knowledge that there would be many young men like him—many Jeffersons—in future generations who would probe the frontiers of knowledge, spread enlightenment, and promote moral development. The dying patriarch may have squandered his estate, leaving his family with next to nothing, but he could think of himself as the "father" and benefactor of rising generations. He would be remembered as a member of the generation of 1776, one of the "host of worthies" who enabled future "sons of liberty" to become fathers themselves.[55]

The fatherhood that Jefferson claimed on his gravestone was abstracted from his own family and reconfigured in line with his conception of generational sovereignty. The gravestone marked his final withdrawal from the affairs of living men, anticipated by his retirement and his retreat into the "tranquillity" of his sanctum sanctorum. This was the ultimate responsibility of the departing generation as it gave way to its self-governing successors, the earth's only legitimate proprietors.

"I consider our relations with others as constituting the boundaries of morality," Jefferson wrote Thomas Law in 1814. "Self-love, therefore, is no part of morality," he explained, for we "can owe no duties" to ourselves, "obligation requiring" at least "two parties." Jefferson's contractual language seems to suggest the primacy of the head's self-interested calculation, but was instead grounded in the heart's capacity for love and sacrifice. "The Creator would indeed have been a bungling artist," Jefferson told Law, "had he intended man for a social animal, without planting in him social dispositions."[56] A good heart, man's natural endowment, could be directed toward good, moral ends in childhood. The family modeled loving relationships, and the discipline exercised by parents as guardians and stewards would inculcate good behavior long before children could rationally calculate their own best interests. Parental authority, not the transcendent authority of a mysterious and inscrutable God, was critical to this moral education, for Jefferson's God acted *through* his creation to make his intentions clear. This is why the young Jefferson railed against conventional religious education for young people. Impressionable children too easily could be led astray and confuse the self-interested mystifications of priestcraft with God's design. Premature leaps of faith could spoil good hearts, perpetuating the darkness of ignorance or superstition.

The moral philosopher's proper sequence was from the fruit to the tree, from good moral actions to a progressively deeper understanding of their source and significance. "For it is in our lives, and not from our words, that our religion must be read," Jefferson wrote Margaret Bayard Smith in 1816. "By the same test the world must judge me."[57] At the end of his day, Jefferson had dismissed the inessential complexities of the theologians. It was clear from his Bible reading that Jesus was a great moralist whose teachings offered the most compelling and accessible account of God's intentions for mankind. The great flaw of conventional and corrupted Christianity was that the priests had mystified the life of Jesus, making him a God-on-earth whose supposed miracles made a mockery of his "father's" original design.

Children should not be indoctrinated in the mysteries of faith at too early an age. As they prepared to assume the responsibilities of adulthood, they instead needed to follow the lead of the moral sense that had been cultivated in their childhood homes. Through the careful study of moral philosophy and ethics, the standard complement—and even replacement—of theology in the curriculum in American colleges, young men would learn how to chart their own way in the larger world. In doing so, they would find Jesus's teachings an increasingly useful guide, for his was "the purest system of morals ever before preached to man."[58] Jesus inculcated "universal philanthropy, not only to kindred and friends, to neighbors and countrymen, but to all mankind, gathering all into one family, under the bonds of love, charity, peace, common wants and common aids."[59]

Good Christians recognized each other—and all men—as brothers, making the idea of family inclusive in a way that resonated with Jefferson's conception of the generation. "We all agree in the obligation of the moral precepts of Jesus," Jefferson told a clerical correspondent in 1809, shortly after he retired to Monticello. "But we schismatize & lose ourselves in subtleties about his nature, his conception maculate or immaculate, whether he was a god or not a god, whether his votaries are to be initiated by simple aspersion, by immersion, or without water." Whereas Jesus preached a gospel of peace, his supposed followers made war on each other: "oceans of human blood have been spilt, & whole regions of the earth have been desolated by wars & persecutions" in his name.[60]

The Old Man's Prayer

Jefferson wrote to the Methodist preacher Miles King in 1814 in language that can be taken as a form of prayer or affirmation of faith.

> I have trust in him who made us what we are, and knows it was not his plan to make us always unerring. he has formed us moral agents, not that, in the perfection of his state, he can feel pain or pleasure from any thing we may do: he is far above our power: but that we may promote the happiness of those with whom he has placed us in society, by acting honestly towards all, benevolently to those who fall within our way, respecting sacredly their rights bodily and mental, and cherishing especially their freedom of conscience, as we value our own.[61]

Jefferson did not retreat to his private quarters in order to ponder metaphysical subtleties, or to achieve some kind of mystical connection with a transcendent reality: "He is," after all, "far above our power." The truths that mattered, about how man should act as a morally responsible agent in the world, were well known to the mature Jefferson, internalized by habits of the heart and reasoning of the head as a kind of second nature. Instead, his energies were directed at reconciling ancient and modern ethical systems, establishing a plausible narrative of Jesus's life, and gleaning his fundamental teachings from the Bible's corruptions. This was important to him, for he understood that religion would remain an important part of life in the American republic. The question was what form this religious engagement would take.

Jefferson's radically edited version of the Gospels was his attempt to create an enlightened, republicanized form of American Christianity. This was a scripture that would be useful in teaching children the fundamental precepts of Christian morality. As a younger man, Jefferson had thought that uplifting and edifying fiction might play a useful role in children's moral education. Now he believed that gospel parables could achieve and improve on that same exalted end, preparing the young to embrace the full implications of Jesus's "universal philanthropy."

Jefferson's labors in culling through the Gospels were another kind of prayer, offered posthumously to future generations of republican children. Yet they may have been something more than this. Perhaps his labors represented the culmination of a faithful republican's efforts to bend toward the common, moral sense of his Christian countrymen. His characterization of Jesus as "a benevolent and sublime reformer" and his translation of Enlightenment moral philosophy into the biblical vernacular authorized his evidently sincere claim to being a "Christian." Yet the decidedly heterodox Jefferson recognized that he remained vulnerable to "the overbearing inquisition of public opinion" until that glorious and enlightened day when, as he wrote to the Unitarian Jared Sparks, "truth will prevail over fanaticism, and the genuine doctrines of Jesus, so long perverted by His pseudo priests, will again be restored to their original purity." "This reformation," like constitutional reform and the end of slavery would "advance with the other improvements of the human mind, but too late for [him] to witness it." It was consoling enough for the aging Jefferson to sustain a prayerful expectation that these good things would one day come to pass.[62]

could the dead feel any interest in Monuments or other remembrances of them, when, as
Anacreon says: Ολίγη δε κεισομεσθα
Κονις, οστεων λυθεντων
the following would be to my Manes the most
gratifying.
On the grave
a plain die or cube of 3.f without any
mouldings, surmounted by an Obelisk
of 6.f. height, each of a single stone:
on the faces of the Obelisk the following
inscription, & not a word more

Here was buried
Thomas Jefferson
Author of the Declaration of American Independance
of the Statute of Virginia for religious freedom
& Father of the University of Virginia.

because by these, as testimonials that I have lived, I wish most to
be remembered. these to be of the coarse stone of which
my columns are made, that no one might be tempted
hereafter to destroy it for the value of the materials.
my bust by Ciracchi, with the pedestal and truncated
column on which it stands, might be given to the University
if they would place it in the Dome room of the Rotunda.
on the Die, might be engraved
of the Obelisk
Born Apr. 2. 1743. O.S.
Died ——

Jefferson's design and inscription for his tombstone. (Library of Congress)

EPILOGUE

A bigail Adams was a parent, and like many parents in the eighteenth century she had lost children. Knowing how it felt to bury one's child, she reached out to Jefferson after she learned that his daughter Maria Jefferson Eppes had died at Monticello in April of 1804. She wrote to him in Washington, DC, on May 20, 1804, commiserating with him on the death of Polly, as her family knew her, following complications from childbirth. Throughout her pregnancy and afterward, Jefferson, from the President's House in Washington, had anxiously followed his daughter's medical condition. A longer than normal session of Congress had kept him in place as Maria's health deteriorated. She had come to her sister Martha's house at Edgehill to have her baby. Watching from afar, Jefferson suggested that Maria might be better off at the more well-appointed Monticello. Determining that a carriage would tax her too much, enslaved men made a litter and carried the young mother up the hill to the place of her birth. Jefferson made it home on April 4, just in time to see Maria. His presence lifted her spirits. For a few days it appeared she might recover, but the hope was illusory. She died two weeks after Jefferson got home.[1]

As the historian Lucia Stanton has noted, Maria's death "shattered" Jefferson. Receiving Adams's letter at such a low moment in his life, no doubt, was like a balm to his wounded spirit. This man longed to have everyone love or, at least, like him—so much so that he was willing to say what was needed to achieve that result. "It is a charming thing," he once wrote to his first three grandchildren, "to be loved by everybody"—and he was serious.[2] Of course, there was no way to even approach the state of being universally loved without often misleading people about one's thoughts and feelings, hiding them or misrepresenting them to head off potential conflict. Adams's missive suggested that she was ready to allow him back into her good graces—to love him again. Jefferson jumped at the chance. This, he hoped, might be the moment when the enduring bonds of friendship between the two families triumphed over the political and philosophical differences that had led to their estrangement. He envisioned a moment like this in his Head and Heart letter to Maria Cosway in October 1786. When a dear friend "loses a child, a parent, or a partner," he then wrote, "we must mourn the loss as if it were our own." Though he and Abigail Adams, writing from Quincy, Massachusetts, were geographically distant, their renewed correspondence could bring them back together. "What more sublime delight," he poetically exclaimed in his letter to Cosway, "than to mingle tears with one whom the hand of heaven hath smitten!"[3]

It was not yet to be. Mrs. Adams shed tears for Polly, recalling the moment when she had met—and parted with—Jefferson's nine-year-old daughter in London in 1787, but she would *not* "mingle tears" with her old friend. When Jefferson sailed for Europe in 1784, he had left Polly in Virginia with her aunt Eppes and her family, from whom she desperately resisted separation; three years later Polly, accompanied by her traveling companion, Sally Hemings, was en route to Paris to be reunited with a father she barely knew. Polly and Abigail Adams formed an instant and intense attachment, setting the stage for yet another emotionally devastating separation. "The tender scene of her seperation from me, rose to my recollection, when she clung around my neck and wet my Bosom with her tears, saying, 'O! now I have learned to Love you, why will they tear me from you.'" Many years later, after Polly departed this earth, Adams confided to

Jefferson, "The powerfull feelings of my heart, have burst through the restraint and called upon me to shed the tear of sorrow over the departed remains, of your beloved and deserving daughter, an event which I most sincerely mourn." Yet "feelings of mutual sympathy" did *not* point her toward reconciliation with Jefferson. He should turn to God, not to her, for "comfort and consolation."[4]

In 1804 Jefferson stood at the pinnacle of political popularity. His successful first presidential term had culminated in the acquisition of Louisiana, a vast hinterland of imperial dimensions that would guarantee "room enough for our descendants" into the foreseeable future—if not "to the thousandth and thousandth generation."[5] As he scanned the political horizon, he could take deep satisfaction in the declining fortunes of the vanquished Federalists and anticipate his landslide victory and vindication in the 1804 presidential canvass. In his second inaugural address, in March 1805, he congratulated his countrymen on the ascendancy of the "truth," "reason," and enlightened self-interest that will "complete their entire union of opinion, which gives to a nation the blessing of harmony, and the benefit of all its strength."[6] For forward-looking Americans, the end of party strife and an ever more perfect union would heal all wounds. Yet some wounds, Jefferson's frustrating exchange with Abigail Adams painfully reminded him, remained open and resisted healing.

Jefferson and John Adams had after all been great allies and friends in 1776, when they took leading roles in the struggle for American independence. When the two patriots served the new nation as diplomats in Europe in the 1780s (together in 1784–85 in Paris, where Jefferson remained until 1789 after Adams moved on to the Court of St. James in London), the Adams family treated the widower from Virginia as a virtual family member. Jefferson and Abigail Adams sustained a lively and affectionate correspondence across the English Channel, mixing high politics with home news and society gossip. There was every reason to expect that the close attachment between the families would flourish when they returned to America and the two men assumed positions in the new Washington administration, with the older Adams serving as vice-president and Jefferson as secretary of state. But unanticipated political divisions soon emerged within the administration and Congress and eventually in an increasingly polarized electorate.

Relations between Adams and Jefferson decidedly chilled as they found themselves more or less unwillingly drawn into party battles that seemed to threaten the fragile new republic's very survival. Adams's narrow victory over Jefferson in the 1796 presidential election made his old friend vice-president, but did not heal the breach. Quite to the contrary, James Madison and other political advisers warned Jefferson that a conciliatory approach to Adams would alienate their political friends and subvert their campaign to redeem the republic from the Federalists' political heresies.[7] The new president and his vice-president instead avoided increasingly vicious party conflict— and each other—as much as they could by spending long stretches of time at their respective homes, in Massachusetts and Virginia. For the Adamses the bitter presidential contest of 1800 marked the final rupture with their former dear friend. With Jefferson's ascendancy to the presidential chair in 1801, there was no need to sustain the faux civility of their shared administration. John and Abigail purposely left Washington, DC, early on the morning of Jefferson's inauguration on March 4; they were not in the audience to hear Jefferson declare an end to partisan controversy and plead with his fellow Americans, "Let us restore to social intercourse that harmony and affection without which liberty, and even life itself, are but dreary things."[8]

After he received Abigail Adams's condolence letter, Jefferson wrote to her three times over the next several months, and she replied at length in a correspondence that she kept secret from her husband. Repeatedly insisting on his undying friendship and esteem for the Adamses, Jefferson attributed the rupture in their relations to partisan excesses. He disclaimed any responsibility for those excesses, congratulating himself instead on magnanimously overlooking Adams's "midnight appointments." (He considered the departing president's last-minute appointments of fellow Federalists to federal offices as an encumbrance on his incoming administration and "personally unkind.")[9] Never one to be easily moved from a firm stance, Mrs.

Adams was not persuaded. The price of reconciliation was much too steep. In effect, Jefferson asked her to accept his protestations of innocence and good faith. She was looking for more, for some acknowledgment of his role in the partisan hysteria that divided the country and destroyed friendships. Had he been prepared to acknowledge them, Mrs. Adams might have forgiven Jefferson's sins against her husband and family. She recognized that the Adamses themselves—including her son John Quincy, who, writing for the press as "Publicola," took the lead in vilifying Jefferson—were hardly free of sin. In an age of political passion, when patriot turned against patriot, no one could claim immunity. The Sedition Act, which Adams signed into law, punished criticism of every public official save the vice-president, the office Jefferson happened to be occupying at the time the act was put in place. People were free to criticize him, and many did so with abandon.

Mrs. Adams tried to open Jefferson's eyes, but "party spirit is blind malevolent uncandid, ungenerous, unjust and unforgiving."[10] She condemned her former friend for an "ardent zeal" that was "derogatory to [his] honour, and independence of Character."[11] Jefferson's unwillingness to acknowledge his own partisan motives and deeds was infuriating, leading Mrs. Adams to catalog grievances that the former lawyer proceeded to explain away. But she would not allow Jefferson to distance himself from the recent—and for her, ongoing—history of partisan combat that had caused her family such suffering. John Adams was a prime victim of that combat, and the wounds he brought home and the pain he shared with his family definitively refuted Jefferson's distinction between politics and domestic life. Fiercely protective of her loved ones, Abigail Adams defended her family. As she mourned Polly Jefferson Eppes's death, she also mourned the death of her friendship with Jefferson. "Faithfull are the wounds of a Friend," she concluded, and those wounds were only deepened by Jefferson's implausible denials. "Often have I wished to have seen a different course pursued by you."[12]

No friend—perhaps no one—had ever said such hard things directly to Jefferson. His pain must have been compounded by the pointed reminder of that earlier time when Polly arrived in London and wondered why her father did not take "pains" to meet her, instead sending his French servant Adrien Petit—"a man whom she [could not] understand"—to take her on to her new home.[13] Both Adamses were deeply upset with Jefferson about his failure to come and get his little girl. Her criticism of her "esteemed friend" was muted then, but unmistakable in retrospect. Adams's discussion of Jefferson's betrayal of the Adamses during their correspondence about the death of his daughter, and her reference to other times he had disappointed her, called into question his role as a father at a crucial moment in Polly's childhood. He had brought his eldest daughter with him to France and left Polly and his youngest daughter, Lucy, behind. When he had the chance to greet her once he decided to bring her to his Paris residence, he neglected to do so. Leaving Polly, only six years old, and Lucy, a toddler, may have seemed, at the time, the prudent thing to do. It would have been natural, however, for Polly to have paused over the fact that her father had taken Patsy and not her. Virginia proved to be no safer for Lucy than Paris would have been. During her tragically shortened life, Polly wondered about her father's love for her, suspecting that he might favor her more accomplished sister Patsy. When she married her cousin Francis Eppes, she returned to her childhood home at Eppington—the home that her widower father could never provide. With heartfelt sincerity Jefferson repeatedly reassured Polly that he loved his daughters equally. So, too, he now reassured Adams, "Neither my estimate of your character, nor the esteem founded in that, have ever been lessened for a single moment, although doubts whether it would be acceptable may have forbidden manifestations of it." His friendship with her husband, John, "began at an earlier date" and "accompanied us thro' long & important scenes" in the new nation's early history. Party politics did not affect their relationship: "The different conclusions we had drawn from our political reading & reflections, were not permitted to lessen mutual esteem."[14]

To Abigail Adams's ear, this was all arrant nonsense. Vicious partisan assaults were fueled by those "different conclusions," and the characters of the two friends were subject to unrelenting abuse. Jefferson deployed the passive voice ("were not permitted") to extricate and insulate party leaders from their followers, but his self-serving distinction was absurdly untenable. Yet the more Adams insisted on the messy and painful realities of the political life that she and her family experienced, the more Jefferson insisted on the absolute and unbreachable wall of separation between private and public, home and world. He would never betray his sacred commitments to family and friends—and particularly to friends like the Adamses who had welcomed him and his daughters into their family. This was something that Jefferson needed to believe about himself in the face of all of the considerable evidence to the contrary. It was the foundation of his patriarchal republican faith.

Jefferson could not find the words that Abigail Adams needed to hear in order to bring about a longed-for reconciliation, precisely because they would have constituted an acknowledgment that his faith was flawed. It was less a question of pride—a sin that New Englanders would readily recognize—than Jefferson's commitment to a conception of American nationhood that depended on the enduring attachments of patriots in an expanding "empire of liberty." The new nation's civic capacity, Jefferson believed, was grounded in republican family life, in the home soil where young citizens' natural sociability and moral sense first took root and flourished. "Every difference of opinion" was not and could not be "a difference of principle," as he told his fellow Americans in his inaugural address.[15] And the principle that bound them together was nothing less than the love that revolutionary patriots bore for each other—and so eloquently expressed in the sacrifices they made to secure American independence.

Jefferson's second presidential term, as so many are, was much less successful than the first, testing and chastening his republican faith. In March 1805, as he took office as president for the second and last time, he could still exult in the progressive fulfillment of the predictions of his first inaugural. The Union had almost fallen apart in the run-up to his "Revolution of 1800," and its future was then by no means secure; the "mighty wave of public opinion" that supposedly swept across the land was less a verifiable, evidence-based description of recent events than a prayer for the future, a testimonial to Jefferson's faith in the wisdom of the people as they emerged from the confusion and darkness of party conflict.[16] Over the course of his second term, American prospects seemed less and less assured: the new nation's security was threatened on land as well as at sea; conflicting sectional interests seemed ever more intractable; if partisan fires dimmed, Jefferson's Republican coalition was disturbingly prone to political and ideological division. Many of his followers hoped he would agree to a third term, precisely because divisions among Americans seemed so intractable. But the old man's time had passed, and he was eager to leave the stage of public life. The time had come for him to look back, to reflect on the course his life had taken.

THE FAILED RECONCILIATION between Jefferson and Abigail Adams in 1804 was evidence of the importance each attached to their relationship. Jefferson insisted that his love for Abigail and her family would endure forever, regardless of the vicissitudes of their troubled times; for Abigail the once strong bond had been irrevocably sundered. But their world was a far different place seven years later when Benjamin Rush of Pennsylvania—a fellow signer of the Declaration of Independence—initiated a successful effort to reconcile Jefferson and John Adams. Rush, who regularly corresponded with both old friends, told Adams that he had had a dream that Adams and Jefferson had reconciled. Once he learned that Adams was amenable, Rush approached Jefferson, who was receptive to the idea, but made it plain that it would be hard for Abigail Adams to be a part of the restoration of good relations. Matters proceeded, and on January 1, 1812, Adams penned a short letter from Quincy to his old friend at Monticello, concluding, "I wish you Sir many happy New years and that you may enter the next and many Succeeding years with as animating Prospects for the Public as those at present before us."[17] Now that the two old men were both retired from public life, they had the leisure to repair a rupture they both long and deeply regretted. And they both understood that their reconciliation had a broader significance for the new nation they had helped bring into existence. The threat of another war with Britain made union among patriots essential, as it had been in 1776. By rising above partisan bitterness and reaffirming their personal union, Adams and Jefferson would set an inspiring example for their countrymen. It would take time, but eventually Jefferson and Abigail Adams also reached a form of rapprochement.[18]

The two old friends found that they could talk about anything—including the political and philosophical issues that had once divided them—in a rich and engaging correspondence that they sustained until their simultaneous deaths, on July 4, 1826. Jefferson could now make good on the claims of enduring esteem and affection that seemed so disingenuous to Abigail Adams in 1804. Though he never assumed any personal responsibility for the "excesses" committed by his partisan followers, Jefferson could acknowledge the legitimacy of the clashing opinions that seemed to loom so large in the 1790s: in the heat of the moment, neither side could see clearly. When some of Adams's more heated and intemperate comments about Jefferson—in private, supposedly confidential correspondence—surfaced many years later, the legendarily thin-skinned Virginian dismissed them peremptorily: "The circumstances of the times, in which we have happened to live, & the partiality of our friends, at a particular period, placed us in a state of apparent opposition, which some might suppose to be personal." Neither should blame the other for the company they once kept. Their opposition was only "apparent"; like the republic itself, their "personal" bond would endure the tests of time.[19]

The two patriots achieved a degree of philosophical detachment by putting their shared labors in the Continental Congress into historical perspective. The party battles of the 1790s receded into the background as they explored formerly contentious issues—most notably, the danger that aristocratic tendencies posed to the republic—in a civil, sometimes even playful way. Patriots could talk about these things without demonizing and threatening each other. Jefferson might still believe that his victory over Adams in the "Revolution of 1800" had saved the republic from imminent peril, but that partisan perspective was tactfully muted in his correspondence with Adams. In any case, by 1812 it was hard for even the most optimistic ideo-logue to imagine that the worldwide republican millennium was near at hand. As they assessed the prospects for republicanism over sub-sequent years, the two men agreed that "ocians" (Adams's term) or "rivers of blood [Jefferson's] must yet flow, & years of desolation pass over" before the nations of Europe gained their freedom.[20] In the meantime Jefferson and Adams cherished the "sacred fire of liberty" that still burned in the United States. They thus revealed themselves to each other to be what we would now call "American exception-alists": patriotism was the deep ground of their enduring friendship.

Jefferson and Adams were acutely aware of their mortality. Solic-itous about each other's health, they reported on their own ailments and waning powers. They also, and assiduously so, tracked the fate of the ever-dwindling number of fellow signers of the Declaration. As long as they lived, they knew they would be revered by their country-men, but they also were consoled with the knowledge that they would be remembered when they were long gone. This theme was implicit in their theological ruminations about the afterlife. As a philosophi-cal materialist, Jefferson could not contemplate absolute nothingness: something beyond failing memories must survive death. For a patriot the idea of the nation itself, and the infinite succession of generations, offered a consoling image of immortality. The devastating personal losses that Jefferson and Adams suffered gave rise to deep longing for some sort of life after death. Commiserating with Adams on the death of his "dear companion" Abigail in October 1818, Jefferson promised his old friend something like a family reunion in heaven: "the term is not very distant at which we are to deposit, in the same cerement, our sorrows and suffering bodies, and to ascend in essence to an ecstatic meeting with the friends we have loved & lost and whom we shall still love and never lose again."[21]

Death promised "ecstatic meetings" with family members and friends, a restoration to the domestic bliss and wholeness that Jefferson cherished in his fireside memories. Yet if his thoughts turned home-ward as he contemplated death, they also anticipated the boundless perspectives, across space and into the future, that were suggested by views from his mountaintop home. It was an article of faith for Jefferson that "nature's God" intended all peoples to be free, including the unjustly enslaved people who worked his plantation: "time, which outlives all things, will outlive this evil also."[22] Jefferson would not be alone in seeing these glorious things come to pass. "You and I shall look down from another world on these glorious atchievements to man," he assured Adams, and they "will add to the joys even of heaven."[23] In death the patriot and the patriarch would achieve his rightful place. When he died and was transported to "another world," the servant of the people prayed that he would finally see the fulfillment of all his hopes for mankind.[24]

PATRIOT AND PATRIARCH: these are the two roles that Jefferson embraced in his lifelong quest to fashion himself. Throughout his adult life, and particularly in his later years, he imagined that self in the view of posterity.[25] He envisioned the nation as an unfolding succession of generations, with each rising generation governing itself—and its share of the "earth"—while preparing the way for its successors. As he approached death, he imagined himself in our place, looking back and taking stock of his generation's "atchievements." We have some idea of what he wanted us to see. What *do* we see? How prophetic was his vision?

The way we have taken Jefferson apart in "*Most Blessed of the Patriarchs*"—exploring the various roles he played and examining his ways of engaging with the world—suggests how we might put him back together, respectful of the self he sought to fashion but sensitive to the constraints and contradictions of his times and to the capacity we all have to tell stories about ourselves that obscure, elide, and overlook unpleasant truths. Things that seemed natural and could be taken for granted in his day are problems for us now: the kind of republican "patriarchy" that Jefferson celebrated and sought to practice strikes us as an arbitrary, privileged status, a "social construction" that we can—and should—live without. Yet our present-day quarrel with privilege should also enable us to recognize and sympathize with Jefferson's crusade against the unnatural and unjust privileges of aristocrats, monarchs, and priests. In the end he never did lead a crusade against slavery. But he certainly recognized the radical injustice of an institution that epitomized despotic rule—and that, he knew, would constitute a fatal flaw in the constitution of republican Virginia.

The slavery problem hit close to home for Jefferson, and that is one of the major reasons that we have spent so much time with him there, at Monticello and in the temporary homes he created elsewhere. It was in his plantation world that Jefferson followed an archaic script, exercising patriarchal authority over his household and brute force over the enslaved people the commonwealth's laws defined as his "property." But the patriarch understood household governance in sentimental terms, fashioning himself as a good man with a sacred responsibility for the happiness and well-being of all of his dependents. And well-governed families, he thought, were the foundation of republican self-government. Genuine consent depended on the independence and autonomy of equal citizens, secure against each other as well as against overreaching, illegitimate governments. Abstracted from the world of plantation slavery, Jefferson's advocacy of individual rights and the broad distribution of authority under federalism still strikes resonant chords for exponents of participatory democracy and local self-government. Jefferson, however, could never tear himself away from his beloved plantation and the people, free and enslaved, who looked out and labored for his happiness. At home, where Jefferson lived, his democratic ideas did not tell an emancipatory story; they instead protected, justified, and perpetuated a regime of unequal domestic relations, including slavery.

Jefferson put his entire self into his home, psychologically as well as financially, and those investments made it increasingly difficult for him to imagine any radical changes in his household regime. Home was his lodestar, a place that existed most vividly in his imagination. Absent for long stretches of time, the master of Monticello had to manage his never-ending construction campaigns from afar, with completion of his dream house always receding into the future.

The mountaintop was a perpetual construction site, and before his final retirement the house itself was often unoccupied. The domestic scenes he imagined materialized only when he was in residence, during his first retirement (1794–97) and periodic vacations when Martha and Maria and their families visited. Jefferson, nevertheless, kept the home fires burning in correspondence with family members, in planning improvements, and in acquiring things for his house.

VISITORS TO MONTICELLO, in Jefferson's time and ours, have interpreted the house as a kind of autobiographical statement. We see it as eloquent testimony to what was so often missing in his life, to the devastating personal losses that marked the passage of years, to evanescent moments of domestic happiness. There is, however, so much about the place that cannot be known. The letters and the records of his plantation, gardens, and accounts form but a small part of his existence. Fawn Brodie suggested that rather than living the life of a lonely bachelor forever pining for the lost wife who had bound him to what could only be described as an outrageous request that he never remarry, the widower Jefferson created a private personal life of happiness with the much younger enslaved half sister of his deceased wife. Brodie had not known of John Hartwell Cocke's diary entries, referenced in an earlier chapter, about his dear friend's domestic arrangements at Monticello with his "substitute for a wife," Sally Hemings. Brodie's idea enraged many—and continues to do so. Contemplating the dynamics of mixed-race–mixed-status families during Jefferson's and Hemings's time is a fraught enterprise. The visionary republican and the future he imagined for other American families, across the continent—a "chosen country" for this rising people—and through time, to "the thousandth and thousandth generation,"[26] could not encompass the family he had with Sally Hemings. They could never be a part of his imagined future for American families, because their existence did not promote the type of harmony Jefferson believed should reign in an ideal family. For the man who believed that every thing and every person had a place in life, Beverley, Harriet, Madison, and Eston Hemings were outside the magic circle of a legal white family, although by Virginia law they were considered "white." As he always intended to free them, these children could take their places as "free white citizen[s] of the United States." This is how the country Jefferson helped create could become home to his sons and daughter. Like the families in his emancipation and expatriation scheme, the mother and father would sacrifice connections with their children for the greater goal of freedom for the coming generations of the family, but in a different place, in another home, besides the slave plantation, Monticello, where they had started life on the lowest rung of the social ladder.

What Jefferson could not see in the great national American home was a place for the enslaved people who worked his fields, built and maintained his house, and sustained community life on his plantation across the generations. His more narrowly focused, self-centered idea of his home at Monticello subsumed these people in the plantation household he governed—benevolently, he imagined, but with a patriarch's absolute authority. Jefferson's slaves disappeared from this sentimental vision of home, as all slaves would have disappeared in fact if his dreamlike solution to the slavery problem—mass emancipation and expatriation—had ever been implemented. Despite his expressed dream, Jefferson never took steps to make it a reality and appears, by the end of his life, to have recognized its ultimate futility. The numbers were too large and were rapidly increasing to the point that millions of fighting black men would simply refuse to leave. In addition, his fellow planters would never agree to his plan to educate enslaved children—females to the age of eighteen and males to the age of twenty-one—to prepare them for departure, with the United States supporting the colony for a time to allow them to get their society in order. Why would they? Unlike other members of his Virginia cohort—James Madison, James Monroe, John Marshall, William Short, and, eventually, Edward Coles—Jefferson never joined the American Colonization Society. Adding his name to the list would not have been onerous, for no one would have expected him, at his advanced age, to do any actual work.

Perhaps formally joining the ACS would have been too much of a spectacle, because it would have raised, in the minds of all who knew Jefferson intimately and loved him—and in the minds of those who hated him—an obvious question: "Mr. Jefferson, are you actually joining in an effort to have your children and their mother expelled from Virginia and sent to Africa?" One can imagine the ridicule this would have provoked. At the end of his life, when actual decisions had to be made in the real world, not the republic of letters, the fantasy of emancipation and expatriation played no more of a role in Jefferson's life than it had in the 1790s when Robert and James Hemings were emancipated. When he freed five men in his will, he did not, as some slave owners had begun to do by this time, free them on the condition that they be expatriated to Africa. Acting in compliance with the 1806 Virginia statute that required freed slaves to have permission to remain in the state, Jefferson requested that the legislature allow these men to stay in Virginia with "their families and connexions." Jefferson could have made no better statement about why all African Americans, who had lived in North America for multiple generations, should have been allowed to remain in the United States. They and their families were bound to the same land that Jefferson loved, with their own hopes and dreams for the future. And he knew that.

As for Sally Hemings, Jefferson was the patriarch to the very end. Israel (Gillette) Jefferson listed her as among the enslaved people Jefferson freed upon his death. This was, evidently, the understanding at Monticello, fueled by her departure from the mountain when Jefferson died. Jefferson did not, however, free her in his will. She was freed informally, as Jefferson's family told his biographer Henry Randall that Wormley Hughes had been or, rather, that Jefferson had instructed Hughes to be freed if he wanted to be. Naturally, they said nothing about Sally Hemings. Hemings appeared as a free white person living in Charlottesville in the 1830 census. She told the taker of a special census, conducted in 1833 to determine which free black people wanted to return to Africa, that she, now designated as a person of color, had been freed in 1826, the year Jefferson died. She declined to make the trip to Africa.

Jefferson's failure to free Hemings formally has been offered through-out the years as evidence that he had no intimate connection to her or, alternatively, that the intimate connection he had with her was mean-ingless. The second interpretation raises the more legitimate question about Jefferson because the first view is internally inconsistent, since it leaves unexplained his emancipation of all of her children. If he had no important connection to them, why free this set of siblings? As we said in the preface to this work, our aim has not been to present Jefferson through the framework of what we think he ought to have done in a given circumstance. It has been to discern what Jefferson thought he was doing in the world. In order to do that, we must know some-thing about that world and consider seriously the context in which he was operating.

In 1826 Jefferson was about to leave the stage, having to make reckonings with his family situation in both economic and emotional terms. To free Hemings in the will he worked on during the final months of his life would have required putting the name Sally Hem-ings in a public document. Then Jefferson would have had to request that the legislature allow her to stay in Virginia. Virginia law did not allow for the emancipation of people under the age of twenty-one, or above forty-five, without an explanation for how they were to be cared for—or how they could care for themselves—in their freedom. Sally Hemings was fifty-three years old in 1826. Jefferson would have had to explain to the legislature and, thus, the world, exactly how he was going to provide for the woman many believed to be his mistress. Long before this point in history, when people said or wrote the name Sally in connection to Jefferson, everyone knew to whom the writer or speaker was referring. A will containing all of these requirements would be a public document that would live in history. Any doubts about Sally and Thomas would have been erased with this very public in-contemplation-of-death gesture.

There was no chance that Jefferson would ever risk his legacy by preparing such a document, or that he would publicly hurt and humiliate the most important person in his life, Martha Randolph. The private domain of Monticello, the world he lived in with Hemings there, was the patriarch's business, not the world's concern. It was his legal family's business only to the extent that he did not flaunt his forbidden connection, and did not treat his children with Hemings as if they were the same as his legitimate white children and grandchildren, which he did not do. Given his attitudes about women, it is unlikely that Jefferson the patriarch would have thought it proper to free a fifty-three-year-old woman. He freed Harriet Hemings because that was what he was supposed to do and she was young. *Partus sequitur ventrem* meant that any child she had in Virginia would be a slave, and slavery was to end for Sally Hemings's line when her children became adults. Jefferson knew the customs and ways of his community. White people in Charlottesville, who had experience with this type of thing, would consider her a free person—and they did. Martha Randolph simply left her half aunt alone. By the time Randolph made her own will, in 1834, and mentioned freeing Hemings, Hemings had already appeared in public documents as a free person.[27]

JEFFERSON TOOK HIS bearings from home when he imagined the nation's future, and it was his faith in the republican family form— replicated from generation to generation, in new farms and plantations across the continent—that enabled him to envision the United States as an ever-expanding "empire for liberty." He believed that American families conformed to the self-evident, natural order in God's design for mankind, modeling the moral sense and sociability that enabled "more perfect unions" within and among families. His conception of the generation extended that idea to the nation as a whole, a great and inclusive family of families. In his famous 1789 letter to James Madison on the rights of the "living generation," Jefferson proclaimed that "one generation is to another as one independant nation to another."[28] Americans did not constitute a people because they were subjects of an all-powerful and protective sovereign, but because they instead identified with each other, recognizing the civic capacity—and kinship—of fellow citizens. The great republic would not fall apart, as fearful critics at home and abroad predicted, collapsing into an anarchic scramble for power and profit. In Jefferson's empire of the imagination, truly independent and autonomous citizens, secure in their rights and therefore with nothing to fear, would be drawn ever closer, forming enduring attachments that would make their government the "strongest" on earth.

It was and still is a bold and inspiring vision. Yet just as Jefferson's self-fashioning project harked back to the age of patriarchs and an archaic conception of self-sovereignty, the "empire of liberty" evoked an idealized past even as it anticipated what a later generation would call the nation's "manifest destiny." Most obviously, Jefferson's new national home depended on the creation of new jurisdictions that secured property rights and the rule of law, so enabling frontier farmers and planters to replicate existing models of labor exploitation.[29] On the dynamic southwestern frontier, the families Americans formed and the homes they built gave racial slavery a vital boost: the value of slaves as property steadily increased even as the institution was progressively domesticated and sentimentalized, incorporated into the quotidian rhythms of life at home. Looking homeward, as Jefferson always did, future generations of slave-owning southerners learned to live with slavery as they benefited mightily from it. Unlike Jefferson, fewer and fewer were troubled by the institution's injustice, though "colonizationists" south and north continued to take comfort from his expatriation fantasy. The result was that the "empire of liberty" became, for long-settled plantation states like Virginia and their expanding western hinterland, an "empire of slavery."

This tragic story is a now familiar, ironic counterpoint to the traditional narrative of westward expansion. Yet again, we can abstract Jeffersonian ideas about republican self-government in settler societies from the lived experience of Indian removal and the expanding ambit of the "peculiar institution": we can and should conceive of our national home—and the homes we make for ourselves—in ways Jefferson could not imagine. Certainly this is an appropriately visionary (and therefore Jeffersonian) solution to our problem with Jefferson. But we might also take a deeper look at the sources of

Jefferson's imperial vision by focusing on the empire he knew and loved when he was a child. The British Empire was seen by patriotic Anglo-Americans—and by no one more so than Jefferson—as an "empire of liberty." Patriot rage against the king was fueled by a sense of betrayal. Rather than embrace and promote Britain's imperial greatness, George III turned away from and made war against his own people. The "sacred fire of liberty" was a precious inheritance, kept alight by the revolutionary patriots of Jefferson's generation. Enlightened, forward-looking republicans would create their own empire, one that was faithful to their understanding of the genius and destiny of the empire the British had forfeited.

Nations have origin stories, and the one Jefferson fashioned in the Declaration of Independence contrasted American freedom and British despotism, New World and Old. The national obsession with newness and exceptionalism drew on patriotic Anglophobia: "Britain" was the antithesis and negative referent for everything that was distinctively "American."[30] Anglophilia came naturally to people—like Jefferson—whose identities and patriotic attachments were forged in the glorious era of British imperial power and prosperity after the great victory over France in the Seven Years' War (1756–63). Jefferson's revolutionary Anglophobia was a close cousin to the younger man's Anglophilia. It was a willful denial and suppression of a much valued family connection. The prophet of a new age was determined to overlook what should be so obvious to us now: much that makes Americans seem exceptional has a British genealogy, from their love of liberty to their faith in the progress of civilization, and even to the precepts and practices of republican self-government, or what we now call democracy. It became the fashion for revolutionary patriots, rebuffed in their efforts to vindicate the rights of Englishmen, to call themselves "men" and claim "the separate and equal station to which the Laws of Nature and of Nature's God entitle them."[31] But they could not and would not have made such claims if they had not seen the world as British provincials saw it, seeing themselves as the saving remnant of a great nation bent on self-destruction.

It would be a mistake for us to conclude on this deflationary note. Of course, it is the fate of historians to explain—and so explain away—the visions of our shortsighted, time-bound subjects, to dwell on what they overlook and we can see clearly. The bright thread that runs through our engagement with Thomas Jefferson is expressed in the key word in our subtitle, "imagination." The Virginian's self-fashioning project is one with which we can identify, though the materials the patriarch had to work with—including the labors and lives of the enslaved people who worked for him—are profoundly alien to our sensibilities and moral sense. In his quest to make something of himself, the son, husband, father, friend, patriot, and seeker of truth looked beyond himself, exercising his sympathetic imagination. Indeed, as his colloquy with John Adams suggests, the faithful republican believed he could see beyond his own life and, in some unimaginable way, participate in the gloriously enlightened future for mankind for which he prayed.

Surely Jefferson was fallible, and we could wish with Abigail Adams that he had acknowledged this. But Jefferson's aspirations were inextricably linked to his limitations: he could not see himself as the kind of false "friend" Abigail, in her fierce identification with her suffering husband, so clearly saw him to be. Jefferson could not admit that he had done anything wrong. As he charted his way through the empire of his imagination, he always believed that the self he fashioned over the course of his life would somehow endure beyond his allotted time on earth. If the "earth belongs in usufruct to the living," past generations live on in the loving memories of current generations, perhaps even in the material substance of the lawful, orderly, and eternal design of nature's God. How this might be was a great mystery that enlightened reason could not finally penetrate.

ACKNOWLEDGMENTS

Thomas Jefferson's indebtedness to his family is a major theme of our book, and we happily acknowledge our debts to our own families: to Annette's husband, Hon. Robert R. Reed, and her children, Susan and Gordon; and to Peter's wife, Kristin K. Onuf, and his daughters, Rachel and Alexandra. They have lived with this project and our focus on Jefferson and Monticello for many years now, and we are grateful for their love, support, and patience. Jefferson has attracted a diverse and growing community of scholars from around the world, most of whom have spent time at the Robert H. Smith International Center for Jefferson Studies at Monticello (ICJS)—and many have become our good friends. We salute Andrew Jackson O'Shaughnessy, the Saunders Director of the ICJS, for his extraordinary hospitality and unfailing good humor, at home in Charlottesville and in conference venues across the globe.

We thank our editor, Robert Weil, for his meticulous attention to the manuscript and enthusiasm, along with others at Liveright, including Bob's assistant, Will Menaker, who helped bring this project to fruition. We were thunderstruck to learn when we handed in our manuscript that the poet we used to help sum up Jefferson's personality, Fernando Pessoa, is the subject of a biography that Bob is editing. This shows the degree to which our minds have met on the question of what types of people in history merit our sustained attention. Faith Childs, our agent, has our thanks for her belief in this project, her insights, her good humor, and support. We would also like to thank Otto Sonntag, who suggested helpful changes to the text for clarity, and worked through our endless revisions with aplomb. We express our deep gratitude to Amanda Cegielski, faculty assistant extraordinaire at Harvard Law School, who helped us both keep on track.

This book was among the projects that one of us (Annette) worked on under the auspices of fellowships from the Dorothy and Lewis B. Cullman Center for Scholars and Writers, the John Simon Guggenheim Memorial Foundation, the Radcliffe Institute for Advanced Study, and with the support of faculty research grants from Harvard Law School.

Finally, our debts to the scholarship of fellow Jeffersonians are apparent and noted in appropriate places in the preceding pages. We particularly thank our friends Christa Dierksheide, research historian at the ICJS, and Francis D. Cogliano, professor of history at the University of Edinburgh, for their careful reading of the entire manuscript and their helpful comments. This book is dedicated to Lucia (Cinder) Stanton, the Shannon Senior Historian Emeritus at Monticello. Cinder's pathbreaking work on Jefferson and the people he enslaved have helped to shape our understanding of "the most blessed of the patriarchs." It is no coincidence that our book and hers, *"Those Who Labor for My Happiness": Slavery at Thomas Jefferson's Monticello* (2012), draw their titles from the letter Jefferson wrote to Angelica Schuyler Church on November 27, 1793.

NOTES

ABBREVIATIONS

Betts and Bear, eds., *Family Letters*	Edwin Morris Betts and James Adam Bear Jr., eds., *The Family Letters of Thomas Jefferson* (1966; reprint, Charlottesville: University Press of Virginia, 1986)
Gordon-Reed, *Hemingses*	Annette Gordon-Reed, *The Hemingses of Monticello: An American Family* (New York: W. W. Norton, 2008)
Gordon-Reed, *TJ and SH*	Annette Gordon-Reed, *Thomas Jefferson and Sally Hemings: An American Controversy* (Charlottesville: University Press of Virginia, 1997)
Papers	*The Papers of Thomas Jefferson*, ed. Julian Boyd et al., 41 vols. to date (Princeton: Princeton University Press, 1950–)
Papers: Digital Edition	*The Papers of Thomas Jefferson Digital Edition*, ed. Barbara B. Oberg and J. Jefferson Looney (Charlottesville: University of Virginia Press, 2009–)
Papers: Retirement Series	*The Papers of Thomas Jefferson: Retirement Series*, ed. J. Jefferson Looney et al., 11 vols. to date (Princeton: Princeton University Press, 2004–)

Peterson, ed., *Jefferson Writings*	Merrill D. Peterson, ed., *Thomas Jefferson Writings* (New York: Library of America, 1984)
Peterson, ed., *Visitors*	Merrill D. Peterson, ed., *Visitors to Monticello* (Charlottesville: University of Virginia Press, 1989)
Randall, *Life of Jefferson*	Henry S. Randall, *The Life of Thomas Jefferson*, 3 vols. (New York: Derby & Jackson, 1858; reprint, New York: Da Capo Press, 1972)
TJ	Thomas Jefferson
TJ, *Notes on Virginia*	Thomas Jefferson, *Notes on the State of Virginia*, ed. William Peden (Chapel Hill: University of North Carolina Press, 1955)

PREFACE

1 TJ to Angelica Church, Nov. 27, 1793, in *Papers*, 27:449.
2 Ibid.
3 TJ to Edward Rutledge, Nov. 30, 1795, in *Papers*, 28:541.
4 Henry Adams, *History of the United States of America*, vol. 1 (New York: C. Scribner's Sons, 1889), 277.
5 *The Selected Prose of Fernando Pessoa*, ed. and trans. Richard Zenith (New York: Grove Press, 2001), 294.
6 Adams, *History*, 445.
7 Ibid.
8 Ecclesiastes 1:9; TJ to Joseph Priestley, March 21, 1801, *Papers*, 33: 394.
9 Henry Adams, *The Education of Henry Adams: An Autobiography* (Boston: Houghton Mifflin, 1918), 457.
10 Randall, *Life of Jefferson*; Dumas Malone, *Jefferson and His Time*, 6 vols. (Boston: Little, Brown, 1948–81).

INTRODUCTION: NORTH AND SOUTH

1 Ellen Randolph Coolidge to TJ, Boston, Aug. 1, 1825, in Betts and Bear, eds., *Family Letters*, 454–57.
2 Ibid.
3 Margaret Bayard Smith's Account of a Visit to Monticello—Aug. 1 [July 29–Aug. 2], 1809, *Papers: Retirement Series*, 1:386.

4   Hamilton W. Pierson, *Jefferson at Monticello: The Private Life of Thomas Jefferson* (New York: Scribner, 1862), 125.

5   Ellen Randolph Coolidge to TJ, Boston, Aug. 1, 1825, in Betts and Bear, eds., *Family Letters*, 454–57.

6   TJ, *Notes on Virginia*, Query 18 ("Manners"), 162.

7   TJ to Chastellux, Sept. 2, 1785, in *Papers*, 8:468.

8   Memoirs of Israel Jefferson, in Gordon-Reed, *TJ and SH*, 252.

9   TJ to John Holmes, April 22, 1820, Library of Congress, http//www.loc.gov/exhibits/Jefferson/159.html.

10   TJ to Ellen Wayles Randolph Coolidge, Aug. 27, 1825, in Betts and Bear, eds., *Family Letters*, 457.

11   Ibid., 458.

12   TJ to James Heaton, May 20, 1826, in Peterson, ed., *Writings of Jefferson*, 1516.

13   TJ to Mary Jefferson Eppes, Jan. 1, 1799, in *Papers*, 30:607.

14   TJ to Martha Jefferson Randolph, June 8, 1797, in *Papers*, 29:424.

15   Although he does not remember saying this, we credit James Romm, Gordon-Reed's colleague at the New York Public Library's Cullman Center for Writers and Scholars, for saying that the Roman writer Seneca used writing to try to create the world as he wanted it to be.

16   Ellen W. Randolph Coolidge to Henry S. Randall, July 31, 1856, in Family Letters Project, Papers of Thomas Jefferson: Retirement Series, tjrs.monticello.org/letter/1989.

17   Ellen W. Randolph Coolidge to Henry S. Randall, July 31, 1856, in Family Letters Project, Papers of Thomas Jefferson: Retirement Series, tjrs.monticello.org/letter/1984.

18   Conor Cruise O'Brien, *The Long Affair: Thomas Jefferson and the French Revolution* (Chicago: University of Chicago Press, 1996), 37.

19   Gordon-Reed, *Hemingses*, 617–18.

20   Gordon-Reed, *TJ and SH*, 15.

21   Lucia Stanton and Dianne Swann-Wright, "Bonds of Memory: Identity and the Hemings Family," in Lucia Stanton, *"Those Who Labor for My Happiness: Slavery at Thomas Jefferson's Monticello* (Charlottesville: University of Virginia Press, 2012), 238.

22   Ellen Coolidge to Joseph Coolidge, Oct. 24, 1858, in Family Letters Project, Papers of Thomas Jefferson: Retirement Series, http://tjrs.monticello.org/letter/1266.

23   Ellen W. Randolph Coolidge to Virginia J. Randolph Trist, Sept. 29, 1826, in Family Letters Project, http://tjrs.monticello.org/letter/1041; Ellen W. Randolph Coolidge to Martha Jefferson Randolph, May 28, 1828, http://tjrs.monticello.org/letter/1132.

24   TJ to Thomas Jefferson Randolph, Feb. 8, 1826, in Betts and Bear, eds., *Family Letters*, 469.

25   Thomas Jefferson Randolph to TJ , Feb. 3 and [16], 1826, in Betts and Bear, eds., *Family Letters*, 467, 472; Francis Wayles Eppes to TJ, Feb. 23, 1826, ibid., 471.

26   Martha Jefferson Randolph to TJ, Jan. 16, 1808, in Betts and Bear, eds., *Family Letters*, 322.

27   TJ to Ellen R. Coolidge, Nov. 14, 1825, in Betts and Baer, eds., *Family Letters*, 461.

28   Joseph Coolidge Jr. to Martha Randolph, Aug. 1825, in Harold Jefferson Coolidge, "An American Wedding Journey in 1825," *Atlantic Monthly* 143 (Jan.–June 1929): 354–66.

29   TJ to Ellen R. Coolidge, March 19, 1826, in Betts and Baer, eds., *Family Letters*, 475–76.

CHAPTER 1: HOME

1   Susan Kern, *The Jeffersons at Shadwell* (New Haven: Yale University Press, 2010), 176.

2   TJ to John Harvie, Jan. 14, 1760, in *Papers*, 1:3.

3   TJ to Thomas Jefferson Randolph, Nov. 24, 1808, in Betts and Baer, eds., *Family Letters*, 362–63.

4   Ibid., 363.

5   Ibid.

6   TJ to John Page, Jan. 19, 1764, in *Papers*, 1:13.

7   TJ to William Fleming, [ca. Oct. 1763], in *Papers*, 1:13. The best account of the Burwell affair is in Jon Kukla, *Mr. Jefferson's Women* (New York: Alfred A. Knopf, 2007), 16–40.

8   TJ to John Page, Jan. 20, 1763; the first quotation is from a postscript dated Feb. 12, in *Papers*, 1:8.

9   Rhys Isaac, "Monticello Stories Old and New," in *Sally Hemings and Thomas Jefferson: History, Memory, and Civic Culture*, ed. Jan Ellen Lewis and Peter S. Onuf (Charlottesville: University Press of Virginia, 2000), 117–18.

10   TJ to John Page, July 15, 1763, in *Papers*, 1:10.

11   Virginia Scharff, *The Women Jefferson Loved* (New York: Harper, 2011), 107.

CHAPTER 2: PLANTATION

1   TJ to Thomas Leiper, Feb. 23, 1801, in *Papers*, 33:50.

2   Herbert E. Sloan, *Principle and Interest: Thomas Jefferson and the Problem of Debt* (New York: Oxford University Press, 1995).

3   The Memoirs of Madison Hemings, in Gordon-Reed, *TJ and SH*, 247.

4   Ibid.; Martha Jefferson Randolph to Ellen Randolph Coolidge, Oct. 22, 1826, in Family Letters Project, Papers of Thomas Jefferson: Retirement Series, tjrs .monticello.org/letter/1058.

5   Hamilton W. Pierson, *Jefferson at Monticello: The Private Life of Thomas Jefferson* (New York: Scribner, 1862), 72.

6   Ron Chernow, *Alexander Hamilton* (New York: Penguin Press, 2004), 315–16.

7   TJ to Martha Jefferson Randolph, July 17, 1790, in *Papers*, 17:215.

8   Thomas Mann Randolph to TJ, Nov. 14, 1793, in *Papers*, 27:377.

9   Lucia Stanton, *"Those Who Labor for My Happiness": Slavery at Thomas Jefferson's Monticello* (Charlottesville: University of Virginia Press, 2012), 74–75; TJ to Stevens Thomson Mason, Oct. 27, 1799, in *Papers*, 31:222.

10   TJ to Maria Jefferson Eppes, March 3, 1802, Library of Congress, 20875.

11   Gordon-Reed, *TJ and SH*, 247.

12   Martha Jefferson Randolph to Ellen Randolph Coolidge, Oct. 22, 1826, in Family Letters Project, tjrs.monticello.org/letter/1058.

13   Christa Dierksheide, *Amelioration and Empire: Progress and Slavery in the Plantation Americas* (Charlottesville: University of Virginia Press, 2014), 50.

14   Thomas Jefferson Coolidge, *The Autobiography of T. Jefferson Coolidge, Drawn in Part from His Diary* (Boston: privately printed, 1901), 3. TJ to Reuben Perry, April 16, 1812, in *Papers*, 4:620.

15   See, generally, Edward E. Baptist, *The Half Has Never Been Told: Slavery and the Making of American Capitalism* (New York: Basic Books, 2014). But see John E. Murray, Alan L. Olmstead, Trevon D. Logan, Jonathan B. Pritchett, and Peter L. Rousseau (2015), review of Edward E. Baptist, *The Half Has Never Been Told: Slavery and the Making of American Capitalism, Journal of Economic History* 75, no. 3 (Sept. 2015): 919–31, http://dx.doi.org/10.1017/S0022050715000996. Olmstead challenges the notion that increased whipping accounted for the dramatic surge in productivity in the antebellum period.

16   *Memoirs of John Quincy Adams*, ed. Charles Francis Adams (Philadelphia: J. B. Lippincott, 1874), quoted at http://www.monticello.org/site/jefferson/quotations-jefferson-conversation#_noted-9.

17   Lucia Stanton, "Perfecting Slavery: Rational Plantation Management at Monticello," in *"Those Who Labor,"* 77–79.

18   TJ, *Notes on Virginia,* Query 18 ("Manners"), 162.

19   Gordon-Reed, *Hemingses*, 381; TJ, in *Papers*, 1:426.

20   Lucia Stanton has written extensively and persuasively about Jefferson's nail factory and what he thought he was accomplishing there. See Stanton, "Perfecting Slavery," 79–89.

21   François Alexandre Frédéric, duc de La Rochefoucauld-Liancourt, *Travels through the United States of North America, the Country of the Iroquois, and Upper Canada, in the Years 1795, 1796, and 1797*, 2d ed., 4 vols. (London: R. Phillips, 1800), 3:157–58.

22 Gordon-Reed, *TJ and SH*, 25–25; Gordon-Reed, *Hemingses*, 577–79.

23 TJ to Paul Bentalou, Aug. 9, 1786, *Papers*, 10:205.

24 TJ to Joseph Dougherty, July 31, 1806, quoted in Lucia Stanton, "A Well-Ordered Household: Domestic Servants in Jefferson's White House," *White House History*, no. 17 (2006): 11.

25 Gordon-Reed, *Hemingses*, 497–99.

26 Ibid., 500.

27 Ibid., 637.

CHAPTER 3: VIRGINIA

1   TJ, *Autobiography*, Peterson, ed., *Jefferson Writings*, 4.

2   TJ to William Duval, June 14, 1806, in Library of Congress, 27898.

3   TJ, *Notes on Virginia*, Query 15 ("Colleges, Buildings, and Roads"), 152.

4   Ibid., 152–53.

5   TJ, *Autobiography*, in Peterson, ed., *Jefferson Writings*, 4.

6   TJ, *Notes on Virginia*, Query 15 ("Colleges, Buildings, and Roads"), 153.

7   Draft Instruction to the Virginia Delegates in the Continental Congress (MS Text of *A Summary View, &c.*) [July 1774], in *Papers*, 1:133, 137.

8   Jefferson's "original Rough draft" of the Declaration [June 11–July 4, 1776], in *Papers*, 1:427.

9   TJ, *A Summary View of the Rights of British America*, in Peterson, ed., *Jefferson Writings*, 113.

10 TJ to William Ludlow, Sept. 6, 1824, in Andrew Lipscomb and Albert Bergh, eds., *The Writings of Thomas Jefferson*, 20 vols. (Washington, DC: Thomas Jefferson Memorial Association, 1903), 16:75.

11 TJ to William Phillips, June 25, 1779, in *Papers*, 3:15.

12 Gordon-Reed, *TJ and SH*, 138–41.

13 TJ to Charles Yancey, Jan. 6, 1816, in Paul Leicester Ford, ed., The Works of Thomas Jefferson, 12 vols. Federal Edition. http://memory.loc.gov/cgi-bin/query/r?ammem/mtj:@field%28DOCID+@lit%28tj110163%29%29.

14 TJ, *Notes on Virginia*, Query 19 ("Manufactures"), 165; Query 8 ("Population"), 85.

15 TJ, *Notes on Virginia*, note to Query 6 ("Productions Mineral, Vegetable and Animal"), 276.

16 Ibid., Query 14 ("Laws"), 148, 146.

17 Ibid., 148.

18 TJ to George Wythe, Aug. 13, 1786, in *Papers*, 10:243; TJ, *Notes on Virginia*, xviii–xix, map reproduced at xxvi–xxvii.

19 TJ, *Notes on Virginia*, Query 6 ("Productions Mineral, Vegetable, and Ani-

mal"), 47, 64–65. Jefferson's "original Rough draught" of the Declaration of Independence, [June 11–July 4, 1776], in *Papers*, 1:426.

20   Ibid., 64–65.

21   Ibid., Query 13 ("Constitution"), 119–20.

22   Ibid., 128.

23   For an engaging study of this difficult period in TJ's life, see Michael Kranish, *Flight from Monticello: Thomas Jefferson at War* (New York: Oxford University Press, 2010).

24   TJ, *Notes on Virginia*, Query 13 ("Constitution"), 128.

25   TJ to Joseph Priestley, March 21, 1801, in *Papers*, 33: 393.

26   TJ, *Notes on Virginia*, Query 18 ("Manners"), 162–63.

27   Ibid., 163.

28   Ibid., Query 19 ("Manufactures"), 165.

29   TJ to James Madison, May 11, 1785, in *Papers*, 8:147.

CHAPTER 4: FRANCE

1   Martha Jefferson to Eliza House Trist, [after Aug. 24, 1785], in *Papers*, 8:437.

2   Ellen Wayles Coolidge Letterbook, 37, University of Virginia.

3   Thomas Jefferson Randolph to Thomas Mann Randolph, June 23, 1806, Library of Congress, http://hdl.loc.gov/loc.mss/mtj.mtjbib016231.

4   The editors of the Jefferson Papers appended this essay outline, undated, to TJ to John Banister Jr., Oct. 15, 1785, in *Papers: Digital Edition*. http://rotunda .upress.virginia.edu.proxy.its.virginia.edu/founders/TSJN-01-08-02-0499.

5   TJ to Madam de Bréhan, May 9, 1788, in *Papers*, 13:150.

6   Winthrop D. Jordan, *White over Black: American Attitudes toward the Negro, 1550–1812* (Chapel Hill: University of North Carolina Press, 2012), 45.

7   Gordon-Reed, *Hemingses*, 16.

8   Stacy Schiff, "Franklin in Paris," *American Scholar* 78 (Spring 2009): 144.

9   Richard Guy Wilson, "Thomas Jefferson and the Creation of the American Architectural Image," in Frank Shuffelton, ed., *The Cambridge Companion to Thomas Jefferson* (Cambridge, UK: Cambridge University Press, 2009), 114.

10   TJ to Charles Bellini, Sept. 30, 1785, in *Papers*, 8:568. Charles Bellini was the first professor of modern languages in an American college. See *William and Mary Quarterly*, 2d ser., 5 (1925): 1–2.

11   TJ to Charles Bellini, Sept. 30, 1785, in *Papers*, 8:568.

12   Lee Alan Dugatkin, *Mr. Jefferson and the Giant Moose: Natural History in Early America* (Chicago: University of Chicago Press, 2009), chap. 6.

13   TJ to James Monroe, June 17, 1785, in *Papers: Digital Edition*, http://rotunda .upress.virginia.edu.proxy.its.virginia.edu/founders/TSJN-01-08-02-0174.

14   TJ to Charles Bellini, Sept. 30, 1785, in *Papers*, 8:569.

15   TJ to Abigail Adams, June 21, 1785, in *Papers: Digital* Edition, http://rotunda
     .upress.virginia.edu.proxy.its.virginia.edu/founders/TSJN-01-08-02-0183;
     TJ to Abigail Adams, Aug. 9, 1786, in *Papers: Digital Edition,* http://rotunda
     .upress.virginia.edu.proxy.its.virginia.edu/founders/TSJN-01-10-02-0135.

16   TJ to Mrs. Trist, Aug. 18, 1785, in *Papers: Digital Edition*, http://rotunda.upress
     .virginia.edu.proxy.its.virginia.edu/founders/TSJN-01-08-02-0318.

17   TJ to John Banister Jr., Oct. 15, 1785, in *Papers: Digital Edition*, http://rotunda
     .upress.virginia.edu.proxy.its.virginia.edu/founders/TSJN-01-08-02-0499.

18   Ibid.

19   Brian Steele, *Thomas Jefferson and American Nationhood* (New York: Cambridge
     University Press, 2012), 53–90.

20   TJ to Eliza House Trist, Aug. 18, 1785, in *Papers: Digital Edition*, http://rotunda
     .upress.virginia.edu.proxy.its.virginia.edu/founders/TSJN-01-08-02-0318.

21   Fawn Brodie, *Thomas Jefferson: An Intimate History* (New York: W. W. Norton,
     1974), 81.

22   Gordon-Reed, *TJ and SH*, 247.

23   TJ to Paul Bentalou, Aug. 25, 1786, in *Papers: Digital Edition*, http://rotunda
     .upress.virginia.edu.proxy.its.virginia.edu/founders/TSJN-01-10-02-0216.
     See also Gordon-Reed, *Hemingses*, 183, on Bentalou and his correspondence
     with TJ.

24   See, generally, Billy L. Wayson, *Martha Jefferson Randolph: Republican Daughter
     and Plantation Mistress* (Palmyra, VA: Shortwood Press, 2013).

25   Cynthia A. Kierner, *Martha Jefferson Randolph, Daughter of Monticello: Her Life
     and Times* (Chapel Hill: University of North Carolina Press, 2012), 58.

26   Ibid., 53, 51.

27   Woody Holton, *Abigail Adams* (New York: Free Press, 2009), 206.

28   As things turned out, the religious atmosphere at the school greatly influenced
     Patsy; for a time she thought of becoming a nun, a choice her father success-
     fully turned aside.

29   TJ to Anne Willing Bingham, Feb. 7, 1787, in *Papers: Digital Edition*,
     http://rotunda.upress.virginia.edu.proxy.its.virginia.edu/founders/TSJN
     -01-11-02-012.

30   Anne Willing Bingham to TJ, June 1, 1787, in *Papers: Digital Edition*,
     http://rotunda.upress.virginia.edu.proxy.its.virginia.edu/founders/TSJN
     -01-11-02-0372.

31   TJ to Anne Willing Bingham, May 11, 1788, in *Papers: Digital Edition*,
     http://rotunda.upress.virginia.edu.proxy.its.virginia.edu/founders/TSJN
     -01-13-02-0076.

32   Gordon-Reed, *Hemingses*, 106–7.

33   Gordon-Reed, *TJ and SH*, 119; Gordon-Reed, *Hemingses*, 88–89, 107. John
      Wayles's parentage of Sally Hemings was talked about among neighbors in
      Virginia and discussed in newspapers. Cocke may have known that Jefferson's
      father-in-law had had a similar relationship with Elizabeth Hemings after the
      death of his three legal wives.

34   Lynchburg *Virgina Gazette*, reprinted in the *Richmond Recorder*, Nov. 3, 1802,
      cited in Brodie, *Thomas Jefferson*, 353.

35   Abigail Adams to TJ, June 27, 1787, in *Papers*, 11:503; *Frederick-Town Herald*,
      reprinted in *Richmond Recorder*, Dec. 8, 1802, cited in Gordon-Reed, *TJ and
      SH*, 64.

36   Kierner, *Martha Randolph*, 70–71.

37   *Frederick-Town Herald*, reprinted in *Richmond Recorder*, Dec. 8, 1802, cited in
      Gordon-Reed, *TJ and SH*, 64.

38   Gordon-Reed, *Hemingses*, 608. See also Gordon-Reed, *TJ and SH*, 193–94.
      Since the publication of this book it has been determined that Sally Hemings
      was the only adult slave who did not sell products to the Jefferson household.

CHAPTER 5: LOOKING HOMEWARD

1   TJ to Charles Bellini, Sept. 30, 1785, in *Papers*, 8:568–69.

2   TJ, *Notes on Virginia*, Query 18 ("Manners"), 162–63.

3   TJ to Samuel Kercheval, July 12, 1816, in Peterson, ed., *Jefferson Writings*, 1397.
      See the excellent discussion of American "spirit" or character in Brian Steele,
      Thomas Jefferson and American Nationhood (New York: Cambridge University
      Press, 2012).

4   TJ, *Notes on Virginia*, Query 17 ("Religion"), 161.

5   Ibid., Query 18 ("Manners"), 162.

6   TJ to George Wythe, Aug. 13, 1786, in *Papers*, 10:243.

7   TJ to Baron von Geismar, Sept. 6, 1785, in *Papers: Digital Edition*, http://
      rotunda.upress.virginia.edu/founders/TSJN-01-08-02-0379. On their rela-
      tionship, see Marie Goebel Kimball, *Jefferson, War and Peace, 1776–1784* (New
      York: Coward McCann, 1947), 40–45.

8   TJ to Charles Bellini, Sept. 30, 1785, in *Papers: Digital Edition*, http://rotunda
      .upress.virginia.edu/founders/TSJN-01-08-02-0448.

9   Charles A. Miller, *Jefferson and Nature: An Interpretation* (Baltimore: Johns
      Hopkins University Press, 1988).

10   TJ to George Wythe, Aug. 13, 1786, in *Papers: Digital Edition*, http://rotunda
      .upress.virginia.edu/founders/TSJN-01-10-02-0162.

11   TJ to James Madison, Oct. 28, 1785, in *Papers*, 8:682; Query 19 ("Manu-
      factures"), 164–65. On Jefferson's "radicalism," see Richard Mathews, *The*

Radical Politics of Thomas Jefferson: A Revisionist View (Lawrence: University of Kansas Press, 1984).

12   TJ, *Notes on Virginia*, Query 6 ("Productions Mineral, Vegetable and Animal"), 60. On Jefferson's understanding of moral progress, see Ari Helo and Peter Onuf, "Jefferson, Morality, and the Problem of Slavery," *William and Mary Quarterly*, 3d ser., 60 (2003): 583–614; Memorandums on a Tour from Paris to Amsterdam, Strasburg, and back to Paris, March 3–April 22, 1788, in Peterson, ed., *Jefferson Writings*, 651–52.

13   TJ to Jared Sparks, Feb. 4, 1824, Founders Online, National Archives, http://founders.archives.gov/documents/Jefferson/98-01-02-4020.

14   TJ, *Notes on Virginia*, Query 14 ("Laws"), 138.

15   Quoted in *Alexander Hamilton* (New York: Penguin Press, 2004), 513, emphases in the original.

16   TJ to William Drayton, July 30, 1787, in *Papers*, 11:647.

17   TJ to Edward Bancroft, Jan. 26, 1789, in *Papers*, 14:492–93. TJ mistakenly dated the letter 1788.

18   TJ to Charles Bellini, Sept. 30, 1785, in *Papers*, 8:569.

19   TJ to James Madison, Oct. 28, 1785, in *Papers: Digital Edition*, http://rotunda.upress.virginia.edu.proxy.its.virginia.edu/founders/TSJN-01-08-02-0534.

20   TJ to George Wythe, Aug. 13, 1786, in *Papers: Digital Edition*, http://rotunda.upress.virginia.edu/founders/TSJN-01-10-02-0162.

21   Bill for the More General Diffusion of Knowledge [1779], in *Papers: Digital Edition*, http://rotunda.upress.virginia.edu.proxy.its.virginia.edu/founders/TSJN-01-02-02-0132-0004-0079.

22   TJ, *Notes on Virginia*, Query 18 ("Manners"), 162–63.

23   Quotations from François Jean, marquis de Chastellux, *Travels in North-America, in the Years 1780, 1781, 1782*, trans. from the French, 2d ed., 2 vols. (London, 1787); Chastellux to TJ, Dec. 27, 1784, in *Papers: Digital Edition*, http://rotunda.upress.virginia.edu/founders/TSJN-01-07-02-0427.

24   TJ to Chastellux, Sept. 2, 1785, in *Papers: Digital Edition*, http://rotunda.upress.virginia.edu/founders/TSJN-01-08-02-0362.

25   See TJ to Baron von Geismar, Sept. 6, 1785, in *Papers: Digital Edition*, http://rotunda.upress.virginia.edu/founders/TSJN-01-08-02-0379.

26   TJ, *Notes on Virginia*, Query 7 ("Climate"), 80–81.

27   TJ to Maria Cosway, Oct. 12, 1786, in *Papers: Digital Edition*, http://rotunda.upress.virginia.edu/founders/TSJN-01-10-02-0309.

28   Gordon-Reed, *Hemingses*, 252–54.

29   Ibid., our emphasis.

30   TJ to Maria Cosway, Oct. 12, 1786, in *Papers: Digital Edition*, http://rotunda.upress.virginia.edu/founders/TSJN-01-10-02-0309.

31 TJ to George Gilmer, Aug. 12, 1787, in *Papers: Digital Edition*, http://rotunda
    .upress.virginia.edu/founders/TSJN-01-12-02-0029.

32 Augustus J. Foster (1807), excerpted from *Jeffersonian America: Notes on the
    United States of America Collected in the Years 1805-6-7 and 11-12 by Sr Augustus
    Foster, Bart.*, ed. Richard Beale Davis (San Marino, CA, 1954), in Peterson,
    ed., *Visitors*, 36–44, 42.

33 Gaillard S. Hunt, ed., *The First Forty Years of Washington Society: Portrayed by the
    Family Letters of Mrs. Samuel Harrison Smith (Margaret Bayard) from the Collection
    of Her Grandson J. Henley Smith* (New York: Scribner, 1906), 387.

34 Dumas Malone, *Jefferson the Virginian* (Boston: Little, Brown, 1948), 160–61,
    434, and passim.

35 We are indebted to the late Rhys Isaac's account of Jefferson's "imagined
    family" and the accumulated "stories" associated with the mountain, in Isaac,
    "The First Monticello," in *Jeffersonian Legacies*, ed. Peter S. Onuf (Charlottes-
    ville: University of Virginia Press, 1993), 77–108.

36 TJ to Maria Cosway, Oct. 12, 1786, in *Papers: Digital Edition*, http://rotunda
    .upress.virginia.edu/founders/TSJN-01-10-02-0309. We are indebted to Andrew
    Burstein's *The Inner Jefferson: Portrait of a Grieving Optimist* (Charlottesville: Uni-
    versity Press of Virginia, 1995) for his superb work on the sentimental Jefferson.

37 TJ to George Gilmer, Aug. 12, 1787, in *Papers: Digital Edition*, http://rotunda
    .upress.virginia.edu/founders/TSJN-01-12-02-0029.

38 Chastellux, *Travels in North-America*, 2:45.

39 Hunt, ed., *The First Forty Years of Washington Society*, 386.

40 Randall, *Life of Jefferson*, 3:544. See the illuminating commentary on Coolidge's
    letter in Jan Ellen Lewis, "'A Beautiful Domestic Character': Sarah N. Ran-
    dolph's *The Domestic Life of Thomas Jefferson*," in Robert McDonald, ed., *Jeffer-
    son's Lives* (Charlottesville: University of Virginia Press, forthcoming).

41 Chastellux, *Travels in North-America*, 2:55.

42 TJ to James Monroe, May 11, 1785, in *Papers: Digital Edition*, http://rotunda
    .upress.virginia.edu/founders/TSJN-01-08-02-0096. For a similar plea see TJ
    to Monroe, Aug. 9, 1788, ibid., http://rotunda.upress.virginia.edu/founders/
    TSJN-01-13-02-0369.

43 TJ, *Autobiography*, in Peterson, ed., *Jefferson Writings*, 4.

44 François Alexandre Frédéric, duc de La Rochefoucauld-Liancourt, *Travels
    through the United States of North America*, 2d ed., 4 vols. (London: Phillips,
    1800), 3:159–60.

45 Randall, *Life of Jefferson*, 3:543.

46 La Rochefoucauld-Liancourt, *Travels through the United States*, 3:157–58.

47 *The Letters and Papers of Richard Rush*, ed. Anthony M. Brescia, microfilm ed.
    (Wilmington, DE, 1980), excerpted in Peterson, ed., *Visitors*, 72.

CHAPTER 6: POLITICS

1   TJ to Mary Jefferson Eppes, Jan. 1, 1799, in *Papers: Digital Edition*, http://rotunda
    .upress.virginia.edu.proxy.its.virginia.edu/founders/TSJN-01-30-02-0415.

2   TJ to Mary Jefferson Eppes, Oct. 26, 1801, in *Papers: Digital Edition*, http://rotunda
    .upress.virginia.edu.proxy.its.virginia.edu/founders/TSJN-01-35-02-0423.

3   For an extended essay on the "Response" and the "Welcome" of prominent
    Albemarle citizens that prompted it, see the editorial note "The Holy Cause of
    Freedom," in *Papers: Digital Edition*, http://rotunda.upress.virginia.edu.proxy
    .its.virginia.edu/founders/TSJN-01-16-02-0094-0001.

4   TJ's Response to the Citizens of Albemarle, Feb. 12, 1790, in *Papers: Digital
    Edition*, http://rotunda.upress.virginia.edu.proxy.its.virginia.edu/founders/
    TSJN-01-16-02-0094-0003.

5   TJ to Samuel Kercheval, July 12, 1816, in Peterson, ed., *Jefferson Writings*, 1398.

6   TJ to Angelica Schuyler Church, Nov. 27, 1793, in *Papers: Digital Edition*, http://
    rotunda.upress.virginia.edu.proxy.its.virginia.edu/founders/TSJN-01-27-02
    -0416.

7   Martha Jefferson Randolph's Recollections, in Randall, *Life of Jefferson*, 1:552,
    our emphasis. Our interpretation of Jefferson's return follows that of Gordon-
    Reed, *Hemingses*, 397–401.

8   Memoirs of Israel Jefferson, in Gordon-Reed, *TJ and SH*, 250.

9   TJ, *Notes on Virginia*, Query 18 ("Manners"), 163.

10 Hamilton to Edward Carrington, May 26, 1792, in *The Papers of Alexander
    Hamilton Digital Edition*, ed. Harold C. Syrett (Charlottesville: University of
    Virginia Press, Rotunda, 2011), http://rotunda.upress.virginia.edu.proxy.its
    .virginia.edu/founders/ARHN-01-11-02-0349. On TJ, Hamilton, and gender
    we are indebted to Andrew Burstein and Nancy Isenberg, *Madison and Jefferson*
    (New York: Random House, 2010). TJ to Thomas Mann Randolph, June 23,
    1806, in *Papers: Digital Edition*, http://rotunda.upress.virginia.edu/founders/
    default.xqy?keys=FOEA-print-04-01-02-3893.

11 Ruth Bloch, "The Gendered Meanings of Virtue in Revolutionary America,"
    Signs 13 (1987): 37–58.

12 TJ to James Madison, Sept. 6, 1789, in *Papers: Digital Edition*, http://rotunda
    .upress.virginia.edu.proxy.its.virginia.edu/founders/TSJN-01-15-02-0375
    -0003. For a brilliant analysis of this letter see Herbert Sloan, "The Earth
    Belongs to the Living," in *Jeffersonian Legacies*, ed. Peter S. Onuf (Charlottes-
    ville: University of Virginia Press, 1993), 261–315.

13 Jan Lewis, " 'The Blessings of Domestic Society': Thomas Jefferson's Fam-
    ily and the Transformation of American Politics," in *Jeffersonian Legacies*, ed.
    Onuf, 109–46.

14 TJ to Benjamin Rush, April 21, 1803, with a "Syllabus of an Estimate of the

Merit of the Doctrines of Jesus, Compared with Those of Others," in Peterson, ed., *Jefferson Writings*, 1125.

15   Our understanding of the importance of friendship for the Jeffersonian Republican opposition is indebted to Joanne Freeman, *Affairs of Honor: National Politics in the New Republic* (New Haven: Yale University Press, 2001).

16   Lance Banning, *The Jeffersonian Persuasion: Evolution of a Party Ideology* (Ithaca: Cornell University Press, 1980).

17   Michael McKeon, *The Secret History of Domesticity: Public, Private, and the Division of Knowledge* (Baltimore: Johns Hopkins University Press, 2006), suggests that bourgeois notions of family life emerged in tandem with an obsessive interest in the "secrets" of court life. Transgressions committed by the privileged, powerful, and leisured against emergent norms of domesticity were juxtaposed to the wholesome and transparent lives of ordinary (middle-class) people.

18   *Journal of William Maclay: United States Senator from Pennsylvania, 1789–1791* (New York: D. Appleton, 1890), 351.

19   Franklin B. Sawvel, ed., *The Complete Anas of Thomas Jefferson* (New York: Round Table Press, 1903), 36–37. TJ also recalled that Hamilton proclaimed "Julius Caesar" . . . "the greatest man who ever lived." Dumas Malone noted that TJ said he offered this story to highlight the differences in the "political principles" between himself "and his famous rival." It was not just about personalities. Malone, Vol. 3, 287.

20   TJ to George Washington, Sept. 9, 1792, in *Papers: Digital Edition*, http://rotunda.upress.virginia.edu.proxy.its.virginia.edu/founders/TSJN-01-24-02-0330.

21   Eugene R. Sheridan, "Thomas Jefferson and the Giles Resolutions," *William and Mary Quarterly*, 3d ser., 49 (1992): 589–609.

22   TJ to Joseph Delaplaine, April 12, 1817, American Memory Website, Library of Congress, Washington, DC, http://memory.loc.gov/master/mss/mtj/mtj1/049/1000/1030.jpg.

23   TJ to Joseph C. Cabell, Feb. 2, 1816, in *Papers: Digital Edition*, http://rotunda.upress.virginia.edu.proxy.its.virginia.edu/founders/TSJN-03-09-02-0286.

24   On the radical republican affinities of Paine and TJ, see Simon P. Newman and Peter S. Onuf, eds., *Paine and Jefferson in the Age of Revolutions* (Charlottesville: University of Virginia Press, 2013).

25   On France's influence and presence in the new nation, see François Furstenberg, *When the United States Spoke French: Five Refugees Who Shaped a Nation* (New York: Penguin Press, 2014).

26   John Marshall to Joseph Story, Sept. 18, 1821, in *The Papers of John Marshall Digital Edition*, ed. Charles Hobson (Charlottesville: University of Virginia Press, Rotunda, 2014).

27   TJ to John Adams, Sept. 4, 1823, in Founders Online, National Archives, Washington, DC, http://founders.archives.gov/.

28   TJ to William Short, Jan. 3, 1793, in *Papers: Digital Edition*, http://rotunda
     .upress.virginia.edu.proxy.its.virginia.edu/founders/TSJN-01-25-02-0016.

29   On TJ's "post-martial" self-presentation, see Maurizio Valsania, *Jefferson's
     Bodies* (Charlottesville: University of Virginia Press, forthcoming).

30   Ellen W. Randolph Coolidge to Henry S. Randall, Feb. 22, 1856, in Fam-
     ily Letters Project, tjrs.monticello.org/letter/1966#XC2B03170-97D3-4628
     -B0A3-DF31BCE07108. Samuel Whitcomb Jr., "A Book Peddler Invades
     Monticello," *William and Mary Quarterly*, 3d ser., 6 (1949): 634–35. Whitcomb
     was a book dealer from Massachusetts.

31   Jay Fliegelman, *Declaring Independence: Jefferson, Natural Language & the Culture
     of Performance* (Stanford: Stanford University Press, 1993). On "homespun" and
     the republican aesthetic, see Kate Haulman, *The Politics of Fashion in Eighteenth-
     Century America* (Chapel Hill: University of North Carolina Press, 2011).

32   So called by the poet Joel Barlow, who sent a copy of a poem with this title
     to TJ, March 18, 1792, in *Papers: Digital Edition*, http://rotunda.upress.virginia
     .edu.proxy.its.virginia.edu/founders/TSJN-01-23-02-0254. See the fine study
     by Francis D. Cogliano, *Emperor of Liberty: Thomas Jefferson's Foreign Policy*
     (New Haven: Yale University Press, 2014).

33   John R. Howe Jr., "Republican Thought and Political Violence in the 1790s,"
     American Quarterly 19 (1967): 147–65; Matthew Rainbow Hale, "American
     Hercules: Militant Sovereignty and Violence in the Democratic-Republican
     Imagination, 1793–1795," in *Between Sovereignty and Anarchy: The Politics of
     Violence in the American Revolutionary Era*, ed. Patrick Griffin et al. (Charlottes-
     ville: University of Virginia Press, 2015).

34   TJ to John Taylor of Caroline, June 4, 1798, in *Papers: Digital Edition*, http://
     rotunda.upress.virginia.edu.proxy.its.virginia.edu/founders/TSJN-01-30-02
     -0280.

35   TJ to Judge Spencer Roane, Sept. 6, 1819, in Andrew A. Lipscomb and Albert
     Ellery Bergh, eds., *The Writings of Thomas Jefferson*, 20 vols. (Washington, DC,
     1903–4), 15:212.

36   TJ to William Duane, March 28, 1811, in *Papers: Digital Edition*, http://rotunda
     .upress.virginia.edu.proxy.its.virginia.edu/founders/TSJN-03-03-02-0378.

37   TJ's inaugural address, March 4, 1801, in Peterson, ed., *Jefferson Writings*, 492,
     496.

38   TJ to Joseph Priestley, March 22, 1801, in *Papers: Digital Edition*, http://rotunda
     .upress.virginia.edu.proxy.its.virginia.edu/founders/TSJN-01-33-02-0336.

39   See Ralph Ketcham's influential study, *Presidents above Party: The First American
     Presidency, 1789–1829* (Chapel Hill: University of North Carolina Press, 1984).

40   Jeremy Bailey, *Thomas Jefferson and Executive Power* (New York: Cambridge
     University Press, 2007).

41   TJ to Henry Lee, May 8, 1825, in Peterson, ed., *Jefferson Writings*, 1501.

42 TJ, second inaugural address, March 4, 1805, in Peterson, ed., *Jefferson Writings*, 519.

CHAPTER 7: MUSIC

1   Hamilton W. Pierson, *Jefferson at Monticello: The Private Life of Thomas Jefferson* (New York: Scribner, 1862), 86.

2   Whenever the words of enslaved people are reproduced from recollections prepared by others, they will be translated. Isaac [Jefferson] as dictated to Charles Campbell, "Memoirs of a Monticello Slave," in James Bear, ed., *Jefferson at Monticello: Recollections of a Monticello Slave and of a Monticello Overseer* (Charlottesville: University of Virginia Press, 1967), 23.

3   "Route to Poplar Forest," https://www.monticello.org/site/research-and-collections/route-poplar-forest.

4   *Jefferson's Memorandum Books: Accounts with Legal Records and Miscellany, 1767–1826*, ed. James A. Bear Jr. and Lucia C. Stanton, vol. 1 (Princeton: Princeton University Press, 1997), p. 297, Nov. 2, 1772: "Pd. Martin at Forest for mocking bird 5/"; p. 343, July 9, 1773: "Pd. Jamey for two mockg. birds 11/6"; p. 508, April 5, 1781: "Pd. Jame for mocking bird £18."

5   Randall, *Life of Jefferson*, 1:64.

6   TJ to Thomas Adams, June 1, 1771, in *Papers: Digital Edition*, http://rotunda.upress.virginia.edu.proxy.its.virginia.edu/founders/ TSJN-01-01-02-0050,

7   TJ to Giovanni Fabbroni, June 8, 1778, in *Papers: Digital Edition*, http://rotunda.upress.virginia.edu.proxy.its.virginia.edu/founders/TSJN-01-02-02-0066.

8   TJ to MJR, July 17, 1790, in *Papers*, 17:215.

9   TJ, *Notes on Virginia*, Query 14 ("Laws"), 148.

10 TJ to Dr. Vine Utley, March 21, 1819, in Peterson, ed., *Jefferson Writings*, 1416: "I was a hard student until I entered on the business of life, . . . and now, retired, and at the age of seventy-six, I am again a hard student."

11 Sandor Salgo, *Thomas Jefferson: Musician and Violinist* ([Charlottesville, VA]: Thomas Jefferson Foundation, 2000), 10.

12 Candida Felici, "Italian Violin School in Mid-Eighteenth Century France: From the Concert Spirituel to Literary Pamphlets," http://www.academia.edu/9929314/Italian_violin_school_in_mid-eighteenth_century_France_from_the_Concert_Spirituel_to_literary_pamphlets.

13 From Nicholas Trist's memoranda, in Randall, *Life of Jefferson*, 1:131; Salgo, *Musician and Violinist*, 10.

14 TJ to Nathaniel Burwell, March 4, 1818, in Jefferson Papers, DLC (Library of Congress), American Memory, http://memory.loc.gov/cgi-bin/query/P?mtj:7:./temp/~ammem_nKRr:.

15 "Memoirs of a Monticello Slave," in Baer, ed., *Jefferson at Monticello*, 23.

16   TJ to William Stephen Smith, Oct. 22, 1786, *Papers*, 10:478.

17   "A Sprig of Jefferson Was Eston Hemings—The Gazette's Delver into the Past
     Brings Up a Romantic Story . . . Was Natural Son of the Sage of Monticello
     . . . Had the Traits of Good Training," *Daily Scioto Gazette*, Aug. 1, 1902,
     quoted in Gordon-Reed, *TJ and SH*, oooTK.

18   Gordon-Reed, *TJ and SH*, 73; Lucia Stanton and Dianne Swann-Wright,
     "Bonds of Memory Identity and the Hemings Family," in *Sally Hemings and
     Thomas Jefferson: History, Memory, and Civic Culture*, ed. Peter S. Onuf and Jan
     Ellen Lewis (Charlottesville: University of Virginia Press, 1999), 168.

19   Randall, *Life of Jefferson*, 1:82.

20   Ibid., 41; TJ to Ezra Stiles Ely, June 25, 1819, in Dickinson W. Adams, ed., *Jef-
     ferson's Extracts from the Gospels*, Papers of Thomas Jefferson, 2d ser. (Princeton:
     Princeton University Press, 1983), 387.

21   TJ to Martha Jefferson, Nov. 28, 1783, in *Papers: Digital Edition*, http://rotunda
     .upress.virginia.edu/founders/TSJN-01-06-02-0286.

22   TJ to Charles Bellini, Sept. 30, 1785, in *Papers: Digital Edition*, http://rotunda
     .upress.virginia.edu.proxy.its.virginia.edu/founders/TSJN-01-08-02-0448.

23   Salgo, *Musician and Violinist*, 7, 24.

24   Ibid., 24–25.

25   Cynthia A. Kierner, *Martha Jefferson Randolph, Daughter of Monticello: Her Life
     and and Times* (Chapel Hill: University of North Carolina Press, 2012), 255; TJ
     to Elizabeth Wayles Eppes, Dec. 15, 1788, in *Papers*, 14:355.

26   Sarah Nicholas Randolph, *Worthy Women of Our First Century*, ed. O. J. Wister
     and Anges Irwin (Philadelphia: Lippincott, 1877), 23–26, cited at http//tjportal
     .monticello.org/cgi-bin?bbid=523; Richard Beale Davis, *Francis Walker Gilmer:
     Life and Learning in Jefferson's Virginia* (Richmond: Dietz Press, 1939), 373, cited
     at http//tjportal.monticello.org/cgi-bin? bbd=1150.

27   Martha Jefferson Randolph to TJ, Jan. 16, 1791, in *Papers: Digital Edition*,
     http://rotunda.upress.virginia.edu/founders/TSJN-01-18-02-0173.

28   Mary Jefferson Eppes to TJ, Dec. 2, 1801, in *Papers: Digital Edition*, http://
     rotunda.upress.virginia.edu/founders/TSJN-01-32-02-0382.

29   TJ to Mary Jefferson Eppes, Feb. 15, 1801, in *Papers: Digital Edition*, http://
     rotunda.upress.virginia.edu/founders/TSJN-01-32-02-0429.

30   Mary Jefferson Eppes to TJ, Jan. 11, 1803, in Betts and Bear, eds., *Family Let-
     ters*, 240.

31   TJ to Francis Hopkinson, March 13, 1789, in *Papers: Digital Edition*, http://
     rotunda.upress.virginia.edu.proxy.its.virginia.edu/founders/TSJN-01-14
     -02-0402.

32   Randall, *Life of Jefferson*, 1:412n.

33   TJ to Maria Cosway, Oct. 12, 1786, in *Papers: Digital Edition*, http://rotunda
     .upress.virginia.edu.proxy.its.virginia.edu/founders/TSJN-01-10-02-0309.

34   See Appendix II, Monticello Music Collection (revised by Emily Gale and
      Matt Jones), in Helen Cripe, *Thomas Jefferson and Music*, rev. ed. (Charlottes-
      ville, VA: Thomas Jefferson Foundation, 2009).

35   We are indebted to Jonathan Gross's *Thomas Jefferson's Scrapbooks: Poems
      of Nation, Family, and Romantic Love, Collected by America's Third President*
      (Hanover, NH: Steerforth Press, 2006) for a generous selection of the 884
      poems in TJ's two scrapbooks and Gross's illuminating commentary.

36   TJ to Cornelia Randolph, Dec. 26, 1808, in Betts and Bear, eds., *Family Let-
      ters*, 373.

37   Sarah N. Randolph, *The Domestic Life of Thomas Jefferson* (1871; reprint, Char-
      lottesville: University of Virginia Press, 1978), 346–47.

38   Stanton and Swann-Wright, "Bonds of Memory," 164.

39   TJ, *Notes on Virginia*, Query 19 ("Manufactures"), 164–65.

40   Bonnie Gordon, "What Did Thomas Jefferson's World Sound Like?, *Slate*,
      May 15. 2012.

41   TJ, *Summary View of the Rights of British America* (1774), in Peterson, ed., *Jeffer-
      son Writings*, 106.

42   TJ to Charles MacPherson, Feb. 25, 1773, in *Papers: Digital Edition*, http://
      rotunda.upress.virginia.edu.proxy.its.virginia.edu/founders/TSJN-01-01-02
      -0071. See the illuminating discussion in Kevin J. Hayes, *The Road to Mon-
      ticello: The Life and Mind of Thomas Jefferson* (New York: Oxford University
      Press, 2008), 133–37, 142–45.

43   François Jean, marquis de Chastellux, *Travels in North-America, in the Years
      1780, 1781, 1782*, trans. from the French, 2d ed., 2 vols. (London, 1787), 2:45.

44   TJ to John Daly Burk, June 21, 1801, in *Papers: Digital Edition*, http://rotunda
      .upress.virginia.edu.proxy.its.virginia.edu/founders/TSJN-01-34-02-0316.
      See the discussion in Gross, ed., *Thomas Jefferson's Scrapbooks*, 5.

45   TJ to Joseph Priestley, March 21, 1801, in *Papers: Digital Edition*, http://rotunda
      .upress.virginia.edu.proxy.its.virginia.edu/founders/TSJN-01-33-02-0336.

46   Gross, ed., *Thomas Jefferson's Scrapbooks*, 19–27.

47   For a generous selection of this correspondence, see Jack McLaughlin, *To His
      Excellency Thomas Jefferson: Letters to a President* (New York: W. W. Norton,
      1991).

48   For a complete treatment and reproduction of the songs and poems related to
      Hemings and Jefferson, see Fawn Brodie, *Thomas Jefferson: An Intimate History*
      (New York: W. W. Norton, 1974), chapters 25 and 26.

49   Michael Fortune to TJ, June 23, 1801, in *Papers Digital: Edition*, http://rotunda
      .upress.virginia.edu.proxy.its.virginia.edu/founders/TSJN-01-34-02-0333.

50   Gross, ed., *Thomas Jefferson's Scrapbooks*, 17.

51   Thomas Moore, Esq., *Irish Melodies* (Philadelphia: M. Carey, 1815).

52   Epistle VII, "To Thomas Hume, Esq., M.D.," *The Works of Thomas Moore*,

Esq., vol. 2, *Epistles, Odes, and Other Poems* (New York: G. Smith, 1825), 161. See the discussion in Brodie, *Thomas Jefferson*, 369–70.

53   Randall, *Life of Jefferson*, 3:119.

54   William Peden, "A Book Peddler Invades Monticello," *William and Mary Quarterly*, 3d ser., 6 (1949): 633.

55   TJ to Benjamin Rush, Sept. 23, 1800, in *Papers*, 32:167.

56   TJ to Mary Jefferson, June 14, 1797, in *Papers: Digital Edition*, http://rotunda .upress.virginia.edu.proxy.its.virginia.edu/founders/TSJN-01-29-02-0339.

57   TJ to Maria Cosway, Oct. 12, 1786, in *Papers: Digital Edition*, http://rotunda .upress.virginia.edu.proxy.its.virginia.edu/founders/TSJN-01-10-02-0309.

58   Jay Fliegelman, *Declaring Independence: Jefferson, Natural Language & the Culture of Performance* (Stanford: Stanford University Press, 1993), 4–28.

59   TJ to Henry Lee, May 8, 1825, in Peterson, ed., *Jefferson Writings*, 1501.

CHAPTER 8: VISITORS

1   William Wirt eulogy, in *A Selection of Eulogies Pronounced in the Several States, in Honor of Those Illustrious Patriots and Statesmen, John Adams and Thomas Jefferson* (Hartford, CT, 1826), in *Boston Lyceum* 1 (Jan.–June 1827): 419–20.

2   From [John Gibson Lockhart,] "Foster's *Notes on the United States*," *Quarterly Review* 68 (June 1841): 42–44, in Kevin J. Hayes, ed., *Jefferson in His Own Time: A Biographical Chronicle of His Life, Drawn from Recollections, Interviews, and Memoirs by Family, Friends, and Associates* (Iowa City: University of Iowa Press, 2012); Merrill D. Peterson, *The Jefferson Image in the Americand Mind* (Charlottesville: University Press of Virginia, 1998), 45.

3   Ellen Randolph Coolidge to Henry Randall, 1857, in Randall, *Life of Jefferson*, 391–92.

4   Margaret Bayard Smith's Account of a Visit to Monticello—Aug. 1 [July 29– Aug. 2], 1809, in *Papers: Retirement Series*, 1:386–87.

5   TJ to William Hamilton, July 1804, in Peterson, ed., *Jefferson Writings*, 1167, 1168–69.

6   George Ticknor to Elisha Ticknor, Feb. 7, 1815, in *Life, Letters, and Journals of George Ticknor*, vol. 1 (Boston: James R. Osgood, 1876), 34.

7   Adam Hodgson, *Letters from North America, Written during a Tour in the United States and Canada*, 2 vols. (London, 1824), reprinted in Hayes, ed., *Jefferson in His Own Time*, 91.

8   François Alexandre Frédéric, duc de La Rochefoucauld-Liancourt, *Travels through the United States of North America*, 2d ed., 4 vols. (London, 1800), 3:137.

9   Margaret Bayard Smith's Account of a Visit to Monticello—Aug. 1 [July 29– Aug. 2], 1809, in *Papers: Retirement Series*, 1:387.

10 TJ, *Notes on Virginia*, Query 15 ("Colleges, Buildings, and Roads"), 153.

11 Margaret Bayard Smith's Account of a Visit to Monticello—Aug. 1 [July 29–Aug. 2], 1809, in *Papers: Retirement Series*, 1:386.

12 Richard Rush to Charles Jared Ingersoll, Oct. 9, 1816, in *The Letters and Papers of Richard Rush*, ed. Anthony M. Brescia, microfilm ed. (Wilmington, DE, 1980), excerpted in Peterson, ed., *Visitors*, 72–73.

13 La Rochefoucauld-Liancourt, *Travels through the United States*, 3:137.

14 Samuel Whitcomb Jr., "An Interview with Thomas Jefferson," May 3, 1824, Special Collections, University of Virginia, in Peterson, ed., *Visitors*, 95.

15 John E. Semmes, *John H. B. Latrobe and His Times, 1803–1891* (Baltimore, 1917), 248–51, in Peterson, ed., *Visitors*, 120.

16 Charles A. Miller, *Jefferson and Nature: An Interpretation* (Baltimore: Johns Hopkins University Press, 1988).

17 TJ to John Adams, Oct. 28, 1813, in Lester J. Cappon, ed., *The Adams-Jefferson Letters*, 2 vols. (Chapel Hill: University of North Carolina Press, 1959), 2:388.

18 Wirt eulogy, in *A Selection of Eulogies*, 421.

19 On TJ's "coldness" see La Rochefoucauld-Liancourt, *Travels through the United States*, 3:157. Francois Jean, marquis de Chastellux, *Travels in North-America, in the Years 1780, 1781, 1782*, trans. from the French, 2d ed., 2 vols. (London, 1787), 2:44; La Rochefoucauld-Liancourt, *Travels through the United States*, 3:157; Francis Hall, *Travels in Canada, and the United States, in 1816 and 1817* (London, 1818), 225–31, in Peterson, ed., *Visitors*, 74.

20 James A. Bear Jr., ed., *Memoirs of a Monticello Slave* (Charlottesville: University of Virginia Press, 1967), 23.

21 Thomas Jefferson Randolph to Randall, in Randall, *Life of Jefferson*, 3:674. On the importance of horses for social status in colonial Virginia, see Rhys Isaac, *The Transformation of Virginia, 1740–1790* (Chapel Hill: University of North Carolina Press, 1982), 98–101.

22 Bear, ed., *Memoirs of a Monticello Slave*, 23.

23 Gordon-Reed, *Hemingses*, 704n14.

24 From John Bernard, *Retrospections of America, 1797–1811*, ed. Mrs. Bayle Bernard (New York: Harper, 1887), 232–43, excerpted in Hayes, ed., *Jefferson in His Own Time*, 108.

25 Henry W. Pierson, *Jefferson at Monticello: The Private Life of Thomas Jefferson* (New York, 1862), 70–71.

26 [John Edwards Caldwell], *A Tour through Part of Virginia in the Summer of 1808* (New York, 1809), 26.

27 TJ to Samuel Kercheval, July 12, 1816, in Peterson, ed., *Jefferson Writings*, 1401.

28 Wirt eulogy, in *A Selection of Eulogies*, 419–20.

29 Martha Jefferson Randolph and Thomas Mann Randolph to TJ, Jan. 31 1801, in *Papers: Digital Edition*, http://rotunda.upress.virginia.edu/founders/TSJN

-01-32-02-0375; TJ to Martha Jefferson Randolph, Feb. 5, 1801, ibid., http://rotunda.upress.virginia.edu/founders/TSJN-01-32-02-0397.

30   Michael McKeon, *The Secret History of Domesticity: Public, Private, and the Division of Knowldege* (Baltimore: Johns Hopkins University Press, 2005).

31   John E. Crowley, *The Invention of Comfort: Sensibilities & Design in Early Modern Britain & Early America* (Baltimore: Johns Hopkins University Press, 2001).

32   George Ticknor to Elisha Ticknor, Feb. 7, 1815, in *Life, Letters, and Journals of George Ticknor*, 36.

33   Randall, *Life of Jefferson*, 3:349.

34   Jared Sparks to Henry Randall, March 30, 1859, collection of the New York Public Library. We thank Edward O'Reilly from the NYPL for bringing this letter to our attention.

35   "Elijah Fletcher's Account of a visit to Monticello," May 8, 1811, in *Papers: Retirement Series*, 3:610.

36   TJ, *Notes on Virginia*, Query 18 ("Manners"), 162.

37   Margaret Bayard Smith's Account of a Visit to Monticello—Aug. 1 [July 29–Aug. 2], 1809, in *Papers: Retirement Series*, 1:396.

38   Randall, *Life of Jefferson*, 3:350.

39   Wirt eulogy, in *A Selection of Eulogies*, 421.

40   On TJ's "coldness" see La Rochefoucauld-Liancourt, *Travels through the United States*, 3:157.

41   Emma Rothschild, *Economic Sentiments: Adam Smith, Condorcet, and the Enlightenment* (Cambridge: Harvard University Press, 2001); Albert O. Hirschman, *The Passions and the Interests: Political Arguments for Capitalism before Its Triumph* (Princeton: Princeton University Press, 1977); TJ, *Notes on Virginia*, Query 18 ("Manners"), 162.

42   *The Private Correspondence of Daniel Webster*, ed. Fletcher Webster, vol. 1 (Boston, 1857), 364–73, reprinted in Hayes, ed., *Jefferson in His Own Time*, 94.

43   Thomas Jefferson Randolph to Henry Randall [1856], in Randall, *Life of Jefferson*, 3:673.

44   TJ to John Adams, June 27, 1813, in Cappon, ed., *The Adams-Jefferson Letters*, 2:337, 335.

45   TJ to Philip Mazzei, April 24, 1796, in *Papers: Digital Edition*, http://rotunda.upress.virginia.edu.proxy.its.virginia.edu/founders/TSJN-01-29-02-0054-0002.

46   Richard Rush to Charles Jared Ingersoll, Oct. 9, 1816, in Peterson, *Visitors*, 72–73.

47   Margaret Bayard Smith's Account of a Visit to Monticello—Aug. 1 [July 29–Aug. 2], 1809, in *Papers: Retirement Series*, 1:396

48   Margaret Bayard Smith, in *Richmond Enquirer*, Jan. 18, 1823.

49   Gaillard S. Hunt, ed. *The First Forty Years of Washington Society: Portrayed by the*

Family Letters of Mrs. Samuel Harrison Smith (Margaret Bayard) from the Collection of Her Grandson J. Henley Smith (New York: Scribner, 1906), 386.

50   TJ's Notes on Patrick Henry, [before April 12, 1812], in *Papers: Retirement Series*, 4:603.

51   Gordon-Reed, *Hemingses*, 625–26.

52   Gordon-Reed, *TJ and SH*, 247.

53   La Rochefoucauld-Liancourt, *Travels through the United States*, 3:157; Joseph Delaplaine, *Delaplaine's Repository of the Lives and Portraits of Distinguished American Characters* (Philadelphia: 1815), 152–53.

54   Margaret Bayard Smith, in *Richmond Enquirer*, Jan. 18, 1823.

55   Ibid.

56   Adams Diary [Nov. 23, 1804], in Hayes, ed., *Jefferson in His Own Time*, 38.

57   Jay Fliegelman, *Declaring Independence: Jefferson, Natural Language, and the Culture of Performance* (Stanford: Stanford University Press, 1993).

58   Randall, *Life of Jefferson*, 3:671–72.

59   Alexander Hamilton to Edward Carrington, May 26, 1792, in *The Papers of Alexander Hamilton Digital Edition*, ed. Harold C. Syrett (Charlottesville: University of Virginia Press, Rotunda, 2011), http://rotunda.upress.virginia.edu.proxy.its.virginia.edu/founders/ARHN-01-11-02-0349.

60   Samuel X. Radbill, ed., "The Autobiographical Ana of Robley Dunglison, M. D.," *Transactions of the American Philosophical Society*, new ser., 53, no. 8 (1963): 26.

61   Francis Hall, *Travels in Canada, and the United States, in 1816 and 1817* (London, 1818), 225–31, in Peterson, ed., *Visitors*, 74–79.

62   Randall, *Life of Jefferson*, 3:674.

63   *The Letters and Papers of Richard Rush*, in Peterson, ed., *Visitors*, 72–73.

64   Radbill, ed., "The Autobiographical Ana of Robley Dunglison," 27.

65   Pierson, *Jefferson at Monticello*, 125.

66   Randall, *Life of Jefferson*, 3:676.

67   From Bernard, *Retrospections*, in Hayes, ed., *Jefferson*, 111.

68   Herbert E. Sloan, *Principle and Interest: Thomas Jefferson and the Problem of Debt* (New York: Oxford University Press, 1995), 13–49.

69   B. L. Rayner, *Sketches of the Life, Writings, and Opinions of Thomas Jefferson* (New York, 1832), 526.

70   Semmes, *John H. B. Latrobe and His Times*, in Peterson, ed., *Visitors*, 120, 122.

CHAPTER 9: PRIVACY AND PRAYERS

1   Gaillard S. Hunt, ed., *The First Forty Years of Washington Society: Portrayed by the Family Letters of Mrs. Samuel Harrison Smith (Margaret Bayard) from the Collection of Her Grandson J. Henley Smith* (New York: Scribner, 1906), 71.

2   Gordon-Reed, *Hemingses*, 614.

3   Gordon-Reed, *TJ and SH*, 247.

4   The best study of Jefferson's retirement years is Andrew Burstein, *Jefferson's Secrets: Death and Desire at Monticello* (New York: Basic Books, 2005). Our indebtedness to Andy's work will be apparent, particularly in our discussion of Jefferson's religious quest.

5   William Howard Adams, *The Paris Years of Thomas Jefferson* (New Haven: Yale University Press, 1997), 109.

6   Margaret Bayard Smith's Account of a Visit to Monticello—Aug. 1 [July 29–Aug. 2], 1809, in *Papers: Retirement Series*, 1:389–90.

7   Ibid.

8   Excerpted from *Jeffersonian America: Notes on the United States of America Collected in the Years 1805-6-7 and 11-12 by Sr Augustus Foster, Bart.*, ed. Richard Beale Davis (San Marino, CA, 1954), in Peterson, ed., *Visitors*, 39.

9   *Life, Letters, and Journals of George Ticknor*, vol. 1 (Boston: James R. Osgood, 1876), chap. 1, quotation on p. 35.

10   Margaret Bayard Smith's Account of a Visit to Monticello—Aug. 1 [July 29–Aug. 2], 1809, in *Papers: Retirement Series*, 1:390.

11   Henry W. Pierson, *Jefferson at Monticello: The Private Life of Thomas Jefferson* (New York, 1862), 86–87.

12   Thomas Jefferson Randolph to Henry S. Randall [1856], in Randall, *Life of Jefferson*, 3:671.

13   Memoirs of Israel Jefferson, in Gordon-Reed, *TJ and SH*, 252, 250; Memoirs of Madison Hemings, ibid., 248.

14   Francis D. Cogliano, *Thomas Jefferson: Reputation and Legacy* (Charlottesville: University of Virginia Press, 2006), 74–105.

15   Thomas Jefferson, *The Jefferson Bible: The Life and Morals of Jesus of Nazareth Extracted Textually from the Gospels in Greek, Latin, French & English* (Washington, DC: Smithsonian Books, 2011).

16   Randall, *Life of Jefferson*, 3: 672.

17   Pierson, *Jefferson at Monticello*, 119.

18   Thomas Jefferson Randolph to Randall [1856], in Randall, *Life of Jefferson*, 3:671–72.

19   This was not strictly true. In 1820 Jeff's sister Ellen Randolph made a copy of TJ's syllabus "of the doctrines of Jesus, compared with others," originally drafted for Benjamin Rush in 1803. Ellen may well have known about her grandfather's Bible. TJ to William Short, April 13, 1820, in Thomas Jefferson and William Short Correspondence, transcribed and ed. Gerard W. Gawalt, Manuscript Division, Library of Congress, Washington, DC; TJ to Rush, April 21, 1803, in Peterson, ed., *Jefferson Writings*, 1122–26.

20 Thomas Jefferson Randolph to Randall, [1856], in Randall, *Life of Jefferson*, 3:671–72.

21 Randall, *Life of Jefferson*, 3: 672.

22 TJ to to A. L. C. Destutt de Tracy, Dec. 26, 1820, and to William Roscoe, Dec. 27, 1820, in Paul Leicester, ed. *The Writings of Thomas Jefferson*, 10 vols. (New York: G. P. Putnam's Sons, 1892–99), 10:174; and Andrew A. Lipscomb and Albert E. Bergh, eds., *The Writings of Thomas Jefferson*, 20 vols. (Washington, DC: Thomas Jefferson Memorial Association, 1903–4), 15:303.

23 TJ to Roger C. Weightman, June 24, 1826, in Peterson, ed., *Jefferson Writings*, 1517.

24 TJ to Peter Carr, Aug. 10, 1787, in *Papers: Digital Edition*, http://rotunda .upress.virginia.edu.proxy.its.virginia.edu/founders/TSJN-01-12-02-0021.

25 Samuel Whitcomb Jr., "An Interview with Thomas Jefferson," May 3, 1824, Special Collections, University of Virginia, in Peterson, ed., *Visitors*, 95.

26 TJ to James Madison, Sept. 6, 1789, *Papers*, 15: 392–94. For a superb discussion of this letter in the broader context of TJ's concern about debt, see Herbert E. Sloan, *Principle and Interest: Thomas Jefferson and the Problem of Debt* (New York: Oxford University Press, 1995), 50–85.

27 As Madison wrote in *The Federalist*, ed. Jacob E. Cooke (Middleton, CT: Wesleyan University Press, 1961), no. 49, p. 340: "frequent appeals would in great measure deprive the government of that veneration, which bestows on every thing, and without which perhaps the wisest and freest governments would not possess the requisite stability." See the discussion in Andrew S. Trees, *The Founding Fathers and the Politics of Character* (Princeton: Princeton University Press, 2004), 107–33.

28 TJ to John Adams, Aug. 1, 1816, in Lipscomb and Bergh, eds., *Writings of Jefferson*, 15:57–58.

29 TJ to William Duane, Oct. 1, 1812, in *Papers:Retirement Series*, 5:367.

30 TJ to John Melish, March 10, 1811, in *Papers:Retirement Series*, 3:440.

31 TJ to John Adams, April 11, 1823, in Lester J. Cappon, ed. *The Adams-Jefferson Letters: The Complete Correspondence between Thomas Jefferson and Abigail and John Adams,* 2 vols. (Chapel Hill: University of North Carolina Press, 1959), 2:592.

32 TJ to Abbe Salemankis, March 14, 1810, in *Papers: Retirement Series*, 2:296; TJ to Caesar A. Rodney, Feb. 10, 1810, ibid., 2:210.

33 TJ to William Duane, March 28, 1811, in *Papers: Retirement Series*, 3:508.

34 TJ, *Notes on Virginia*, Query 18 ("Manners"), 163.

35 Ibid.

36 TJ to Martha Jefferson Randolph, Dec. 1, 1793, in *Papers*, 27:467.

37 TJ to St. George Tucker, Aug. 28, 1797, in *Papers*, 29:519.

38   Samuel Whitcomb Jr., "A Book Peddler Invades Monticello," *William and Mary Quarterly*, 3d ser., 6 (1949): 633.

39   TJ to Edward Coles, Aug. 25, 1814, in *Papers: Retirement Series*, 7:603.

40   Edward Coles to TJ, Sept. 26, 1814, in *Papers: Retirement Series*, 7:704.

41   TJ to James Heaton, May 20, 1826, in Peterson, ed., *Jefferson Writings*, 1516.

42   TJ to John Holmes, April 22, 1820, in Peterson, ed., *Jefferson Writings*, 1434-35.

43   For a detailed discussion of the facts and legal aspects of the case, See *Ennis v. Smith*, 55 U.S. 14 How. 400 (1852), and Louis Ottenberg, "A Testamentary Tragedy: Jefferson and the Will of General Kosciuszko," *American Bar Association Journal* 44, no. 1(1958): 22–25. For a critical view of the matter, see Gary B. Nash and Graham Russell Gao Hodges, *Friends of Liberty: Thomas Jefferson, Tadeusz Kościuszko, and Agrippa Hull: A Tale of Three Patriots, Two Revolutions, and a Tragic Betrayal of Freedom in the New Nation* (New York: Basic Books, 2008).

44   "Thomas Jefferson v. The Heirs of Bennett Henderson, 1795–1818: A Case Study in Caveat Emptor," *Magazine of Albemarle County History* 63 (2005): 7–8.

45   TJ to Joseph C. Cabell, Feb. 2, 1816, in Peterson, ed., *Jefferson Writings*, 1380–81, and for next paragraph.

46   Revisal of the Laws, no. 79, A Bill for the More General Diffusion of Knowledge, June 18, 1779, in *Papers: Digital Edition*, http://rotunda.upress.virginia .edu.proxy.its.virginia.edu/founders/TSJN-01-02-02-0132-0004-0079.

47   TJ to Joseph C. Cabell, Jan. 24, 1816, Lipscomb and Bergh, eds., *Writings of Jefferson*, 14:413.

48   TJ to Samuel Kercheval, July 12, 1816, in Peterson, ed., *Jefferson Writings*, 1399.

49   TJ to Joseph C. Cabell, Feb. 2, 1816, in Peterson, ed., *Jefferson Writings*, 1380.

50   TJ to William Short, April 13, 1820, in Gerard W. Gawalt, ed., Jefferson and Short Correspondence, Library of Congress, http://memory.loc.gov/cgi-bin/ query/r?ammem/mtj:@field%28DOCID+@lit%28ws03101%29%29.

51   TJ to Joseph C. Cabell, Feb. 2, 1816, in Peterson, ed., *Jefferson Writings*, 1380.

52   TJ to Dr. Benjamin Waterhouse, July 19, 26, 1822, in Dickinson, ed., *Jefferson's Extracts from the Gospels*, 407.

53   TJ to Benjamin Waterhouse, June 26, 1822, in Peterson, ed., *Jefferson Writings* 1459.

54   TJ to John Adams, April 11, 1823, in Peterson, ed., *Jefferson Writings* 1469.

55   TJ to Roger Weightman, June 24, 1776, in Peterson, ed., *Jefferson Writings*, 1516.

56   TJ to Thomas Law, June 13, 1814, in Peterson, ed., *Thomas Jefferson Writings*, 1336-37.

57   TJ to Margaret Bayard Smith, Aug. 6, 1816, Lipscomb and Bergh, eds., *Writings of Jefferson*, 15:59–61.

58   TJ to William Baldwin, Jan. 19, 1810 (draft not sent), in *Papers: Digital Edi-

tion, http://rotunda.upress.virginia.edu.proxy.its.virginia.edu/founders/TSJN -03-02-02-0124-0002.

59   TJ to Dr. Benjamin Rush, with a syllabus, April 21, 1803, in Peterson, ed., *Jefferson Writings*, 1125.

60   TJ to James Fishback, Sept. 27, 1809 (draft not sent), in *Papers: Digital Edition*, http://rotunda.upress.virginia.edu.proxy.its.virginia.edu/founders/TSJN -03-01-02-0437-0002.

61   TJ to Miles King, Sept. 26, 1814, in *Papers: Digital Edition*, http://rotunda .upress.virginia.edu.proxy.its.virginia.edu/founders/TSJN-03-07-02-0495.

62   TJ to Jared Sparks, Nov. 4, 1820, in Lipscomb and Bergh, eds., *Writings of Jefferson*, 15:288.

EPILOGUE

1   Gordon-Reed, *Hemingses*, 588.

2   TJ to Anne Cary, Thomas Jefferson, and Ellen Wayles Randolph, March 2, 1802, in *Papers*, 37:20.

3   TJ to Maria Cosway, Oct. 12, 1786, in *Papers: Digital Edition*, http://rotunda .upress.virginia.edu.proxy.its.virginia.edu/founders/TSJN-01-10-02-0309.

4   Abigail Adams to TJ, May 20, 1804, in Lester J. Cappon, ed., *The Adams-Jefferson Letters: The Complete Correspondence between Thomas Jefferson and Abigail and John Adams*, 2 vols. (Chapel Hill: University of North Carolina Press, 1959), 1:268–69.

5   TJ, first inaugural address, March 4, 1801, in Peterson, ed., *Jefferson Writings*, 494.

6   TJ, second inaugural address, March 4, 1805, in Peterson, ed., *Jefferson Writings*, 522–23.

7   TJ to James Madison, Jan. 1, 1797, with enclosure, TJ to John Adams, Dec. 28, 1796 (not sent); Madison to TJ, in http://rotunda.upress.virginia.edu.proxy.its .virginia.edu/founders/TSJN-01-29-02-0196-0002 and http://rotunda.upress .virginia.edu.proxy.its.virginia.edu/founders/TSJN-01-29-02-0190-0002.

8   TJ, first inaugural address, March 4, 1801, in Peterson, ed., *Jefferson Writings*, 493.

9   TJ to Abigail Adams, June 13, 1804, in Cappon, ed., *The Adams-Jefferson Letters*, 1:271; see also TJ's letters of July 22 and Sept. 11, 1804, ibid., 275–76, 280.

10   Abigail Adams to TJ, Aug. 18, 1804, in Cappon, ed., *The Adams-Jefferson Letters*, 1:277.

11   Abigail Adams to TJ, Oct. 25, 1804, in Cappon, ed., *The Adams-Jefferson Letters*, 1:281.

12   Abigail Adams to TJ, July 1, 1804, in Cappon, ed., *The Adams-Jefferson Letters*, 1:274.

13   Abigail Adams to TJ, July 6, 1787, in Cappon, ed., *The Adams-Jefferson Letters*, 1: 183–84; Gordon-Reed, *Hemingses*, 203–8.

14   TJ to Abigail Adams, June 13, 1804, in Cappon, ed., *The Adams-Jefferson Letters*, 1:271.

15   TJ, first inaugural address, March 4, 1801, in Peterson, ed., *Jefferson Writings*, 493.

16   TJ to Joseph Priestley, March 21, 1801, in *Papers: Digital Edition*, http://rotunda .upress.virginia.edu.proxy.its.virginia.edu/founders/TSJN-01-33-02-0336.

17   John Adams to TJ, Jan. 1, 1812, in *Papers: Digital Edition*, http://rotunda.upress .virginia.edu.proxy.its.virginia.edu/founders/TSJN-03-04-02-0296-0002. See the editorial note ibid., http://rotunda.upress.virginia.edu.proxy.its.virginia .edu/founders/TSJN-03-04-02-0296-0001.

18   See Andrew Burstein's evocative study *America's Jubilee: How in 1826 a Generation Remembered Fifty Years of Independence* (New York: Alfred A. Knopf, 2001), esp. 255–86.

19   TJ to John Adams, Oct. 12, 1823, Founders Online, National Archives, Washington, DC, http://founders.archives.gov. For further discussion, see Peter S. Onuf, "Founding Friendship: John Adams, Thomas Jefferson, and the American Experiment in Republican Government, 1812–1826," in *Companion to Nineteenth-Century American Letters and Letter-Writing*, ed. Celeste-Marie Bernier et al. (Edinburgh: Edinburgh University Press, forthcoming).

20   Adams to TJ, Sept. 18, 1823; TJ to Adams, Sept. 4, 1823, in Founders Online, http://founders.archives.gov.

21   TJ to Adams, Nov. 13, 1818, in Founders Online, http://founders.archives .gov.

22   TJ to James Heaton, May 20, 1826, in Peterson, ed., *Jefferson Writings*, 1516.

23   TJ to John Adams, Sept. 4, 1823, in Founders Online, http://founders.archives .gov.

24   TJ to Angelica Schuyler Church, Nov. 27, 1793, in *Papers: Digital Edition*, http://rotunda.upress.virginia.edu.proxy.its.virginia.edu/founders/TSJN-01 -27-02-0416.

25   Francis D. Cogliano, *Thomas Jefferson: Reputation and Legacy* (Charlottesville: University of Virginia Press, 2006).

26   TJ, first inaugural address, March 4, 1801, in Peterson, ed., *Jefferson Writings*, 494.

27   Gordon-Reed, *TJ and SH*, 38–43; Gordon-Reed, *Hemingses*, 657–60.

28   TJ to Madison, Dept. 6, 1789, in *Papers: Digital Edition*, http://rotunda.upress .virginia.edu.proxy.its.virginia.edu/founders/TSJN-01-15-02-0375-0003.

29   Christopher L. Tomlins, *Freedom Bound: Law, Labor, and Civic Identity in Colonizing English America, 1580–1865* (New York: Cambridge University Press, 2010).

30   Peter S. Onuf, "American Exceptionalism and National Identity," *American Political Thought* 1 (2012): 77–100.

31   Declaration of Independence as Adopted by Congress, July 4, 1776, in *Papers*, 1:429.

INDEX

Page numbers in *italics* refer to illustrations.

ABOUT THE AUTHORS

ANNETTE GORDON-REED is the author of the National Book Award and Pulitzer Prize–winning *The Hemingses of Monticello: An American Family* and is the Charles Warren Professor of American Legal History at Harvard Law School, Professor of History in the Faculty of Arts and Sciences at Harvard University, and the Carol K. Pforzeheimer Professor at the Radcliffe Institute for Advanced Study. She lives in New York City and Cambridge, Massachusetts.

PETER S. ONUF is the Thomas Jefferson Foundation Professor of History Emeritus at the University of Virginia and Senior Research Fellow at the Robert H. Smith International Center for Jefferson Studies at Monticello. Winner of the American Historical Association's Nancy Lyman Roelker Mentorship Award in 2012, Onuf is cohost with Ed Ayers and Brian Balogh of the popular public radio program *BackStory with the American History Guys*. He lives in Portland, Maine, and Virginia.